Travel

WRITING

DON GEORGE
with Charlotte Hindle

LONELY PLANET OFFICES

Australia
Head Office
Locked Bag 1, Footscray, Victoria 3011
☎ 03 8379 8000, fax 03 8379 8111
talk2us@lonelyplanet.com.au

USA
150 Linden St, Oakland, CA 94607
☎ 510 893 8555, toll free 800 275 8555
fax 510 893 8572, info@lonelyplanet.com

UK
72–82 Rosebery Ave,
Clerkenwell, London EC1R 4RW
☎ 020 7841 9000, fax 020 7841 9001
go@lonelyplanet.co.uk

Travel Writing
1st edition March 2005
ISBN 0 86442 742 5

Published by Lonely Planet Publications Pty Ltd
ABN 36 005 607 983
text © Lonely Planet 2005 and authors as indicated
photographs © photographers as indicated 2005
'Las Vegas' by Simon Calder © The *Independent*
'Sri Lanka' by Harriet O'Brien © Traveller / The Condé Nast Publications Ltd
'Guitar Central' by Christopher Reynolds © 2001, *Los Angeles Times*
Reprinted with permission.

Front cover photograph: Ross Barnett, Lonely Planet Images

Printed through The Bookmaker International Ltd
Printed in China

CONTENTS

THE AUTHORS

DON GEORGE

Don George has been a pioneering travel writer and editor for 25 years. Currently the Global Travel Editor for Lonely Planet, Don was Travel Editor at the *San Francisco Examiner & Chronicle* and founder and editor of Salon.com's celebrated travel site, Wanderlust. He has visited more than 60 countries, and published more than 600 articles in magazines and newspapers around the globe. Don's stories have been selected to appear in numerous collections, and he has edited four travel anthologies, including Lonely Planet's acclaimed *The Kindness of Strangers* and *A House Somewhere: Tales of Life Abroad*. Don has won numerous awards for his writing and editing, including the Pacific Asia Travel Association's Grand Award for best travel article of the year and the Society of American Travel Writers' Lowell Thomas Award.

Don has lectured on travel writing and travel literature at conferences and workshops around the world. He is a visiting lecturer in travel writing at the University of California, Berkeley, Graduate School of Journalism, and the co-founder and chairman of the Book Passage Travel Writers & Photographers Conference, held annually near San Francisco. Complementing his travel writing and editing, Don often appears as Lonely Planet's global spokesperson on TV and radio and in print. Don has worked as a translator in Paris, a teacher in Athens, and a television talk show host in Tokyo. He now lives in the San Francisco area with his wife and two children.

CHARLOTTE HINDLE

Charlotte Hindle travelled overland to Australia from the UK after graduating from university, and stayed on to work at Lonely Planet's head office in Melbourne for three years. In 1991 she returned to England to establish Lonely Planet's UK office, which she managed until June 2002 when she decided to change career to become a freelance travel writer, photographer and mum. Over the years Charlotte has written for many Lonely Planet guides, including *The Gap Year Book, The Career Break Book, Australia, Mediterranean Europe, Walking in Britain, England* and *Britain*. She also writes for the *Independent* and *Wanderlust* magazine. Her photographs are sold by Lonely Planet Images (LPI) and regularly appear in Lonely Planet's guidebooks, newspapers and magazines.

DAVID ELSE

David Else is a professional travel writer based in the UK, specialising in guidebooks for independent travellers of all budgets. David also contributes to travel and outdoor magazines, and works as a consultant for travel companies, tourism bodies and specialist mountain-trekking operators.

Since the early 1980s David's travels have taken him to India, Mexico, the Arctic and much of Europe (among other places), but his great love is Africa. He has travelled, trekked, worked and written across the entire continent, from Cairo to Cape Town, from Sudan to Senegal, via most of the bits in-between.

David's Lonely Planet guidebooks include *West Africa, Southern Africa, Gambia & Senegal, Zambia, Malawi, Trekking in East Africa* and the legendary backpacker bible, *Africa on a Shoestring*. He has also written guides to Zanzibar and Kenya for other publishers, and contributed to numerous compilation titles, such as *African Safari*, published by Insight Guides and the Discovery Channel.

When not tramping the globe, David turns his attentions closer to home. With a team of co-authors he has written several editions of Lonely Planet's guides to *Britain* and *England*, and he still manages to get his boots dirty by researching and writing *Walking in Britain*.

Contributing Author

Janet Austin has worked in the travel publishing industry for 11 years, as an editor and writer. Her particular focus is travel literature, and writing and researching for travel and lifestyle publications. She has written on Italy for Lonely Planet's *Western Europe* guide, and provided content for a range of print and Web publications. Janet is based in Melbourne with her husband and two grey cats.

INTRODUCTION

Twenty-five years ago, a very successful man twice my age leaned toward me at a cocktail party and said, 'Let me get this straight. You're travelling around the world. You're not spending any of your own money. And you're being paid to do this?'

That was a conversation I'll never forget. I'd been hired six months earlier by the *San Francisco Examiner & Chronicle* as a travel writer, and had been describing my first two commissioned trips: the first to a Mexican fishing village and its neighbouring resort, the second a one-week cruise around the Caribbean. 'Son,' he said, looking me straight in the eye, 'that's not a job, that's a *dream*.'

Travel writer. The title does conjure exotic scenes: lying on a chaise longue on a white-sand beach by an aquamarine ocean, palm trees rustling in the salt-tinged breeze; sipping a *café crème* in a Parisian café, scribbling impressions in a battered notebook; bouncing through the African bush, snapping photos of gazelles and lions, and ending the day by listening to spine-tingling tales over gin and tonics in the glow of a campfire.

And yes, I have been lucky enough to be paid to do all these things. In the past quarter-century, my work has taken me to more than 60 countries. I have slept under the stars on pine needles and in thousand-dollar-a-night hotel suites. I have eaten fresh-sliced sashimi on a rocking Japanese fishing boat, billy tea and damper in the Australian bush, and steak tournedos with truffles and foie gras on a sun-dappled terrace overlooking the terracotta roofs of Provence. I have met Kenyan woodcarvers and Caribbean boat-builders, Welsh poets and Balinese puppet-makers, Fijian farmers and Californian vintners, Greek chefs and Jordanian archaeologists. But most important of all, I have experienced first-hand the incredibly rich diversity of culture, creativity and connection that graces our globe.

There is, of course, a flip side to the above. Being a travel writer means enduring long hours in front of a blank computer screen, experiencing stress attacks induced by looming deadlines, receiving rejection letters, bedding down in fleabag hotels, surviving endless journeys in storm-tossed ferries and nights when you spend more time in the bathroom down the hall than in your own bed... They're all part of the picture, too – and part of the reason for this book. The life of the travel writer is certainly not all glamour and glory; it's disciplined, demanding work that requires a mix of talent and tact, pluck and luck. Making a living solely as a travel writer is very difficult, but travel writing can be a part of your life at many different levels – from the odd travel article written when you return from your holiday to a commission checking out five-star hotels for a glossy magazine.

Wherever and however you intend to travel, the rewards of travel writing – and of approaching travel with the travel writer's mindset – are numerous. First and foremost, you become a better traveller. You arrive at your destination having already learned something of its history, culture and important sites, making you far better able to explore and appreciate what it has to offer. Also, as you will be on the lookout for trends, unique places to visit and hot spots, you gradually build up a store of knowledge, becoming more and more of a travel expert.

When you are on the road, travelling as a travel writer will force you to pay attention. You will look more closely, listen more clearly, taste more carefully – and continually reflect on what you're experiencing. As a result, your travels will be deeper and richer. In addition, you will often be able to go behind the scenes at a restaurant, shop or hotel, to take advantage of special access to a historical site or museum exhibit, and to speak with intriguing people – from archaeologists and curators to chefs and shamans – whom everyday travellers would not be able to meet.

Finally, even after you have returned home, you will be able to relive your journey over and over in the course of writing about it. And when your account is published, sharing your experience with others will further multiply your pleasure. All these effects will broaden and extend the significance and depth of your travels.

These riches come with a corresponding responsibility, of course. As a travel writer you will have a fundamental commitment to your reader to explore a place deeply and fully, and to report the information your reader needs to know by writing an honest, fair, objective and accurate portrayal of that place.

So my cocktail-party acquaintance was only half-right all those years ago: travel writing really *is* a means of making a living, but it's up there with the globe's other dream jobs. That doesn't mean it's beyond your reach. The world of travel writing is open to everyone – if you love to travel and you love to write, it's a natural. No one can guarantee that you'll be successful, but I *can* guarantee that you'll never be successful if you don't try.

Reading this book will get you started – wherever you may be and wherever you may be travelling. Lonely Planet's *Travel Writing* is a truly global collaboration, intended for would-be and practising travel writers around the world. These pages interweave my own hard-won advice, earned and learned from 25 years on both sides of the travel editor–writer relationship, with insights and information from Charlotte Hindle in the UK and Janet Austin in Australia. In addition to our words, you'll find a treasure trove of tips and tales, including interviews with 28 prominent UK, US, Canadian and Australian travel writers and editors, presented at the end of each chapter; seven exemplary published travel articles that illustrate the principles discussed throughout the book; and an in-depth chapter on writing for guidebooks, written by one of Lonely Planet's most experienced guidebook authors, UK-based David Else. The appendix provides an extensive compilation of UK, US and Australian resources, from publications and publishers to writers' groups and websites, reference books and travel literature classics, that will nurture and guide you on your journey.

One last point about that journey. This book is not intended solely for aspiring professional travel writers, but for writing travellers of all kinds – from postcard-scribblers and journal-jotters to blog-abonds and tome-raiders. In the end, you don't have to make money to profit from travel writing; sometimes the richest rewards are in the currency of experience. The goal of this book is to reveal the varied possibilities that travel writing offers, and to inspire all travellers to take advantage of those opportunities. That's where the journey begins; where it goes is up to you.

– Don George
San Francisco, October 2004

TRAVEL WRITING THEN & NOW

A (VERY) SHORT HISTORY

People have been producing accounts of their journeys ever since they first began to travel. The earliest wall paintings can be seen as a kind of travel 'writing', the prehistoric predecessors of Bill Bryson and Paul Theroux recounting their adventures in the larger world. The first travel book is generally credited to the Greek historian Herodotus, whose *History of the Persian Wars*, produced in 440 BC, contains vivid accounts of sites and rites in foreign lands. Through the ensuing centuries, traders and explorers from Marco Polo and Christopher Columbus to Henry Morton Stanley and Charles Darwin have written diaries and dispatches that make illuminating armchair reading. They all wrote with the goal of sharing their knowledge and experience so that others could appreciate the world more deeply – especially those parts most readers could never even dream of visiting.

It wasn't until the 20th century that travel writing flourished as an independent genre. For the first time, a number of extraordinary writer-travellers emerged who devoted themselves almost exclusively to this art: Patrick Leigh Fermor, Wilfred Thesiger, Eric Newby, Colin Thubron and Jan Morris prominently among them. Modern travel writing is a field of nonfiction whose primary focus is a particular place and whose primary purpose is to illuminate something about that place and about the experience of travel. While travel writing incorporates elements of many other kinds of nonfiction – the personal essay, journalistic reportage and critical reviews, for example – the quality that distinguishes it from other kinds of nonfiction is that it is always fundamentally about *place*.

Stylistically, the travel writer can also utilise various elements of the fiction writer's craft, such as character and dialogue, plot development, conflict and resolution. The travel story has been described as being just like any other short story, in that it traces the development of the relationship between the writer and a second main character – the difference in the case of the travel story is that the other character is the place itself. Given this relationship, it's easy to understand why many of our best travel writers have also been fiction writers, from Henry Fielding and Mark Twain to Bruce Chatwin and Paul Theroux.

The emergence of travel writing as a fully fledged genre was accompanied by a number of distinctive developments. The most important was the expanding popularity of the first-person narrative. While travellers have been sending back personal dispatches from the road for centuries, the first-person narrative – shaped like a work of fiction, with a beginning, middle and end – has really come into its own only in the last 50 years or so. Many critics trace the watershed to the publication of Paul Theroux's first travel book, *The Great Railway Bazaar*, in 1953. A bestseller, it introduced a curmudgeonly narrator for whom travel was not all plush beds and fine dinners but who nonetheless revelled in the eccentricities of the world. Theroux's book showed that travel writing can observe with a cynical eye, speak with a prickly voice, and combine humour with pathos and passion – and all in a popular way. It was a pivotal part of a widespread movement that liberated travel writing from the confines of pure guidebook writing, and began to equate first-person narrative with literary art. Over the ensuing decades, first-person travel writing became so pervasive that the majority of travel writing published today in America and Australia, and to a lesser extent in the UK, is written in the first person.

Another important development was the wide-ranging expansion of travel options. During the 20th century, transportation of all kinds became more affordable, accessible and widespread, bringing more and more of the planet into the traveller's – and so the travel writer's – reach. Destinations that had once been purely for armchair travel were now being promoted in glossy adventure-travel company catalogues. Writing about off-the-beaten-path places came into vogue, and mainstream publishers were no longer restricting their travel accounts to the planet's well-trodden trails. From Bruce Chatwin in Patagonia to Eric Hansen in Borneo, Wilfred Thesiger in Arabia to Redmond O'Hanlon in the Congo, travel writing in the 20th century increasingly pushed the geographical limits. Virtually the entire globe was opened up to travellers, and if you could get there, you could write about it. As a result, travel writing today presents a wider world of subject possibilities than ever before.

PUBLISHING OPPORTUNITIES

Today's travel writers can choose not only from a greater range of potential subject matter but also from a more extensive and varied range of publishing opportunities than ever before. Here is a quick overview of these possibilities; we will cover them in detail in Chapter Six.

Newspapers

Newspapers have radically increased their number of travel pages over the past few decades, and they often publish separate sections devoted exclusively to travel. In the US most major newspapers have separate travel sections that are published every Sunday, ranging in size from four to 30 pages. In the UK most quality newspapers have travel sections of between four and 42 pages on Saturdays and Sundays, and some also feature travel during the week. Major Australian newspapers also feature separate travel sections on Saturdays and Sundays, ranging from four to 24 pages. In addition to these, local newspapers often include some travel coverage in their pages.

Magazines

Magazines focusing on travel have also proliferated, and general interest/lifestyle magazines regularly include travel coverage in their pages. In addition, a whole host of new magazines that publish travel writing have emerged: virtually every airline has its own in-flight magazine which publishes articles about the destinations to which it flies, and niche publications that focus on specific subjects, activities or regions often feature travel pieces. With all of this explosive growth, subcategories within the travel world have developed audiences and outlets of their own; for example, family travel, business travel, gay and lesbian travel, and adventure travel.

Electronic Publishing

With the advent of the Internet, a protean new place for the dissemination of travel writing was born. Though the Net has not resulted in the flourishing of a thousand high-quality

FACT BOXES

Most destination articles include a Fact Box or Fact File (also called a sidebar in the US) that presents essential travel information: how to get there, where to stay and eat, where to get more information etc. An editor will tell you if they are planning to publish a Fact Box with your story, but if you are not working in advance with an editor, it is always a good idea to include one.

What should you include in the Fact Box? Ask yourself what a reader would need to know in order to duplicate your experience. This essential information, tailored to the subject of your story, should be enough. If you're writing about food stalls in Singapore, you don't need to tell readers how to get to Singapore, but you do want to tell them how to get to the stalls you mention in your story, the days and times they are open, and particular specialities to look out for. If you're writing about discovering the riches of Riga, your editor will most likely want to tell readers the best way to get there, and the best places to stay and eat. For some examples of Fact Boxes, see the articles we've reproduced in Chapter Five.

Web magazines as once was hoped, there are a number of websites that publish travel articles from freelancers (though often for little or no pay), and the medium also offers extraordinary new possibilities for self-publication.

Travel Literature

The book publishing world has launched a number of series specifically devoted to travel literature, reflecting an increase in the genre's popularity. Many major publishers produce works of travel literature on a regular basis; these tend to come from writers with already established reputations, but some newcomers break into the ranks every year. Smaller publishers represent much better opportunities for writers who are not already well known. In the US, for example, a number of publishers have begun producing travel anthologies of original unpublished stories; these anthologies are now among the most promising outlets for narrative travel writing. See p223 of the US Resources section at the back of this book for more information on relevant publishing houses.

Guidebooks

Guidebooks continue to grow in scope and speciality, offering writers a wide range of opportunities, from proposing and writing new books to updating subsequent editions of already published titles. Guidebook publishers are constantly on the lookout for excellent writers and fresh ideas from knowledgeable travellers. See Chapter Eight for a detailed look at this rich and varied field of travel writing.

Other Avenues

There are hundreds of 'alternative' outlets for the budding travel writer, from product descriptions for a travel clothing manufacturer to travel brochures for tourist boards and catalogue copy for tour operators. These opportunities are covered in more detail in Chapter Six.

TYPES OF TRAVEL STORIES

Just as travel writing's subject possibilities and markets have expanded over time, so too have the types of travel articles become more varied. We will look at the art and craft of good travel writing in Chapters Three and Four, and provide examples of different types of articles in Chapter Five. Very broadly speaking, however, travel writing can be sorted into three categories: 'service' stories, destination stories and personal essays.

Service Stories

The primary purpose of service stories is to provide essential practical information that will enable a reader to travel more efficiently or more enjoyably. The broad umbrella of service stories covers how-to pieces, thematic round-ups, news-in-brief digests (summarising the most important travel-industry news), equipment reviews, restaurant reviews, book reviews and investigative stories.

Destination Stories

Many travel articles published today come under the category of destination stories. These pieces take a number of forms, but in general they attempt to portray a place and provide the reader with a concrete sense of what it is like to be a traveller there. Some of the most popular genres of destination stories include historical articles, cultural stories, food-focused pieces, slice-of-life stories, environmental/conservation articles, outdoor/activity accounts, journey and road-trip stories, personal narratives and special-interest stories such as family travel, business travel or travel for the physically challenged.

Personal Essays

Essays are personal reflections that draw larger lessons from a travel experience. Humour pieces are a specialised form of this type of work, and while a specific place may be an integral element of the story in this instance, the focus is more on the humorous particularities of the author's experience there.

As you can see, the travel writer's world is bigger, broader and brighter than ever before. There are more places to write about, more outlets for that writing, and more ways in which to depict and share your experiences.

So just what does it take to be a travel writer? We'll talk about that in Chapter Two.

INTERVIEW WITH PICO IYER

Pico Iyer is the author of Video Night in Kathmandu, The Lady and the Monk, Falling off the Map, Global Soul *and numerous other books. He writes for* Time, Harper's *and* Condé Nast Traveler, *among other magazines. Originally from the US, Pico is now based in Japan.*

How did you start off in your career as an author of travel literature?

I was lucky to be a traveler from birth, and I quickly found that whenever I went on vacation, I started keeping voluminous diaries – as I never did at home. Clearly, I was so quickened and filled up by what I was seeing and experiencing that I needed to get it out in some form. And after I began noticing the pages begin to fill up – I would routinely write 200 pages after a two-week trip – I decided that if I were writing all this for myself, I might as well inflict it on someone else, in something more than just letter form.

So I began looking for practical ways to get my records out into the world – the best, because most strenuous, of which was working for two summers while at grad school for the Let's Go series of guidebooks for young travelers in Europe. I wrote parts of seven of those books, traveling through 60 cities in 70 days, having to visit every site and hotel and restaurant in every one (theoretically) and then having to reel back to my resting-place and copy them all down on carbon paper. The opposite of a vacation – and an ideal training for the living-by-traveling I tried to do later.

What is the best way of establishing yourself if you're just starting out in your career as a travel literature author?

Just write, write, write – and if you're trying to write for a living, you have to believe that quality will show, that what you have to offer fills a niche and meets a need (if you don't believe that, it's hard even to begin). For me, the great advantage was that I was always writing as a way to travel – writing simply in order to sponsor and give shape and meaning to the journeys I wanted to take in any case; which meant that the writing was a means to an end and not an end in itself.

There's no substitute for writing, if you want to be a writer. In travel writing, the main thing you have to address is what you can say – how you can approach Kyoto or the Pyramids or Machu Picchu as no one has ever done before, and as few could do today. What do *you* bring to the dialogue you conduct with these immortal places?

But the main thing is just writing – for the free supermarket handout, for the non-paying alternative newspaper in town (as I did), for magazines that may never dream of hiring you, or even for just friends and family.

As a travel writer, how do you get the numbers to add up in terms of an income?

Quite simply, you don't – and you never will. If you're going to try to write about place, I think you have to surrender at the outset any idea of doing it for the money; all the rewards will be internal ones. There was a boom in the publishing of 'travel literature' a few years ago, and there will always be a market for travel pieces in magazines and newspapers, but really it can only be something on the side. To take an example, I have to write 10 pieces a month (on subjects other than travel) just to pay the bills; and although I've published eight books now, I can still only afford to live in a two-room flat in the countryside in Japan, paying rent as when I was a student, without bicycle or car or printer or almost anything. And I will get as much income from three weeks of covering the Olympics as from writing a book that almost kills me over a period of two years.

Even the most distinguished writers have trouble finding a publisher – most of the writers of travel I know and read do it only as a sideline, a vacation, as it were, from the real business of life. Jan Morris is an inexhaustible journalist; Paul Theroux is a professional historian who publishes five or more novels every decade; Bruce Chatwin worked at Sotheby's before he took to the road. For me, part of the beauty of travel and writing about travel is that it forces you to see all material things inwardly: you're not going to get rich and comfortable doing it, but you are going to have experiences and memories and challenges that could put Bill Gates to shame.

What tips would you give to budding travel writers?

Do it for the love of it, and always begin by asking yourself what you have to bring to the Taj Mahal or the Grand Canyon or Venice that no one has brought before. What is particular about your experience and background and interests that will allow you to see and describe things that most of the rest of us could never see?

Maybe you're a jeweler, and so can read meanings into the lapis and coral of the inlay work at the Taj that few of the rest of us could discern; maybe you're of Islamic descent and so can see how the gardens outside the Taj reproduce the outline of the Islamic paradise; maybe you're an architect, and so can explain to the rest of us how science and craft can produce wonder. But you have to begin with something more arresting than just the place and the emotions it arouses in you.

And having chosen a focus – as specific as possible – and decided what will be your angle and your structure, having asked questions of both the place and yourself, and having taken down all the details you could want and more, then you have to work out how to shape the piece and how to find a voice that will make it compelling and fresh to a reader who has no interest in you and never wants to see another piece about the Taj Mahal. Tell your experience and observations as if you were trying to convey them to a friend with whom you long to share your passion; but do so as if you had to win that friend over every time, with your enthusiasm, your clarity and your specificity.

And write it all up even if there's going to be no guaranteed publication, and no reader other than your mother, your partner or your best friend, at the end of it. You won't regret it.

Are there any courses or any training that you would recommend a budding travel writer to undertake?

None whatsoever. The only training for writing is writing – and reading and reading and writing some more. Writing can't be taught, it can only be done; and reading the masters of the trade is a good way of seeing how it can be done in myriad voices and contexts. All the worthwhile training I've done is private, and at my desk; by contrast, I studied literature and nothing but literature for eight years, and feel that that has only hindered and encumbered me as a would-be writer.

What are the most common mistakes that travel writers make in their manuscript?

I don't think you can presuppose that the reader is interested either in you or in the subject matter; and I think you have to remember that your enthusiasm can only be conveyed through specifics. You have to take the reader by the hand and lead them into the place you're describing, and then lead them into the wonder or terror or mixture of the two it evokes in you.

Which is a way of saying that the easiest mistake, especially when you're starting out, is to forget that there's a reader at the other end, and that your first obligation is to them. And it's wise, I think, to read much that's already been written on the subject so you know what *not* to do, what's been done already.

The question I always ask myself before undertaking a project is, 'How can I ever begin to justify the time and heartache and effort I am going to put into this, and tell myself it's bringing something new into the world, or at least into a friend's apartment?' There is a justification, always, but it's often a rigorous or subtle one.

What, in your opinion, constitutes 'good' travel writing?

Travel writing, more than any other kind of writing, has to transport you, has to teach you about the world, has to inform you, and, ideally, has to take you into deeper and deeper questions about yourself and the world. The writer's job, as Milan Kundera once told Philip Roth, I think, is to get the reader to see the world as a question. And travel writing has to hold your attention, first, and then take you into a dialogue between yourself and the world that tells you something new about both and compels you more powerfully than any other dialogue around.

It hardly matters what you call it or what impels the writing – much of the best travel writing is offered by Graham Greene and D. H. Lawrence and, these days, John le Carré, in their novels just because they are driven by a curiosity about the world – other cultures and other people – and because they have refined and developed that curiosity so that they can seize other places and people quickly; they have trained their instincts. These are travelers who are consistently eloquent and perceptive on place, as opposed to those, like Heinrich Harrer in *Seven Years in Tibet*, who stumble into an experience so transcendent and moving that they give voice to what they know is a once-in-a-lifetime adventure.

What constitutes 'bad' travel writing?

Something that doesn't hold the reader.

What are the rewards of travel writing as a career?

All the rewards are inner. They have to do with coming to a better understanding of the world and of oneself, of learning more sharply what one can appreciate about home, and what one is lacking there, of being able to see life as a pilgrimage and journey in which no answer is ever final and one is really moving from question into deeper question, from one way station to the next.

Writing of any kind is a way of making a clearing so as to make sense and shape out of the world, and to take all the rubble of one's experiences and emotions and observations and piece them together into a kind of stained-glass whole. It is a way of removing oneself from the world, and sometimes from the self, so as to see both more clearly. But travel writing is different because it engages with the world in a very urgent and specific way, keeps (ideally) one's eyes constantly fresh, confers on life the sense of an adventure and reminds you that every moment is provisional, every perception, local, ready to be thrown over by the next epiphany.

It keeps you on the move, teaches you (enforces) alertness and makes you more attentive than when you are at home, or blurred by the familiar. As Thoreau famously said, it doesn't matter where or how far you go – the farther commonly the worse – the important thing is how alive you are. Writing of every kind is a way to wake oneself up and keep as alive as when one has just fallen in love.

What has been the downside for you?

The drawback of travel writing comes when the traveling seems part of a job – something to get done rather than something to do – and one cannot embark on it with the freshness and excitement of a possibly life-changing adventure. Then, often, it's time to stay home, or write about things closer to home. (Thoreau, after all, did all his traveling and travel-writing at Walden while staying still, and these days our hometowns are often more exotic and full of new curiosity than Timbuktu or Easter Island.)

Traveling is about freshness and going out into the unknown; if it starts to become known, if you begin to have too clear a sense of where you're going, or if it even begins to resemble a routine, then you have to rethink what you mean by 'traveling'.

How did you get your first book published?

I started taking holidays from my otherwise all-consuming job in Rockefeller Center in New York, and as soon as I did, I found I was so quickened, so stimulated and engaged, by what and whom I had met, that all I wanted to do was return to them, in person or in memory and imagination. So I started writing out my travels, on the basis of the exhaustive notes – or diary-entries, really – I would keep while on the road.

And then, determined to spend even longer traveling, I made up a three-page proposal – asking myself, again, what was special about my background and perspective that would allow me to bring something new to Japan and China and India and elsewhere – and, not knowing better, just sent it out to 'Nonfiction Editor, Random House', 'Nonfiction Editor, Simon & Schuster', and eight other unsuspecting nobodies in the 10 biggest publishing houses I could think of.

Seven never replied to me; but at three houses I got letters from editors who said that I might be onto something interesting, and asked me to send them a sample chapter. I did that, and they were sufficiently intrigued – though not persuaded – to ask for another sample chapter, and then for me to start revising what I'd sent them.

I should stress that this was all hard work, as hard as the work that followed. My regular job often kept me in the office till 4am, and then had me back again at dawn even on Saturday mornings, so it hardly seemed as if I had time to write anything on the side. But

I kept on hammering away, using all my free time for six months, every weekend and slow morning, till I had two sample chapters done, and, at the end of that, with much skepticism but a touching leap of faith, one editor offered me the lowest advance then available – but enough for me to take a six-month leave of absence to write my first book.

· Once I took those six months off, I still had to support myself, of course, so while I was traveling around 10 countries in Asia, writing my first book, *Video Night in Kathmandu*, I holed up in a tiny hotel in Manila, and wrote a long article on the 12th-century Assassin sect of Persia and Syria in order to finance my travels beyond the small advance.

My first book found a few readers and friends, but nonetheless, when I went to my editor to suggest a second, he did not recommend an advance and told me he couldn't begin to guarantee that he would have a place for it.

How long does it take to write your books?

It generally takes me two years, though to say that is to make it sound easier than it is. My last book really consumed me for nine years, even though the writing of it took two. And during one of those years of writing, I was so preoccupied with it that I barely slept, and was staggering through life like an insomniac madman.

Before I began writing – and when I wrote that first book in the second half of a six-month leave from work – I figured it would be easy to do since I had no trouble covering space when writing my diary or knocking off letters to friends. But writing, when I began to do it properly, seems very different from that. One of the chapters in my first book went through 300 drafts – and that was the book I wrote most quickly! And many passages in every book go through 30 drafts or more, to catch the right feeling or slant of light.

My sense is that the longer you put into a book, the longer it will stay with you. A book that takes six months to write is often forgotten six months later; one that claims a decade of your life has a greater solidity to it, and feels more durable.

Do you have an agent, and how important do you think they are?

I do have a wonderful and brilliant agent, though even she, being a wonderful and brilliant agent, often tells me that she can't begin to send out the manuscripts I give her, and they are best kept to myself.

When I wrote my first book, I didn't have an agent – and the advance was so small, and so welcome, I was more than happy to accept it just as an act of faith, in both directions. And I was well-embarked on my second book before an agent or two approached me, through recommendations or pieces of mine they had seen in magazines.

These days it does seem more and more imperative to find an agent, to the point where it can be harder to find an agent than an editor and when you've got the former, you can often suppose that the hard part is behind you. But, alas, no agent can work wonders if the quality isn't there. A good book sells itself, with no intermediaries needed; even the best agent in the world can't sell a weak book.

I always tell my friends not to worry about agents, or editors, let alone publication, until they have truly made their work as good as possible. In any case, the joy and adventure all come in the writing; everything thereafter can sometimes feel like sales tax.

WHAT IT TAKES TO BE A TRAVEL WRITER

THE QUINTESSENTIAL QUALITIES

While travel writing can be one of the most agreeable professions on the planet, it's not for everyone. In fact, trying to make a living as a travel writer can be extremely demanding and daunting, requiring a particular temperament and setting limits on your lifestyle.

What are some of the qualities you need?

Flexibility

One of the hallmarks of the travel writer's life is its general instability and spontaneity. This is equally true both at home and on the road. At home, you have to be able to drop everything and take off for a far-flung destination at a moment's notice. Your life is dictated by the whims of editors and printer deadlines. To a certain extent, you can negotiate timelines with editors, but often their deadlines just cannot be adjusted – and then, if you're not flexible, you risk losing the commission (or assignment, as it is called in the US). You might also risk building yourself a reputation for saying 'No', which you definitely don't want to have in the close-knit travel editorial world.

On the road you also need to leave room for the unexpected. You may need to alter your itinerary to take in a once-every-seven-years festival you hadn't known about, or to spend an impromptu afternoon with the wine-maker who promises to make a fascinating subject for your article.

The moral is this: the more flexible you are, the better.

Adaptability

The second quality is a corollary to the first. If you want to maximise your chances as a travel writer, you have to be equally ready to explore the heart of Paris and the heart of Papua New Guinea. This means that you have to have a closet full of suitable clothing and accoutrements, but even more important, you have to have a head full of suitable attitudes. Are you equally at home on high seas and low roads? Can you keep your cool in hot situations? Is your stomach strong, or are you susceptible to illness? Could you hop from an expedition ship in Antarctica to a $15-a-night hut on an isolated South Pacific island and then into a five-star hotel in London? To take the maximum advantage of such opportunities, you have to be adaptable.

Frugality

Let's get this out of the way right now: it's not likely that you're going to get rich as a travel writer. Not in terms of money, anyway. You will certainly accumulate an uncommon wealth of experience, but to be a travel writer, you need to be able to live on a precarious income. If you are a freelancer you never know how much you're going to earn in a year, and you don't know when the money you *have* earned is going to come in. Some publications will pay you on acceptance of a piece, while others may not pay you until your piece has been published – and that could be many months or even years after your initial outlay. Some publications will pay automatically and on time; others will have to be reminded many times before you finally receive your payment. As a result, the commitment of significant, regular, ongoing expenses – a mortgage or school fees, for example – does not fit well with the freelance travel writer's life. If you are lucky enough to get a staff job as a travel writer, you will at least have a regular income you can count on, but generally speaking, the travel writer's lifestyle is a frugal one – and you need to be content with that. We'll talk in more detail about money matters later in this chapter.

Understanding Family & Friends

The here today, gone tomorrow nature of the travel writer's life takes a significant toll on friendships, and of course on more permanent and intimate relationships. You have to have an extraordinarily understanding and supportive partner who is able to carry on without you virtually at the drop of a hat, for uncertain, and sometimes prolonged, periods of time. If you have children, the situation is multiply compounded. The wife of a UK travel journalist (who wishes to remain anonymous) recently complained:

In 2003 my husband managed to be away for my 40th birthday, our sixth wedding anniversary (he was also away for our fifth), our first daughter's third birthday and my brother's wedding. These are all dates he'd had in his diary for months and months, but we just can't afford to turn down work due to prior family commitments.

Even friends can become irritated by your comings and goings, and feel that they can't rely on you – they'll complain that they just don't know if you'll be there for them. In addition, when you *are* there you seem to be working all the time – working long hours is one of the only ways you can make travel writing pay. All in all, in committing yourself to the travel writer's lifestyle, you relinquish a certain amount of control over your own life – and the people in your life have to be satisfied with that.

Curiosity

Curiosity is one of the prime characteristics common to all great travel writers – they are constantly studying the world around them, asking how things work and why they appear the way they do. They always observe and absorb, and they always talk to people – waiters, taxi drivers, sales assistants, fellow travellers. It is essential to have a passionate and insatiable curiosity about the world, and it is equally essential to keep recharging this curiosity so that you bring a fresh eye and enthusiasm to each new place and story. It will set your research, reporting and writing apart from the pack.

Pluck

Travel isn't easy, especially when you're on a mission to track down information and experiences that will make good travel stories. No matter how exhausted and overwhelmed you may be, you have to keep plugging on, overcoming cultural differences, leaping over language barriers, smoothly swallowing stomach-tumbling foods. You have to find the courage to talk with people you've never met, and to learn to trust the kindness of strangers. Time after time, place after place, you can't give up until you've got your story and then you can't give up until you've written it down and the editor has accepted it. And then it's time to start the next story.

Self-Motivation & Discipline

If you are a freelancer you are your own and only boss, and procrastination is your enemy. You have to make yourself sit down at your desk every day, organise your material, plan your story and write. You need the self-motivation to repeatedly rework and resubmit your articles, and the organisational skills to manage travel schedules, workloads, deadlines, finances and networking. On the road you need the discipline to be continually researching, interviewing, taking notes and gathering information. Wherever you are, travel writing can be a relentless, ongoing, time-consuming balancing act that requires unstinting dedication.

Perseverance

Think of your favourite travel writer. Whoever they are, at some time in their life they were unknown, struggling to get a foothold in the writing world, just as you are today. They faced rejection, probably many times, but they always persevered, continuing to send in their proposals and stories to editors. To survive as a travel writer, you too need the confidence, ability and just plain thick skin to bounce back from rejection after rejection. You need a tenacious faith in yourself and an inventive perseverance. The same applies for temporary setbacks on the road. If an avalanche has closed the route to your destination, you hire a horse. If the local tourism office doesn't have the information you need, you track down the long-time resident who is happy to spend an hour telling you neighbourhood tales. Somehow you find a way to accomplish what you need to do.

Passion

Finally, and fundamentally, you have to have passion – passion for people, passion for the world, passion for the whole business of travelling and for exploring and integrating your discoveries into precise and palpable prose. Travel writing is essentially a lonely profession, and it is your passion that will sustain and reward you.

THE GLAMOUR VERSUS THE HARD WORK

So there you are on the African savanna, notebook in hand, camera around your neck, bouncing through the bush in hot pursuit of the king of the beasts. Later that night, you sit around the campfire recounting the day's exploits while sampling the local beer.

Sounds wonderful, doesn't it? But to get there, you had to fly for a day and a half, squeezed into an economy-class seat between an apprentice sumo wrestler and a man whose personal beliefs forbid bathing. You spent a skin-slapping night on a flea-infested mattress, then had your bones rearranged on a bus bounding over a potholed highway. Your stomach hadn't adjusted well to all the time and temperature changes, so you subsisted on bottled water and biscuits.

And now, while others snore blissfully away, you sit in your tent scribbling into your notebook by lamplight, having cursed the flat battery in your laptop. The following afternoon, while others nap, you interview the driver and the cook. And on the day when everyone sleeps in after the late-night bush trek, you get up before sunrise to photograph the tawny dawn light. Now, is that glamour tarnishing just a bit?

While travel writing certainly has the reputation of being an alluring profession, 95 per cent of the job involves a lot of hard work. It's gathering minute details on hotels, bus timetables, restaurants and walking tours. It's researching which god did what, which ruler took over from whom and when, and what is signified by the curious ceremony that's performed every third Friday in May. It's waiting for planes and trains, buses and ferries, *tuk-tuks* and trishaws. It's swatting mosquitoes and squatting over hole-in-the-floor toilets. It's eating alone night after night, while whispering couples glance piteously your way. It's enviously eyeing all the people languorously sunning themselves on the beach and realising that you've got six more beaches to check out before lunch.

Being a travel writer can be lonely, exhausting and depressing. You're always on the lookout for a useful anecdote or scoping an angle. You can't ever let up, because you're always working. And that's just the travelling part. After the trip you have to sell your piece – and that can be a very time-consuming process. Even if your work has been commissioned beforehand, you have to be patient until the editor finds time to read it, and you may have to rewrite your article substantially after they've read it.

BURNOUT

Burnout is a major factor in the travel writer's life. You grow tired of gruelling travel schedules; of airports, train stations and bus depots; of late departures and late arrivals; of packing and unpacking; of trying to drum up the enthusiasm to explore some new uncomfortable corner of the world; of juggling home life and road life. You have to strive constantly to balance fickle earnings with fixed expenses in order to pay your bills and maintain ongoing accounts. You have to set aside money for unexpected expenses and, in the US, take care of your own health care. Both personally and practically, it can feel like you're always playing catch-up.

It's important to heed the warning signals, and to structure your life accordingly. One antidote is to take a purely pleasure trip at least once a year. If you find yourself burning out in the middle of a trip, try to turn off your mental note-taking machine for a morning and

OVERCOMING WRITER'S BLOCK

Sometimes I get up in the morning and just can't think of anything to write, or what I do write comes out all wrong. In my early writing days when this happened, I would while away an hour staring into the void – or clean the refrigerator for the 10th time or check yet again to see if the mail had come – but over the years I've found two techniques that help get the words flowing. The first is to write about my writer's block: 'Today, for some reason, I just can't get started writing. I'm not sure why. I wonder if it's because of the pizza I ate last night, or maybe it's just because I don't know how to get where I know I need to be in my story today. The problem is bringing that village back to life. Here's what I remember…' Suddenly, I've forgotten about my writer's block and started writing my piece again.

The second technique follows the model that John Steinbeck used when he wrote *East of Eden*. He kept a notebook. In the left-hand pages of the notebook he wrote a daily diary – this was his way of warming up his writing engine. In the right-hand pages of the same book he wrote the novel itself. I have adapted a version of this. If I simply can't get going on my story, I start writing about whatever comes to mind – the Yosemite hike we did over the weekend, the Borges story I read the night before, the glistening cheesecake in the refrigerator, the Polynesian beach I wish I were lying on… I just start writing about whatever is occupying my mind, and somehow this unlocks me and liberates my imagination to get back into the story again.

– Don George

just wander at will, for pleasure, or laze on the beach. Most successful travel writers ground themselves by building in a certain number of months at home between trips; they catch up on relationships and bills, write the pieces they've researched, and recharge their batteries.

SOME STRAIGHT TALK ABOUT EARNINGS

If all the people on the planet who make a living solely from their travel writing (excluding travel guidebook writers) were brought together in one room, they would number only around three dozen. Most of the guests at this globe-girdling gathering would write books for a living, and their income would be a mix of advance payments for their new books and royalties from their old ones, supplemented by a few travel magazine or newspaper pieces a year. Only a very few would make a living exclusively from writing articles for magazines and newspapers – there simply isn't enough work to go around, and it just isn't well paid enough.

In today's publishing world, many travel writers outlay their own time and money up-front without any guarantee that they'll ever see any money. Even if and when their article is finally published, if they were to calculate the hours that went into the travel, research and writing of the piece, they'd need a magnifying glass to see their hourly wage.

Another factor to consider is the lack of any Freelancers Retirement Fund Limited that will squirrel money away for you and dole it out after you've stopped wandering and scribbling. You have to do that yourself. Many travel writers in their 50s and 60s are only thinking about this now, and realising that they should have started saving for this phase of life decades ago.

The fundamental caveat is that you must be realistic about the amount of money you can earn as a travel writer – but if you are able and willing to try to make travel writing your primary source of income, more power to you. And good luck!

Earnings in the UK

Pay varies enormously in the UK, and how much you can earn in a year will depend on who you write for, how often your pieces are published, and how hard you work. As the quality newspapers have a weekly or bi-weekly travel section, freelance travel writers often find themselves writing more pieces for newspapers than for magazines, which are normally published monthly. Pay for newspaper articles varies from £200 to £500 per 1000 words; for travel magazines the rate ranges between £150 and £400 per 1000 words (of course, well-known writers or regular contributors are paid more). However, the length of a standard destination piece in the UK is around 1000 to 2000 words, so this needs to be factored in when you're calculating how many articles you need to write to make a living. Sometimes you might be commissioned to write 3000 words or more, especially for a magazine, but it's rare.

Expenses are rarely paid on top of your article fee, because it is assumed you'll be negotiating 'freebies' – trips arranged for low or no cost with airlines, hotels and other travel providers in return for coverage in the article you write, usually in the fact box (or sidebar, as it is called in the US) accompanying your story. (The attitude towards freebies is very different in the US, and is discussed in greater detail in Chapter Six.) Procuring such deals with airlines and hotels can take up a prodigious amount of your precious time. Of course, travelling also takes up a lot of your time, and days when you're travelling are days when you are not earning – in effect, you are paid to write, not travel. This is why you need to write as many articles as you can from one trip. Another point to consider is that many articles are commissioned 'on spec' – this means that a travel editor has said they like the idea of what you might write but will only agree to run it (and pay you) once they have seen your copy. It is also much more difficult to negotiate free travel or accommodation with an 'on spec' piece as there are no guarantees of coverage for the service provider.

Earnings in the US

A very few US-based freelance writers might make more than $100,000 a year, but the vast majority earn in the vicinity of $15,000 to $40,000 a year. A very good scenario would see you being lucky enough to receive six assignments from major magazines in one year. If each assignment was for an article of 3000 words, and the magazines paid an average of $1.50 a word, plus expenses, that would come to $4500 per story and a grand total of $27,000. That would be it, and you'd still have all your life expenses to cover, from housing and food to medical costs and phone bills. Unlike the situation in the UK, you would at least be compensated for any expenses incurred, but could you possibly survive on this amount?

To be even more realistic, few US magazines would pay $1.50 a word to a new writer. Top magazines would most likely start you at $1 a word for articles ranging from short pieces (250 words) published at the beginning of the magazine to longer features (4000 words) in the middle sections. And some magazines pay dramatically less than this, down to 10 cents a word.

Major newspapers pay considerably less than major magazines, with most of them paying between $200 and $500 for articles of 1000 to 2500 words. Rates do vary, however; for example, in July 2004 the *New York Times* paid around $850 for a lead story, the *Washington Post* and the *Los Angeles Times* paid up to $800 for features and between $250 and $500 for most inside stories, and the *Chicago Tribune* and the *San Francisco Chronicle* paid $500 for a lead story and $150 to $250 for inside stories.

Earnings in Australia

Most Australian newspapers pay a rate of 50 cents a word, rising to perhaps 70 cents if you're very lucky. Features range from 1500 to 3000 words, and inside pieces vary between 700 and 1000 words. Metropolitan and smaller regional newspapers can pay a set fee of as little as $50. Magazines vary wildly, from a set fee of $350 to as much as $1 per word from the majors. As in the UK, expenses are rarely paid, reviewers for publications such as restaurant guides being the fortunate exception. Making a living solely from travel writing is tough in a relatively small market such as Australia, and most writers end up looking for staff jobs.

Travel Literature

If you are writing a literary travel book on contract you will at least get some money up front from the publishers – this is called an 'advance' and the publishers award it in the hope that sales of your book will recoup that sum and more. An advance for your first book from a major publisher will probably be in the region of £10,000 in the UK, $15,000 in the US or $20,000 in Australia, though there are plenty of first-time writers who have published a book for much less, and smaller publishers will pay correspondingly smaller advances. Unless you have a supplemental income, this advance will have to fund your travels and your general living expenses for the length of time it takes to write your book – generally one to two years. Of course, if your first book is a success and you want to write a second, the financial picture can brighten considerably.

Travel Guidebooks

Many travel guidebook authors write full-time, either for one publisher or for a variety of companies, with only one- or two-day gaps in between assignments (see Chapter Eight for more information on fees for guidebook authors). The formula for paying guidebook writers depends on where you are researching (for example, whether it is a cheap or expensive destination), how well the publisher calculates the book is going to sell (the author of a guide to Thailand will be paid more than the author of a book on Vanuatu), and on your reputation to deliver a sparkling manuscript to length and on time. As with newspapers and magazines, some guidebook publishers pay better than others, and some take expenses into consideration while others don't. Very roughly, a full-time guidebook writer can expect to earn between £10,000 and £25,000 per year in the UK, from $20,000 to $45,000 in the US, and approximately $30,000 to $50,000 in Australia.

IN-HOUSE VERSUS FREELANCING

There are two main avenues for making travel writing your career: either working as a salaried staff member for a newspaper or magazine, or working as a freelancer.

Working As a Staff Writer

To be brutally realistic, staff writing jobs are as elusive as the creature Peter Matthiessen seeks and never quite finds in his classic work of travel literature, *The Snow Leopard*.

There are in total perhaps three dozen full-time travel writer jobs at newspapers in the US, the UK and Australia, and these positions are usually occupied by long-time staffers who have cut their teeth on the city desk and the business beat, for example, before being offered the plum of travel. Even the best of these jobs require a good deal of decidedly unglamorous desk-bound work making telephone calls and Internet expeditions to research car-rental rates and single-traveller supplements for the kinds of practical pieces the staff writer is frequently called on to produce.

The picture is the same for the very few staff writing jobs on travel magazines: the staff writers for the most part fill in the holes in the magazine's editorial picture-puzzle, writing news-oriented pieces, industry stories, book and product reviews and the like. Occasionally a staff writer may be allowed to take a long weekend to some nearby or far-flung locale, but those meaty middle-of-the-book stories are often written by freelance writers. In terms of travel and writing, probably the best gig you can hope for is to become a contributing editor (despite the name, this means someone who writes regularly for one publication; it actually has nothing to do with editing) – but these coveted spots go to people who already have a reputation (and who actually enhance the magazine's reputation by appearing on its masthead and in its pages). And while the contributing editors may be guaranteed some kind of annual stipend from a publication (usually in exchange for a specified number of articles or for enhanced rates of pay for what they do write), they do not enjoy the perks of full-time employment.

An added complication is that in-house travel writing jobs or travel desk jobs at newspapers and magazines are rarely advertised. Travel publishing is a very small world and most jobs go to internal candidates or are advertised by word of mouth to colleagues in the industry. The plain truth is that if you are just starting out as a travel writer it will be extremely difficult for you to score a staff writing job. Even if you have a few published articles under your belt, the same applies. However, if you start off as a freelance writer, become known, get a good reputation and move in the right circles, then you may hear of a job on offer or be tapped on the shoulder.

Another way of breaking into salaried employment – and occasionally to get your name in print – at a newspaper or magazine is to apply for unpaid work experience on the travel desk. In the US such work experience is called an internship and is only offered by newspapers, usually in affiliation with an academic program. Working on a travel desk means that you are the office anchor, doing all the administration that goes along with the travel pages – answering the phone, dealing with reader queries, organising travel arrangements etc. It may also include some commissioning, editing and a little writing. Although a work experience intern on the travel desk is often at everyone's beck and call, it's a wonderful training ground for any would-be travel writer. If you show initiative and flair, you might be asked to do some research on a piece and to write it up – and suddenly, *voilà!*, your name's in print. Doing unpaid work for a busy travel desk also gives you a foot in the door and means that you could be 'in the right place at the right time' when a suitable position comes along. From here the only way is up, heading towards your long-term goal of becoming a staff travel writer.

The benefits of a staff job, as opposed to freelance travel writing, are a steady income, health coverage (in the US at least), the camaraderie of office life and regular publication of your work. Writing as a staffer means you avoid the frustration, uncertainty and general agony of freelance life – continually pitching to editors for work, never knowing where or if your articles will be published, never knowing when your money will come in, and hardly ever taking a holiday because it is unpaid. In some ways, having a reliable outlet for your work is even more valuable than having the steady income.

So what could possibly be the downside of working in-house? There are the problems and pitfalls – the Machiavellian minutiae – of office politics, for one thing. Also, like all other office workers, you essentially have to go to work every day (when you're not travelling for work), and you don't have a lot of control over what you do. If you're told to write 1000 words on the history and highlights of consumer taxes, you do it.

However, as an in-house writer you'll have access to some fantastic travel opportunities. And more importantly, working in-house, even if it is only for a short period of time, is an invaluable way of building up your contacts if you later want to go freelance. The bottom line is that as a novice travel writer you'd be crazy to turn down a staff job if you were offered one. Take it, learn everything you possibly can, network like mad and then decide if you want to remain on staff or go freelance.

Working As a Freelancer

For most writers who choose the freelance life, the freedom of setting their own schedule far outweighs the benefits and perks of a salaried position. As a freelancer you can work when you want, on what you want; you usually have the freedom to write for several publications (as long as they are noncompeting), as opposed to only one; you can write all night and sleep all day if you wish. You are your own boss, and in control – and this is a rarity in the working world.

On the other hand, unless you have some sort of independent income, you're always wondering where your next payment is coming from. That is the hardest truth of the free-lancer's life: the lack of certainty, stability and regularity. Even the most famous freelancers cannot assume a steady income. When Paul Theroux, perhaps the best-known travel writer in the US, was researching his latest book on Africa, *Dark Star Safari*, he proposed Africa-related articles to virtually all the major magazines in the US – and did not get one commission.

One thing you'll definitely need to develop as a full-time freelancer is fiscal discipline. You may receive one big sum in January and not get another until July, so you need to develop a system to make your money stretch through the lean periods. If you're writing a travel literature book, there's the problem of making an advance last until your royalties kick in – which they will only do if your book sells well. Similarly, if you're working on a guidebook, payments normally come in three instalments, months apart: there's an up-front fee for signing the contract, a payment upon acceptance of your work and the final cheque upon publication.

If you're writing for newspapers and magazines, smaller amounts of money will be coming in on a very ad hoc basis and you'll never know from one day to the next whether you'll be rich or poor that week. Some newspapers pay at the end of the month after the month of publication – so if your story appears in the first week of July, you won't see the cheque until September. The bottom line is that as a freelancer you need to set up an efficient article- and payment-tracking system to ensure you don't fall into a predicament financially.

Part-Time Travel Writing

Using travel writing as an additional occupation to supplement your earnings and career is much more common than depending on full-time travel writing work. Some part-timers teach (those long school holidays can be spent on the road); others expand their speciality by writing restaurant or book reviews, personality profiles or feature stories on the arts and culture. Some write corporate copy – year-end reports, catalogue texts, corporate brochures or press releases, for example. Some of them work as editors, copy editors or fact-checkers; some as flight attendants or booksellers.

In many ways, it makes a lot of sense to try to make travel writing a complement to the job that you depend on for your livelihood. You can research travel articles during holiday periods and on weekends. This takes the pressure off your travel writing and allows you to ease into it. It also gives you more flexibility to pursue and write the stories you really want to do, knowing that you're not dependent on their sale to put bread on the table and a roof over your head.

Whether your travel writing is a full-time profession or a part-time passion, you need to know how to find and focus the story that's just right for you. We'll discuss this in Chapter Three.

INTERVIEW WITH FRED MAWER

Fred Mawer is a UK-based freelance travel journalist for the Mail on Sunday *and the* Daily Telegraph.

How did you start off in your career as a travel writer?

Firstly, I wouldn't, and don't, call myself a travel writer. The title sounds too fancy and creative. I call myself a travel journalist.

I started out with *Holiday Which?* – the magazine produced by the Consumers' Association. I replied to an ad for a job as a researcher there, and stayed for about three years. It was a very good grounding in researching topics and destinations thoroughly and accurately.

What is the best way of establishing yourself if you're just starting out in your career as a freelance travel journalist?

I went freelance after that time with *Holiday Which?* I sent out letters to virtually every guidebook publisher in the UK, and got work from a couple in the first year. So this practice can work if you have some experience.

I also wrote a couple of uncommissioned articles for newspapers' weekend travel sections. I managed to get a couple of things accepted, but breaking into this field is a hard slog. I only started getting regular commissions after a few years – basically when old colleagues had got commissioning positions on the papers.

In regard to submitting uncommissioned pieces – do submit uncommissioned pieces, but don't be too optimistic. Also, make sure they're not too long – under 1500 words for the quality papers.

How have you managed to get your name known as a freelance travel journalist?

Lots of cold calling initially. Trying not to say no to any work offered, at first. Going to a few media events – PR lunches etc – but be selective, as many are a waste of time.

As a freelance travel journalist, how do you get the numbers to add up in terms of an income?

I work long hours. I'm lucky enough to work for two of the better-paid papers – the *Mail on Sunday* and the *Telegraph*. I don't know how those who work regularly for less well-paid newspapers can make ends meet. I also do as little travelling as possible! The bane of a travel journalist's life is having to travel – you're paid for writing, not travelling. I'm lucky that much of the stuff I do is consumer travel articles, which you can, and often have to, do from your desk.

What tips would you give to budding travel writers?

Develop a few niches/specialties – country, destination, topic.

Write to length.

Be accurate – check all your copy (phone numbers, even if abroad; websites) before submitting it.

Write notes on the spot, not at the end of the day (or trip).

Avoid press trips – you end up doing stuff that is clichéd, and get the PR spin.

Don't do too many trips with your partner/family: travelling for work is usually hard work, and not much fun for companions.

Are there any courses or any training that you'd recommend a budding travel writer to undertake?

I've never gone on a course. I wish I'd learnt to touch-type and had shorthand skills.

What are the most common mistakes that travel writers make in their copy?

Making themselves the focal point of the piece. It's the subject matter that should be the focus.

Making mistakes that would be easy to avoid with a few checks.

Not being judgmental enough.

What are the main differences between travel writing for a newspaper as opposed to a magazine?

Not that much. Newspaper pieces are more time dependent – they often need to be more newsy, topical. Magazine pieces have to be submitted longer in advance before publication.

What, in your opinion, constitutes 'good' travel writing?

Writing that is opinionated, judgmental, that focuses on the place not the writer.

Awareness of audience – being selective about what is and isn't interesting.

What constitutes 'bad' travel writing?

Stuff that is clichéd, inaccurate, out of date, lifted from guidebooks.

What are the rewards of travel writing as a career?

Being your own boss. Being able to work from home.

Travelling a lot – though the perks of this diminish after a while. The travel is often a chore, not a perk.

The combination of having a desk job and a job that gets you away from your desk.

What has been the downside for you?

A lack of work colleagues: it's a pretty lonely existence.

A lack of career structure: unless you move into the editing side of things, it's hard to know where to take your career.

The money: it's not a well-paid job – even by journalistic standards. Most guidebook work in particular pays appallingly badly.

INTERVIEW WITH HARRIET O'BRIEN

Harriet O'Brien is a UK-based freelance travel writer and author. She was Weekend Editor of the Independent *(1994–99) and Managing Editor of* Condé Nast Traveller *(2000–02). She won the Travelex Best Daily Feature Award in 1997.*

How did you start off in your career as a travel writer?

I started in book publishing – after university I worked for *The Bookseller* magazine. This didn't pay very well and it was tedious so I found a job as assistant to the editor of a new magazine called *Business*, which was a real 1980s venture. This gave me a good editorial background so I understood how the word gets on the page, what a sub actually does, how the pages get laid out, who commissions what etc.

Then I worked for several small publishers where I did everything (editing, picture researching, writing, commissioning).

I then wrote a book on Burma because I grew up there. After that I joined the *Independent* newspaper.

What is the best way of establishing yourself if you're just starting out in your career as a freelance travel writer?

It's a real chicken and egg situation. You need to get yourself published, but that's not easy the first time.

I'd advise getting a job or doing work in an office of a travel publication, even voluntary work. You get your face known, people might trust you with the odd small commission and it can be a launching pad for your career.

How have you managed to get your name known as a freelance travel writer?

I would only be freelance now with the contacts I have made over the last 10 years. I wouldn't start off as a freelance travel writer with no experience or outlets for my work.

As a freelance travel writer, how do you get the numbers to add up in terms of an income?

I think the short answer is that you don't. A lot of people who write either have a private income or another job. While I've been freelance travel writing I've also been doing editing jobs and writing things totally unrelated to travel.

What tips would you give to budding travel writers?

Don't limit yourself to travel. Think of yourself as a writer first and foremost so that you can turn your hand to feature pieces while on your travels.

Are there any courses or any training that you'd recommend a budding travel writer to undertake?

Experience counts for more than any course – do your apprenticeship on the job. I think it is really important to learn how a publication is put together so that as a writer you understand the whole process and don't get too precious about your copy.

What are the most common mistakes that travel writers make in their copy?

Unreliable spelling and incorrect facts. Those are unforgivable.

What are the most common mistakes that travel writers make when pitching to you?

Pestering too much is very annoying. If you don't want a story then there's nothing a writer can do to change your mind. They've got to understand that it might not fit.

What are the main differences between travel writing for a newspaper as opposed to a magazine?

Deadlines. Newspapers work to very tight timetables because they are daily or weekly, and magazines tend to be monthly.

Also, you are much more likely to get a commission from a newspaper because of the volume of material they need.

What, in your opinion, constitutes 'good' travel writing?

A sense of place, definitely, but beyond that just a very good feature.

I don't see that there's much difference between a travel piece and a feature piece – a travel piece is simply a feature about travel.

What constitutes 'bad' travel writing?

Awful clichés – 'a land of contrasts', for instance. A writer putting too much of themselves into the piece.

And I also find that humour can be really difficult – something that you find hysterical in a trip can sound very unfunny when you write it up.

What are the rewards of travel writing as a career?

You travel and you write. Those two things in themselves are very rewarding.

What has been the downside for you?

Being away at a moment's notice, often for several days, and mostly not being paid much for the piece you write.

INTERVIEW WITH ALISON RICE

Alison Rice is a UK-based freelance travel writer, broadcaster and presenter. She was Editor of BBC Holidays *magazine (1992–95), and Director of Programmes for Travel Channel (1995–2000).*

How did you start off in your career as a travel writer?

I was a magazine editor and had a weekly BBC Radio 1 program and got fed up with being an editor. I went freelance and was advised to have a speciality. I had written some travel pieces as an editor (editors get the pick of travel trips and I'd done some travels around the East off my own bat) and I thought there was a gap in the market (this was 1983) for a specialist on mass-market travel. A bloke who liked my writing and radio stuff offered me a gig as travel editor on TV-am. The bloke was Greg Dyke (ex Director-General of the BBC).

What is the best way of establishing yourself if you're just starting out in your career as a freelance travel writer?

Be very knowledgeable in a certain type of travel. You can't be all things to all people.

If at all possible, don't freelance until you've spent time as a staffer in some form of publishing/media and developed your own network of editors. Do your homework about the publication before offering ideas to the editor.

How have you managed to get your name known as a freelance travel writer?

Because I started when I was already known – as an editor and broadcaster. Because I worked bloody hard for the first 15 years and really got to know the travel industry. Because after about the first five years I found a style that was mine and that suited me and that people seemed to want.

As a freelance travel writer, how do you get the numbers to add up in terms of an income?

I don't. You have to work very hard and be very well established to make a decent living just from travel writing, and I think only a very few achieve this – all well-established and knowledgeable gurus.

After 20 years in the field I don't want to produce the number of features I'd need to write for what I think is a decent living, so I use my experience and expertise in other ways to produce the sort of income I want.

What tips would you give to budding travel writers?

If you want to be a travel journalist, get a job in the media first. If you want to produce 'travel literature' à la Thubron, Lewis etc, get a private income or downsize from taxi to bus, high mortgage to bedsit. Develop your own fresh, unclichéd look on the world.

Are there any courses or any training that you'd recommend a budding travel writer to undertake?

No. Andy Soutter's (andy@cellan.freeserve.co.uk) summer schools might be a chance to see whether you really have that fresh look on the world or whether you're better sticking to writing great emails on your holidays and keeping the day job.

What are the most common mistakes that travel writers make in their copy?

Clichés. Tired stereotyping. No spirit. Kowtowing to tourist boards, PRs. Believing the hype they're offered. Never checking facts…shall I go on?

What are the main differences between travel writing for a newspaper as opposed to a magazine?

Deadlines. News. Some magazines treat travel pages as no more than payback for free staff holidays. Dire.

What, in your opinion, constitutes 'good' travel writing?

Something that so conjures up the spirit of the place I can smell it. Some of the best travel writing makes me know I'd never want to go to the place. Something unexpected that's sharp and fresh and might make me laugh or cry.

What constitutes 'bad' travel writing?

Much easier to answer – clichéd, lazy, 'what I did on my holidays' stuff and the belief that because the destination is 'exotic' the feature must be good. They rarely are. Trying to cover everything about a place in one feature.

What are the rewards of travel writing as a career?

The reward of travel journalism is that sometimes you really can make a tiny difference – for the better – to the way that the extraordinary travel industry conducts itself.

And sometimes your advice really can mean some family has a better holiday. The reward for travel writing is that around the world you get to peep through doors that are locked to nonwriting travellers/holidaymakers.

What has been the downside for you?

The downside of freelancing is occasionally having some of what I thought was good work 'changed' by staffers. Still, I've learnt to try not to worry as long as they get my name on the cheque right.

INTERVIEW WITH ROLF POTTS

Rolf Potts is the author of Vagabonding: An Uncommon Guide to the Art of Long-Term World Travel. *Based in the US, he has written for* Salon.com, National Geographic Traveler *and* Condé Nast Traveler, *as well as National Public Radio.*

How did you start off in your career as a travel writer?

My career started, as most do, with failure. Right after university, I saved up my money and spent eight months traveling around North America. When I got back, I decided I was going to write a book about the experience, and that this book would be the biggest thing since Kerouac's *On the Road*. The problem, of course, is that I hadn't considered my audience. What was interesting to me was not always interesting to the people who read these travel tales. After months of writing and unfruitful attempts to attract agents and editors, I came to the difficult realization that I would have to learn how to tell a story and evoke a place and an experience through the details.

A couple of years after I quit that failed book, I was able to rewrite one of its chapters (a story about Las Vegas) and sell it to the on-line magazine Salon.com. I was living and teaching English in Korea at the time, so I began to write Korea travel tales for Salon as well. Eventually, I built up a working relationship with the editor, after proving my ability to work hard and write well. When I left on a two-year trip around Asia (funded by my years of teaching in Korea), I was able to talk the editor into making me a travel columnist for Salon.com. That exposure led to being published in other magazines, and my career took off from there.

What is the best way of establishing yourself if you're just starting out in your career as a freelance travel writer?

There are several things you can do to get your name out there. One is to write a lot, and to write well. Another is to market yourself with a website that selectively showcases your stories and photos and publications. But, as much as anything, the best way to get your name out there is to write in a very distinctive way. Some people do this by writing stories that are funny. Other writers are good at evoking the human essence of the travel experience. Other travel writers become experts on certain countries, or on travel planning, or on certain types of travel, like adventure travel. If you can combine a talent for more than one of these elements, of course, you will do well.

How have you managed to get your name known as a freelance travel writer?

My website (http://rolfpotts.com) has been a big help. It was an integral part of my initial pitch as a columnist at Salon.com, and has showcased my writing ever since. It includes links to on-line stories and radio pieces, as well as photos and interviews and advice. In the past year I have even started a weblog of travel-related information and trivia. In this way, if you provide people with new and interesting travel information and stories, they will come back again and again to see what you are saying.

Of course, it is essential to write well.

As a freelance travel writer, how do you get the numbers to add up in terms of an income?

Through simplicity, and not spending very much. That allows me to get by just fine on a minimum of money. It also allows me to concentrate on the kind of stories I like, the kind of stories I excel at. I mean, I could supplement my income by writing a lot of travel news and service articles for newspapers and magazines, but these kinds of stories don't interest me as much as more involved, in-depth features. Thus, I write fewer stories in a given year than your average travel journalist, but I enjoy them more, and I think my writing benefits from this kind of focus.

As for keeping things simple and saving money, I've found that the easiest way to do this is to live overseas, preferably in a less-expensive region, like Asia or Latin America. Not only does this save me money on day-to-day living, but it also increases my chances of getting work writing about those regions for newspapers and magazines.

What tips would you give to budding travel writers?

Travel a lot. Write a lot. Read a lot. Don't do it for the money, because there are better ways to make money. Don't even do it for the travel, because there are better ways to fund and facilitate travel. Do it because you love to write, and you love to write about travel. Do it because it is your passion and obsession. Don't ever do it just because you think it will make you seem cool or sexy, because it will never match your expectations.

Are there any courses or any training that you'd recommend a budding travel writer to undertake?

I think the most important thing as a writer is to read well. Be familiar with good writing (not just travel writing, but creative nonfiction, novels and poetry), and try to recognize what makes it work. Also, don't be afraid to fail, so long as you learn from your mistakes and always work at getting better. The best training in the world is the school of hard knocks.

What are the most common mistakes that travel writers make in their copy?

First, they assume the reader will be as interested in their travels as they are. Second, they stick too hard to chronology, without ever telling a story. All the worst stories are just a bland recounting of events.

Thus, while travel writing should never be fictional, it *should* emulate the best techniques of fiction, such as character, action, plot, foreshadowing, dialogue and payoff. Character and dialogue are especially important, since they bring the story to life. Think about it: do we enjoy *Seinfeld* or *Cannery Row* or *American Pie* for the setting and descriptions? Of course not – we are drawn to their *characters* and what these characters do and say. Thus, be an extrovert as you travel, and color your story with the people you meet. Provide action and dialogue, setup and payoff. Draw the reader into the story with these elements.

What are the main differences between travel writing for a newspaper as opposed to a magazine, or for the web versus print?

Newspaper features tend to be shorter and more service-oriented – though this will often depend on the taste of the editor. Newspapers are more likely to publish 'destination' pieces, something that magazines rarely do. Magazines like a bigger theme or news hook to the story, and rarely take a standard piece about a 'place'. Web writing is harder to pin down. As a rule, web writing is short – but then some of my longest pieces have appeared on line. The web is very flexible, of course, and often allows for the kind of storytelling that you couldn't get away with in magazines and newspapers.

What, in your opinion, constitutes 'good' travel writing?

Engaging stories that evoke people and places around the world in a personal way. Naturally, they must also be well-informed and well-researched.

What constitutes 'bad' travel writing?

Bad writing often comes from bad traveling – and bad travel is unimaginative, uninformed and unoriginal. Thus, to write well, you have to get into adventures and meet people. You have to try new things, or experience old things in new ways.

Of course, people can have good adventures and still write poorly, if they don't tell a story (with a beginning, middle and end), evoke characters, and put themselves in the shoes of their readers.

What are the rewards of travel writing as a career?

The ability to see the world, live creatively, and express yourself through the written word. Each new day is an adventure.

What has been the downside for you?

Travel writing doesn't pay well, if at all, and it is often a solitary pursuit that your friends and families and lovers don't understand. I have personally come to terms with all of this, of course; I'm just mentioning these factors to those who think there is some way around the bad pay, frequent solitude, and lack of life consistency. There isn't.

But I love it just the same.

INTERVIEW WITH DAISANN McLANE

Daisann McLane is the author of Cheap Hotels. *Based in the US, she wrote the Frugal Traveler column for the* New York Times *travel section and writes regularly for* National Geographic Traveler *magazine. She has also written for* Rolling Stone, Vogue, *the* Village Voice *and* Harper's Bazaar.

How did you start off in your career as a travel writer?

I've been working at writing and journalism since before I graduated from college. I began as a rock critic and feature writer, working for *Crawdaddy* magazine and later for *Rolling Stone* and the *Village Voice*. *Rolling Stone* sent me all over the world to go on the road with rock bands like Fleetwood Mac, Cheap Trick and Peter Frampton. When I look back on some of those old stories, like the one I wrote about Cheap Trick's phenomenal tour in Japan (where they were greeted as if they were the second coming of the Beatles, with young shy Japanese girls suddenly screaming and throwing themselves over the band's motorcade cars!), I realize that I'd started to write about travel way back then and I didn't even know it.

Later I went to live on the island of Trinidad for a while, and got interested in the great musical culture there (calypso and soca). I eventually became a calypso singer myself, and made a couple of records. The incredible experience of participating in someone else's culture really launched my career in a different direction. When I went back to New York, I wasn't very interested in rock and roll or celebrity culture anymore. I started writing about the music I loved, from the Caribbean, from Latin America and from Africa. The term 'world music' hadn't been coined yet.

Articles about such things were a hard sell back then, even in New York, where so much of the action was going on in the ethnic enclaves of Brooklyn and Queens. So I stumbled onto a strategy to finance my travels – when I wanted to go, say, to the Dominican Republic to learn more about the local music, I'd call up some of the travel magazines and ask if they wanted a story on the destination. In this way, I built up a portfolio of travel articles, although I wasn't really thinking of travel as my main interest as a writer, it was a sideline to writing about music. (Selling those music stories did get easier after a while – I became world music columnist for the *Village Voice*, then for

Rolling Stone, and did articles for *Vogue, Harper's Bazaar, US Weekly*, the *New York Times Magazine* and the Sunday Arts and Leisure section.)

I was in graduate school at Yale, studying Caribbean culture and freelancing on the side, when quite by chance, an opportunity came up to try out to write the Frugal Traveler column at the *New York Times*. The editor of the column had worked with me before as a music writer, and so she already knew my work. They sent me to Budapest, liked what I came back with, and thus began a frantic merry-go-round of traveling that has pretty much taken over my life for the past five and a half years.

As you can see, I've poked around at a lot of things in my life, following what interested me at the moment. I don't recommend this approach to others! But it somehow has worked out for me. And in a wacky way, every stage I have passed through, from rock to world music to cultural studies at the university, seems to have been a terrific preparation for what I do now.

To me it's funny that now people think of me as a 'travel writer' since for most of my career I was doing something else.

What is the best way of establishing yourself if you're just starting out in your career as a freelance travel writer?

This is a question that I don't really have an answer for, since 'travel writing' is truly something I stumbled into. I've never been good at selecting career goals and then aiming for them, and I never set out to do what I'm doing today. I still don't think of myself as a 'travel writer', but as a writer with an overdose of curiosity about other people's cultures and how they live. The other day Keith Bellows, my wonderful editor at *National Geographic Traveler*, said to me: 'You aren't a travel writer, you are a writer who travels.'

I'm very lucky that I started out as a writer more than 20 years ago. I've had a lot of practice, and many years in which to make contacts, and establish a professional reputation. That makes things easier for me than for someone just starting out. If I were just starting out today, and certain that travel writing was my biggest interest, I'd probably try one of two things – getting an editorial job with a travel-related magazine to get my foot in the door, or moving to another country that totally fascinated me from top to toe, while writing a book that I'd hope would blow everyone away.

How have you managed to get your name known as a freelance travel writer?

I'm terrible at self-promotion, so I mostly just do my work and hope for the best. I'm not the sort of personality who will send 150 emails out to my dearest 'friends' every time I have a piece coming out somewhere. I don't maintain a website or do Letterman. But I did notice that there was a jump in my career when I put out my book *Cheap Hotels* in 2002. Having a book out in the market makes a big difference to magazine and newspaper editors, I think. It gives you more heft, more presence. It also makes a great hostess gift.

As a freelance travel writer, how do you get the numbers to add up in terms of an income?

It never really adds up. Some years are good, others are disasters. I know that just about every writer has a similarly discouraging tale, so I'll just leave it at that.

What tips would you give to budding travel writers?

Besides marry an investment banker? Seriously, I think that if you want to do this, you should be prepared to cut yourself loose and go on adventures. Go to places you adore, and immerse yourself in the people and their culture. Be open and humble. If someone invites you to come home with them and sleep on their floor, go. Put yourself in vulnerable situations and then come back home (or stay out there) and write marvelous stories. Do it because you love it, not because you see it as a way to make a fortune or be famous. Do it because you want to look back in 30 or 40 years on an amazing life lived.

Are there any courses or any training that you'd recommend a budding travel writer to undertake?

Absolutely. Learn another language. Two would be even better! Learning a foreign language is the best way to break through the wall between you and the place you are writing about. There's a quantum difference between a piece that is written by a writer fluent in the language and culture, and a piece written by someone who's just dropped in.

Living abroad for a spell is another great way of stretching your imagination, and acquiring a different point of view that will set you apart from the rest of the would-be travel writers pitching stories. Although I have to admit that if I read another article by a travel writer about teaching English in Asia or working in the Peace Corps, my eyes will glaze over. Both those activities are fantastic living-abroad experiences, but don't fall into the cliché of writing only that story – find a way to make other connections with the place you're in.

Studying and becoming expert at something that is identified or connected with another culture or place – say, for example, martial arts, or yoga, or French cooking – will give you an insider's edge for an article about India, China or France.

What are the main differences between travel writing for a newspaper as opposed to a magazine?

I think it's very hard to generalize the differences between magazines and newspapers. I think that the editor is more crucial than the format. Some newspaper travel sections allow writers to use their own voice freely, others will slice and dice your copy until it fits their mold. Some travel magazines are very tightly formatted, and print mainly service features that are edited and focus grouped and worried to death so much that by the time the thing gets printed you don't even want to have your name on the piece. Other magazines love it when you dance and dazzle and give you all the freedom you could want.

Over 20 years of writing, I've had four, maybe five editors who really clicked with me and understood and supported my writing. The editor makes all the difference in this work. When you find a good one, keep them in your life by any means possible. Remember their birthdays. Send chocolates from Belgium, silks from Vietnam. Offer them the name of your favorite massage therapist in Thailand.

What, in your opinion, constitutes 'good' travel writing?

This is really a matter of personal taste. Off the top of my head, here are some books that I love: *The Middle Passage*, by V. S. Naipaul; *Miami*, by Joan Didion; *Iron and Silk*, by Mark Salzman; everything by Ryszard Kapuscinski. Oh, my old buddy Mikal Gilmore's *Shot in the Heart*, and as long as we're talking memoir, the first 200 pages or so of Gabriel Garcia Marquez's *Vivir Para Contarla*. None of these writers is specifically a 'travel writer' yet each takes the reader on amazing journeys to other places, from a village in China to Mormon Utah; decodes other ways of life with great authority, empathy and understanding; makes other cultures, other belief systems accessible to the general reader. All of these writers have fascinating minds, strong points of view, and great passion – whether positive or negative – for the cultures they are traveling in. This is what turns me on about them.

Of the old school travel writers, I adore Norman Lewis, and have a soft spot for Patrick Leigh Fermor.

What constitutes 'bad' travel writing?

Again, this is very personal. I am not particularly interested in 'light' travel writing – you know, those 'I spent a year with the wife and kids in a Mediterranean village and look at all the wacky and tender things that happened' kind of books. There's a market for such books and they have their place, but it isn't on my bookshelf. I'm also put off by the travel genre I'd call 'Cynic on the Road' – I see a lot of stuff out in the market these days that is witty, but doesn't really have much to say, except that the author thinks that he (and it is nearly always a 'he') is cleverer and sharper than the people he is using as material.

What has been the downside of travel writing as a career?

There's no security in this career, and that can be really scary. On the other hand, when you travel to so many different places, and you see how people live outside of your little bubble, you realize how ridiculous the very idea of security is, from a global perspective. Empires come and go, personal fortunes rise and fall, the river waters flood and recede, and people somehow keep going. When I catch myself freaking out about my lack of a 401(K) plan, I slap myself back with a reality check: most people in the world don't have anything to catch them if they fall except their will and their determination to press on.

The other downside, at least in the last couple of years, has been witnessing first-hand and close-up the disintegration of America's image in the rest of the world. It's depressing to know that so many people around the world think my country's government is foolish at best, warmongers at worst – and even more depressing that I have to agree with them. When George W. Bush was running for president, my biggest objection to him wasn't his position on taxes or abortion – it was that he was a man who had almost never traveled abroad. Spending time in a different place watching the world from an unfamiliar (and, perhaps, uncomfortable) perspective should be a requirement for all our leaders. I hope that America's next president will be someone who knows how to speak at least one foreign language!

FINDING & FOCUSING YOUR STORY

THE RIGHT SUBJECT

The first step in writing a good travel story is finding the right subject. If the topic is right, the chances of getting your piece published will be maximised.

A good topic is usually a marriage of passion and practicality. As a writer, you want to choose a subject that will allow you to infuse your story with a sense of connection and conviction; at the same time, you need to write about a topic that will capture an editor's attention and will fit well with the publication you've targeted.

Today's publishing world offers a bountiful variety of outlets for travel writing, and so it is critically important to know the market. Study the publications you'd like to write for, reading several issues closely to analyse the focus, tone, approach and length of the articles they publish.

At the same time, it is equally important to know yourself, and to focus on subjects or places that especially interest you. Are you particularly drawn to food, crafts, festivals or nightlife? Do you prefer five-star resorts or no-frills motels? Do you like to explore the heart of a city or its far-flung hinterlands? Finding your passion will help you narrow the publication targets for your stories – but don't narrow your field too much. If you love luxury resorts, you may think that you couldn't possibly write for a budget travel magazine – but what about a story on finding luxury for under £50 a night? If you're not passionate about food, you probably wouldn't think of approaching a food and wine magazine, but a humorous piece on surviving a week in Tuscany with a fervent foodie could be right on target.

TRAVEL TRENDS

There are three kinds of trends you should monitor in order to find good story ideas and to get to know your market.

Objective Travel Trends

Objective travel trends reflect traveller behaviour: where people are going, how they are getting there and what they are doing when they get there. For example, are ski resorts in America suddenly all the rage with Europeans? Are more Americans barging their way along European waterways than before? Is Austria a hot destination for Australians? Does camping have a new cachet for Canadians? Is train travel booming around the globe? Are airlines or tour operators opening operations in any new destinations?

Whenever possible, anticipate these trends. If you know that a country is planning a major tourism campaign in six months, pitch a story about that country right now. When a city is chosen as a future Olympics site or as a future European Capital of Culture, you know that travellers – and editors – will be interested in knowing more about them as their time in the spotlight approaches.

STAYING UP TO DATE WITH TRAVEL TRENDS

Finding fresh material, spotting travel trends and keeping up to date with industry and consumer changes are essential facts of life for all travel writers. The Resources Chapter at the back of this book contains a wealth of global and regional information sources, and is a good place to start.

Scanning newspaper travel sections and travel magazines will give you a feel for what your competitors are writing about, and will give you ideas for new stories. If you follow this practice you will also avoid the embarrassment of offering an editor a story similar to one that has just been run. Reading one or two industry magazines a week will keep you informed of what airlines, tour operators, hotel groups etc are up to. In the UK, subscribe to *Travel Weekly* and *Travel Trade Gazette*, or read www.travelweekly.co.uk and www.ttglive.com (much cheaper). In the US, subscribe to the American version of *Travel Weekly* or peruse its website, www.twcrossroads.com. In Australia, read *Travel Week* (www.travelbiz.com.au) and the fortnightly *Traveltrade* travel news magazine for Australian travel professionals.

Various on-line publications and websites are also important to watch, such as the UK-based TravelMole (www.travelmole.com) and Lonely Planet's travel forum, the Thorn Tree (http://thorntree.lonelyplanet.com). Other on-line resources that provide excellent updated information and analysis include Joe Brancatelli's informative free newsletter (www.joesentme.com), Frequent Flyer (www.frequentflyer.oag.com), Leisure Travel News (www.ttgweb.com) and the World Travel Watch website produced by James O'Reilly and Larry Habegger (www.worldtravelwatch.com). An extensive list of on-line travel trade publications can be found at www.ehotelier.com/browse/magazines.php.

You should also look regularly at websites that provide tourism facts, figures and statistics; for a comprehensive list by region, see the Facts, Figures & Statistics sections of the Resources Chapter. Major websites for UK travel writers include National Statistics Online (www.statistics.gov.uk), the UK Tourism Industry website (www.visitbritain.com) and the European Travel Commission (www.etc-corporate.org). In the US, try the Office of Travel and Tourism Industries

Subjective Travel Trends

These trends are anecdotal and often qualitative. Are the travellers who once flocked to Thailand now heading to Vietnam? Does the up-market traveller consider the spa resorts in the Maldives passé and, if so, where are they going instead? Is Panama the new Costa Rica, Krakow the new Prague? Are baby boomers turning to volunteer vacations to add meaning to their lives? Are honeymoon cruises suddenly in vogue?

Editorial Travel Trends

Editorial trends are indicated by changes in the weight of coverage given to different regions or types of travel. For example, these days almost every serious British newspaper regularly devotes a page to European city breaks – a sharp contrast from a decade ago when coverage was very patchy. Stories on luxury spas might be on the decline while articles for older travellers are on the increase.

YOUR PROFESSIONAL NICHE

To make a decent living as a travel writer, you need to be able to turn your hand to a variety of travel articles. However, it can be very much to your advantage to find the niche that best fits your expertise as a writer. By narrowing your field, you can focus on a particular slice of the travel world and so become an authority on it. Travel editors, and possibly (http://tinet.ita.doc.gov/research/reports/basic/index.html) and the Travel Industry Association of America (www.tia.org/Travel/default.asp). Useful Australian websites include the Australian Bureau of Statistics (www.abs.gov.au) and the Research & Stats pages of the Tourism Australia website (www.tourism.australia.com).

It's also a good idea to visit the websites of the World Health Organization (www.who .int/en), the UK's Department of Health (www.doh.gov.uk), the US Centers for Disease Control (www.cdc.gov) and the Australian Department of Foreign Affairs & Trade (www.smartraveller .gov.au). Also compare the foreign office websites maintained by the governments of the UK, the US, Australia and Canada. Sometimes the differences in these offices' respective travel advisories can be eye-opening.

Another useful way of finding out about what's happening in the travel world is by joining the press mailing lists of several travel companies. Ring up the companies you're interested in and speak to their PR departments, but try to be selective because you don't want to be flooded with press releases. Jaded travel writers or editors will tell you that 99 per cent of what you will be sent will go straight into the rubbish bin, but if that remaining one per cent forms the basis of a fresh travel article that you can sell, then it's worth it. And don't discount the fact that perusing a press release and learning about a new travel initiative adds to your overall body of travel information and may well be valuable one day.

Identifying a trend can become the nucleus for a story. You may create a story about the emergence of the trend itself – or you may be able to adapt that trend to a place you want to write about. For example, if you see that an editor has published a cover story on farm stays in Portugal, consider if there is a version of the farm-stay experience in perhaps New Zealand or Argentina that might interest the same editor. If the publication routinely features articles on extreme adventures, come up with an adrenalin-charged story in a destination they haven't covered yet. It's also important to remember that most newspaper travel sections are inundated with stories on hard-to-get-to places halfway around the globe, but are desperate for great writing on easy-to-visit places closer to home. Try proposing a long-weekend story – they're easier and cheaper to research, and your odds of getting published are considerably higher.

broadcasters, will begin to recognise your expertise, and will think of you when they are looking for a story or comment on your subject. Specialising in this way should mean *more* paid work, not less, because your particular expertise will be recognised. In addition, writing on something that you know about means less research, and less research means more time to write and, as we've said before, writing is what you're paid for.

Choosing a niche will involve looking for a decent gap in the market – there's very little point in specialising in a subject that everyone else has chosen as their particular field. Obviously, you also need to select something that really interests you and fits your lifestyle; it might be travel with children, no-frills airlines, a particular form of transport or a specific part of the world. Travel guidebook writers are in a great position to become experts on a region or country and its beliefs, customs and lifestyle. In addition, many journalists who are successful at being recognised as an authority in their area have done so by writing a book about their subject. Of course, your niche may also change over time, as you adapt to changes in your own life.

DEVELOPING YOUR STORY

Whether you specialise or widen your view, each new trip poses the same question: how do you develop a story from scratch? You've researched the publications that interest you, the passions that arouse you and the subjects that are currently popular. Now it's time to put your research to work.

A fundamental issue, particularly for aspiring newspaper and magazine writers, is the question of timing. Should you come up with story ideas before you travel or after you return? In the beginning you may find it easier to pitch articles from trips you've already taken – you know the place, and know exactly what you want to write about, making it infinitely easier for you to write a convincing proposal, or query letter, for that article. (We'll talk more about proposals and query letters in Chapter Six.)

As you develop a collection of published articles (known as a 'clip file') and a reputation, you may want to try pitching ideas for subjects and trips you haven't yet made. The difficulty is knowing what exactly you want to write about before you've made the trip. To be convincing, you'll need to do a good deal of research so you can paint a compelling portrait of your subject and of its relevance to the publication in question without having experienced it. (A more advantageous situation is when you have visited a place in the past and are returning to update your impressions and experiences.)

Pre-trip Research

Whether you're hoping to pitch your story pre- or post-trip, in order to get the most out of your journey you'll need to do some research. Start by buying a few good guidebooks and thoroughly studying the place you're planning to visit – everything from history and cultural background to specific events and attractions. These days many destinations have English-language newspapers or magazines. You may be able to track down copies before you leave home, depending on the destination, and many of them have websites. Reading these publications, whether in print or on line, will give you a sense of local flavour and help you discover what news stories and events are capturing residents' interest. Reading travel literature set in the country you're planning to visit can also open up story ideas and offer deeper insights into the character of the place.

After you've done all this research – studied the markets, the trends, yourself and the place you're preparing to visit – you should have a well-grounded idea of what you're likely to find in that place and what experiences or topics are most likely to impassion you. One more factor to consider, however, is that the best travel stories are often the un-anticipated ones that you stumble onto when you're actually in a place. The best practice is to have a story idea in mind before you take your trip, and at the same time to be open to discovering an even better story while you're there. Having a pre-conceived idea will give your trip preparations and itinerary a focus and framework. And of course, if you've interested an editor in a particular story pre-trip, you'll usually need to write about that. But if you find something extraordinary on the spot, all the better – your article possibilities will have doubled.

Researching on the Road

Of course, all that pre-trip research is just the prelude to the journey itself. Once you're aboard the train, bus, ferry or plane, the real work begins. As you travel, stay alive to the world around you. Cultivate encounters. Ask questions. Gather brochures and other printed information. If something catches your fancy, follow it. When you can, let serendipity be your guide.

Use your camera to capture the look of a place; use your audio recorder to capture conversations, evocative sounds and snatches of your own impressions when it's impractical to write them down; use your journal to record on-the-spot notes that will bring your experience back to you later. (For more about these essential tools of the trade, see Chapter Seven.) Absorb as much as you can, but remember to constantly filter what you're absorbing, so you retain and focus on the aspects of the trip that most appeal to you and offer the best potential story subjects.

EFFECTIVE NOTE-TAKING AND INTERVIEWING TECHNIQUES

Central to the success of your travel research and writing is the ability to take good notes and to carry out efficient, effective interviews.

Taking Notes

There is no substitute for notes taken on the spot. These provide reliable and vivid building blocks for your story, but they are also poignant keys that can unlock a rich flood of images and details from a particular place and experience – even when you're sitting down to write your story half a year later. Your notes don't always need to be complete sentences; fragments often do the job just fine. You might just write 'red poppies, white columns' or 'pine scent, silvery sea' or 'grandmother in blue fur, lilac perfume, Mozart from window'. You just need a few words that capture the essence of the thing you want to remember. At other times you will want to stop and write a more complete portrait of a moment, as the words written on the spot are inevitably the most vivid depictions of all.

One of the secrets to good note-taking is simply paying attention. Another is to slow down and take the time to stop, absorb and reflect on your surroundings and on the things that have happened so far on your journey.

Interviewing Techniques

Effective interviewing is an art of a different kind. Before you begin, you need to know what you want to get out of the interview. In many cases you will simply be trying to gather hard information, and so these interviews are not likely to be particularly controversial or confrontational. But since the interview will most likely be your only opportunity to talk with this particular individual, you need to make sure you have thought out in advance everything you want to learn from your meeting.

Basically, your interviews will fall into one of two types: the official and the unofficial. The official, or expert, interview involves anyone who represents a place. This might be a museum curator or the director of an archaeological site; a tourism official or tour guide; a hotel owner or restaurant chef. In every case, your job is to glean as much relevant information from this expert as possible. You want to be friendly and nonthreatening, but you also want to be sure to get the information you need. If you ask a question and don't get a satisfactory answer, ask it again. In this kind of formal interview it's vital to use an audio recorder. This will liberate you from note-taking so that you can focus on the answers and your follow-up questions. Whenever possible, try to get contact information so you can follow up if a question occurs to you long after your meeting.

If you have a particularly intransigent interview subject, one trick is to turn off your recorder, put away your notes and prepare to leave. Then stop and say, 'You know, one more question has just occurred to me.' This may be the question you walked into the interview most wanting to ask, but if you had asked it directly during the formal part of the interview, you would not have received a useful response. Now, in that unguarded setting, you may get just the candid answer you need.

The unofficial interview is usually a conversation with a fellow traveller or a local. These are often used to provide a different perspective and voice for your story, and sometimes to fill in background information. In these cases, your interviewing technique can be more indirect and conversational. You may decide not to use an audio recorder, so the person you're talking to will feel at ease and converse freely. (Writers who are just starting out may feel that using an audio recorder or notebook will make them seem more 'professional'. This is not necessarily the case, and if such equipment makes your subject more nervous or self-conscious, you may not get the free-flowing stories, information and quotes you're hoping for.) Ask for anecdotes that illustrate a point. Ask for memories. If you are not using an audio recorder or taking notes during the interview, write down all the important points from your conversation as soon as you possibly can.

If you are planning to name and quote your interviewee you should let them know before you begin the interview. In an informal situation where you won't be naming the speaker, you don't necessarily need to say that you're interviewing them for publication, but sometimes it's easier to approach someone if you say you're gathering information for a story. If you're using an audio recorder or taking notes, you will certainly want to explain why. And, of course, there are times when you will be interviewing people by phone or by email, as many travel pieces these days are researched and written from home. Finally, if you do quote someone (without naming them) in a story on a sensitive topic, be very sure that they cannot be recognised from your writing. You do not want to inadvertently imperil someone because they gave you important information or freely expressed their views to you.

In all cases, it is absolutely essential for you to be accurate in quoting people you've interviewed, and it is important to have records from your interview – either audio or extensive notes – which you can give to an editorial fact-checker, if asked, to verify the authenticity of your quotes.

FINDING YOUR FOCUS

We have already discussed a number of ways to help you narrow your focus before and during your trip, but now let's consider the aftermath of the trip. You've just returned from three weeks in France and everything was great – every day brought new discoveries and treasures, and you want to write about them all. Writing about everything you did on holiday should be kept strictly between you and your diary; you need to find the theme that will interest an editor. If you sounded out a few travel editors before you set off, you'll already know which stories might be of interest to whom. But if you didn't, or if you want to try other editors now that you've returned, how do you decide what to write about?

Ask yourself this simple question: what most impassioned you? When you meet people and they say, 'So, how was France?', what's the first story that comes to mind? Focus on that story, because for some reason your internal filter has decided that that particular story embodies the quintessence of your trip. Analyse why the story especially appeals to you, and ask yourself if other people would be interested in reading about it. Also ask yourself why you are choosing to describe that particular aspect of your trip. Think about the connection and resonance your focus has created. Does it capture an illuminating characteristic of French culture or French manners or French food? Does it tie in neatly with something that's highly topical today or with something that will be news in the future, such as an anniversary or event? Or is it so unusual that it stands out simply as an extraordinary travel experience?

This is the seed of your story: seize it, explore it, look at it from different angles, draw it out. Think about what it means to you, but remember that the story isn't about yourself. A very common mistake that inexperienced travel writers make is to put too much of themselves into a piece; your job as a writer is to be the reader's portal into a deeper understanding of the place and of the experience of being a traveller there.

Now, think about other experiences from the trip that support this aspect or in some way complement it. You can begin to fashion your story in this way, establishing a central theme and then building on it. Your final piece will be an exploration of this theme and how it was present in your trip, and ideally you will lead up to it step by step. If you feel you've got many seeds from your trip, then that's great – you'll be able to write a variety of different articles covering each one for a range of different outlets.

This process should help you avoid one of the most common traps for travel writers: the fear of the known. Writers often feel paralysed when trying to write about a familiar subject. How can I write about Paris, they say, when a million stories have already been written on the subject? A million stories *have* been written about Paris, it's true – but there could be a Paris you experienced that no one else has ever known. Let's say you love puppets and you stumbled onto a dusty puppet-maker's shop in an alley in the 13th *arrondissement*. You spent an hour talking about puppets and puppetry with the white-haired owner, who looked a little like a puppet himself. Here's the perfect subject for your story, a subject no one else could write about with as much authority, presence and passion as you.

Ultimately, travel is all about connections – connections outside us and connections inside us. If you can bring those connections to life in your work, readers who may have never been to Paris or who may not care a whit about puppets will be brought in touch with similar connections they have made in other countries, in other places. They will connect with your sense of connection, and so the piece will in some metaphorical way build a powerful bridge and remind us all over again of one of the great and fundamental joys of travel: the stretching of personal boundaries, the flinging of bridges across cultures.

To achieve this connection we move to the next stage: the writing. You've done your research, analysed the market, studied yourself and found a subject that marries publishability with passion. Now you need to write to that passion. Explore it, savour it, draw it out in your prose – paint such a complete, compelling, sensually full description that your readers will experience it just as you did. We'll discuss how to do this in Chapter Four.

INTERVIEW WITH RORY MACLEAN

British travel writer Rory MacLean (www.rorymaclean.com) is the author of Stalin's Nose, Under the Dragon, The Oatmeal Ark, Next Exit Magic Kingdom *and* Falling for Icarus.

How did you start off in your career as an author of travel literature?

I'd always dreamed of being a film director. To that end I wrote dozens of movie scripts, following every trend, choosing 'saleable' subjects rather than stories that moved me. The result was a series of flops, tame thrillers and busted blockbusters. But after each movie, to regain my sense of self, I went travelling. And soon I realised that I loved journeying into territory unknown (to me) and writing about the people and places met along the way.

What is the best way of establishing yourself if you're just starting out in your career as a travel literature author?

Win a prize. I'm not being flippant. There are dozens of travel writing competitions run by newspapers and magazines. Researching and writing a travel article forces you to focus. Winning a competition opens the door to agents and publishers. Alternatively, marry the son or daughter of a newspaper baron.

As a travel writer, how do you get the numbers to add up in terms of an income?

To be honest, for the first book they rarely add up. But if you're serious about writing, you just have to take the risk. I was lucky. My first book, *Stalin's Nose*, made the UK top 10. It meant that the advances paid for my second and subsequent books have been enough to survive on.

What tips would you give to budding travel writers?

Write. Write. Write. Then write some more. And if you feel you've had enough, it'd probably be a better idea to do something sensible like becoming a dentist or raising rabbits.

Are there any courses or any training that you'd recommend a budding travel writer to undertake?

In the UK, the Arvon Foundation (www.arvonfoundation.org) offers writing weeks tutored by experienced, professional authors.

What are the most common mistakes that travel writers make in their manuscript?

First, many first-time travel writers choose subjects because of their perceived popularity. Second, some of them don't engage their imagination or sense of wonder. Third, many don't check their spelling.

What, in your opinion, constitutes 'good' travel writing?

A book that is written from the heart. As a reader, I want to know how a journey affected the writer, what he or she learnt through the trip, and how he or she was changed by the experience.

What constitutes 'bad' travel writing?

Writing to catch – or cash in on – a trend.

What are the rewards of travel writing as a career?

The opportunity to try to understand peoples, societies and histories. Then to communicate that passion with others.

What has been the downside for you?

No office Christmas parties.

How did you get your first book published?

I won the *Independent*'s first travel writing competition. That enabled me to approach publishers with an idea for a book on Eastern Europe. Then Gorbachev was kind enough to knock down the Berlin Wall, making my subject highly topical.

How long does it take to write your books?

Usually just under two years: three months' preparation, three months' travel and about 15 months bent over blank sheets of paper.

Do you have an agent, and how important do you think they are?

An agent is vital. To find one, scan the *Writers' & Artists' Yearbook* or look up the name of your favourite travel writer's agent and approach him or her. Books submitted directly to big publishers often go unread.

INTERVIEW WITH STANLEY STEWART

Stanley Stewart is the author of Old Serpent Nile, Frontiers of Heaven *and* In the Empire of Genghis Khan. *Based in the UK, he has twice been winner of the prestigious Thomas Cook Travel Book of the Year Award.*

How did you start off in your career as a travel writer?

My own start was unusual. I began with a book. I set off up the Nile for nine months, without a publishing contract, wrote an account of the journey and sold it to a publisher when it was complete. The success of the book opened doors for travel journalism which helped to feed, financially, more books.

What is the best way of establishing yourself if you're just starting out in your career as a freelance travel journalist?

Try to find an area in which you can specialise, or to which you bring unique experience, like cycling in the Alps or conservation in Africa. Try as well to master the more mundane nuts and bolts of travel journalism – how to get a cheap airfare or good hotel package. The best way to get started is to land a job on a newspaper, however junior – answering the phone, opening the post. You will then be on hand to pick up those assignments that someone else has just dropped on Thursday afternoon when copy is due for the Sunday paper. They will be so desperate to have someone cover it, they won't notice you haven't written before. You will also learn how it all works from the inside, on the desk, where the decisions are made. When you go freelance, you will not only have the inside dope, but you will have the best kind of contacts – personal ones.

As a freelance travel journalist, how do you get the numbers to add up in terms of an income?

With difficulty. At the beginning, you are likely to be working for a pittance. But hang in there. As you become better known, and as your polished prose becomes more ad-mired, rates will go up and you will be able to pitch to higher-paying journals. Travel writers need to be able to double up – so when you are in Rome doing a story about riding a Vespa along the Appian Way for newspaper X, you are also getting the info together for a restaurant story for magazine Y and a piece on the Coliseum for news-paper Z. And think about other markets, different ways to use the same material for other journals, as well as selling the same story to different newspapers abroad.

What tips would you give to budding travel writers?

Be persistent. Don't be put off by rejection. In the end, landing a junior job at a paper, or a commission for your first story, will largely be a matter of luck and timing. Keep at it until you call or knock at just the moment when the editor is at their wits' end trying to find someone to do that piece on Greek island ferries or that feature on shopping in Milan.

Are there any courses or any training that you'd recommend a budding travel writer to undertake?

I am not aware of any. Better to travel, and to read. It may sound blazingly obvious, but the best preparation for a career in travel writing is travel. Take a year off and travel round the world. When you come to pitching a story about the hot springs of Iceland, you will have the advantage of sounding like someone who knows what they are talk-ing about. But remember that you must be able to write. And the best education for a writer is to read, as widely as possible.

What are the most common mistakes that travel writers make in their copy?

They forget that travel stories must be stories, not merely descriptions of a destination. It is not enough to enthuse about the blue seas or the difficulties of the hike or the charm of the old quarter. What you write must be able to stand as a good story when all the 'colour' and atmosphere are stripped away.

What are the main differences between travel writing for a newspaper as opposed to a magazine?

Length. A magazine will often allow you to write to a much longer length, up to 3000 or 4000 words, and that allows you to write a piece with greater depth and complexity. At least that is the theory. In practice, economy can give birth to some wonderful writing.

What, in your opinion, constitutes 'good' travel writing?

Good travel writing is done by good writers who travel. It is not enough to have swum through piranha-infested waters to the source of the Amazon. You must be able to write well to convey that experience. When you have learnt the craft of writing, you can a make a stroll through your own suburban neighbourhood interesting, even exciting. Good travel writing needs much the same ingredients as any good story – narrative drive, characters, dialogue, atmosphere, revelation. Make it personal. Let the reader know how the place and the experience are affecting you.

Good travel writing is just good writing. It must have literary merit. The most important journey you will make as a travel writer is the journey of a good sentence. Without that, your close encounter with the piranhas is wasted.

What constitutes 'bad' travel writing?

Bad travel writing is done by travellers, often good travellers, who mistakenly believe they can write. There seems to be an awful lot of them about. Their prose is littered with clichés, their sense of narrative timing is inept and their characters, whether themselves or people they encounter, are clumsily portrayed. Too many travel writers seem to believe that the journey 'makes' the story. It doesn't. In the end, anyone can travel to Timbuktu, but only a few people will write about the journey well. Bad travel writing is just bad writing.

What are the rewards of travel writing as a career?

To travel the world and get paid for it. And hopefully along the way to understand a little more about other peoples and other cultures, and thus about yourself.

What has been the downside for you?

Too much travelling can put a strain on relationships and families.

INTERVIEW WITH ANTHONY SATTIN

Anthony Sattin is the author of many books, including The Pharaoh's Shadow, Shooting the Breeze *and* The Gates of Africa. *Based in the UK, he contributes regularly to the* Sunday Times.

How did you start off in your career as a travel writer?

Writing other things. I spent years in London writing fiction (and publishing some of it), but then had the urge to see and do and write about something new. I went to live in Cairo, lured by love. Before I went, I persuaded my editor to commission a book about a novelist's eye on the city.

What is the best way of establishing yourself if you're just starting out in your career as a travel writer?

It may seem obvious, but writing is the best way forward. First get your book commissioned, written and into production. Once it is on its way, then try getting your name about in other ways – travel features for newspapers or magazines, book reviews, radio features all help.

As a travel writer, how do you get the numbers to add up in terms of an income?

You don't, unless you are Bill Bryson or one of a very select band of best-sellers. If you want to make money, take some advice and try your hand at banking. Travel writing has other rewards. Having said that, it is possible to make some sort of a living writing books and contributing to newspapers and magazines.

What tips would you give to budding travel writers?

Be original and be true to yourself. Only write what you really want to write, not what you think will sell.

Are there any courses or any training that you'd recommend a budding travel writer to undertake?

The nearest I got to training was taking a Masters in Creative Writing. My only thoughts were for fiction in those days, but the novel I was working on was set abroad. It must have started something.

What do you think are the most common mistakes that travel writers make in their manuscripts?

Although there are more travel books being published these days, very few stand out. Often this is because few progress beyond telling us what happened on the journey. The best books have their own distinct angles, or characters, or have something beyond the journey that makes the story unique and involving.

What, in your opinion, constitutes 'good' travel writing?

Something that moves and amazes me. I want to feel the wonder – or the horror – of the world. And I want to have a sense that the writer has looked for the universal in the particular story they have told.

What constitutes 'bad' travel writing?

I don't need to read about what you did on your holiday. Or how macho you are.

What are the rewards of travel writing as a career?

Not often financial (see above). One of the biggest rewards is having the opportunity to see the world, and often in a way of your choosing, whether through the filter of a historical character or while floating along a river.

What has been the downside for you?

Travel writing is too easily dismissed by some editors, booksellers and readers as a lesser form of writing. I find that frustrating. Like the best novels, histories or any other sort of writing, the best travel writing has the power to cast light on the essential things in life and to move us.

How did you get your first book published?

The usual route: I had already published short stories and reviews. I wrote a proposal and my agent hawked it around the likely editors.

How long does it take to write your books?

How long is a piece of string? I tend to write quickly and can get a story down in a few months, but the re-writing, which is just as important, can take a lot, lot longer. One book took more than 10 years from gestation to print but definitely benefited from the wait.

Do you have an agent, and how important do you think they are?

Agents have become increasingly necessary in the time I have been writing. I have always had one, simply by getting them to read my work. But as they have become more powerful, so they have put up more barriers. It helps if you are approaching an agent who handles the sort of writing you want to produce. A good agent can be a big help and can do everything from helping to shape a proposal, providing encouragement when things are going bad, to being there at publication celebrations.

INTERVIEW WITH JOHN FLINN

Based in the US, John Flinn is the Executive Travel Editor for the San Francisco Chronicle.

How did you start off in your career as a travel editor?

Like most travel editors, I just fell into it accidentally. I'd been with the newspaper for many years and had carved out a niche for myself as a good feature writer. On my time off, I traveled a lot. When the travel editor job came open, it seems as if just about everyone on the staff applied for it. It came down to me and an assistant business editor. Previously we'd both taken year-long leaves of absence: he went off to Missouri to study some weighty journalism issues and I goofed off and vagabonded around the world. And in the end, that's what made the difference.

What is the best way of establishing yourself if you're just starting out in your career as a freelance travel journalist?

The great thing about travel writing, particularly at the newspaper level, is that it's pretty much a meritocracy. If your stuff is good, you'll get published and recognized. Maybe not immediately, but quickly. As an editor, I don't care where (or whether) you went to college, what your résumé looks like or whether you've previously had a dozen cover stories in *National Geographic*. I don't even look at clips. All I care about is the manuscript you've sent me. If it's good, I'll publish it. If it's not, I won't. And once an editor publishes you, don't assume that you're now 'in' and can slough off on your next story. Make sure the next story you send that editor is even better than the first. And that your third story is better still.

How do you think freelance travel journalists get the numbers to add up in terms of an income?

If you're writing for newspapers, you've *got* to be able to re-sell a piece three or four times, or more. Successful freelancers have an instinct for stories that have broad appeal, and the really good ones tweak their stories slightly to appeal to different editors and markets.

What tips would you give to budding travel writers?

Don't become a travel writer. Become a writer. Most of the top travel writers have lots of experience writing in other genres. Paul Theroux is a novelist who turns out an occasional travel book. Jan Morris spent most of her career as a foreign correspondent covering wars, revolutions and the like. Bill Bryson has written two books on the history of the English language and one about science. Tim Cahill started out writing for *Rolling Stone* and has written a book about a serial killer. The skills you pick up writing in these other genres make your travel writing immeasurably better. I always say I'm looking for writers who dabble in travel, rather than travelers who dabble in writing.

Are there any courses or any training that you'd recommend a budding travel writer to undertake?

I'd recommend taking some basic college-level journalism news- and feature-writing courses, and also some classes in essay or memoir writing. And once you're competent at writing, take a course in travel writing to learn the idiosyncrasies of this particular genre. The four-day Book Passage Travel Writers & Photographers Conference has an amazing track record for turning out writers who get published. But there's a limited amount a writer can learn from courses. To learn writing you pretty much have to lock yourself in a room and keep pounding away at the keyboard until you don't suck anymore. There's really no substitute for this.

What are the most common mistakes that travel writers make in their copy?

They send in stories about their vacations. Trust me: no one wants to read a 2000-word account of your vacation, any more than you want to go over to the reader's house and sit through four carousels of their vacation slides. Remember those 'what I did on my summer vacation' essays you used to write in fourth grade? Your teacher had to be *paid* to read those. Now that you expect people to pay for the privilege of reading your words, you have to give them something of value. A lot of destination stories are written in the first person, but if you look at them carefully the writer is merely using their experiences to preview what the reader's trip will be like. As Arthur Frommer says: 'Don't tell me about your vacation; tell my readers about *their* vacations.' The difference is subtle but crucial.

The other big mistake is not taking the craft seriously enough. A lot of would-be travel writers get into it because they think it's an easy, less-demanding genre. Nothing could be more wrong. A good travel story – whether it's a destination piece, an essay or a memoir – is very difficult to write, and the competition is intense. You have to have a really good command of structure, tone and style, and above all have a really compelling story to tell.

What are the most common mistakes that travel writers make when pitching to you?

First, I have to say that like most US newspaper travel sections we don't take queries, only completed manuscripts submitted on spec. Which isn't to say we don't get dozens of pitches every week. A typical one is: 'Hi. I'm going to Asia. Want any stories?' Wrong! It's the writer's job to come up with a compelling angle, and in essence this person is saying, 'Will you please do part of my job for me?'

What are the main differences between travel writing for a newspaper as opposed to a magazine?

In my experience, a well-written newspaper destination story is almost identical to a magazine destination story. They have precisely the same structure (introductory hook, overview, anecdote, anecdote, anecdote, conclusion), although a magazine story might be a little longer. Which either means another anecdote or two, or else airing out your hook and overview a little. Since magazines generally pay more, they expect better craftsmanship – more research, a more finely honed style, more 'writerly' touches. But that's about it.

What, in your opinion, constitutes 'good' travel writing?

Stories that capture the spirit of the place – the *genius loci* – and provide important context and perspective. Stories that tell my readers about a fascinating destination they've never heard of before, or a new way to experience a familiar destination. Stories that keep me interested all the way to the ending.

What constitutes 'bad' travel writing?

As I said earlier, accounts of the writer's vacation. Also, 'immature' stories about 'mature' destinations. ('I just got back from Paris and they have these amazing things called cafés, where people sit out on the sidewalk and drink coffee and watch people walk by.') Stories with no context, that make every place sound the same.

What are the rewards of travel writing as a career?

As Paul Theroux once said, it's not a great living, but it's a great life.

What has been the downside for you?

It's a great life, but it's not a great living! Seriously, though, the problem with making your hobby or your passion into your job is that it's now work, rather than your hobby or passion. I tend to be in 'writer' mode whenever I travel – even on vacation – and it's hard sometimes to just slow down and enjoy the experience.

INTERVIEW WITH K. C. SUMMERS

Based in the US, K. C. Summers is the Travel Editor for the Washington Post.

How did you start off in your career as a travel editor?

I was already a journalist at the *Post* (I'd reported and edited for various sections including Outlook, Weekend and Style). The Travel section had an opening for an editor and I thought it sounded like fun.

What is the best way of establishing yourself if you're just starting out in your career as a freelance travel journalist?

Start writing stories and submitting them to newspapers and magazines, get some clips. Try to establish a relationship with an editor by coming up with original ideas, giving them problem-free copy and anticipating their needs. I guarantee you will quickly become indispensable.

How do you think freelance travel journalists get the numbers to add up in terms of an income?

Have a trust fund? Based on what we pay, it's not a very lucrative profession. Our no-freebies policy rules out a lot of starving freelancers.

What tips would you give to budding travel writers?

Be a writer already, before you set yourself up as a travel writer. Pay your dues – learn how to report, write and edit by working for small publications and writing about nontravel-related topics. Then, when you know how to report and write a story, you can get all lyrical on us.

In terms of getting a piece accepted, be familiar with the publication you're submitting to so you can see how they do things, what formats they use etc. I'm constantly amazed by the number of pitches I get from people who have clearly never seen the section and have no clue how we do things. When I get a story that not only reads well but also has an 'if you go' box attached with all the little 'getting there' and 'where to stay' info filled out, I almost break into tears – they actually took the trouble to follow our format!

In terms of professional development, clip writers you admire and study their techniques.

Are there any courses or any training that you'd recommend a budding travel writer to undertake?

Not specifically, but any good writing course taken through a college or university would help – it doesn't have to be travel-related. A journalism school would be good because it would emphasize good reporting and accuracy as opposed to flowery writing.

What are the most common mistakes that travel writers make in their copy?

Not coming up with an original angle. Not having a fresh voice or a sense of humor. Not having people in their stories. Putting too much of themselves into the story – forgetting that the story should be about the place, not about them.

What are the most common mistakes that travel writers make when pitching to you?

Being too broad ('Would you like a story about Spain?'). Not being familiar with the section (pitching a story on a place we've recently written about). Not knowing the ground rules (eg taking comp trips, which we don't allow). Not proofreading their cover letter (sending a piece to the *Post* that begins, 'I've always wanted to write for the *Times*…').

What are the main differences between travel writing for a newspaper as opposed to a magazine?

Newspapers are timelier, pay less, have more space restrictions, have a rough-and-tumble layout and editing process that may require last-minute changes (prima donnas need not apply), and – in our case at least – have more of a consumer, news-you-can-use bent. Oh, and our reproduction is lousy.

What, in your opinion, constitutes 'good' travel writing?

Any travel story that keeps the reader reading. That's harder than it sounds. So many travel stories are the written equivalent of someone's vacation slide show – you fall asleep halfway through. A fresh voice and original angle helps. Travel stories are like any other story – they benefit greatly from the use of quotes, humor, conflict etc. Many travel stories don't meet these basic minimum requirements.

What constitutes 'bad' travel writing?

Travelogues that are either too focused on the writer (it's all about me!) or that, conversely, could double as encyclopedia entries. Stories without humor, suspense or people in them. Stories that plod through the person's trip chronologically. Stories that use, with no sense of irony, phrases like 'unspoiled gem', 'tropical paradise' or 'breathtaking vista'.

What are the rewards of travel writing as a career?

Aside from the obvious – getting paid to travel – knowing that you're going to write about a place tends to sharpen your observations, forcing you to see a place more clearly and to seek people out – to take chances you wouldn't ordinarily take. You're more acutely aware of your surroundings, in a way you wouldn't be if you were merely relaxing and enjoying a place.

What has been the downside for you?

I am now incapable of taking a vacation without taking notes.

INTERVIEW WITH TIM CAHILL

Tim Cahill is the author of Jaguars Ripped My Flesh, Pecked to Death by Ducks, Pass the Butterworms, Hold the Enlightenment *and many other books. Based in the US, he writes for* National Geographic Adventure *and* Outside, *among other publications.*

How did you start off in your career as an author of travel literature?

I was an editor at *Rolling Stone* magazine. The editor/publisher wanted to create a magazine that would appeal to those who went outside. As one of the only two people in the office who ever went outside, which is to say, who backpacked, I was picked to help decide what the future magazine should look, feel, and be like. This was in 1975. I thought we should have a travel/adventure story in each issue of the magazine that eventually became *Outside*. In fact, I created my own job.

What is the best way of establishing yourself if you're just starting out in your career as a travel literature author?

My suggestion would be to publish with the local newspaper, in what is generally a weekly travel section. This allows you to travel, to write, to work with professional editors and understand, from the get-go, that travel isn't a high-paying career.

As a travel writer, how do you get the numbers to add up in terms of an income?

I try to write very good magazine stories. The stories, if I do them right, can then be collected in a hardcover anthology. Then it goes to paper. In effect, I get paid three times for some stories.

What tips would you give to budding travel writers?

I'm not being sarcastic, but the major thing I can say is *write*. No one can give you the magic bullet that, once fired, will make you a writer. Writing is like anything else: the more you do it, the better you get at it.

Are there any courses or any training that you'd recommend a budding travel writer to undertake?

I have a Masters degree in English/Creative Writing. I always thought the two years I spent earning that degree were wasted and that I learned a lot more from working with good editors. But who is to say? Did my academic career lay the groundwork for my professional one? I don't know.

If I was starting out today, I believe I'd try to write for a year or two. I'd check such magazines as *Writer's Digest* for appropriate 'writer's conferences'. These are meetings where professional editors lecture and look at your work; where you will meet publishers and agents. Book Passage, a bookstore in Corte Madera, north of San Francisco, hosts a travel writers' conference I attend almost every year.

If, after two years, you haven't sold and are still convinced of your talent, try the academic route.

What are the most common mistakes that travel writers make in their copy?

When I was editing, the most common mistake I saw writers make was submitting their journal. A day-by-day chronicle of events, as seen in a journal, is raw material. One needs to think about that raw material. Hold it to the light and turn it this way and that until you see a prism. When I read a story that begins: 'January 19th: The plane descended over neat cultivated fields that reminded me of a child's blanket…' I can be almost sure that I'm going to read a journal. Which means that this has been submitted by someone who hasn't thought much about what happened. Such manuscripts travel to the circular file, posthaste.

What, in your opinion, constitutes 'good' travel writing?

Good writing is good travel writing. Travel is a forgiving medium – as soon as you walk out the front door, you're traveling.

At *Outside*, we discovered early on that the world's best ice climber may not be the person you want to write about ice climbing. He or she will be consumed by their passion for ice, not writing. They will tend to address their (very few) peers, not a general audience. No, you want someone who can write.

Do you need to do extreme things? Naw. Lots of people do extreme things and are never published because they can't write. Writing is the key. Better a well-written travel story about a picnic in the backyard than a tedious story on someone who did cartwheels up Mount Everest.

What constitutes 'bad' travel writing?

A chronological recounting of events is usually not good. (There are exceptions, of course.) People who can't find the story and hope description will carry them.

What are the rewards of travel writing as a career?

Obviously, travel. I get to go wherever I want to go, do what I want to do. Because much of what I do is physical, I have to stay in some kind of shape, which is good. I never spend money on a foreign vacation. My idea of a vacation is staying home.

What has been the downside for you?

Poor pay, a little too much travel early on that wasn't good for my social life or my love life.

How did you get your first book published?

In 1984 I published a book about a serial killer that became a best-seller. That gave me the clout to publish what I wanted next, which was a collection of my outdoor travel pieces.

How long does it take to write your books?

A book takes anywhere from one to three years, depending on the research involved and how scared I am.

Do you have an agent, and how important do you think they are?

I have an agent. They are important for books. You can get one by submitting a query and/or manuscript to the list of agents who accept manuscripts found in the back of *Writer's Market 2005* (or whatever year it is: the book, as you may have guessed, comes out yearly).

An agent is familiar with contracts (which are, in my case, 80 pages, single spaced). In the contract, the publisher takes everything. An agent knows what can be crossed out without a fight, how much of a fight this deletion will entail, and what clauses the publisher will not delete under any circumstances. You need this expertise. Otherwise, believe it or not, a publisher will screw you.

THE ART & CRAFT OF TRAVEL WRITING

Whether you're writing a piece for a newspaper or magazine, or penning a work of travel literature, the same principles of crafting a story apply. The differences in terms of pitching, content and deadlines are analysed in Chapter Six.

WHAT CONSTITUTES GOOD TRAVEL WRITING?

What makes a wonderful travel story? In one word, it is *place*. Successful travel stories bring a particular place to life through a combination of factual information and vividly rendered descriptive details and anecdotes, characters and dialogue. Such stories transport the reader and convey a rich sense of the author's experience in that place. The best travel stories also set the destination and experience in some larger context, creating rings of resonance in the reader.

Crafting a Structure

A good travel article is shaped like a good short story, with a clear beginning, middle and end. Broadly speaking, and of course varying with the overall length of the story (travel stories for the UK and Australian markets tend to be shorter than those for the US market), the beginning is made up of approximately the first two to seven paragraphs. The aim of the beginning is to create a thematic or narrative lead (spelled 'lede' in the US) that immediately interests and engages the reader, drawing them into the article. Often the beginning will set the story's scene, and sometimes it will hint at why the writer is there, but the prime purpose of the beginning is to grab the reader's attention. The middle is the long and winding road of the story, where the destination is brought alive for the reader, using your experience there as a filter. The end – and again, this is usually no more than the last two to seven paragraphs or so – wraps the story up and offers a kind of closure, tying the story back to its beginning but with a larger, enhanced sense of the whole.

Five Compelling Beginnings

Let's study five leads from published pieces that work well and in differing ways. The stories are reprinted in their entirety in Chapter Five.

An article by British travel writer and editor Simon Calder, published in the *Independent* newspaper, begins with this quirky angle on Las Vegas:

Neon: you need to know two things about this gas. The first is that it is, in elementary terms, a relative newcomer; even though it is present in small quantities in the air we breathe, it was identified only a century ago by a French scientist named Georges Claude. The second is that, being inert, neon is intrinsically dull. Oh, unless you pass an electric charge through it, as M Claude did. Do that, and it can light up the desert and dazzle the world.

Las Vegas was just a flicker in the eye of the San Pedro, Los Angeles and Salt Lake City Railroad when M Claude announced his discovery. The first neon sign in North America was sold in 1923 to a Packard dealership in Los Angeles.

At the time, the Mormons mistakenly thought they had discovered a promised, and morally safe, haven in the middle of the Mojave Desert. By the Thirties, they had lost faith with Las Vegas – and the rest of the world had lost interest in the fact that neon glows red in the dark and that, when mixed with a little mercury, its elementary cousin argon turns bright blue. But Las Vegas had barely begun to experiment with the extreme right-hand side of the Periodic Table of Elements.

Helium radiates a lurid magnolia when suitably fired up; krypton issues a steely silver; while xenon emits the palest blue. These elementary truths helped Las Vegas find its place in the world.

By presenting Las Vegas in this unexpected light, Calder prepares us for – and entices us into – a new appreciation of this much-described city.

CREATING A COMPELLING BEGINNING

So how do you create a compelling hook that will capture your readers' attention and propel them into the middle of your story? A few writers I know refuse to write any other part of their piece until they find that attention-grabbing introduction. I've sometimes found that a beginning will occur to me as I'm shaping the piece in my mind. When that happens I write it down immediately, as the beginning can be a kind of key that unlocks the rest of the story for you.

In most cases you won't find the beginning right away – you'll only find it in the process of writing the story. So my advice is to move on, and not get stuck on the start. You can, as Douglas Adams said so memorably, 'stare at a blank piece of paper until your forehead bleeds', but if you're waiting for the perfect beginning to arrive, you may never get your story written. So just start writing.

You'll find that as you are writing, all sorts of ways to start your article may pop into your mind. Write them down and leave them at the top of your screen or page until they become so compelling that you feel forced to stop writing the body of your article to start writing its beginning. Sometimes you might have too many ideas for beginnings; sometimes none. If the latter happens, one trick I often use is to think of the most telling moment of my trip and start with that.

– Don George

The following opening by British writer William Gray, from an article published in *Wanderlust* magazine, powerfully pulls us into an electric moment on a jungle expedition in India, and keeps us there:

It was almost as if the tiger had flicked a switch in the forest. One moment it was quiet and calm – the trees swathed in webs of early morning mist – the next, the air was charged with tension. Gomati had heard the distant alarm calls – the shrill snort of a spotted deer, the indignant bark of a langur monkey – and her mood suddenly changed. She blasted a trunkful of dust up between her front legs, then shook her head so vigorously that I had to clutch the padded saddle to keep my balance. Gomati's mahout, sitting astride her neck, issued a terse reprimand before urging the elephant into the tangled forest. There was no path; Gomati made her own. Soon the air was infused with the pungent aroma of crushed herbs and freshly-bled sap. Spiders and beetles drizzled from shaken trees; our clothing became wet with dew and stained by moss and lichen. We sounded like a forest fire – crackling, snapping, trailblazing. But through all the noise came a single piercing cry. Gomati stopped and we heard it again – the tell-tale alarm call of a spotted deer.

Manoj Sharma, my guide, leaned towards me. 'When the tiger moves, the deer calls,' he murmured. 'We must be close.' I nodded slowly, my eyes chasing around the shadows of the forest. Sunlight sparked through chinks in the canopy, but the understorey was still a diffuse patchwork of muted greens and shadows-within-shadows – the perfect foil for tiger stripes. Apart from an occasional rumble from Gomati's stomach, the forest was silent. No one spoke or moved.

Gray's beginning offers an example of a compelling literary technique called *in medias res*, which sets you right 'in the middle of things'. This technique has a long and honourable literary pedigree – Milton employed it in *Paradise Lost*, beginning the epic right in the middle of the story.

Former US Poet Laureate Robert Hass employs the technique to riveting effect in his powerful story about Korea, 'The Path to Sokkuram', which originally appeared in *Great Escapes* magazine. Hass takes a couple of notable risks in his opening. He begins with a very long first sentence that propels the reader into the story with a stream-of-consciousness momentum, and he begins his narrative with a character in mid-speech:

'The thing you need to understand about Korea,' said the dissolute, cheerful-looking British shipping agent I had run into at six in the morning in the fish market in the harbour at Pusan – we were drinking coffee at an outdoor table in the reek of fish and the unbelievable choral din of the fish merchants, beside tanks of slack-bodied pale squid and writhing pink and purple octopus – 'is that it's Poland. I mean, as a metaphor it's Poland. Caught between China and Japan for all those centuries like the Poles were stuck between the Russians and the Germans. The Japanese occupied the place from 1910 to the end of the war, and in the '30s they simply tried to eradicate Korea as a nation. Outlawed the language. Everybody in the country over 40 went to school when the teaching of the Korean language was forbidden.'

An old woman pushed past with a cart full of fist-sized reddish-green figs. McEwan, the shipping agent, called her over. 'Try one of these,' he said. 'Damned good.' They were, red-fleshed, packed with seeds. McEwan was waving down a waiter with one hand, clutching a torn-open fig with the other. 'They demand soju, don't they?' Soju is a transparent, fiery, slightly sweet Korean brandy, perfect with figs, I was sure, but beyond me at that moment. I had been out the night before with a surprisingly hard-drinking lot of professors from Pusan National University, and wandered afterward rather aimlessly through the night market. Just before leaving America I had come to the end of a long marriage, and I had spent my first few days in Korea, when I did not have to concentrate on a task, in a state of dazed grief. In the night market the families had fascinated me, at one in the morning shutting down their produce stalls, loading up their boxes of fennel and cabbage and bok choy, moving swiftly in and out of the arc of light thrown by a hanging propane lamp, husbands and wives and drowsy children, working easily side by side. I drank beer at a stall and watched the market close down, and then went back to my hotel and couldn't sleep, and so got up again and walked down the hill in the pre-dawn coolness to the wharf.

Not all travel stories need to begin so dramatically, however. Here's a good example of a thematic beginning from an article that UK author Stanley Stewart wrote about rodeo-hunting in the American West for the *Sunday Times*:

At the rodeo you notice that horses and cowboys are kind of alike. Horses stand around a lot, flicking their tails, breaking wind, doing nothing in particular. Cowboys are like that. They lean on fences, looking at horses. Sometimes they spit, sometimes they don't. With their hats tipped down over their eyes, it is never easy to tell if they are asleep, like horses, on their feet. The similarity disguises a major difference of temperament. Cowboys are soft-spoken mild-mannered fellows. In the West it's the horses that are the outlaws.

To the newcomer, cowboys are the surprise of the American West, like finding Romans in pleated togas waiting for the trolley buses on the Via Appia. Towns like Laramie and Cheyenne and Medicine Bow and Kit Carson are full of people who seem to have wandered off the back lot at MGM. They wear boots and ten gallon hats and leather waistcoats. In town they drink in saloons with swing doors and stand around on street corners in a bowlegged fashion. Back at the ranch their nearest neighbours are miles away. The men are lean laconic figures with lopsided grins. The women look like their idea of a good time would be to rope you and ride you round the corral awhile. The women are rather chatty. With cowboys there is a lot of silence to fill.

The West is America's most vibrant sub culture with its own music, its own fashions, its own political orientation and its own folklore. They care nothing for the suburban world that is the American mainstream. They talk of Washington and back east as if they were part of Red China. It is one of the pleasures of Wyoming to find Americans who are as cantankerous and as sceptical as the regulars of any Yorkshire pub. If the West is the spiritual home of America's ardent individualism, it is the landscape that is to blame.

Between the Missouri River and the Rocky Mountains lies a vast swathe of country that early cartographers called the Great American Desert. They were wrong but you can see where they got the idea. The West is a landscape of skies and infinities. In the loneliness of this place, self-reliance becomes a kind of religion. When the first settlers tried to farm this land, it broke their hearts. The West did not take kindly to the idea of fields. It was a vast sea of grass, a landscape for horses.

The rodeos that are held in small towns all over the West are like church fetes with Budweiser tents and bullriders, a chance to meet the neighbours and complain about the government. They are also the moment for the big showdown between the cowboys and the horses.

With this beguiling beginning, Stewart introduces a multifaceted theme: visiting rodeos is a singular method of developing an appreciation for the history, quintessential qualities and contemporary culture of the American West. Through five spare paragraphs he paints a vivid and compelling portrait of the ensuing tale's main characters: cowboys, horses, and the infinite landscape they inhabit. By the end of that beginning, Stewart has already given us a good notion of where he's going – in search of rodeos – and a seductive sense of the riches and mysteries we'll find if we accompany him on the ride.

Finally, an example of a beginning that combines the narrative and thematic approach comes from a story of my own, which was published in *Signature* magazine:

There are no tavernas, no discotheques, no pleasure boats at anchor. Nor are there churches, windmills, or goatherds. Delos, three miles long and less than one mile wide, is a parched, rocky island of ruins, only 14 miles from Mykonos, Aegean playground of the international vagabonderie. Once the center of the Panhellenic world, Delos has been uninhabited since the first century AD, fulfilling a proclamation of the Delphic oracle that 'no man or woman shall give birth, fall sick or meet death on the sacred island.'

I chanced on Delos during my first visit to Greece. After three harrowing days of seeing Athens by foot, bus and taxi, my traveling companion and I were ready for opens seas and uncrowded beaches. We selected Mykonos on the recommendation of a friend, who also suggested that when we tired of the Beautiful People, we should take a side trip to Delos.

On arriving in Mykonos, we learned that for under $3 we could catch a fishing trawler to Delos (where the harbor is too shallow for cruise ships) any morning at eight and return to Mykonos at one the same afternoon. On the morning of our fourth day we braved choppy seas and ominous clouds to board a rusty, peeling boat that reeked of fish. With a dozen other tourists, we packed ourselves into the ship's tiny cabin, already crowded with anchors, ropes and wooden crates bearing unknown cargo.

At some point during the 45-minute voyage, the toss and turn of the waves became too much for a few of the passengers, and I moved outside into the stinging, salty spray. As we made our way past Rhenea, the calluslike volcanic island that forms part of the natural breakwater with Delos, the clouds cleared, and the fishermen who had docked their caiques at the Delos jetty greeted us in bright sunlight.

At the end of the dock a white-whiskered man in a navy blue beret and a faded black suit hailed each one of us as we walked by: 'Tour of Delos! Informative guide to the ruins.' A few yards beyond him a young boy ran up to us, all elbows and knees, and confided in hard breaths, 'I give you better tour. Cheaper too.'

This approach is more purely chronological than the *in medias res* method. It provides a thematic framework for the piece, promising that the rest of the story will detail how my experience in Delos offered encounters and lessons that deepened my appreciation of Greece.

Each of these beginnings successfully draws the reader into the story and induces them to keep reading because they are intrigued by the possibilities and want to know what happens next. Each hook promises that the reader will be entertained if they continue reading, and introduces questions that can only be answered by plunging deeper into the text.

What beginning will work best for you? Think about where you want the reader to be at the start of your story. How do you want your tale to unfold? What is the main point of your story? What's the best way to get that point across?

However you structure your beginning, remember that it's the doorway to your story – and that in the eyes of an overworked editor, it's also your calling card. It's your one chance to inspire the editor to read more. Many editors read hundreds of submissions a week; in effect, when they take your story in hand, they are looking for a reason to reject it as quickly as possible. If your beginning doesn't work, the editor will not read any further.

The Middle Section

Most travel stories are structured by following either a thematic or narrative strategy. If your story is thematic, you will develop the middle section as an ascending succession of examples leading to your overriding point. If it's a narrative, you will most likely develop the central section of your story as a chronological sequence of anecdotal incidents that embody and reveal the main points of your piece.

MODULATING YOUR MIDDLE

Let's say I want to write a thematic article expressing my conviction that Croatia is the next big destination for travellers to visit. First, I'd ask myself why I feel this way. Well, let's see: it's beautiful, it has a rich history, the people are warm and unjaded, and it's great value. Now I've isolated four salient points to support my theme, so the next question is their order of importance.

I've decided to organise my story in terms of accelerating emotional connection, so I'll lead with the point about value for money as it's the least emotional and most practical or logical consideration. History begins to involve the heart but is still fundamentally intellectual, so that would be second. Beauty is a more emotional consideration, drawing readers into the story via their soul. Finally, the people connection represents what I think is the climax of my trip, and is the climax of travel itself, so that would be the final point I would want to make in my story. My final point is the top of the pyramid, but every step along the way contributes to my story's overall resonance and effectiveness.

Next, I'll search through my notes and draw out the experiences that really brought these points to life. There was the hostel in Dubrovnik that cost just £15 a night, or that extraordinary meal under the stars that was £5. That's where I really learned how inexpensive the place was, relatively speaking. The historical richness of the country came to life most poignantly in Dubrovnik, when I walked along the walls of the old city and saw the old roof tiles shattered during the war lying side by side with the new roof tiles that have been built to replace them – a shining and poignant reminder of the presence of the past wherever we go, but also an inspiring example of how tourism can help rebuild a place.

Croatia's beauty was obvious from the start: the rocky coast and the shadowing cypresses, the wildflowers in bloom and not a person in sight. And then it all came together for me on my last night in Dubrovnik, when I went out to dinner with a local tour guide and she told me about her family and how they had suffered during the war, how the entire country had suffered, but how there was now new hope blooming in the land and a new sense of the future.

On reviewing these experiences and thoughts, I realise that the historic part of the piece has more emotional resonance for me than the beautiful landscape. So, in keeping with my strategy of accelerating up to the greatest emotional resonance, I decide to rearrange the segments. I'll start with the prices, then move on to the beauty and the history, and end with my meal with the tour guide. It's a smooth movement. I'll have to make sure I pay attention to the transitions between the sections, but the piece is already taking shape in my mind. I've figured out how to structure the middle, and now it's just a question of bringing the individual examples to vivid life.

– Don George

As you'll see when you read the complete stories in Chapter Five, most of the pieces we've chosen to reproduce are organised along chronological, narrative lines, with the authors focusing on selected moments to draw out the most important aspects of their tales. In the Korea story, for example, Robert Hass takes us through his explorations, journeying deep into the countryside to visit the ancient capital of Kyongju, interweaving the themes of alienation and independence, pain and passion, introduced in the story's first paragraphs. Along the way we are presented with indelible portraits of people and places, history and culture, all interconnected in the unfolding of the author's experience – and all culminating in unexpected revelations and resolutions before the Buddha of Sokkuram. The result is an exemplary illustration of a moving, multilayered travel tale.

Conclusions That Lead to New Directions

The end of your article needs to achieve three intricately related objectives: it has to bring the focus of your piece to a satisfying conclusion; it has to tie the story back to its beginning; and it has to deliver the reader back to the world.

The article about Las Vegas by Simon Calder quoted earlier in this chapter concludes with a reference that nicely brings the piece full circle:

Thanks to the physical properties of neon, a trip to Las Vegas can have much the same effect as expensive designer drugs.

The home town of indulgence looks and feels like Toytown for tycoons. But beware staying here too long. On my last evening I got so lost trying to find a way out of Binion's Horseshoe Casino that I had to ask for directions back to real life.

A similar effect informs the Delos story. The extract reproduced earlier in this chapter ended with the introduction of an old man and a young boy, both of whom offered a tour of the island. The story goes on to describe how I spontaneously decided to miss the boat back to Mykonos in order to spend the night on the island, and depicts a raucous dinner with a Hungarian physicist who is also spending the night there, concluding with this description of the following morning:

Streaming sunlight awakened me. I turned to look at my watch and disturbed a black kitten that had bundled itself at my feet. In so doing, I also disturbed the ouzo and retsina that had bundled itself in my head, and I crawled as close as I could to the shadow of the wall – 6:45. I pulled my towel over my head and tried to imagine the windy dark, but to no avail. The kitten mewed its way under my towel, where it took to lapping at my cheek as if it had discovered a bowl of milk.

I stumbled down the stairs and soaked my head in tepid tap water until at last I felt stable enough to survey the surroundings. Behind the pavilion a clothesline led to the rusting generator. Chickens strutted inside a coop at the curator's house. Rhenea stirred in the rising mist.

Again I wandered through the ruins, different ruins now, bright with day and the reality of returns: The tourists would return to Delos, and I would return to Mykonos. I ate a solemn breakfast on the terrace with the physicist, then walked past the sacred lake and the marketplace to the Terrace of the Lions. Standing among the five lions of Delos, erected in the seventh century BC to defend the island from invaders, I looked over the crumbling walls and stunted pillars to the temples on the hill. Like priests they presided over the procession of tourists who would surge onto the island, bearing their oblation in cameras and guidebooks. As the trawler approached, a bent figure in a navy blue beret hurried to the dock, and a boy in shorts raced out of the curator's house past the physicist, past me, and into the ruins.

You can see how the story circles back to its beginning – the old man and the young boy rushing to meet the new day's potential clients – but everything else has changed. The reader has spent 24 hours on Delos with me, and so now has an entirely different impression of the island. At the end of the story, readers are led back to the world outside Delos and outside the article – but with an enhanced understanding of Delos and, ideally, with a renewed appreciation of the planet.

THE ACCORDION THEORY OF TIME

Students often ask me how to craft a description of an entire trip in a few words. Say you have between 1500 and 2500 words to write about a five-day journey. If you tried to write about everything that happened on that journey, you would have the travel equivalent of *War and Peace*. (You would also end up with a piece that was more suited to your personal travel diary than the very public pages of a newspaper or magazine.) So what you have to do is edit your reality. You have to think about all the pertinent experiences in your trip and then you have to choose those very few – three or four – that embody and illuminate the main points you want to make about your journey.

In order to do this well, you are going to end up focusing very precisely on those four experiences, and skimming over all the other experiences of your trip. This is where the accordion theory of time comes in. Your narrative focus moves in and out, in and out. You expand the accordion to full arm's length in order to focus closely on a moment in time, then you push it in to skim over whole days; then you draw it out again to focus on the next significant experience, then push it in to jump over more days.

Study almost any travel narrative, and you'll see that the author is playing the accordion of time. The writer isolates the cardinal events in their experience, analyses how they fit into the pattern of meaning they are trying to evoke, and focuses on the details of those events to render them in a way that will enable the reader to live them just as they did. They may lavish three pages on an incident that happened in five minutes, then summarise the next five days in five sentences. The narrative proceeds in this way – in and out, in and out – singling out for scrutiny and expanded description the events that form the building blocks of the story. The full meaning and impact of the story is created through the accumulation, organisation and integration of these event blocks.

– *Don George*

Finally, it's critical that you pay special attention to the last word of your story. This is where you leave the reader, literally and figuratively. It is your – and your story's – last point of connection with the reader, and the reader's threshold to the world outside the story. Where do you want to leave the reader? What do you want their last – and lasting – impression of your story to be?

Elements of Structure

Here are some important elements to consider when shaping your story.

Building Blocks

Think of each story as a set of building blocks. The beginning lays the foundation, and the middle builds on that foundation. It is essential that each part of the story builds upon the part that came before. This building is logical – that is, the progression of ideas and events in the story has to make sense – but it is also thematic and emotional.

When you are editing your own article, ask yourself if each section advances the story in the direction it needs to go, and whether each section builds upon the one before. In order to answer these questions, you need to be clear about your article's overall aim – this is absolutely fundamental to a successful travel article. As long as you know your story's goal, you'll be able to tell if your story is proceeding clearly and powerfully, block by block. With each new addition, ask yourself: does the reader need to know this? Does this take the reader one step closer to the overall point? If you stray from your overall aim, you'll lose your reader.

Transitions

In crafting a story, transitions are one of the writer's most important tools, linking one paragraph to another, and one section of a piece to the next. If you think of your article as a journey, the transitions are the stepping stones or tiny bridges that help the reader along – without them, the reader would fall into the chasm of incomprehensibility. Transitions give your piece coherence; they make sure your story follows logically from one step to the next, and they make sure you don't lose your reader along the way.

Transitions from one paragraph to another usually pick up a detail, image or theme from the last sentence in the preceding paragraph. In a chronological description, the sequential rush of events provides its own transitions, but when you leap from one event to another, you need to make sure the reader leaps with you. Occasionally, you will find that there is no appropriate transition at a particular place in a story, or that you don't want to craft a transition – you want to make a clear break. This is the place to use a section break, indicated in the text by a line break or a graphic element, which signals to the reader that you have ended one sequence and are beginning another. The reader will leap with you over the break, but without that visual cue, the reader will expect you to lead them along by the hand.

Bringing Your Story to Life

How do you bring your story to life with the kind of lively prose that editors say they want? Here are some of the most important tools and principles.

Dialogue

Dialogue helps to enliven a piece aurally, varying its rhythm. On another level it can be used to humanise a story, injecting characters into your article in a way that creates warmth and resonance for the reader. It can also help to illuminate a place. Remember how Robert Hass began 'The Path to Sokkuram'? He employed dialogue to push the story thematically along. His account ends at another café with dialogue of a different kind:

The waitress returned with a little paper packet of roast silkworms. On the house. She pointed at a shy boy at the next table and bit her lip before proceeding very deliberately. 'My friend is so exciting only to have this opportunity to speak practical English and having sharing Korean culture.' I understood. He was treating me to the silkworms. We were going to argue about politics. I ordered another bottle of wine and gestured him over. He sat down opposite me. Two of the waitresses joined us. The silkworms tasted vile, and I smiled gratefully trying to get one down. The girls laughed and the wine came. 'Korea,' the young man began, and shook his head. He said the word as if it were a synonym for life. Then he sighed happily and said it again. 'Korea, Korea, Korea.'

Dialogue gives a piece human context and contact. It can also help supply critical information in a nontextbook way. For example, a local resident or museum attendant can enter the story to reveal the history of the town or the special qualities of the painting on display. And dialogue can introduce human quirks – turns of phrase, words, patterns of speech – that help warm a story as well. The key is to use dialogue sparingly, keeping it crisp and authentic.

Dialogue should never be invented or embellished to suit your purpose. If you are altering reality in any way – compressing sentences spoken by three different people at three different times into one cocktail party dialogue, for example – then you have to make it clear that you are doing so. It's perfectly acceptable to clean up dialogue by removing repetitious pauses such as 'um' and 'ah', but you must adhere scrupulously to the truth of what the person is saying. You must not distort their words or misrepresent their meaning.

Characters

The introduction of characters is often critical to the success of a travel piece. Characters can illuminate places, and often help to propel and enliven a story. The human connection is arguably the most powerful element of travel, spanning cultures and backgrounds. Conveying a sense of human connection through the effective introduction of character is a great and powerful art. So pay attention to characters and don't shy away from bringing local people – or fellow travellers – into your story. Their presence in a story creates a human bridge between the story and the reader, just as they themselves are a human bridge between their home and you.

Illuminating Details & Anecdotes

Details hold the key to a good description and can be full of meaning, embodying the most important characteristics you want to convey. The more precise you can be in identifying and isolating the right details, and the more fully you can evoke those particular details in the reader's mind, the more powerful, compelling and effective your description will be.

You can never squeeze all the details of a place into a description. If you tried to do so minutely, you could write a book as long as *Ulysses* about the room you are sitting in now. You have to edit reality. You have to isolate the most telling details, asking yourself which ones most powerfully and precisely convey whatever it is about the scene that is most directly relevant to your story, which details will best establish the points you want to make.

In Simon Calder's description of neon, he didn't tell you everything he knows about neon, just the facts that pertain to his eventual point about Las Vegas. And in Robert Hass's depiction of his Korean pilgrimage, he doesn't add extraneous details about the country or his experience there – he focuses solely on the information the reader needs to know in order to relive his journey.

Anecdotes are simply a larger, expanded version of details. Just as a scene is composed of myriad details that need to be filtered, so a journey is composed of myriad anecdotes. Your job is to choose just those anecdotes that capture, crystallise and convey the point of your piece.

Accuracy

One especially critical element in re-creating a travel experience is accuracy. Travel pieces must be accurate in two ways. First, they must be factually accurate in their reporting. This means getting the population of the African village right, precisely conveying the colour of the church in Nova Scotia and getting the year that the Spaniards settled on the coast correct. There is simply no excuse for getting your facts wrong, and you should not expect sympathy (or future work) from an editor if you do.

The second kind of accuracy is perception and description. It is far more difficult to capture, but is equally critical to the depth and success of travel writing.

Let's say you are trying to describe a field in France. You write, 'I saw a field in France.' Does this bring any image of the field into the reader's mind? No. So you think some more about the field and write, 'In France I saw a field the size of a football pitch.' This helps a little – at least we have a sense of size – but we still don't see the field. So you dig back into your memory – and your notes – and write: 'In France I saw a field the size of a football pitch, filled with red poppies.' Suddenly the image blazes to life. We can *see* the field, the poppies extending toward the horizon. Now you're back in the scene, remembering the morning, and you write: 'In France I drove by a field the size of a football pitch, filled with red poppies and bordered on three sides by rows of lavender, whose sweet scent so filled the air that I had to stop.' Now we're right with you. Not only do we have a sense of size and colour, we also have another sense involved – the sense of smell – and the action of you stopping. You've engaged us.

A good travel story is basically the accumulation of such details of perception and description. But you can't put these descriptive details into your stories unless you experience them first. You have to experience the world with a fearless curiosity, and then render that curiosity and the discoveries it brings in clean, clear, compelling prose. Do that and you'll get somewhere. And you'll take the reader with you.

Use All Your Senses

Most travel articles include good visual descriptions of the places where the stories are set, but writers far too frequently ignore their other senses. Think of it: when you walk into an Italian restaurant, what are the first senses that accost you? Not sight, but probably sound and smell. There's the raucous ruckus of the patrons, the waiters pushing through the crowd, the garlicky snap and sizzle of food flipped in frying pans. The aromas may be the first sensory impression of all: the garlic that insinuated itself into the preceding sentence's sizzle, the mozzarella and tomatoes wafting from the kitchen, the mingled smells of veal piccata and pasta al pesto. So if you are going to describe this Italian restaurant in your article, you could begin with its smells and sounds, not forgetting, of course, the tastes.

When we travel we experience the world with all of our senses – so why do we focus so exclusively on sight in our articles? Pay attention to all the senses. Let your ears and nose and taste buds and fingers do as much work as your eyes. How can you cultivate this art? Here's a little exercise that should help. Think of a place or situation from the past and describe it in no more than 300 words, using as many of the five senses as you can. Then read your piece of writing aloud and see how using all the senses in your description brings the place to life – it's more satisfying for you and for your reader.

Show, Don't Tell

If you've ever taken a creative writing class, you will have had this maxim drilled into your head. Don't tell what your characters are feeling – show it. Reveal their inner selves through what they do and say. Let the reader draw the conclusions. The same is exactly true for travel writing. Your piece will be much more powerful and successful if you engage the reader in the creative process of figuring out how the people in your tale are being affected. By the same token, don't spell out the fact that *you* were moved by an experience – make the reader moved by the way you describe the experience. Re-create the experience so that the reader is in your shoes – and is moved just the way you were.

Avoid Clichés

Clichés have a way of creeping into our writing – it's difficult to come up with something fresh every time. Sometimes, without our even realising it, a well-worn phrase that we've picked up from who-knows-where slips surreptitiously into our prose. Reread your writing with your cliché-meter on high, and avoid those tired descriptions – land of contrasts, tropical paradise, bustling thoroughfare… Whenever you come to a phrase that sounds wooden, stop and ask yourself if there might be a better way of expressing what you want to say, one that more truly reflects your take on it.

One of the culprits editors most frequently cite when they talk about bad travel writing is the use of clichés. So be a vigilant self-editor. Always make your words and descriptions your own.

Elements of Style

The following critical elements also help to determine the success – or failure – of a travel story.

Voice

Travel stories need a warm human voice. Don't try to write like a fact-checker or reporter who is simply recording their surroundings, without any sense of engagement. You are undertaking a fundamentally human adventure – encountering new people and a new culture, whether it's in a different region of your own country or somewhere halfway around the world. Your humanity should be one of the fundamental strengths of your story.

Your voice should be a reflection of your personality and style, whether romantic, reflective, funny, sarcastic or informative. Read the examples in Chapter Five, and note how each writer employs a different tone. Over time you will come to be identified with the voice you project in your stories, so it is imperative to write in a way that feels natural to you and to the particular story.

Another aspect of voice is its use to express opinion and judgment. Readers – and editors – are relying on your expertise and discernment to steer them away from scams and disappointments, and to point them in the direction of the best on-the-road experiences. Informing your voice with opinion when appropriate is an essential part of your job.

Pacing

What kind of pace do you want your story to have? It can be headlong and breathless or slow and measured. Make sure the pace fits your piece, and that you're in control of the pacing of your story. It's fine to speed up and slow down – it can make the reading a richer experience – just don't let the story careen out of control like a South American mountain bus crossing a snow-patched pass and then heading downhill when suddenly the brakes give out and the driver can't stop and the landscape is whizzing dizzyingly by and before you know it the reader is gone – *pfff!* – like that bus into the South American sky.

Attend to the Music of the Language

Think of English as a musical instrument. You are using that instrument to create great music. Read your writing out loud, and listen to the music of your writing. What kind of mood are you creating? Are you keeping the pace lively or is it wooden? Are you varying the tempos in your writing? Are you using devices such as internal rhyme and alliteration?

Take any book by Jan Morris, open it at random and begin to read aloud. Listen to the way she modulates your journey through the story. Revel in her masterful use of the intrinsic music of our language.

Make Your Verbs Act & Your Words Count

One of the biggest traps for novice writers is the urge to make prose powerful by over-writing, using high-flown adjectives and adverbs. You can feel the sentences collapsing under the weight of such words. Use active verbs, and don't use three words when you can use one. Rather than writing 'He walked as quickly as he could up the crater', write 'He raced up the crater' or, even better, 'He scrambled up the crater'. Reread your work slowly, and ask yourself if you really need each word. Remember that less is more.

Consistent Verb Tense

You would be amazed how many writers, even very established writers, mix up their verb tenses in their stories. Unless you're doing this on purpose and with a sure sense of control, you shouldn't begin your story in the present tense and then flip into the past tense, and then into the present tense and then back into the past tense again. You might think this is an obvious point, but just watch yourself the next time you write a travel piece. Reread it very carefully and see if at some point you too don't fall prey to inconsistencies of tense.

Writing in the present tense has become something of a vogue recently, largely due to the Internet and the more immediate prose the medium has encouraged and cultivated. Somehow, the Web feels like a present-tense medium. But writing in the present tense can have its pitfalls. As a narrator you can have no more sense of what's coming than your reader. You cannot possibly know what happened two days after the day you're describing, and you need to take particular care not to let that knowledge colour your narrative in any way. You have to re-create the ignorance you had at the moment you are describing, and never divulge more about your trip than you knew at that time.

Writing in the past tense, on the other hand, liberates you. You already know what happened at the end of the trip, so in that sense writing in the past tense is a much more natural choice. But it's up to you – just be sure to be consistent and in control of your choice. If you're not, the reader will get lost – and your piece won't get published.

WHICH TENSE SHOULD YOU WRITE IN?

When I was just starting out, I wrote a commissioned piece for an American magazine. I was pretty naive about the business of travel writing at that stage, and fashioned myself an artist – a poet of the road. And so I purposefully crafted my work in the present tense.

The editor liked my submission, but asked me to rewrite it in the past tense. After initially exploding with righteous anger (note: this is not recommended as a way to impress an editor and start a sympathetic relationship with them), I recast the piece and discovered that in fact it made hardly any difference at all. I had written it in the present tense because I wanted to convey a sense of immediacy to the reader; I wanted the reader to feel that they were right there with me. But the truth is that the reader will feel that way when the piece is written in the past tense as well.

– Don George

Rewriting & Self-Editing

Different writers have different strategies for rewriting and self-editing. Some rewrite as they go along; others wait to rewrite until they've completed a first draft of the entire piece.

A good practice is to write three drafts of an article. In the first draft, try to get down everything that's in your mind about the story – all the important incidents, impressions and lessons. In this phase it's best to write as quickly as possible, rather than pausing to rewrite.

The second draft is the macro-editing phase. Read the story for flow and logical development, possibly moving sections in order to clarify and refine the movement and development of the piece. Remove sections that don't add to the story and identify gaps that need to be filled. Ask yourself if you've supplied all the information a reader needs to know to re-create that experience. Does the story build up coherently to its main point?

The third draft is the micro-editing phase, where you read very slowly and precisely, paying close attention to the style of the prose. Have you made every word count? Are you re-creating your experience as vividly and truly as possible? Are all the transitions there? How about the music of the piece?

After the third draft you should be ready to send the story to an editor. At this stage many experienced writers show their work to a trusted reader before sending it off to be published – sometimes even the most capable writers are too close to their work to see something that an objective eye can pick up. Of course, after the editor has read it, you may need to rework the piece further, but that's an essential part of the process, too. The editor will have their own view of the piece, and of where and how it fits into the puzzle of their publication. It is the writer's job to work with the editor to come up with a story that satisfies both parties. If you feel very strongly that you don't want to make an editorial change, you should discuss that point with the editor by all means, but you should be careful not to alienate them. Just as finding a great story entails a marriage of passion and practicality, so too publishing a story entails marrying the editor's and the writer's views of the story. We'll look at some successful examples of this marriage in Chapter Five.

INTERVIEW WITH LYN HUGHES

Based in the UK, Lyn Hughes is the Editor and co-founder of Wanderlust *magazine.*

How did you start off in your career as a travel editor?

I started my own magazine! Back in late 1992, my partner, Paul Morrison, and I were frustrated by the lack of travel magazines. We were heading off to South America for the winter, and on the flight were bored so started scheming out our ideal magazine. The idea stuck, so despite having no previous publishing experience, we launched *Wanderlust* in our spare bedroom a few months after we returned.

What is the best way of establishing yourself if you're just starting out in your career as a freelance travel journalist?

Be as professional as possible, sending editors well-thought-out proposals that demonstrate that you understand their publication and what makes their readers tick. This might sound basic, but it's surprising how many people fall down at this first hurdle.

How do you think freelance travel writers get the numbers to add up in terms of an income?

Some freelance travel writers have a sideline; eg as a guidebook writer, a tour leader or a freelance sub-editor. Others are so prolific and proficient that they sell several articles from every trip they do. For instance, this year I sent one of my freelances, Jasper Winn, to do a story in Malawi. To date he has sold five different pieces from that trip to different publications and radio stations. Importantly, all were very different from the *Wanderlust* article, so I had no objections there.

What tips would you give to budding travel writers?

a) Know the market: which magazines and newspapers run travel articles, what style of article they go for and who they are aimed at.
b) Think laterally: about where to send your idea or article, and about the angle.
c) Read. Read travel articles of all types. Understand what makes a good piece.
d) Does your idea pass the 'so what?' test. You say you could write an article on Thailand. So what? So could thousands of other people. Why should we go for you?
e) What are editors going to be looking for? What's in the news? What is going to be a hot destination and why?
f) Don't claim to be 'funnier than Bill Bryson'. People who claim that invariably aren't.

Are there any courses or any training that you'd recommend a budding travel writer to undertake?

The one-day courses run by TNT give a good introduction and flavour, and give you a chance to put your questions to editors and successful freelancers. Any course that gives you a chance to get your work critiqued won't be a waste of time. Like any craft, travel writing needs a lot of practice to develop and improve.

What are the most common mistakes that travel writers make in their copy?

Diary-style articles rarely work, so don't even consider those unless agreed by an editor. Avoid tired clichés – snow-capped mountains, sun-kissed beaches, cacophony of sound, the heat hit me like a sauna. Avoid exclamation marks!!! And make sure you've got an eye-grabbing intro and an interesting last paragraph, too – your article is a story, not a school essay.

What are the most common mistakes that travel writers make when pitching to you?

Not understanding who our readers are. Or saying something along the lines of 'I'm off to Peru – would you like an article?' If it's Peru that you're going to, think of two or three different angles or ways to treat a story that would suit my publication. Tell me why they would be of interest to my readers. And why should I use you and not the dozen other people who have just written in with ideas on Peru?

What are the main differences between travel writing for a magazine as opposed to a newspaper?

Magazines have much longer lead times than newspapers and tend to plan much more in advance. Therefore, it is no use pitching an idea on Christmas breaks in November – you should have been suggesting it the previous February or March.

Likewise, rather than responding to topical items in the news, think ahead to what the trends and newsworthy topics will be in six to twelve months' time. Magazines like to think of themselves as setting the trends and influencing their readers. It is absolutely key that you understand who those readers are and what makes them tick.

Photographs are much more important to a magazine – they use more of them and usually in colour. So, even if you can't supply the photos, they are more likely to go for a story if it's going to be visually interesting.

What, in your opinion, constitutes 'good' travel writing?

Good travel writing should transport the reader to the destination or situation that you're describing. They should be able to hear the sounds, smell the smells, and feel the atmosphere.

What constitutes 'bad' travel writing?

I can't stand 'ego' pieces which are about the author, rather than about the place or the experience. The author is there to guide, inform and entertain the reader, not to be the equivalent of the pub bore.

At the other end of the pendulum, very dry articles that are crammed with facts and figures are equally indigestible.

What are the rewards of travel writing as a career?

You get to see places, have experiences and meet people that you may not have achieved under your own steam. Having a notebook gives you the perfect excuse to nose around and ask questions in a situation where you may have felt too shy or overawed.

What is the downside?

If you want to make travel writing pay, you have to very much treat it as a job cramming extraordinary trips into just a few days. Your idea of a dream trip might not involve inspecting every hotel in town or having a very boring dinner with the local head of tourism.

And once you're a travel writer, you might find it impossible to ever take a proper holiday again – the temptation to just knock up a piece in your notebook or on your laptop will be too much.

INTERVIEW WITH CATH URQUHART

Based in the UK, Cath Urquhart is the Travel Editor of the **Times.**

The most important thing to me is that the writer pitching stories has a strong, new angle and is telling me something I haven't heard before. The number of (unsuccessful) pitches I get in which people say, 'Do you want something on Paris?' never ceases to amaze me. The answer is always: yes, I want good ideas.

Clearly you're going to stand a far better chance of success, therefore, if you are a properly trained journalist and know what constitutes a good story, and/or have a particularly strong knowledge of a place and can see what is new/interesting/different about it.

I strongly believe that travel writing, for newspapers at least, is fundamentally no different from any other branch of journalism, in that the best preparation is to be a reporter or otherwise trained journalist, so you know what makes a story, how to interview people, and preferably know law for journalists and have decent shorthand. Many of the writers who contribute to the *Times* have this background, as do all the commissioning editors on the desk.

INTERVIEW WITH AMANDA JONES

Amanda Jones is a New Zealand–born writer whose articles and photographs have appeared in Travel & Leisure, *the* Los Angeles Times, *the* London Sunday Times, Condé Nast Traveller *and* Vogue, *among other publications.*

How did you start off in your career as a travel writer?

Travel writing was the forth incarnation of my career. I began in neurophysiology, moved to fashion and quickly realised I was a failed fashionista. But that horrific stint did get me into working for a magazine (*Vogue*). I then became the editor of an art magazine, quit after two years, and pondered what to do next. Travel was in my blood, and one of my all-too-few skills was writing, so I resolved to try combining the two. I started at the very bottom writing for small, little-known adventure publications.

What is the best way of establishing yourself if you're just starting out in your career as a freelance travel journalist?

Perfect your art by writing much and often, get feedback, attend conferences and workshops, then send your pieces out to editors. The very best way to get known is to get published, and the one way to get published is to write engaging, lively and informed articles on topics that haven't been covered a million times before. Editors love people who can actually write. Even if they don't need the topic of your first submission, if they enjoyed your style, they will invite you to submit on other destinations.

How have you managed to get your name known as a freelance travel journalist?

Perseverance, luck and the occasional decent story, I suppose.

As a freelance travel journalist, how do you get the numbers to add up in terms of an income?

Herein lies the rub. I am now, after many years, in the lovely position of being able to write for publications that pay well and cover expenses. There was a time when I lost money at travel writing, which eventually brought me to a fiscal epiphany. I could no longer do stories that *cost* me money. From then I made a fast rule that I would only write stories that would pay well enough for it to make sense. And now, to supplement my income, I have also taken up photography. And after any embargos are honoured, I try to re-sell my stories to as many outlets as possible, or recycle them for various publications, both domestic and foreign. (An embargo is a contracted period of time during which the original assigning publication forbids you to reprint the story. This is generally about three to six months and only happens with magazines. Newspapers do not typically have embargos.)

What tips would you give to budding travel writers?

Write, write, write. This is the only way to improve.

Read other fiction and nonfiction writers and notice strong, original descriptive phrases and elegant use of narrative.

Make sure the transitions between all your paragraphs are smooth. They should not be jarring. Paragraphs should flow together logically, even if you are changing directions within the story. A sure sign of a green writer is jarring paragraph transitions.

Read the magazine or newspaper section to which you are submitting. Know their style, the demographic of their reader, their article length, their voice, their comfort zones. Make sure your pieces are in accordance with their style. For example, you can get away with using slang if you are writing for *Outside* magazine, but not for *Town & Country Travel*.

Fact-check everything you write. Nothing angers an editor more than false information. The Internet is a powerful tool. Take the time.

Prune any lines you don't feel 100 per cent comfortable with. Anything you struggled with should probably go away.

Read a printed version of the story to yourself before submitting it. When you stumble, re-write.

Lastly, *spellcheck*…even if you do nothing else, do this.

After *several rounds of editing*, send your work out to editors at newspapers and magazines. Contrary to popular wisdom, I think it is a mistake to blanket the market with the same story at the same time. Although you may think it bodes well for your abilities, editors absolutely loathe being told you sold the story to another publication while simultaneously soliciting them. Start with your A Team list. If they reject it, move to your B Team list.

Make sure you spell the name of the editor correctly. It is incredible how many aspiring writers don't bother with these rather important details.

Don't focus only on the major national titles. Look for 'vertical' publications, or niche titles. If you have a hobby, a passion, a skill, a sport or an art, there is bound to be a magazine catering to people with similar interests. Say, for example, your passion is collecting quilts. There is very possibly a magazine that would like a story on shopping for quilts in Prague's flea markets. These things sound esoteric, but they sell, and are a good way to get your name in print.

Are there any courses or any training that you'd recommend a budding travel writer to undertake?

Why, the Book Passage Travel Writers Conference, of course. Personally, I have not taken any others. I recommend doing them, however. They are a powerful hub for learning and networking.

What are the most common mistakes that travel writers make in their copy?

Most budding writers do not pay enough attention to their first few paragraphs. This is a tragic mistake, as this is generally all the editor will read. If they don't like the lead, the ugly truth is that your manuscript is tossed. If they are compelled, they will read on. Take your most interesting or exciting sentence and try working it into the beginning.

New writers often make the mistake of engaging in what we call 'purple prose' – florid, overblown, descriptive phrases or excessively emotional personal musings. Your goal is to write a piece that can be read fluidly. It is not to demonstrate the extremes of your vocabulary. Use evocative, concise description.

Often writers don't include enough dialogue in their stories. Readers and editors love dialogue, and they adore developed characters that help 'people the landscape' you are writing about. Experiment with these techniques.

What are the main differences between travel writing for a newspaper as opposed to a magazine?

As a whole, newspapers want shorter pieces. And they commonly want replicable information – in other words, the reader needs to be able to do your trip almost word for word. Personal heartbreaks, epiphanies and mishaps don't have much place in the newspaper travel section piece unless it is in an essay form. However, first-person commentaries can be more acceptable in magazine pieces. Newspapers are a great place to start your career. They need 52 cover stories a year, whereas most magazines need only 12.

What are the rewards of travel writing as a career?

When Mick Jagger was recently asked what career he would have chosen had he not become a rock star, he answered that he would have liked to have been a travel writer. Travel writing, when it works, is truly one of the most enviable jobs in the world.

As a travel writer, you will have experiences that few can have, you will see things most will never see, and you will meet people, go places and learn things that will change you forever. However, the chance of becoming wealthy is slender. Egregiously slender. You will have to satisfy yourself with different riches – those of experience.

What has been the downside for you?

Mercifully, there have been very few downsides. Sometimes I must write stories that bore me, but that's my own fault. Occasionally I have had a bad experience with an editor, or an editor has eviscerated my work distressingly, but I generally don't write for those people again. After I had children (although that can hardly be called a downside), travelling extensively became more difficult. I have figured out ways around that, however (I take them with me, or I don't go for as long). Naturally we all wish the job of a travel writer paid as well as that of an investment banker, but I willingly chose this life and I am delighted with it. I would not change my experiences for that of any other profession.

INTERVIEW WITH ANDREW BAIN

Andrew Bain is an Australian-based adventure-travel writer, journalist and photographer whose articles appear regularly in the Age *and the* Sydney Morning Herald. *His recent book,* Headwinds, *describes his around-Australia cycling experiences.*

How did you start off in your career as a travel writer and journalist?

I studied and received a degree in journalism, then began in the usual journalistic fashion – regional media, city media, branch out. I spent about five years as a sports writer then set off on the standard backpacking tour through Europe. As it is for so many people, travel writing began as a lark to fund more travel, until eventually the writing became the purpose of travel.

What is the best way of establishing yourself if you're just starting out in your career as a freelance travel journalist?

Choose destinations that aren't already clogging the pages of travel sections and magazines. Skip New York, London and Paris, and look for lesser-known places with appealing quirks. If you must stick to the blue-chip destinations, find a different way to look at them. Develop a specialty – food, spas, outdoor adventure – that will gain you a niche market, then supplement it with general stories.

As a freelance travel journalist, how do you get the numbers to add up in terms of an income?

It's a risky business. I determine how much a certain trip will cost me, then calculate how much I'll need to earn to justify the journey. I break this down into the number of stories required from the trip and then scurry about making certain I come up with at least that number of stories. Then comes the problematic bit: selling them. It's difficult at the beginning of your travel-writing career to make accurate forecasts on expenses and profit because you're not sure how much a certain story will bring in, but eventually you get a feel for the markets you're targeting.

What tips would you give to budding travel writers?

Avoid clichés. Have you ever *really* seen a view that sucks the breath from your throat? Then why do so many travel writers insist on 'breathtaking' views? Look at places, not the brochures. It's not your job to write a marketing piece but to find the words that accurately describe your experience and reaction to a place or activity. People already know that Paris is 'pretty' and 'romantic'. Tell them something unique about your particular visit and your interaction with a place. Explore your mind and discover that you did indeed experience more than 'fright' on a bungy jump. Now explain it to a reader who wants to know exactly what it was like.

What are the most common mistakes that travel writers make in their copy?

Not knowing the publication's market or style. Some magazines refuse first-person stories; others are devoted to luxury travel or outdoor adventure. It's pointless sending them something different. Read several issues of a publication and you'll also get a feel for the breadth of its interest. It might cover the world or it might show a preference for local material. Tailor your work to suit the market.

How did you get your first travel literature title published?

Books are a long, slow process…and that's even after the writing's complete. As *Headwinds* was my first book, I completed the manuscript before making any approaches to agents or publishers. It's then a marketing battle – to convince a few people that this book will reap a profit to any publisher. I found an agent who thought the book had potential and she then found it a publisher.

Do you think it's important to have an agent?

I think it's invaluable. Publishers receive so many manuscripts, and the endorsement of an agent is often the only way to get your manuscript read. It tells the publisher that the manuscript has already been considered by somebody whose opinion they hopefully respect.

Are you in a better position as a travel journalist because of your ability to provide photographs?

Photos are crucial. Your stories are competing with such a huge slush pile on an editor's desk that you need any advantage. If editors are choosing between a story that requires photos from a library, and a story presented with good photos, they're likely to go for the complete package every time, especially for writers new to them. And photos invariably boost your earnings.

Have you written for genres other than adventure travel? Does having a specialisation help or hinder finding work?

To be too specialist can be a hindrance as it shuts you out of certain markets, so I do range widely in subject matter. Certainly, adventure is my primary focus but I complement this with general travel pieces. If I'm trekking in the Andes, for instance, why not also spend some time in a nearby city and write about it? To have a specialist field is useful for earning respect with a core of publications, but diversity is critical if you're to make a living from travel writing, especially at the outset of a career.

What, in your opinion, constitutes 'good' travel writing?

Good writing is fresh, with observations that are clearly personal. I don't want to read about 'towering skyscrapers' or 'quaint villages'; that's as obvious as calling an elephant 'large'. Good writing incorporates simile and metaphor, and goes easy on adverbs and unnecessary adjectives, to paint pictures of language. Don't forget that every place on earth has now been written about, so what is it we are trying to achieve by adding to the pool? It can only be our own insight. It was well expressed in a quote from Neal Cassady (Jack Kerouac's travel mate): 'I think one should write, as nearly as possible, as if he were the first person on earth and was humbly and sincerely putting on paper that which he saw and experienced and loved and lost…with careful avoidance of common phrases, trite usage of hackneyed words and the like.'

What constitutes 'bad' travel writing?

Brochures and travel writing…never the twain should meet. Too many writers seem to think that they have to be glowing in praise for a place for a story to be marketable. In doing so, they veer dangerously towards writing brochure-style sentences. You get 'sparkling lakes', 'pristine beaches' and the people are always the 'friendliest on earth'. You can like a place without using lazy language. There's a particular danger of over-effervescing from writers who travel on junkets. To criticise or even parody a place might threaten future freebies so it's clear they often write what their hosts will want to read.

What are the rewards of travel writing as a career?

Travel is its own obvious reward, and without being a travel writer I wouldn't have seen half the mountains and deserts that so inspire me. Equally, the writing, both as a process and a product, is enormously rewarding. To create what you consider a perfect sentence (until you read it later in print – they always seem terrible by then), to have a lightning flash of inspiration…it's nearly as good as summiting a peak.

What has been the downside for you?

Behind all things glamorous there's the everyday tedium: actors learning their lines, models waxing their backs, and writers spending hours wrestling with a sentence. It happens, and more regularly than we'd all like. And while everybody else at the Grand Canyon is oohing and aahing about the view, you're quietly fretting about how your story is progressing and wondering how you're going to express the scene in words – 'words cannot describe…' will never suffice. Everything you now see and do will be tainted slightly by the knowledge that you'll later be sitting at your computer re-creating what you wish you never had to re-create.

EXAMPLES OF GOOD TRAVEL WRITING

In previous chapters we discussed the different categories of travel articles, and the qualities and strategies that make travel writing successful. In this chapter we have chosen seven exemplary travel articles that have been published in a variety of publications. Selections from some of these stories have already been referred to and analysed in earlier chapters.

We hope our selection will inspire you by revealing the literary spectrum that travel writing encompasses. We also hope it will help you consider what kind of writing best suits you, or suits the subject of a particular piece you are trying to write.

Choosing these stories was a daunting task, and we do not mean to suggest in any way that they are the best travel stories published in the past decade. They are simply representative stories that illustrate many of the principles of successful travel writing that we have discussed throughout this book. Pick up the current issue of any of the newspapers or magazines mentioned in these pages and you will find other excellent examples of travel writing.

Listings of classic works of travel literature are included in the Resources section at the end of this book. In particular, we recommend that you peruse the works of the following writers, who are contemporary masters of travel writing and who publish in both periodicals and books: Jan Morris (you can learn from anything she's written, but take a look at the essays collected in *Journeys* and *Destinations* for a starter); Paul Theroux (his first travel book, *The Great Railway Bazaar*, remains his best but *Fresh Air Fiend* offers a stimulating sampling of his essays and articles); Tim Cahill (his collections are audacious and illuminating; as an appetiser, try *Pass the Butterworms*); and Pico Iyer (all his books are elegant and insightful, but begin with *Video Night in Kathmandu*, which still pulses with an eclectic, electric intelligence and passion decades after its publication).

LAS VEGAS

by Simon Calder

Simon Calder is the Senior Travel Editor of the *Independent* newspaper, where this story was first published. This deceptively fact-packed article offers a witty illumination of neon's past and presence in Las Vegas. As already noted in Chapter Three, the story's surprising beginning signals that we are in for an intriguing and offbeat approach to a city we may usually feel we already know too well. We learn midway through the article that the piece is pegged to a specific exhibition on neon at the Nevada State Museum, but the larger point Calder makes is that all of Las Vegas is an 'amorphous neon museum'. Also note Calder's lively use of puns – 'the fall-out of constant re-invention' in a paragraph on Nevada's nearby atomic explosions; 'tuition is better than intuition' – and the way he compresses and connects ancient (Luxor) and modern (the Mormons, the railroad company, the atomic tests) history with the timeless character of the city itself. Calder uses the 'Neon Unplugged' exhibit to reveal the entire city in a new light.

Neon: you need to know two things about this gas. The first is that it is, in elementary terms, a relative newcomer; even though it is present in small quantities in the air we breathe, it was identified only a century ago by a French scientist named Georges Claude. The second is that, being inert, neon is intrinsically dull. Oh, unless you pass an electric charge through it, as M Claude did. Do that, and it can light up the desert and dazzle the world.

Las Vegas was just a flicker in the eye of the San Pedro, Los Angeles and Salt Lake City Railroad when M Claude announced his discovery. The first neon sign in North America was sold by M Claude's own company in 1923 to a Packard dealership in Los Angeles.

At the time, the Mormons mistakenly believed Las Vegas presented a promised, and morally safe, haven in the middle of the Mojave Desert. By the Thirties, they had lost faith with Las Vegas – and the rest of the world had lost interest in the fact that neon glows red in the dark and that, when mixed with a little mercury, its elementary cousin argon turns bright blue. But Las Vegas had barely begun to experiment with the extreme right-hand side of the Periodic Table of Elements.

Helium radiates a lurid magnolia when suitably fired up; krypton issues a steely silver; while xenon emits the palest blue. These elementary truths helped Las Vegas find its place in the world.

Whatever your desire, especially if it was illegal and/or frowned upon in the rest of the US, it could usually be found in Nevada's largest city. Drinkers could slake their thirsts, gamblers could stake their shirts and lovers could make (or fake) their vows. In short, it was a gas, with neon at the top of the elementary tree.

'Welcome to Fabulous Las Vegas' shrieks the iconic sign. When you see the city's emblem close up, in the unforgiving glare of a Nevada noon, it looks pitifully plain. You spot it as you head north along Las Vegas Boulevard at the intersection with Main Street. Las Vegas Boulevard is stripped down to 'the Strip' by almost everybody. All the grand monuments from the turn of the 21st century, from the Venetian to Camelot (not a lottery operator, but a re-enactment of the court of King Arthur), cling to the southern part of the Strip.

Downtown Las Vegas is where M Claude's new gas found its raison d'être, and helped the city claw an identity from the shadowy desert. Neon helped to define Las Vegas, and now the city is returning the favour. Time in Las Vegas seems to revolve around 33 times faster than real life. So the relics that have seen the city through since its foundation in 1905 are, relatively speaking, as ancient as the antiquities in Luxor – established in Egypt 1570 BC, established in Las Vegas 1993. This was the same time as the Dunes – a shining light on the strip – was snuffed out. It was imploded to make room for Bellagio, the flashy Italianate hotel-casino (that hyphen welds the two together with a permanence not often found in Las Vegas) where Europe meets America and gambles away the rest of the night.

Las Vegas did not always have such global pretensions. In the early days, the city experimented freely with newly discovered elements on the blank canvas of the Mojave Desert.

Evidence of innovation is scattered around the city, but you have to raise your gaze from the baize gaming tables to see it. Downtown is like an amorphous neon museum, whose exhibits are scattered around the streets. The first item was the horse and rider from the Hacienda, now frozen in mid-leap at the corner of Fremont Street. Other exhibits, such as the flame that illuminated The Flame Bar and Grill, are tucked away in culs-de-sac.

But this month, the definitive exhibition of electrical potential has plugged itself into the traveller's need to know. For the rest of this year, 'Neon Unplugged' is on show at the Nevada State Museum, a modest (for Las Vegas) building in Lorenzi Park, a couple of miles west of Downtown.

'Elvis slept here' used to be the boast of the Normandie motel, whose sign has been recovered from the boneyard (scrapheap) to play a leading part in the new exhibition. 'If you wish to bet,' goes the catchy slogan of another exhibit, El Rancho, 'there's nothing better than roulette.'

There is, actually. Place a bet on Oxford to be selected as European Capital of Culture 2003, at the outrageously long odds of 10 to 1, then spend your winnings on a flight to Las Vegas to see the new exhibition. It opens with the long and ridiculously curly R of the Desert Inn – a 1950s casino demolished to make way for La Reve, the city's latest $5bn venture. You can see images of Moulin Rouge, 'The resort wonder of the world', now a dowdy shell on Bonanza Avenue but about to be replenished as Las Vegas rediscovers its roots.

Neon wasn't the only experimental element to feature in Las Vegas. In the Fifties, above-ground atomic explosions on the Nevada Test Site, north (but not very north) of Las Vegas were regarded as tourist attractions. Thousands of citizens and tourists flocked to Mount Charleston, 45 miles north of the city, for a radioactive picnic. Binion's Horseshoe Casino produced postcards of the events, while the Sands Motel staged a 'Miss Atomic 1957' parade. The fall-out of constant re-invention is the continuous scrapping of Las Vegas heritage. Happily, some of the most ancient signs are preserved in Fremont Street, together with a free light show that puts the 'o' into ostentatious.

Among the bright lights, there is a dark side to Las Vegas. Paradise: that was what the destination board on the front of the bus promised. But as the CAT ('Citizens Area Transit') bus lurched from stop to stop along Paradise Avenue, which carves a messy track through the south-eastern wastes of suburban Las Vegas, my self-appointed tour guide in the next seat was not instilling confidence.

'Go any further east along Fremont and it's just crack-heads and whores,' she cautioned. 'We'll be passing by Crack Alley in a minute or two.'

A New Yorker who had just blown $4300 (£3000) in a marathon, four-day roulette session, insisted on spelling out in words, as well as figures, the measure of his personal catastrophe: 'Forty-three hundred dollars.'

Las Vegas takes the world to extremes. Spending time in Las Vegas without spending money in the casinos is to defy the purpose of the place; hey, everyone, let's chip in – you should see the size of the electricity bill. But when it comes to serious gambling, tuition is better than intuition. To help gamblers lose money more slowly, Caesar's Palace offers free blackjack lessons every morning. So long as you understand that the odds are against you, and that in the unlikely event of your being ahead you should quit, there are few more pleasurable ways of losing the odd $50. But bear in mind the gambling maxim: if, after half an hour at the table, you can't spot the sucker – it's you.

Thanks to the physical properties of neon, a trip to Las Vegas can have much the same effect as expensive designer drugs.

The home town of indulgence looks and feels like Toytown for tycoons. But beware staying here too long. On my last evening I got so lost trying to find a way out of Binion's Horseshoe Casino that I had to ask for directions back to real life.

Traveller's Guide

Getting there: the only airline with non-stop services between the UK and Las Vegas is Virgin Atlantic, which flies from Gatwick on Thursdays and Sundays. A return fare is typically £500.

Staying there: rates for most Las Vegas hotels are very flexible. At quiet times, particularly midweek, you could pay $79 (£53) for a room in a top hotel such as New York New York. On a Saturday night, the price could rise to $259 (£165).

Neon Unplugged: this exhibition runs until 4 January next year. It is part of the Nevada State Museum; call 001 702 486 5205 for more information, or visit www .nevadaculture.org.

NEW DAWN

by Harriet O'Brien

Freelance writer Harriet O'Brien wrote this article for the UK's *Condé Nast Traveller* magazine. The piece is an excellent example of how a writer can skilfully interweave what is essentially a densely informative 'service story' on accommodation options in Sri Lanka with a spare but vivid evocation of the country. The first few paragraphs effortlessly immerse us in history and place – who can resist the brilliant beginning? – then O'Brien reveals the point of her piece: a hotel tour of this newly alluring destination. As she leads us on this tour, O'Brien uses very specific details to bring to life the unique characters and amenities of each hotel. Note how she avoids the kind of fawning, purpled prose hotel critiques often inspire in less-seasoned writers; rather, she presents her own judgments about each place in an authoritative way, grounded in fact and precise description, so that we end the story with an overall impression of the island's varied attractions and a specialised appreciation of what each property offers.

In the afternoon sunshine a couple of little brown monkeys sprawled indolently beside the king's swimming pool. Belly up, the small sunbathers looked preposterously human, as if deliberately apeing the insouciance of the monarch and his courtiers who enjoyed this leisure centre back in the 5th century. With their imperial airs, the resident creatures appeared to be the de facto inheritors of the colossal palace complex of Sigiriya, disdainfully ignoring larger visiting primates who clambered slowly up steep stairways and exclaimed in awestruck tones at the jungle panoramas that rewarded their efforts.

Such effusion is inevitable. The views at Sigiriya are astounding, while the remains of its pools and fortress constructions beggar belief: moats, ramparts, water gardens and, towering above them, the vestiges of a 1500-year-old citadel built into, and on top of, a mighty granite rock, its caverns still adorned with frescoes of big-breasted women. Yet this is by no means the only jaw-dropping sight in Sri Lanka. The interior of the island is strewn with ancient Buddhist shrines and with other excavated remnants of historic kingdoms. And quite apart from these is the promise of more forgotten riches lurking undiscovered in the undergrowth where snakes as well as monkeys now preside.

Other wildlife casually adds colour to this antique land. Bee-eaters flash iridescent plumage as they dart across rice fields; kingfishers perch on electricity wires, scrutinising irrigation ditches for tiny fish; brilliant white egrets stalk the shallows of lakes festooned with the pink bloom of lotus flowers. Less ubiquitous are the leopards that still roam Sri Lanka's mountain forests and the herds of wild elephant which periodically cause havoc in lowland villages. Meanwhile black eagles soar over tea estates that exude an atmosphere of the British Raj and around the island's coastline are coral reefs harbouring at least 1000 species of fish.

With its beaches, beasts and age-old emblems of a spiritual culture rooted in the very soil, Sri Lanka presents a halcyon package. Much of the island is reasonably accessible; prices are for the most part low, yet the abject poverty of the country's gigantic neighbour India is mostly absent; and the Sri Lankans themselves are courteously old fashioned and welcoming. About the size of Ireland, the island is traditionally described as a pearl, pear or tear drop off the south of India. Until recently the lachrymose image was the most apposite: like Ireland, the country has, of course, been troubled. Driving around the island, I was struck by the number of lottery ticket vendors sitting at the roadside in tricycles modified to allow propulsion from cranklevers on the handlebars. These landmine victims provide abrupt reminders of the civil war that has riven Sri Lanka.

However, prospects are promising. The Norwegian-brokered ceasefire between the majority Singhalese and the northern Tamils demanding a separate state has held for more than a year. Local opinion is optimistic – and also pragmatic. 'So far so good, but we've still got a long way to go,' commented one hotel owner and resident of the capital, Colombo. 'Peace talks are being negotiated, and at the moment we seem to be inching towards some sort of federalism. But there is a possibility that violence could flare up again. That said, it would probably be contained within northern and eastern parts dominated by the Tamil Tigers – the main holiday regions are unlikely to be affected.' With conciliatory enthusiasm, others are quick to point out that the Tamil secessionists were among the first to provide aid to the mainly Singhalese area around the southern city of Ratnapura when recent floods nearly devastated the region.

Natural disasters aside, the mood is buoyant and business is starting to boom. Alongside familiar advertisements for perfume and cosmetics, the June issue of SriLankan Airlines' magazine *Serendip* somewhat eccentrically included at least five large notices inviting passengers to invest in real estate. Meantime the travel industry is falling over itself to acquire property in Sri Lanka and quite apart from a rash of new openings, many old colonial hotels, oozing nostalgia, are being snapped up. Rumours are rife that Amanresorts is moving into the market, although the Hong Kong–based luxury hotel group is reticent about such interests. Not that Sri Lanka has been entirely lacking stylish accommodation: given the troubles, a surprising number of plush hotels were established in the 90s, many of them designed by the country's renowned architect Geoffrey Bawa who died in May this year. While some properties in the tea-clad hills are being refurbished and a few eastern beach areas are opening up to tourism, for the moment the finest places to stay are concentrated in Sri Lanka's cultural interior and along stretches of its relatively undervisited south-west coast.

Culture

The country's historic heartland, now known as 'The Cultural Triangle', contains a mind-numbing array of ancient sites with impossible looking names. Highlights include Anuradhapura and Polonnaruwa, respectively capitals from the 3rd century BC and the 11th century AD; Mihintale, a sacred monastic centre of caves and temple ruins; the great cave complex of Dambulla, housing hundreds of Buddha images, its walls coated with 16th-century paintings; and the extraordinary rock palace of Sigiriya. Other, less visited places range from the monumental Aukana Buddha, a vast statue hewn out of a solid rock face purportedly in the 5th century, to the royal hunting fortress of Ritigale, so hidden in dense forest it remains a semi secret. It would require superhuman effort to take in more than a few of these shrines, palaces and monuments, and besides, in the sapping heat the density of history and legend becomes bewildering – which makes relaxing accommodation all the more desirable.

Set more or less in the middle of the Cultural Triangle, between Sigiriya and the Dambulla caves, Elephant Corridor opened in March this year. The 22-suite hotel has been carefully constructed to make minimal impact on its 200 acres of wilderness and has recently acquired a resident naturalist to advise on planting so as to attract more birdlife – peacock, drongo, bulbul and more. Facing the jungle and offering fine views of the weird and wonderfully shaped Kandalama hills, separate thatched chalets, each with plunge pool and outdoor area, have been built on a slight ridge so as to deter larger wildlife intrusions – a herd of elephants roams the area, hence the hotel's name. Nature in super luxury is the theme. Co-owner Susanne Filippin is an Al Maha enthusiast and describes the hotel as a jungle version of the desert eco-resort in Dubai. She is keen to emphasise that this is a sanctuary: there are no plans for more building save, possibly, for a helipad and an organic dairy farm. Meanwhile, privacy and seclusion are the catchwords of the management team, although given the large landholding it seems something of an oversight that most

of the accommodation is grouped together like a line of up-ended dominoes, gardens well within earshot of each other. Not that there is any sense of being cramped: bedrooms, containing every conceivable amenity of TV, CD player and mini-bar (there is no eco-fastidious hold-back here), are large, bathrooms huge if hot. Fine tuning, though, should soon improve ventilation and other slight design flaws such as overly discreet lighting. The 'romantic' suite I stayed in had a four-poster bed complete with mirrored ceiling (not entirely welcome), which blocked out the overhead lights. Requests for a table lamp so as to avoid reading in bed with a torch failed to be understood. With 120 employees, and a staff-to-guest ratio of 4:1 (far more in low season), service should be a shining feature but at the time of my visit in late May it was lacking in finesse. However, teething problems aside, Elephant Corridor is a stylish retreat, remote yet offering easy access to some of the most stunning sites in Sri Lanka. And with its dramatically sited restaurant, ayurvedic spa with swimming pool, archery, golf putting and small stable, it provides an agreeable range of resort facilities.

On the shores of Kandalama Lake nearby, the Kandalama Hotel is less exclusive although equally as spectacular, in an idiosyncratic way. At first sight the exterior looks like an urban complex from the 70s literally gone to seed and sprouting great fronds of greenery. It is, though, a mid-90s design by Sri Lanka's architectural giant Geoffrey Bawa who devised the hotel as an eco-resort that would embrace the surrounding nature. Birds flit through the open-sided corridors and bar areas, which at times pulse with so much wildlife that it seems as if the building has germinated from the jungle around it. Other environmentally friendly efforts are less visible and are concentrated where they matter most: water treatment and garbage disposal. The 162 slightly boxy bedrooms are replete with mini bar, TV and all the expected accoutrements of an international, quality hotel. And with three swimming pools, tennis courts, and an ayurvedic health centre, facilities match those of other luxury establishments. Although guests are not brow-beaten over eco-concerns, nature watching is encouraged, with guided bird-spotting tours on offer every morning and elephant-back safaris readily available.

It is no coincidence that many hotels in the region share an eco-focus. Not only is the area rich in wildlife, most of the accommodation has been built in the last 10 years, during which environmental issues have become a big consideration. Over on the western fringes of the Cultural Triangle Ulpotha offers perhaps the ultimate blend of relaxation and ecological commitment. This hidden haven is not designed to appeal to everyone, but those seeking chill-out tranquillity tend to become hooked – when I was there one guest was on her third visit from Britain within less than a year. It is a working village rather than a hotel, whose community was founded on an abandoned coconut plantation in the mid 90s: the mission being to develop the surrounding farmland so as to revive traditional agricultural practices for the benefit of both the land and the people. Since 1997 paying guests have been welcomed for just a few weeks of the year, helping to fund the non-profit making operation and joining the rural lifestyle – one without electricity, hot running water or alcohol. All of which may sound absurdly ascetic, particularly given that a holiday here does not come cheap by local standards. Yet this is far from being a back-to-basics bootcamp. Traditional accommodation has been adapted for considerable comfort. The open-sided mud-hut bedrooms are beautifully and simply furnished with local fabrics,

rush mats and pottery. Each grouping of three huts shares a stylish bathroom area complete with wooden-seated flush loos and outdoor showers where, in the heat, the water is naturally tepid. Meanwhile the lack of electricity seems a bonus in the soft lamp-lit evenings. There are no waiters or maids, yet the discreetly attentive hospitality of the villagers during my stay rivalled the best service offered by Sri Lanka's formal hotels. In a health-farm-meets-houseparty atmosphere, meals are nutritious, vegetarian feasts served communally to guests (the maximum capacity is 19) in a central pavilion. Yoga, mainly led by teachers from London, is the chief attraction for most visitors, however there is no pressure to join the classes. Reading, snoozing in hammocks, swimming in the reservoir, visiting the local temple, and receiving massage and ayurvedic treatments are the other principal entertainments. Occasionally day trips are arranged to Sri Lanka's great archaeological sites and to the pretty city of Kandy.

At the southern tip of the Cultural Triangle, Kandy is beautifully situated in a bowl of green hills. The last bastion of Buddhist power before the country was fully annexed by the British in 1815, it is still the lively centre of Sri Lanka's performance arts and contains a number of fine old buildings dating back over the last three centuries. Not least of these is the Dalada Maligawa, the octagonal Temple of the Tooth, housing Buddha's left eye-tooth. This sacred and much travelled relic attracts a steady stream of tourists and pilgrims who come to pay homage during daily, frangipani-filled ceremonies. Given the volume of visitors, the city's limited choice of chic accommodation is surprising.

Helga's Folly, famously atmospheric and eccentric, has long been a favourite with British travellers. The 40-bedroom home of the illustrious de Silva family has attracted a glittering list of celebrities – Zandra Rhodes being one of the more recent visitors. Awash with colour and flamboyant murals, the hotel is either hilariously outré or simply too much. 'A trip, a dream – who knows, who cares?' reads one entry in the visitors' book. Whatever the answer, the food here is a serious plus: dinner of aubergine salad with a kick and delicately seared tuna was the best meal I ate in Sri Lanka.

On the other side of town, Stone House Lodge is a model of peaceful understatement. A plantation-style bungalow lined in teak, it is furnished with antiques and wicker, its spacious garden filled with hibiscus and birdsong. For the moment, the elegance is unmatched elsewhere in Kandy, although plenty of properties have promising potential. Most notable of these is the Queens Hotel, a splendid 1844 building in the centre of the city, aching for a makeover and currently the subject of negotiations over new ownership.

Coast

Although for the most part unspoilt, Sri Lanka's southern beach area is not the pristine-white idyll of the coral coasts around the Maldives further west in the Indian Ocean. Frankly, it's not that bland. From toddy tappers in the canopies of coconut palms to fishermen perched on stilts in the sea, looking like human herons, and great Buddha statues peacefully presiding at busy road junctions, the shores are packed with local activity. And dotted with emblems of the country's colonial past, too. Although the Dutch never conquered the entire island, in the 17th and 18th centuries they dominated maritime trade and many of their substantial forts are still thriving, if crumbling, seaside towns.

A few kilometres east of the dusty old fort of Matara, Tangalle has become the beach area of choice for those in the know.

Empty, pink-tinged sandy bays border a cheerfully unassuming little town with a large Methodist church and a bustling main drag. There are just a few hotels in the locality – as well as an increasing choice of villas providing truly exclusive accommodation. Commanding spectacular views over sweeping, palm-fringed sands, Lansiya is one of the latest private properties being developed here. Owned by Colombo residents Anitra and Dirk Caldera, the villa has been designed to take full advantage of its ample, secluded grounds, with wide balconies and a shower room set outdoors in an attractive courtyard. A congenially laid-back atmosphere is in part attributable to the cook, Dilip, a jolly ex-mariner with a penchant for chatting and a considerable talent for concocting superb meals which are presented with due flourish.

Service is a more formal matter at the neighbouring Beach House, giving the villa the air of a private hotel rather than a holiday house. With its play of blue-and-white furnishings, its open-air master bathroom splendidly featuring a tub on claw feet, and its magical infinity pool set in an elysian, agave-filled garden, it would be difficult to improve on the sheer sense of style here. The colonial, four-bedroom villa was bought in the 1990s by the late Douglas Johnson, an American painter whose artworks still hang on the walls and who painstakingly restored the property with the help of his friend and mentor Geoffrey Bawa.

The Beach House is now run by Geoffrey Dobbs, an English entrepreneur with a string of equally glamorous properties along the south coast. Taprobane, west of Matara, is an almost impossibly romantic island-villa eccentrically accessible only by wading through the sea. Further west, just outside the walls of the Dutch fort of Galle, the Sun House is an elegantly refurbished mansion built by a Scottish spice merchant in the 1860s. Opposite is Doornberg, or the Dutch House, a 1712 building once home to the commander of the Netherlands's forces garrisoned in the old town below.

This four-suite boutique hotel opened last year to much acclaim. It has been beautifully and sensitively developed, a new wing added to the original ochre-washed building and a sublime infinity pool positioned at the edge of the hotel's tree-clad hilltop. Furry black monkeys were pinching mangoes overhead as I took a dreamy dip here, while beside the loungers a glass of lime juice appeared as if by magic, provided by evanescent staff. The subtle attentiveness is reflected in the care over detail. Two varieties of lawn grass carpet the neatly clipped gardens. Raffia sun hats for guests' use hang in the spacious bedrooms, which feature capacious four-poster beds and are filled with antiques – a huge hunt took place to find just the right period doors. The large bookshelves in my room offered an eclectic supply of reading material, from *Running in the Family*, Michael Ondaatje's reminiscence of a childhood in Ceylon, to the *Mini Owner's Workshop Manual*. Flower-filled bathrooms are thoughtfully supplied with such imaginative amenities as cinnamon body scrub and ayurvedic toothpaste. However, a possible downside to the hotel is the lack of a dining room, yet it is not much of a hardship for guests to pop across the road for dinner in the excellent restaurant at the Sun House.

Beach zealots, though, might find the location of both hotels disappointing. The principal attraction of Galle itself is the architecture of the old fort: lined with time-worn Dutch buildings, its quiet streets offer an absorbing meander while its north walls provide a good vantage point for watching cricket matches in the stadium below. But the nearest sizeable stretch of sand with safe swimming is Unawatuna Bay about 5km away. Once rated among the world's top 12 beaches, the golden shores are now perhaps a little too crowded with daytrippers and are peppered with busy cafes.

On the long strand of Bentota Beach, equidistant from Galle and Colombo, are two quietly elegant properties, both developed in the 70s by Geoffrey Bawa. One was an existing Dutch villa he restored and re-devised; the other he built next door in the same style for his friend, the hotelier S M A Hameed, whose family home it became. Both houses have since been turned into small hotels. Management of the former, Villa Mohotti, has recently been taken over by Ajai Zecha. Operating independently of his father, Adrian Zecha of Amanresorts, he is taking this already beautifully decorated and furnished residence even more upmarket. The latter, Club Villa, is not quite as stylish but exudes cheerful charm – and is a great deal cheaper. Both villas are well placed not just for beach activities but also for boat trips along the Balapitya River and for excursions to the glorious garden of Brief, the creation of Bawa's brother, Bevis. And both villas also have a railway line cutting a clanking path between their long lawns and the beach. For some guests the intrusion is disconcerting; others, however, find that the periodic appearance of rusty, tooting trains adds a certain wacky charm, entirely in keeping with the intrinsic spirit of Sri Lanka.

How to get there

SriLankan Airlines (020 8538 2001) flies direct from Heathrow to Colombo: return fares in November around £620 including taxes. Emirates (0870 243 2222) flies from Heathrow or Gatwick to Colombo via Dubai: return fares in November around £560 including taxes.

Tour operators

Colours of Sri Lanka (298 Regents Park Road, London N3 2TJ; 020 8343 3446; www.partnershiptravel.co.uk) offers tailor-made holidays taking in any of the above destinations and properties: prices for a 10-day holiday with accommodation at Elephant Corridor, Helga's Folly, Lansiya and the Dutch House from £1668 per person (based on two sharing) including international flights and private transport in Sri Lanka.

Other tour operators providing tailor-made travel to Sri Lanka include: Handmade Holidays (First Floor, Carpenters Buildings, Carpenters Lane, Cirencester, Glos GL7 1EE; 01285 642555; www.handmade-holidays.co.uk); Scott Dunn (Fovant Mews, 12 Noyna Road, London, SW17 7PH; 020 8682 5010; www.scottdunn.com); and Carolanka (01822 810230).

Where to stay
CULTURAL TRIANGLE

Elephant Corridor, Sigiriya (00 94 66 83333; hotel@elephantcorridor.com; www.elephantcorridor.com). Suites from US$150 (accommodation only and excluding service charges and government tax).

Kandalama Hotel, Dambulla (00 94 66 84100; kandalama@aitkenspence.lk; www.aitkenspenceholidays.com). Double rooms from US$121 (accommodation only, including service and tax).

Ulpotha (bookings through Neal's Yard Agency, BCM Neal's Yard, London WC1N 3XX; 0870 444 2702; info@ulpotha.com; www.ulpotha.com). Open to guests from late May to early July and from November to March. Holidays are for two-week periods (although occasionally one-week stays are offered), with an all-inclusive cost of £980 per person earlier in the year and £1200 high season for the fortnight. The price includes group transfers from the airport and all yoga, massage and ayurvedic treatments.

Other options include Culture Club on the shores of Kandalama lake near Dambulla (00 94 66 31822; cdchm@sltnet.lk; www.connaissanceceylan.com). Less happy-clappy than the name (and website) suggests, the hotel takes Sri Lankan traditions of hospitality as its guiding theme. Accommodation is in 92 chalets and 11 new 'eco-lodges' while facilities include an ayurvedic health centre, swimming pool, tennis courts and jogging track. Double-room chalets from $77 (room only, excluding service and tax).

KANDY

Helga's Folly, off Mahamaya Mawatha (00 94 8 234571; chalet@sltnet.lk; www.helgasfolly.com). Double rooms from $90 Nov–Dec, $100 Jan–Oct (room only, including service and tax).

Stone House Lodge, 42 Nittawella Road, Nittawella (00 94 8 232769; stonehse@sltnet.lk). Double rooms from $55 (room only, excluding service and tax, credit cards not accepted).

Other options include Earl's Regency, Kundasale (00 94 8 422122; erhotel@sltnet.lk; www.aitkenspenceholidays.com). In lush greenery yet within easy reach of the centre of town, the 85-room hotel offers every comfort in slightly unimaginative surroundings. Double rooms from $75 (room only, excluding service and tax).

COAST
Tangalle

Lansiya (book through Colours of Sri Lanka, 020 8343 3446). Sleeps two, although a further three bedrooms are due to be added during the low season next year. £140 per person per night including all meals.

The Beach House (enquiries through The Sun House, 00 94 74 380275; sunhouse@sri.lanka.net; www.thesunhouse.com). Accommodation for seven people. The rate of $495–

$1000 per night depending on low/high season includes tax, staff costs (except tips) and a traditional Sri Lankan curry on arrival, other meals are between $10–$15 per person.

Other options include Mahawella, at the end of an unspoilt beach about 7km from Tangalle (enquiries to Tim and Sarah Jacobson at sarahjac@netvigator.com). Owned by a Hong Kong–based family, this is the last private house to be designed by Geoffrey Bawa, with gardens sweeping down to the beach, a courtyard swimming pool, shady verandahs and five double bedrooms. Rental prices per night range between $550–$750 depending on the season (meals, prepared by five resident staff, are extra). Eva Lanka (00 94 47 40940; eva .lanka@mail.ewisl.net; www.eva.lk), an Italian-run hotel set on a hillside overlooking a sandy bay, is well equipped for families, with three swimming pools and a long waterslide in addition to an open-sided restaurant, a bar and an ayurvedic health centre. Accommodation is in 29 chalets from $75 per night for two people (room only, extra bed for children up to 12, $5. The rate includes service and tax).

Weligama, near Matara

Taprobane (00 94 9 22624; sunhouse@sri .lanka.net; www.thesunhouse.com). Accommodation for up to eight people. The rate of $750–$2000 per night, depending on high/ low season, includes tax, staff costs and a welcoming Sri Lanka meal; all other meals as well as drinks are extra.

Galle

Doornberg/The Dutch House, 23 Upper Dickson Road (00 94 9 22624; sunhouse@ sri.lanka.net; www.thesunhouse.com). Double room from $330 per night inclusive of breakfast and afternoon tea as well as tax. Dinners at the Sun House are around $30 per person.

The Sun House, 18 Upper Dickson Road (00 94 9 22624; sunhouse@sri.lanka.net; www .thesunhouse.com). Double rooms from $120 including taxes.

Other options include Lighthouse Hotel and Spa, Dadella (00 94 9 23744; hotels@ jetwing.lk; www.jetwing.net). The 163-room hotel looks down over quiet but at times rough beaches where the Indian Ocean can put on a spectacular show. It is another 90s building by Geoffrey Bawa, with comfortable if pricey rooms and extensive facilities including two swimming pools, a large spa and tennis and squash courts. Ideal for an active holiday but this is no hideaway. Double rooms from $180 (room only including service and tax). The Secret Garden, just off Unawatuna Bay (00 94 74 721007; secretgardenvilla@msn.com; www.secret gardenvilla.lk). This secluded villa and chalet complex has a separate pavilion for yoga practice, and can be shared with other guests or privately rented in entirety. Villa, sleeping seven to nine plus two children from $210 per night; double-room chalet from $35 (accommodation only and including maid service as well as service and tax; meals, provided by the resident cook, are extra).

Bentota

Villa Mohotti Walauwa (00 94 34 75311; reservation@thevilla.eureka.lk). Doubles from $195 high season (room only, excluding service and tax).

Club Villa (00 94 77 362984; clubvilla@ itmin.com; www.club-villa.com). Doubles from $90 high season (room only, excluding service and tax).

Other options include Taru Villas Taprobana, 146/4 Galle Road, Robolgoda (00 94 34 75618; taprobana@taruvillas.com; www.taruvillas .com). In quiet gardens just off Bentota Beach, this boutique hotel has recently been refurbished by fashion designer Taru. The nine bedrooms, furnished with antiques, are set off a central pool area and elegant, Mediterranean-style pavilion. Double rooms from $145 (B&B, including service and tax as well as afternoon tea).

Colombo

Due to arrival and departure times of international flights, a night in or near the capital may be necessary. Colombo in any case boasts much fine if decrepit colonial architecture as well as temples, markets and gardens. Shopping has become something of an artform at Barefoot (704 Galle Road) offering homewares and brilliantly coloured cottons and linens designed by Sri Lankan artist Barbara Sansoni, and at Paradise Road (213 Dharmapala Mawsha), a type of upmarket, Sri Lankan version of Habitat, while designer-label clothes (Armani, DKNY and the like) are exceptionally good value at Arena (338 Darley Road) and Odell (5 Alexandra Place).

The Galle Face Hotel, 2 Kollupitiya Road (00 94 1 541010; gfh@diamond.lanka.net; www.gallefacehotel.com) is a splendid edifice straight out of the British Raj – oozing atmosphere and in need of a makeover. Doubles from US$50 (room only, excluding service and tax).

Renting a private villa is a peaceful alternative to staying in town. Java Moon, on the banks of Bolgoda Lake, is about three quarters of an hour from Colombo. The three-bedroom villa with infinity pool and beautifully kept grounds is furnished with antiques, its walls hung with works by Sri Lankan artists. (Book through Colours of Sri Lanka, 020 8343 3446.) £98 per person per night including all meals.

THE WONDERFUL THING ABOUT TIGERS

by William Gray

Sri Lanka is not far from India, but this article by British freelancer William Gray is worlds away from Harriet O'Brien's piece. This story, written for the UK magazine *Wanderlust*, is designed to yank us out of our comfortable living rooms and drop us in the middle of a tiger-hunting expedition in the Indian jungle. The beginning accomplishes just this, presenting an accumulation of wonderfully rendered sensual details ('shrill snort', 'indignant bark', 'pungent aroma of crushed herbs and freshly bled sap', 'a diffuse patchwork of muted greens and shadows-within-shadows') that root us in the scene and make us accomplices in the effort to decipher the jungle's clues. As you read the piece, note how Gray plays the accordion of time. How many moments does he choose to focus on? How much of his trip has he left on the editing floor? And note, too, how, even though this is a chronologically organised account, Gray ends his piece by looping back to the beginning of the trip, for dramatic purposes. Also note how he modulates his last four paragraphs, culminating in that magical last sentence.

It was almost as if the tiger had flicked a switch in the forest. One moment it was quiet and calm – the trees swathed in webs of early morning mist – the next, the air was charged with tension. Gomati had heard the distant alarm calls – the shrill snort of a spotted deer, the indignant bark of a langur monkey – and her mood suddenly changed. She blasted a trunkful of dust up between her front legs, then shook her head so vigorously that I had to clutch the padded saddle to keep my balance. Gomati's mahout, sitting astride her neck, issued a terse reprimand before urging the elephant into the tangled forest. There was no path; Gomati made her own. Soon the air was infused with the pungent aroma of crushed herbs and freshly-bled sap. Spiders and beetles drizzled from shaken trees; our clothing became wet with dew and stained by moss and lichen. We sounded like a forest fire – crackling, snapping, trailblazing. But through all the noise came a single piercing cry. Gomati stopped and we heard it again – the tell-tale alarm call of a spotted deer.

Manoj Sharma, my guide, leaned towards me. 'When the tiger moves, the deer calls,' he murmured. 'We must be close.' I nodded slowly, my eyes chasing around the shadows of the forest. Sunlight sparked through chinks in the canopy, but the understorey was still a diffuse patchwork of muted greens and shadows-within-shadows – the perfect foil for tiger stripes. Apart from an occasional rumble from Gomati's stomach, the forest was silent. No one spoke or moved.

Gradually, the tension slipped from our bodies. The woodpecker stopped drumming, and Gomati grabbed a nearby branch and stuffed it into her mouth. I reached forward to stroke the elephant's neck; there was a soft patch, free of wrinkles and bristles, behind her ear.

Corbett was always going to be the more challenging of the two Tiger Reserves on my Indian safari. Over 1,300 sq km of forest and grassland tucked into the Himalayan foothills, it's home to about 135 Bengal tigers. But compared with Ranthambhore, further south, the cats in Corbett are shy and elusive. 'Some people have been coming here for years and have never seen a tiger,' Manoj had told me earlier. To expect to see one on my first visit to India, let alone on my first elephant ride in Corbett, was perhaps asking too much. Still, I was happy enough tickling Gomati behind the ear. And at that moment, none of us realised just how close the tigress – or her cubs – really were.

They say tigers make the orchestra of the jungle play and, suddenly, several species seemed to launch into a gusty rendition of 'I can see a tiger!' Sambar and spotted deer began whistling to our left, while langur, babblers and others pitched in with a well-rehearsed repertoire of coughs, grunts and chatters.

Guided by the commotion, Gomati waded into the undergrowth once more. After 50m or so the alarm calls ceased, but now Gomati's trunk was raised and she began to hesitate. The mahout dug his heels in, but she shuffled to a halt. For the first time that morning, the elephant let out a deep, resonating rumble. Clearly, Gomati was going no further.

Moments later we saw why. Less than a dozen metres ahead, the vegetation thrashed from side to side as three tigers burst from cover. The two cubs kept low to the ground, melting into the forest like wisps of smoke. But the tigress paused to glance over her shoulder. For a second or two, she stared straight at us – her eyes locked on ours with the intense scrutiny of a supreme predator. Then she turned and vanished.

It was the briefest of encounters – an exchange of glances that jolted the senses, seared the mind. 'You are very lucky,' Manoj told me as Gomati trundled back to the rest house. 'Not one tiger, but three!' Somehow, though, numbers seemed irrelevant. I began to realise that it wasn't the glimpse of the tigers that had moved me, so much as the supercharged atmosphere of their native forest stronghold. Spotting the tigers had merely reaffirmed their beauty; tracking them had revealed their spirit.

Later, during our afternoon elephant ride, we heard and saw nothing – no alarm calls pulsing through the forest, no pug marks on the sandy tracks that led from the rest house. The following dawn, Manoj took me out in a jeep to explore a wider area of the reserve. But again, no tigers. The forest seemed to be guarding their whereabouts, a silent reminder of their secrecy and rarity.

Leaving the forest, we drove out onto the floodplain of the Ramganga River, where tendrils of mist squirmed in the gathering heat of mid-morning. A large herd of spotted deer, perhaps 200 strong, grazed peacefully, while families of wild boar snuffled amongst them. It was a scene more reminiscent of Africa: a tawny grassland peppered with game; vultures wheeling overhead; a pair of jackals on the lookout for an easy meal. There were even wild elephants, far across the plain, looking for all the world like giant river boulders except for the occasional puff of dust that rose above them.

Quietly and methodically, like a holy man reciting a mantra, Manoj totted up a list of nearly 100 bird species that he had either seen or heard that morning. A huge variety were concentrated around a lake at the heart of the reserve. Herons, plovers and stilts tip-toed around basking gharial crocodiles, while pied kingfishers hovered overhead.

If anything, my next destination should have provided an even greater avian spectacle. Travelling overnight on the sleeper train to Agra, I hired a car and driver to take me the short distance to Bharatpur Bird Sanctuary, a former royal hunting estate. During the breeding season Bharatpur is usually throbbing with painted storks, ducks, pelicans and other waterbirds, but the monsoon had failed in 2002 and the network of lagoons had all but dried up. 'The storks arrived as usual,' said local ornithologist Dilip Saini. 'But they took one look and left again.' With patience, and Dilip's keen eye for birds, we still managed to notch up several dozen species, including a lone pelican squatting dejectedly beside a muddy waterhole that should have been a sparkling lake.

The Rajasthan countryside on the drive between Bharatpur and Ranthambhore was equally arid. Cattle-drawn ploughs struggled through the hard-baked soil while women, balancing metal water pots on their heads, queued at every village water pump. Numerous camel trains were on the move, their masters leading them, grim-faced, in search of new water and forage. The brick factories lining the roadside only added to the sense of desiccation.

Ranthambhore had not escaped the drought either. In the 400 sq km national park (at the core of the tiger reserve), the lakes were dry and the dhok forest – usually lush after a monsoon soaking – was scantily clad with brittle, golden leaves.

Ironically, the parched conditions boded well for tiger viewing. Ranthambhore's tigers would be more visible in a forest deprived of its seasonal rejuvenation of leaves and grasses – or so I was told.

There are no elephant-back safaris in Ranthambhore. Instead, a controlled number of vehicles is granted access to specific routes on the park's network of tracks. Each vehicle has a driver and guide, and there are strict rules for minimising disturbance to wildlife, such as speed limits and bans on off-road driving or deviations from allotted routes. A sound system, in principle. However, I quickly learned that the route scheme had a drawback. Eager to clinch their 'double tips' for a tiger sighting, drivers often treated their routes like race tracks. When the park gates opened at 6.30am there was a jostle for pole position – the first jeeps desperate to locate any fresh tiger prints before other traffic obliterated them. By imposing invisible barriers in the wilderness, the route system relied less on fieldcraft and more on chance. You were either lucky enough to have a tiger on your patch or not.

By my fourth game drive in two days, we had seen no tigers. On several occasions we had hurtled at over 60km per hour to beat another jeep to a junction simply so we wouldn't be following in its dust trail. Langurs, peacocks and spotted deer were literally leaping out of our path.

There were, of course, several moments of pure Ranthambhore magic – a wonderful encounter with a lolloping sloth bear and a glimpse of a rare wild dog. We watched ring-necked parakeets raiding a fig tree and witnessed sambar deer stags locking antlers in a rutting contest. But, ultimately, it seemed that the success of our game drives was determined by whether or not we had seen a tiger.

On my fifth and final drive I did see one – a tigress lying in the shade of a narrow gully – but, by then, too much of Ranthambhore's wildness and spirit had been compromised. If I had so desperately wanted to see a tiger, I could have gone to a zoo. To my mind, the whole essence of tiger reserves like Ranthambhore is that they embody some of the few places left on earth where you can still sense the aura of wild tigers. With its magnificent 12th century fort and ancient chhatris (memorials) and temples, Ranthambhore's importance as a refuge for some of India's last 3000–3500 tigers (believed to be an optimistic estimate) seemed especially poignant. It is a rare place indeed where the crumbling remains of human presence are juxtaposed against a thriving population of one of the world's most endangered species.

Ultimately, the most thrilling tiger encounter of my safari was not actually an encounter at all. It took place several days earlier when Manoj and I were leaving Corbett Tiger Reserve. It was a quiet morning. The sal forest had shrugged off its blanket of morning mist and Manoj was happily scanning the trees for tawny fish owls – one of the few bird species that had eluded us.

When a jeep approached us from the opposite direction we paused to chat to the driver, but he hadn't seen the owls either – so we headed on towards the park gates. A short distance further, Manoj suddenly stiffened and pointed to the dirt track ahead. 'Tigers.' With one word, he transformed our laid-back birding rambling into an edge-of-the-seat drama. There, clearly imprinted over the tyre marks of the jeep we had just passed, were the pug marks of a tigress and her three young cubs. Less than five minutes had elapsed since we saw the other vehicle and, in that time, the cats must have emerged from the forest, strolled along the road a short distance and disappeared into the trees again.

We took a long, hard look around us. A rustle of leaves spun our heads, but it was just a pheasant scrabbling about on the forest floor. Manoj thought he heard the alarm call of a babbler, but whatever it was stopped almost immediately. He signalled to our driver to reverse up the track. About 100m beyond a sharp bend, we found more tiger prints – this time overlaying our own tyre tracks! Again, we stopped and listened. Somewhere, very close, a family of tigers was probably doing the same.

We never did see them. And yet it felt as though we had been directly interacting – pitting our wits and senses against each other. It had been an exhilarating experience – a moment of heightened awareness that stirred some primordial human instinct: part fear, part respect. I had discovered how it feels to fall under the spell of the tiger.

India: Footnotes

VITAL STATISTICS

Capital: New Delhi
Population: Over one billion
Time: GMT+5.5
International dialling code: +91
Visas: British nationals require a visa, which costs £30 and is valid for six months. Contact the High Commission of India, India House, Aldwych, London WC2B 4NA (0906 844 4544, www.hcilondon.net).
Language: Hindi is the most national Indian language, but there are 18 official languages.
Money: Indian rupee (Rs), currently Rs77.4 to the UK£. Take UK£ or US$ travellers cheques. Credit cards are widely accepted in cities and larger towns, and can also be used to get cash advances in rupees.

WHEN TO GO

The dry season begins in November when national parks and reserves reopen after the monsoon. Vegetation is lush and the rain has cleared the air of dust. From February to late April, leaves fall, grasses wither and water sources recede in the tiger reserves, providing the best opportunities for seeing wildlife.

GETTING THERE

Numerous airlines serve Delhi from London, including British Airways (0845 773 3377, www.britishairways.com) and Air France (0845 0845 111, www.airfrance.com). BA flights from Heathrow to Delhi start at £545 including taxes.

GETTING AROUND

Local transport ranges from auto-rickshaws, cycle-rickshaws and tongas (horse-drawn carriages) to trains, cars and buses. Hiring a car and driver is straightforward and is probably the best option for reaching Corbett Tiger Reserve, an eight-hour bus ride from Delhi. At some stage of your trip, be sure to experience the Indian railway system – a great way to see the country and meet its people. There are several classes with varying degrees of comfort. For overnight journeys, a second-class, four-berth sleeper cabin is a good option.

Sawai Madhopur, on the main Delhi–Mumbai line, is just ten kilometres from Ranthambhore National Park. You'll find numerous taxis and auto-rickshaws at the station, but agree a price before setting off. Elephant rides are available in Corbett for around Rs250 per person. Try to book Ranthambhore 4WD safaris in advance. You have two options: five-passenger 4WDs, which cost around Rs875 for the vehicle (including guide entrance fee); or 20-seater trucks which enter the park twice a day and cost around Rs110 per person (including entrance fee).

SAFARIS

There are several reserves and sanctuaries in India that can be incorporated into a wildlife safari. Wildlife Worldwide (020 8667 9158, www.wildlifeworldwide.com) offers an 18-day Tiger Tiger itinerary combining the national parks of Kanha, Bandhavgarh and Ranthambhore with a visit to Agra and the Taj Mahal. It costs from £2195 including flights, transfers, guided activities and most meals. Other wildlife hot spots in India include Sasan Gir wildlife sanctuary (the last stronghold of the Asiatic lion), Periyar Wildlife Sanctuary (a beautiful reserve with a lake and forest in southern India) and the Keoladeo Ghana Bharatpur National Park (a world-renowned birdwatching location near Agra).

ACCOMMODATION

Flights from Europe tend to arrive during the early hours of the morning, so it's worth arranging an early check-in at your hotel to freshen up before spending the day sightseeing. Delhi has a wide range of accommodation; try www.india-accommodation.com for details.

Many of the tiger reserves and wildlife sanctuaries also offer a variety of places to stay. In Corbett, Dhikala Rest House (tiger camp@wildquestindia.com) is superbly located in the heart of the reserve with rooms from around Rs1500 and dormitory beds from just Rs200. There is also an excellent value restaurant. Outside the reserve, Ramnagar has several small resorts which charge Rs3500–5000. Ranthambhore also has accommodation to suit most budgets – from modest guesthouses to luxurious tented camps like Sher Bagh (sherbagh@vsnl.com) where the double occupancy rate is US$180 full board.

HEALTH & SAFETY

Malaria is present in India, so you should consult your doctor for advice on an appropriate course of prophylactic tablets, as well as vaccinations against typhoid, tetanus, polio and hepatitis. Many of India's larger cities are highly polluted and travellers with respiratory ailments may wish to take precautionary measures.

FURTHER READING

There are numerous guidebooks to the subcontinent, including *India* (Lonely Planet, 2001) and *India* (Rough Guides, 2001). For wildlife-themed travel guides, try *Indian Wildlife* (Insight Guides, 2001) and *Traveller's Guide: Wildlife of India* (Collins, 2001).

If elephant-riding in Corbett Tiger Reserve inspires you to greater things, be sure to read Mark Shand's *Travels on my Elephant* (Penguin, 1992), which describes his 1000km elephantine journey across India.

For a passionate account of Indian natural history, plus stunning photography, look no further than Valmik Thapar's *Land of the Tiger* (BBC Books, 1997).

FURTHER INFORMATION

Visit the official website of the Indian Ministry of Tourism at www.tourismindia.com.

GUITAR CENTRAL

by Christopher Reynolds

It may seem a long way from hunting tigers in the Indian jungle to hunting guitars in the Mexican hinterlands, but in fact, this story by Christopher Reynolds – a former travel writer for the *Los Angeles Times*, where this story first appeared – is fundamentally similar to William Gray's piece. Both are essentially 'quest' stories. In each, the writer is specifically in search of something – stripes or strings – and that quest frames the resulting narrative. There is much to admire in Reynolds' account. He begins by planting questions in the reader's mind. What's the extra luggage? Why does he need the money? What is this 'guy who knows a guy' trafficking in, anyway? Where are we riding in this rental car? Before we become too frustrated, Reynolds provides the answers and reveals that he is writing to a personal passion. We may not particularly care about Mexico or guitars, but Reynolds does such a masterful job in bringing to life the people and places he encounters on his quest that we are compelled to read on. In particular, note his use of dialogue and character, and his interweaving of fact, history, anecdote and description. By the end of the piece, we have learned more than we had ever imagined we would want to know about guitars and a little town devoted to their creation. Reynolds' story is very personal, but he never drags us into the abyss of egregious self-revelation; he uses himself and his quest as a portal to a deeper understanding and appreciation of Paracho, and Mexico, and finally, of the treasures – figurative and literal – that he will bring back from that town of guitars in the mountains.

It is a mild day in the mountains of middle Mexico, a fine day for chasing butterflies or lingering on cobbled side streets, neither of which I'll be doing. I am here to sniff sawdust and engage in arcane conversations with old men in dim, cluttered rooms.

I step down onto the runway of the Morelia airport – the old colonial state capital of Michoacán, midway between Mexico City and Guadalajara – with one less piece of luggage than I expect to take home. In a hidden compartment beneath my belt, I carry a large amount of cash. In my wallet, I carry an address given to me by a guy who knows a guy.

I rent a car and head southwest. As darkness falls on the colonial buildings of Pátzcuaro's main plaza, I corner a wizened man named Raúl, who in a few moments will be singing and playing 'Guadalajara' to a restaurant full of Mexican and American tourists. I nod at his guitar, and in my Spanish, which has been compared with President Bush's English, I say something like: The guitar you are playing, is Paracho from it, that town of guitars in the mountains?

Um, yes, says Raúl in Spanish, half-surprised.

I am going to Paracho this week, to see the festival, and to buy a guitar. Is there a guitar player, no, a guitar-maker, whom you can recommend? The man from your guitar?

'Amezcua,' says Raúl. But he adds that he couldn't afford an Amezcua himself. He's been playing this Velazquez for about eight years now. Anyway, Raúl says, I can find both on the main street. ...

Now it's a Sunday afternoon. The big cities and colonial scenery are behind me, and under a sky full of dramatic clouds, I'm racing along a two-lane highway, passing cornfields, crawling up pine-stubbled slopes, rolling at last into Paracho, guitar-making capital of North America.

Above the town looms a jagged mountain peak, Tare Tzuruan, which in the indigenous Purépecha language might mean Big Hill or Eagle Mountain, depending on whom you ask. But I can't take my eyes off the shop windows: Taller de Guitarras. Barajas Guitarras. Jesús H. Fuerte Guitarras. Casa Amezcua Guitarras...

Inside I see guitars large and small, whole and half-built, hung on hooks, strangled in twine (to hold the wood in place while the glue dries) and cradled in the arms of makers wielding files and hammers and saws and rags and other tools whose purposes I can only guess.

The Morelia airport is about a three-hour drive, perhaps 100 miles, but it seems much farther. Down the street my rental car creeps, past shops advertising guitars, produce, guitars, wooden curiosities (including guitars), gifts (including guitars), food, guitars, toys (including guitars), guitar-making tools, an Internet cafe (hey, this is rural Mexico, not the dark side of the moon), an auto repair garage and more guitars.

Although it's a town whose population wouldn't quite fill Staples Center, Paracho in early August practically seethes. Its annual fair has just begun. In search of a parking spot, I crawl south to north the length of the main drag, which changes names twice in its eight blocks. The buildings are one or two stories, except for the church tower, which looks over the main plaza and a cultural center. At the north end of town, perhaps a five-minute walk from the central plaza, the raw countryside resumes.

'This not just a guitar festival. This is the whole town throwing its summer festival –

people all over the streets doing all sorts of stuff,' a Paracho veteran named Kenny Hill told me before I headed south.

Hill, a professional guitar-maker and player who spends most of the year in Santa Cruz, is the only American with a workshop in Paracho. He's been a regular visitor or part-time resident for two decades, and he estimates that there are more guitar-makers in Paracho than in the entire United States. Guesses range from 1200 to 3000.

Paracho's population, including neighboring settlements, was put at 31,003 in the 1999 Mexican census. By some estimates, it produces as many as 80,000 guitars a year.

Search for it on the Internet and you'll find precious little; I only heard of it a few years ago, from a friend who'd wandered through on a backpacking trip in the '80s. But Paracho is not quite invisible. Last year, the National Geographic Society published a children's book on Paracho and its guitars by Peter Laufer and Susan L. Roth. Titled 'Made in Mexico' and filled with wildly colorful paper collages, it features a blurb by singer Linda Ronstadt. Years before she began exploring her Mexican heritage in her 1987 'Canciones de Mi Padre' recordings, Ronstadt recalls, she first learned to play guitar on an instrument from Paracho.

The town's specialty goes back at least 80 years, but beyond that, the history gets hazy. Some local boosters (and some travel guidebooks) would have you believe that the craft of guitar-making was specifically assigned to Paracho by Michoacán's beloved 16th century bishop, Don Vasco de Quiroga. In fact, many sources agree that the bishop did assign specialties to several towns near the banks of Lake Pátzcuaro. But when it comes to Paracho in the mountains, the documentation gets

thinner, and some locals take a more skeptical view.

'In the history book, Quiroga never came here,' says Francisco Navarro Garcia, whose workshop is on the north end of Calle Independencia. In those days, neither the town nor the guitar existed in anything like their current form. Though the term 'guitar' apparently originated in 16th century Spain, it then described a four-string instrument with different tuning and shape than most modern guitars.

Either way, the reputation that Paracho developed through the 20th century was for the quantity, not quality, of its guitars. But since the mid-1990s, a handful of workshops have begun concentrating on high-quality instruments, which require more time and costlier materials. While the factories on the edge of town crank out 100 largely machine-made guitars or more a day, a fine craftsman might spend weeks on a single big-ticket instrument. Thus you can spend $50 on a Paracho guitar, or $3000, and it behooves a buyer to visit several shops before making any commitments.

Navarro has been a guitar-maker for 18 of his 38 years. He speaks as bluntly about Paracho's output as he does about its history. 'About 10% of guitars here are of high quality,' he tells me. 'Ten years ago, none were.'

Navarro aims for the high-end market, making about 70 instruments a year and selling most through a dealer in Houston, at prices around $1,800. I linger a long while in his workshop, listening to town gossip and guitar theory, and noodling on one of his instruments. Since we've cut out shipping and the middle man, he might be able to make me a deal.

I'm eager to buy; when I'm home I pick up a guitar nearly every day. But the truth is I don't play particularly well – simple folk and blues songs, no classical compositions. So I hand the guitar back to Navarro and ask him to give it a workout.

He hesitates, picks a few notes, then declines.

'Guitarrero o guitarrista,' he says. 'You either make guitars, or you play guitars. You don't do both.'

A great pink cloud hovers before me: pink cotton candy, carried aloft by a tiny vendor. Like the vendor, everyone on the street seems to be 5-feet-6 or shorter, and a native of Mexico. And the later it gets, the busier the sidewalk becomes.

Campesinos converge from nearby towns – the men in white cowboy hats, the women in their traditional black-and-blue shawls – for their biggest spending binge of the year. Far-flung children, now grown, have come back from their jobs and new lives in el norte to renew their ties. Technicians are fiddling with a PA system in the plaza, and some of the streets are blocked.

Tonight, brass bands will march and the town pooh-bahs will burn a castle made of sticks. Tomorrow, all the town's craft-makers will march around the plaza, then take the stage and toss special party favors to their neighbors, provoking a scramble no less raucous than the annual skirmishing over Mardi Gras beads in New Orleans.

While this goes on at street level, the town's elite are staging a semi-separate second celebration: the National Guitar Festival. Now nearly 30 years old, it features master classes, competitions among guitar-makers and young guitar players, and free performances by classical guitarists from Cuba, Paraguay, Bosnia, the Czech Republic and Mexico, all in the 150-seat auditorium of the Center for the Investigation and Development of the Guitar (CIDEG, in local language), two blocks from the plaza.

But since the town is so small, the street fun and salon seriousness end up scrambled, so that the student guitarists, carefully coiffed and clad in black suits to help the judges focus on their performance, find themselves tiptoeing around tuba players and churro vendors on the way to their appointments with destiny in the recital hall. Somewhere amid all this, I know, a guitar waits for me.

Soon I stand before José de Jesús Reyes Alvarez, who is sanding the top of a guitar (the tapa, they say here) while a black-and-white Marilyn Monroe poster peers down over his shoulders. With an apprentice boy awaiting orders in the background, Reyes, a slight man of 45 with rolled-up sleeves, drops his tools, pulls up a stool, guides me to it, places an instrument in my hands. I begin the questioning.

You have how many years? When of those did you start the making of guitars? The business is how long?

The questions puzzle him, as if I've asked a dog how long it's been barking.

'All my life,' he says.

The workshop is an oversized Picasso montage. Shaped wood is everywhere in suggestive, incomplete forms. The walls are papered with Marilyn and carnicería calendars. The air is heavy with sawdust. Against the walls lean stacks of wood from far-off lands. The guitar in my hands feels comfortable. The top and sides, Reyes says, are palo escrito, a handsome Mexican wood; the bridge, rosewood from India. This is one of his best, he says, and he's hoping it will sell for 5000 pesos – that is, around $525. I gulp and change the subject.

Then Reyes barks an order to the apprentice and leads me out of the shop, down the street and into the heart of guitardom: Paracho's cultural center, where the courtyard is festooned with paper decorations cut in guitar shapes, where schoolchildren have made a 15-foot-high guitar out of plywood, cardboard and paint, where a grill full of carne asada smolders.

The courtyard teems with artisans from surrounding villages peddling pottery, textiles and woodwork. Farther back, the mountains jut up beyond the rooftops, and the pines stand in mist like an invading army at attention. Reyes leads me to a door and points inside. Arrayed on tabletop stands is this year's batch of entrants in the guitar-building competition. Precisely joined wood, elaborate inlays. Most are for sale, at prices from $160 to $750.

Looking closely at a guitar is like trying to count all those bones in your inner ear. Most instruments involve more than 100 bits of wood, large and small, which may have come from four continents. To complicate matters, Americans and Mexicans have developed their own intimate terms for types of wood and principal parts.

Americans refer to the neck, where the frets (trastos) are, and head (where the strings are wrapped around the tuning keys). Mexicans refer to el brazo (the arm) and la palma (the palm). On the back of the guitar, where the neck/arm meets the main body, there's a wooden brace that Americans call the heel, and Mexicans call the nariz (nose). Everybody uses 'bridge' (puente) for the crucial strip of hard wood against which the strings are stretched. But while Americans call the opening next to it the 'sound hole,' Mexicans stick with body language. That, they say, is la boca. The mouth.

In the Velazquez shop, I find a broad range of instruments and wooden souvenirs, all the way down to toy mini-guitars priced at about 90 cents each. But nothing speaks to me. In the Amezcua shop nearby, I find Gerónimo Amezcua Gómez, 50 years old and a third-generation guitar-maker, gently pounding trastos into a brazo. Behind him, his late grandfather peers out from a 1923 photo, guitar in hand.

The living Amezcua before me, a gruff, dedicated fellow who could pass for Det. Sipowicz's Mexican twin, made his first guitar at 13. He turns to point out a dusty old instrument mounted on the wall: his first guitar. Amezcua massages the new instrument in hand. 'A guitar like this,' he says, 'I make about four a week.' The price is about $200.

A few more doors down, José Luis Díaz Reyes retreats to a back room and returns with an odd steel-string guitar. Like most of his competitors, Díaz usually makes nylon-string guitars. But this is a one-of-a-kind innovation. The front and sides are bent so that the sound box, where the strings resonate, is extra large. Díaz, 62, says he started out to be a violin-maker but switched to guitars when he was 14.

'You hear the nice tone?' he asks, strumming the extra-large guitar. 'This guitar exists in no other place in Paracho.'

Between shop visits, I duck into the auditorium to hear the students play and wander among artisans under the arches of the cultural center.

The biggest risk in buying a Paracho guitar, I have been told, is making sure that it's not made of newly cut wood. The best guitars are made from the oldest, driest wood, which is less prone to warping and cracking.

Also, certain types of wood, not all of them grown in Mexico, are most suited to certain parts of a guitar. So, as the quality of Paracho's guitars improves, the local specialty takes on a global scope. Even the humdrum $50 guitars around Paracho are likely to feature foreign wood, and probably metal tuning keys from Asia.

In the unadvertised upstairs workshop of Kenny Hill, where a team of builders produces some guitars for his label and some for themselves as side projects, most of the wood arrives by way of the San Diego-Tijuana border. Most finished guitars leave the same way, and the best end up fetching $2000 or more.

That's beyond my budget. But Manuel Hernández, who runs the Hill workshop, is happy to show me around all the same. The machines that dry the wood, the blueprints the makers follow, the rich tone that comes from the low E-string on a well-made instrument.

The low notes, I tell Hernández, they are sounding much pretty.

Most American visitors, if they find their way into Michoacán at all, head straight for the old architecture, craft vendors and lake vistas around the town of Pátzcuaro, about an hour southwest of Morelia, or to Angangueo, at the state's eastern edge, where monarch butterflies cluster in a mountain sanctuary each winter.

Paracho lies on neither path. As the crow flies, it's about 30 miles west of Pátzcuaro, about 20 miles north of Uruapan, on the Mesita Purépecha, a severe but beautiful plateau of forests, cornfields, free-ranging livestock and rugged little towns.

The Purépecha, also known as the Tarascan, are the indigenous people whose ancestors retreated farther and farther into these mountains once the Spanish began their advances here in the 16th century. They raise corn, zucchini, apples and lentils, manage livestock and make crafts for the markets. If Cortez and company had never arrived, the Mesita Purépecha might not look much different today.

Winters can be bitterly cold. Illiteracy is sufficiently widespread that municipal ballots in Paracho offer candidates' photographs instead of names. Unemployment is severe enough that Michoacán rivals Jalisco and Guanajuato among the Mexican states that send the most immigrants to the U.S. In Paracho, skilled guitar-makers might earn as little as $40 per week, perhaps as much as $200.

But in summer, between cloudbursts, the freshly rinsed countryside is something to see. The plateau is more than 7000 feet above sea level, hemmed in by jagged volcanic peaks. Round a corner on one of the roads up here and you may find a pair of Purépecha women ambling along the roadside, shoulders swaddled in black and blue, hands cradling scythes. Twin reapers, their faces and their chores straight out of the 16th century.

Out beyond Angahuan, no more than 20 miles from Paracho on a good blacktop road, you can hire a horse and guide to explore the low slopes of Paricutín, a volcano that rose from a cornfield in 1943, erupted and buried most of the nearest town in lava. On the three-hour horseback trek, you can reach the spot where a buried church tower protrudes like a giant tombstone from a stark black lavascape.

These are illuminating sights – especially for somebody who's never seen beyond those 'I love Michoacán' bumper stickers that turn up so frequently on the freeways of Southern California. (To add a soundtrack to that vision, you need only approach a mariachi guitarist in Los Angeles and ask for 'Caminos de Michoacán.' Part love song, part anthem of homesickness, it tells of a narrator who searches for his lover from town to town throughout the state, from Zitácuaro to Huétamo and Apatzingán to Morelia.) In Paracho itself, there are about 55 hotel rooms, including 16 at the plain and central Hotel Hermelinda, where rates for singles are about $24.

But I want more creature comforts and a bit more distance between me and the revelry on the plaza. So I do my sleeping at the Hotel Mansion del Cupatitzio, a pleasant, river-side hacienda-style hotel at the northern end of Uruapan, right on the road that climbs and winds 20 miles to Paracho. (The hotel's owners, the Monroy family, also control a major guitar factory in Paracho and have thrown their weight behind CIDEG and the guitar festival.)

Summer daytime temperatures hover around 70 degrees. Downpours come mostly in brief bursts, trapping the market vendors under blue tarps with their mangoes and avocados – although one afternoon the pelting continues so long and strong that as I sit outside on a sheltered bench alongside the plaza, I see a 55-gallon drum positioned beneath a faulty rain gutter fill to overflowing in less than an hour.

Monday night. Night of the parade of the torneros, or craft-makers. I stand amid a throng in the plaza, snapping pictures of merrymaking while a master of ceremonies intones the names of Paracho's largest, oldest families. Onstage, the fair's queen and princesses dance with their fathers.

Down in the mosh pit, as I snap away, a boy of about 8 approaches, shyly bearing a wooden toy. For me. A few minutes later, a little girl arrives with a similar trinket. Then a teen-age boy, whose hair is partly dyed blond, singles me out and hands over a handsome pair of maracas.

These gifts are the same party favors that celebrants have been tossing from the stage deep into a surging, hand-waving audience. I keep bowing and saying gracias and passing smaller gifts on to smaller children nearby. But what's up?

Here's what: I am the only readily identifiable foreign tourist. These families are sending their children to make me feel welcome. And now one of the parents approaches. 'My family would like to invite you to join us dancing on the stage,' says Leticia Herrera Bentley, speaking perfect English. 'We would like to show you Paracho's hospitality.'

To the stage we go, and the crowd titters while I attempt to shift my weight rhythmically from foot to foot. Then our party, about 40 people, not counting the 20-piece brass band that will follow us through the evening, lurches to a corner of the plaza. Apparently, I am now an honorary Herrera.

Leticia Bentley, it develops, was born in Paracho, one of 11 children, the only one to leave Mexico. Now she lives in Moab, Utah, with an Irish American husband and three children. She teaches and does social work with Navajo families in connection with the public schools there. But every summer, she comes back for five weeks.

In the last two decades, 'the population has doubled, and you see a lot more professionals,' she says. The week of the Paracho festival, with its reunions and celebrations of roots and community, is so gratifying for her that it's excruciating. 'I told my husband I felt like I wanted to rip up my [return] ticket and never go back,' she says.

Before long, I'm introduced to the rest of the extended family, beginning with Leticia's niece, Carmen Herrera Padilla, a general-practice physician in Zitacuaro. Then more dancing. Then a bottle of tequila surfaces.

Then it's off to the cultural center, where the bottle makes further rounds. One of my new relatives, in a touching gesture of fraternity, proposes to drink three tequila shots for every one of mine. Grinning loopily, he looks like Diego Rivera, drunk, at 20.

'No,' I tell him. 'You are clearly a professional. I am just a tourist. It is better for me to watch and teach. And learn. To watch and learn. Also, I am working. Must take pictures. Look! Taking pictures now!'

So I have blurry snaps of the plastic cup looming, and my brethren guffawing as another new relative proposes, between shots, to discuss geopolitics. 'El globalismo!' he hollers.

He's in favor of it. I have to agree. From the cultural center, the Herreras and I migrate to a private home, where the wives and mothers serve posole, a hearty stew of pinto beans, hominy, ham hocks and peppers. Fathers and daughters dance, my new friends explain some subtleties of Paracho society, and the tequila is joined by a corn liquor known as charanda. I eat heavily, dance with the doctor and her son, dodge the alcohol and take great secret gulps of mineral water.

Midnight finds me strolling across the town to find my car. Now all the sensitive classical guitar types are gone. A band blares in the plaza, fireworks bloom overhead, and bodies lurch merrily on the streets and sidewalks.

But not me. Not only do I have a Herrera retinue to guide me – one social worker, one physician, five teenagers, one 6-year-old and one 3-year-old – I have sobriety on my side. Which is good, not only because of the drive down the hill, but because it wouldn't do to choose a guitar while fighting a hangover.

Tuesday afternoon. Flight home tomorrow. Deal today.

Back in the Kenny Hill workshop, Manuel Hernández and his guys have finished a side-project guitar that was nearly done when I showed up in town. Its sides and backs are made of gorgeous striped palo escrito. Its neck is cedar; the bridge, rosewood from India; the fingerboard, ebony from Brazil. And, of course, the elbow grease is all Paracho. This, I later learn, is the sort of instrument that Kenny Hill calls 'a concert guitar for the student' and carries a $1,200 price tag in music shops. But that's after Hill buys it from Paracho, and Paracho ships it to California, and Hill sells it to a retailer. 'Listen,' says Hernández in Spanish, leaning over the unlabeled instrument. 'This is your guitar.'

He plucks the top and bottom strings, which fill the small room with twin E notes, two octaves apart. You can almost see the sawdust trembling in the air.

We agree on $400 in pesos – a tremendous discount, as long as I don't dwell on the $600 cost of my plane ticket, not to mention hotels and meals. I close the case carefully, shake hands with Hernández and step back out into downtown Paracho, where the rain has mercifully ceased. The fair continues in all its glory, guitarreros and guitarristas eyeing one another's instruments and lazing in the shade.

Now all I have to do is get mine safely home, and then learn some new songs to do it justice. I believe I'll start with 'Caminos de Michoacán.'

Guidebook: Guitar Hunting in Mexico

Telephone numbers and prices: The country code for Mexico is 52; the regional code is 4. All prices are approximate and are computed at 9.5 pesos per dollar. Room rates are for a double for one night. Meal prices are for two, food only.

Getting there: Mexicana has direct service to Morelia from Los Angeles. Though often pricier than in the US, rental cars give you flexibility in exploring the countryside, and they can be reserved at the Morelia or Uruapan airport.

Where to stay: In Morelia, Hotel & Suites Villa San José, Patzimba 77, Colonia Vista Bella, Morelia; telephone 315-1738, fax 324-4545, www.villasanjose.com.mx. Forty-three rooms on hillside overlooking the city. Great view from restaurant, with playfully arranged, well-tended grounds. Rate: $128.

In Uruapan, Hotel Mansión del Cupatitzio, Parque Nacional Eduardo Ruiz; tel. 523-2100, fax 524-6772, www.mansioncupatitzio.com. Fifty-seven rooms in a hacienda-style setting next to Cupatitzio National Park, a river that runs into the city. Courtyard pool popular with families. Rate: $96.

In Paracho, the Hotel Hermelinda, Ave. 20 de Noviembre, No. 239; tel. 525-0080. Hotel with 16 plain rooms is on the main drag near the center of town; rooms in back may be quieter. Rate: $24.

Where to eat: In Paracho, La Casona, Portal Jesús Díaz, No. 110; tel. 525-0830. A rambling restaurant next to the main square that serves great, hearty Tarascan soup; $20.

In Morelia, La Fonda Santa Mar'a restaurant at the Hotel & Suites Villa San José offers sweeping city views and a few Italian dishes along with a Mexican regional menu. My favorite dish: a cold avocado soup with tomato chunks and a hint of tequila; $25.

When to go: Because of their high-altitude settings, Paracho, Uruapan and environs are cool – and frequently wet – through the summer and chilly in winter. As for Paracho's annual festival, discovering specific dates is like trying to hold water in your hands. But innkeeper Gerónimo Villafán at Hotel Hermelinda says it's always the first two weeks of August, with most festivities (including fireworks and bonfires) on Friday and Saturday nights.

For more information: Mexico Tourism Board, Mexican Consulate, 2401 W. 6th St., Los Angeles, Calif., 90057; tel. (213) 351-2069, fax (213) 351-2074, www.visitmexico .com. Also, Mexico's Ministry of Tourism Office (Mexico City), (800) 482-9832, www. mexico-travel.com.

JUST FOR KICKS

by Stanley Stewart

This article by British freelancer Stanley Stewart, which was first published in the travel section of the *Sunday Times*, is also a kind of quest story, but in this case the quest is less precise and more ethereal. Essentially, Stewart is travelling in search of the American West. In Chapter Four, we noted how Stewart's vivid beginning introduces the themes of his piece and suggests the mysteries and riches that await the reader on this rodeo ride. There are other qualities to savour in this story. For example, the way Stewart palpably juxtaposes past and present ('To the newcomer, cowboys are the surprise of the American West, like finding Romans in pleated togas waiting for the trolley buses on the Via Appia'), and seamlessly illustrates his opinions ('The West is America's most vibrant sub culture with its own music, its own fashions, its own political orientation and its own folklore') with subsequent information and anecdotes. Stewart also skilfully and coherently develops metaphor (rodeos 'are like church fetes'; 'the Bronco snorted and took off across the plains while I clung weakly to the steering wheel'; 'a huge sky decorated with mare's tail clouds' – have you ever seen clouds depicted this way before?), interjects humour ('These horses were dangerous and bad to know, the kind of horses you warn your daughter's pony about') and cleverly uses quotation ('Welcome, laygeezeengenelmen, to the Greatest Show on Dirt'). Also note the way he vividly portrays the cowboys with just a few deft strokes of detail, and where he chooses to place us at the very end of our Wild West ride.

At the rodeo you notice that horses and cowboys are kind of alike. Horses stand around a lot, flicking their tails, breaking wind, doing nothing in particular. Cowboys are like that. They lean on fences, looking at horses. Sometimes they spit, sometimes they don't. With their hats tipped down over their eyes, it is never easy to tell if they are asleep, like horses, on their feet. The similarity disguises a major difference of temperament. Cowboys are soft-spoken mild-mannered fellows. In the West it's the horses that are the outlaws.

To the newcomer, cowboys are the surprise of the American West, like finding Romans in pleated togas waiting for the trolley buses on the Via Appia. Towns like Laramie and Cheyenne and Medicine Bow and Kit Carson are full of people who seem to have wandered off the back lot at MGM. They wear boots and ten gallon hats and leather waistcoats. In town they drink in saloons with swing doors and stand around on street corners in a bowlegged fashion. Back at the ranch their nearest neighbours are miles away. The men are lean laconic figures with lopsided grins. The women look like their idea of a good time would be to rope you and ride you round the corral awhile. The women are rather chatty. With cowboys there is a lot of silence to fill.

The West is America's most vibrant sub culture with its own music, its own fashions, its own political orientation and its own folklore. They care nothing for the suburban world that is the American mainstream. They talk of Washington and back east as if they were part of Red China. It is one of the pleasures of Wyoming to find Americans who are as cantankerous and as sceptical as the regulars of any Yorkshire pub. If the West is the spiritual home of America's ardent individualism, it is the landscape that is to blame.

Between the Missouri River and the Rocky Mountains lies a vast swathe of country that early cartographers called the Great American Desert. They were wrong but you can see where they got the idea. The West is a landscape of skies and infinities. In the loneliness of this place, self-reliance becomes a kind of religion. When the first settlers tried to farm this land, it broke their hearts. The West did not take kindly to the idea of fields. It was a vast sea of grass, a landscape for horses.

The rodeos that are held in small towns all over the West are like church fetes with Budweiser tents and bullriders, a chance to meet the neighbours and complain about the government. They are also the moment for the big showdown between the cowboys and the horses.

In Denver I hired a car called a Bronco, and headed north on Interstate 28. The road and the landscape emptied and the sky took over. Here and there wooden houses hove into view afloat on the swells of grass. Antelopes bounded away over the brows of hills. I passed four men in an old Chevy, sprawled in the seats, their cowboy hats bumping the windows. The boot of the car, tied down with baler twine, was bulging with saddles. They were rodeo cowboys heading for Caspar.

They looked like clean living guys with big chins, ready to tame the wild equine forces of the West.

Rodeo cowboys have taken over from outlaws and bashful sheriffs as the heroes of the modern West, footloose fellows who struggle to make a living from the competitive world of bronco riding and bull wrestling. Lift a handful of their names from the program notes and they seem to describe a way of life: Lance, Cody, Chance, Skeeter, Shane, Chuck, and Rusty. In their pickup trucks and old cars, the cowboys tour the rodeo circuit from Texas to Montana, from Arizona to South Dakota. They often drive a thousand miles between rodeos, compete in the bronco riding for an afternoon, wave at the cheering crowds, then get back in the truck to drive all night to another rodeo in another town in another state. Their only income is the prize money they win. If they do well, it might cover their expenses. It is the kind of reckless itinerant life I dreamt about when I was fifteen – the American West, the open road, horses and prairie towns miles from nowhere, late-night bars and girls in tight blue jeans.

In Caspar, the banners over Main Street welcomed me to the Central Wyoming Fair and Rodeo. Most of the buildings on Main Street were hardly older than my father. At lunch in a turn of the century hotel I was served by a riverboat gambler with slick hair, a pencil moustache and shiny waistcoat. He looked like he had just stepped off the stage from Carson City. I asked him if he was from Caspar. He said he was just passing through.

In the late afternoon I headed out to the fairgrounds. Pens of horses and steers and a car park of pickup trucks surrounded the open-air grandstand. Just inside the gate I was greeted by one of those tall young men with perfect teeth and day-glow tans

who make a living in America on afternoon soap operas. When the romantic leads run out, they turn their hands to running the country.

'Hi, I'm John Thune, and I'm running for Congress.' John gave good handshake. He wore cowboys boots and a T-shirt that said 'Thune!'. 'I want to get government off the peoples' backs,' Thune! said. 'I sure hope I can count on your vote.' I thought Thune! might make a start by getting off my back. But he was already on to the next punter. 'Hi, I'm John Thune!…'

The only people with shinier smiles than Thune! were the rodeo royalty. I was still struggling to gain my seat with a plastic beaker of beery foam and a hot dog the size of Idaho when the Queens arrived.

'We have five visiting Rodeo Queens here today,' the announcer boomed over the loudspeakers. 'And I jes know you're gonna want to give 'em a big Caspar welcome.' The Queens, in spray-on Levis and shiny shirts, galloped in on white horses. They were dazzling figures. There was Miss Country & Western Music, Miss Rodeo Iowa, Miss South-west County Fair and Livestock Show, Miss Rodeo South Dakota. They cantered past in a blur of fixed smiles, big hair and royal waves. The minor royalty tended to outshine the major players. With high-voltage eyes and a hairstyle with fins, Miss Laramie Feed and Hardware Store had more than a little of Princess Michael of Kent about her.

'Welcome, laygeezeengenelmen, to the Greatest Show on Dirt.' The announcers, the D.J.'s of the rodeo, had the honeyed tones of the revivalist tent. They made jingoism an art form. The National Anthem was their big moment.

'We're here for a good time laygeezeengenelmen. We gonna forget our troubles, let our hair down, go a little wild with the wild west rodeo…[crowd roars]…but first, I'm gonna ask you to pause for a moment. [crowd noise subsides]…I want us to remember just how lucky we are…[crowd is silent] The Good Lord blessed us with this Great Land of Ours, we must never take for granted the Freedoms that We Fought so Hard to Win…I am gonna ask you to stand now, laygeezeengenelmen, for the most beautiful colours on earth, the red white and blue of Old Glory. God Bless America, laygeezeengenelmen, the Greatest Country on Earth.'

I prided myself in being able to get through these introductions without resort to the sick bag.

Behind the chutes the cowboys were warming up. Some were stretching like ballerinas, others were rocking on saddles on the ground, working the resin into the leather. One was performing a practise mime of bull riding, one hand above his head, snapping his back in slow motion. Another was trying to make his peace with God. He stood with his hat tipped down against the top rail of a corral, praying. A massive bull with a cynic's face and testicles the size of basketballs, eyed him malevolently from the other side of the fence.

I said howdy to Randy, a rancher I knew from the hills back of Kaycee where the Butch Cassidy gang used to hide out after raiding the Union Pacific railroad. Randy was a bony taciturn cowboy with pale eyes and red cheeks. He was so soft-spoken, in that cowboy way, that conversations became a series of furtive whispers. He had been a bronc rider himself until a horse had thrown him over a wall, breaking his back. He missed the rodeo, and he hung around behind the chutes, chatting to the cowboys, like the ghost of rodeos past.

The bucking horses arrived, snorting and pawing the ground like demons as they were herded into the stalls. A row of cowboys climbed up on the buckboards to set and adjust the saddles. One of the horses snorted and reared in the box, and a tall cowboy in a white hat shot backwards like a cartoon character, coming to rest against the front row of the grandstand. The horse had caught him with a powerful left hook and broken his jaw. It was a sobering moment. These horses were dangerous and bad to know, the kind of horses you warn your daughter's pony about.

When the broncs were saddled and the judges ready, a cowboy lowered himself gingerly onto the first horse. There was a moment of anxiety as he settled himself. Gripping the head rope, the cowboy leaned back, adjusted his hat, stuffed a wad of chewing tobacco in his mouth and nodded to signal he was ready. When the chute gate swung open, all hell broke loose. As the horse charged into the arena, it hardly seemed to touch the ground, and the cowboy, flesh and blood but a moment ago, was whipping back and forth like a rag doll.

The idea is to hang on for just eight seconds, a feat which barely half of the cowboys manage. Hanging on would be enough to occupy most people, but the cowboy must also meet certain criteria to score well, including spurring the bucking horse in the requisite manner, rather like stepping on the accelerator when the car is already out of control. Two of the other rough stock disciplines, bareback bronc riding and bull riding, have the added difficulty of remembering, when you are thrown, to fall off the right side. If you come off the wrong side, opposite to the way your hand grips, your hand is trapped in the rigging with consequences too grim to describe.

For bull riders of course their troubles only just begin when they hit the ground.

The bulls make the horses look like teddy bears, and they tend to bear a grudge with people foolish enough to ride on their backs. Part of the job of the rodeo clowns, who entertain the crowd between events, is to distract the bull while the rider makes a hasty escape over the boards. In the world of comedy this is trial by fire; if the bull isn't taken with the clown's stand-up routine, he doesn't just heckle.

I asked Randy why they did it. It is wonderful entertainment but one could understand a young cowboy preferring a quiet career yee-hawing at a herd of docile cows.

'It's a western thing,' Randy whispered. 'They've been around horses all their lives and they like the challenge. They also like the independence, life on the road, nobody telling 'em what to do. Lot of guys when they stop ridin' and get some job somewhere, long for the days when they were a poor young cowboy, driving across Wyoming to the next rodeo.'

I was impressed. I had never heard Randy talk so much. He seemed kind of tuckered out by his monologue, and retired to the beer tent. When I looked round the steer wrestling had begun. Ostensibly this is a more sedate event for cowboys who might have second thoughts about climbing aboard deranged livestock. They chase runaway steers instead, jumping on their backs when they have reached full speed. Participants liken it to driving along a road at about forty miles an hour and then stepping out the passenger door to embrace a passing tree. The cowboy is meant to throw the steer but the fun lies in the fact that it is often the other way round.

The next morning I hit the road in the Bronco. I drove west to Laramie where the rodeo was in a windswept grandstand with a view of the Medicine Bow Mountains. I went north to Belle Fouche in South Dakota where a bronc rider broke his arm and the post-rodeo street party was washed out by a freak storm out of Nevada. I turned west again into Montana to the night rodeo at Billings where I learnt that the cowboys have their own union, the PRCA, the Professional Rodeo Cowboys Association. Presumably health care is one of the comrades' chief priorities.

Montana has dispensed with speed limits, which are nothing but a Washington conspiracy to deprive the American citizen of his inalienable right to see if he can get his pickup airborne. The Bronco snorted and took off across the plains while I clung weakly to the steering wheel. I was in Idaho before I knew what had happened. The next day I was back in Wyoming, barrelling down the Platte River Valley beneath a huge sky decorated with mare's tail clouds. I was heading for Cheyenne and the 'Daddy of 'Em All', the Cheyenne Frontier Days, the country's biggest and oldest rodeo.

Cheyenne is the product of the Union Pacific Railroad, the Black Hills Gold Rush of the 1870's and the cattle wars of the 1880's. It's an archetypal cowboy town, with wide streets and plain flat-faced buildings. The pawn shop was full of saddles, and the jukeboxes in the bars were devoted to Garth Brooks and Dolly Parton.

Begun in 1896, Frontier Days takes place over ten days in July and attracts almost 20,000 spectators a day. All the best cowboys come here, and all the best riding stock. The bucking horses are wild creatures from a ranch in the Rattlesnake Hills of Colorado and the bulls, part Brahma, are as big and as ornery as you are ever gonna see.

The climax of each day's events were the wild horse races. The idea is simple enough.

The cowboys compete in teams of three. A herd of wild horses is released into the arena, and each team runs out to lasso and saddle one. The cowboy who has drawn the short straw then gets to ride the horse round the track. That's the theory anyway.

Few of the teams even get so far as saddling the horses. As the mustangs charged into the arena, white-eyed and wet-muzzled, a blur of dust and horse-flesh, the cowgirl behind me become hysterical. She was trying to explain the finer points of the race to a friend. To her it was a simple imbalance in male hormones. 'It's testosterone,' she shrieked. 'It's pure testosterone. It's madness.'

She seemed to be on a first name basis with most of the testosterone-laden competitors. 'Come on Cody. Come on Tuff. Get him Skeeter, get him. Wrassle 'em, Duane,' she cried.

The cowboys were doing their best but the horses were winning. One took off down the track dragging a hapless cowboy at the end of a rope. It was an impressive burst of speed but sadly he was going the wrong way. The cowboy reappeared, later in the afternoon, limping badly. Another horse head-butted one of the cowboys then swung round and chased the whole team into the grandstands before taking off to terrorise the suburbs. A third simply bit everyone who came near him. Half an hour later when they were all herded back into their corral, they were as frisky as children, whinnying their pleasure at such a jolly outing. The cowboys limped away, their hats crushed, their clothes covered in dust, their levels of testosterone seriously depleted.

That evening at the Hitching Post Inn the car park was full of stretch pickups loaded with saddles and hay. The Hitching Post was the happening place after hours. In the saloon bar it was wall to wall cowboy hats. Cowboys clean up real nice, and they were all turned out in their best shirts. It is said that cowboys have three pairs of jeans. A size too big for practise; the right size for the rodeo itself; and a size too small for the dances afterwards.

The next morning in the western outfitters I bought a handsome Stetson from a sales girl with a mean pair of boots and a serious chewing gum habit. A sign by the till read 'It's Never Too Late to be a Cowboy'. I had already decided it was too late for me. I wasn't sure the testosterone levels were up to it. I put on my hat and went out into the wide streets of Cheyenne. I was happy to walk the walk and talk the talk but there was no way I was going near those horses. They were the real thing, the last remnant of the Wild West.

A NIGHT WITH THE GHOSTS OF GREECE

by Don George

This was the first of my travel stories to be published in a national travel magazine. The magazine was *Signature*, which was subsequently bought by Condé Nast and transformed into *Condé Nast Traveler*. I recently asked the editor who bought the piece why she had liked it. She replied: 'First of all, I liked the uniqueness of the idea – you spent a night on an island where no one was supposed to be. That caught my attention. Second, I liked the way you gave us just the history we needed to know – you didn't weigh the story down with history – and then brought both that past and the present of the place to life with the specific details you chose to describe (and which you described with colour and precision). I liked the small, humanising touches (the lizard slithering over your boot, the cat lapping your cheek in the morning, and of course your encounters with the physicist and the pavilion owner), the humour ('the universal tongue of Loquacious Libation'), the way you imparted a sense of the place's effect on you without overdoing it, and I liked the way you kept a certain sense of mystery throughout the piece. Also, I liked the circular structure of the story, where the end comes back to the beginning – but of course, you (and by extension, we) are part of the island now and so we see it all with new eyes. For *Signature*, this was a very satisfying and unexpected appreciation of a little-ballyhooed Greek island. It fitted our sense of our own style – and of our readers' tastes and interests – perfectly.'

There are no tavernas, no discotheques, no pleasure boats at anchor. Nor are there churches, windmills or goatherds. Delos, three miles long and less than one mile wide, is a parched, rocky island of ruins, only 14 miles from Mykonos, Aegean playground of the international vagabonderie. Once the center of the Panhellenic world, Delos has been uninhabited since the first century AD, fulfilling a proclamation of the Delphic oracle that 'no man or woman shall give birth, fall sick or meet death on the sacred island.'

I chanced on Delos during my first visit to Greece. After three harrowing days of seeing Athens by foot, bus and taxi, my traveling companion and I were ready for open seas and uncrowded beaches. We selected Mykonos on the recommendation of a friend, who suggested that when we tired of the Beautiful People, we should take a side trip to Delos.

On arriving in Mykonos, we learned that for under $3 we could catch a fishing trawler to Delos (where the harbor is too shallow for cruise ships) any morning at eight and return to Mykonos at one the same afternoon. On the morning of our fourth day, we braved choppy seas and ominous clouds to board a rusty, peeling boat that reeked of fish. With a dozen other tourists, we packed ourselves into the ship's tiny cabin, already crowded with

anchors, ropes and wooden crates bearing unknown cargo.

At some point during the 45-minute voyage, the toss and turn of the waves became too much for a few of the passengers, and I moved outside into the stinging, salty spray. As we made our way past Renea, the calluslike volcanic island that forms part of the natural breakwater with Delos, the clouds cleared, and the fishermen who had docked their caiques at the Delos jetty greeted us in bright sunlight.

At the end of the dock a white-whiskered man in a navy blue beret and a faded black suit hailed each one of us as we walked by: 'Tour of Delos! Informative guide to the ruins.' A few yards beyond him a young boy ran up to us, all elbows and knees, and confided in hard breaths, 'I give you better tour. Cheaper too.'

I had read the Delphic oracle's proclamation the night before and wondered what these people were doing on the island. I asked the boy, and he pointed to a cluster of houses on a knoll about a thousand yards away. 'I live here. Family.'

At first glance Delos seemed the quintessential ruin: broken bits of statues, stubby pillars, cracking archways and isolated walls. Nothing moved but the sunlight, glinting off the fragments like fish scales scattered over a two-acre basin.

Other movements had once animated the alleys and temples before us. Legend has it that Delos was originally a roving island when Leto, mistress of Zeus, landed there racked with birth pains. Poseidon anchored the island in its present position while Leto brought forth Artemis and Apollo, the Greek sun god and protector of light and art. Apollo eventually became the most revered of the Greek gods, and religious devotion, coupled with the island's central, protected situation, established Delos as the thriving center of the Mediterranean world, religious and commercial leader of an empire that stretched from Italy to the coast of Asia Minor.

Wandering the ruins of this once-boisterous center, we found temples both plain and elegant, Greek and foreign; massive marketplaces studded with pedestals where statues once stood, now paved with poppies; a theater quarter with vivid mosaics depicting actors and symbolic animals and fish; a dry lake ringed with palm trees; a stadium and a gymnasium; storehouses and quays along the waterfront; and an ancient suburb where merchants and ship captains once lived: the haunting skeleton of a Hellenistic metropolis.

At 12:45 the captain of the trawler appeared at the end of the dock and whistled once, twice, three times, then waved his arms. He repeated this signal at 12:50 and 12:55. My friend left, but something about those deserted ruins held me, and I decided to spend the night on the island. I watched from the top of Mount Cynthus, the lone hill, as the boat moved away toward the mountains of Mykonos on the northeast horizon. Looking around, I felt at the center of the Cyclades: to the north, Tinos, to the northwest, Andros, then Syros, Siphnos, Paros and Naxos, and beyond them Melos and Ios – all spokes in the sacred chariot of the sun god.

Below me the ruins were absolutely desolate, shimmering silently in the midday sun. A lizard slithered over my boot. The boat crawled farther away. The wind sighed. Droplets of sweat seemed to steam from my forehead.

I walked down the hill to the shade of the tourist pavilion, the one concession to tourism (besides a three-room museum) on the island. I walked inside and asked the owner, a large, jolly man with a Zorba mustache, what he was offering for lunch. He looked surprised to see me. 'You miss the caique?'

'No, I wanted to spend the night here.'

'Ah.' He looked beyond me into the glaring, baked ruins. 'We have rice, meat, vegetables.'

'Do you have any fish?'

'Fish? Yes.' He directed me to a case in the back room, opened it and took out five different fish, each caked with ice. 'Which do you want?' I pointed to one. 'Drink?'

'A beer, please.'

He nodded, pointed out the door to a terrace with tables and chairs scattered at random like dancers at a Mykonos discotheque, and said, 'Sit, please,' motioning me into a chair.

The heat hung in the air, folding like a curtain over the pillars and pedestals, smothering the palms and reeds. Occasionally a dusty-brown lizard would scuttle from one shadow into another. The owner moved from kitchen to terrace like a man who has never waited, never worried about time, wiping off the table, bringing a glass of cold beer, then fish, fried potatoes and a tomato salad.

Eventually, two old men dressed in the same uniform as the man who had greeted us that morning walked up carrying two pails filled with water. One went inside and began to talk animatedly with the owner.

The other sat down on the edge of the terrace, dipped his callused hands and pulled out a white and black octopus. He rolled the octopus in a milky white liquid from the other pail, twisting and slapping its tentacles against the cement until he was satisfied it was clean. Then he laid it aside, and dipped in again, pulling out another slippery creature. He cleaned five octopuses in all, leaving them oozing in the sun, their tentacles writhing and their suction cups puckering for water.

At 4 p.m. a cock crowed. What is he doing here? I wondered. And, more important, why is he crowing at 4 p.m.? The sound broke the silence with an eerie premonition. I looked at the bottles, chairs, tables, heard the reassuring murmur of voices inside. Beyond the terrace, in the light and heat, seemed another world.

An hour later I walked into the ruins, following the wide central avenue (the 'Sacred Way') toward the waterfront, the theater district and the hillside temples. On my way I passed columns carved with line after line of intricate symbols with no breaks between the words; sacrificial altars; huge cisterns for storing rainwater and oil; and vast foundations outlining meeting halls and marketplaces by the wharves. I explored the remains of private houses, passing from room to room, trying to imagine where their inhabitants had cooked, eaten and slept, awakened from my reverie only by an occasional spider web or lizard trail. As I walked on and the setting sun cast the halls and walls in an orange-pink light, the ruins seemed to take on a strange life all their own.

What had been eerie desolation became an intense timelessness, a sense of communion with other peoples and other eras. My boots crossed rocks other sandals had crossed; my hands touched marble other hands had touched. When I reached the mosaics, they seemed a living thing, green-eyed tigers and blue dolphins, flowers of every shape and color, the same to me as they were to the countless merchants and artisans who had admired them centuries before. I continued up the hill to the temples of the Syrian and Egyptian – as well as Greek – gods, and reflected how many different cultures had met in that silent hollow below.

While I was sitting in the temple to the Egyptian gods, a figure appeared walking up the hill toward me. It was not the owner of the pavilion, nor any of the fishermen I had seen previously. This was a man in shorts and a Western shirt, with a satchel and a walking stick. We exchanged waves and wary glances until he came up and sat next to me. 'You are English?'

'American.'

'Ah, good.' He stuck out his hand.

He was a physicist from Hungary, on leave from a national research project for two weeks. 'I have been saving my passes for this trip,' he said. 'Isn't this wonderful? Yesterday I examined all the ruins from there' – he waved a finger toward the stadium at the distant end of the basin – 'to here. Today I have walked the circuit of the island.' He paused to catch his breath, his cheeks as grainy as the rocks on which we sat. 'There really isn't that much else to see.'

The mountains were turning purple over the poppy-red water. The ruins were fading into shade. I wanted to explore further before darkness set in, so we agreed to meet for dinner.

When I entered the tourist pavilion, the owner greeted me like a long-lost friend and brought out three glasses and a bottle of ouzo. 'We drink.' The Hungarian appeared through another doorway that, I learned later, led to the pavilion's four 'guest rooms,' distinguished by the presence of a mattress and wash basin. We finished one bottle and began another, talking in Greek, Italian, French, German and English about everything, and soon thereafter about nothing. When one language failed, we tried another, until we were all speaking in the universal tongue of Loquacious Libation.

In another hour or two the owned fixed us a feast of fish, lamb, fried potatoes, rice, tomatoes and cucumbers, with baklava and rice pudding for dessert. While we ate, the physicist and I talked. I learned that the cluster of houses I had seen earlier had been built by the French School of Classical Studies when it was digging on Delos in the 1950s and '60s. When the last archaeologists left, the curator of the museum moved in with his family. It was his son I had met that morning. The old man who had hailed our arrival was a fisherman from a local island who turned to guiding when the fishing was slow.

After finishing our second bottle – compliments of the owner – of sweet, resiny retsina, we drank a good night toast of thick Greek coffee. Then the physicist retired to his room, preceded by the owner's wife, who had drawn a pitcher of cold water for his use in the morning. I was traveling on a backpack budget, however, and when the owner offered me the use of his roof for 30 drachmas (under $1) – half the cost of the guest rooms – I gladly accepted.

I walked up two flights of cement stairs to a cement roof enclosed like a medieval fortress with a 4-foot-high wall. The stars glinted like a nighttime mirror of the marble ruins. I unrolled my sleeping bag in a protected corner, thankful that the lizards could not reach me at that height,

and rummaged in my backpack for soap, toothpaste and a toothbrush.

'Could you use this?' The physicist held out his flashlight. 'I've come to ask you to hurry in preparing your toilet. The owner wants to turn off the electricity.'

After I had washed and brushed and stumbled back up the stairs to my sleeping bag, I heard a scuffling of footsteps; voices thundered back and forth through the blackness, and the lights went out.

The footsteps returned, a door squeaked and banged shut, chairs scraped. Then everything was silent. No machine sounds, no human sounds, no animal sounds. Absolute silence. I lay in my sleeping bag, and the ruins encroached on my dreams – the swish of the lizards scrambling over the rocks, the moist coolness of the marble at sunset, the languid perfume of the poppies dabbed among the fluted white fragments.

Streaming sunlight awakened me. I turned to look at my watch and disturbed a black kitten that had bundled itself at my feet. In so doing, I also disturbed the ouzo and retsina that had bundled itself in my head, and I crawled as close as I could to the shadow of the wall – 6:45. I pulled my towel over my head and tried to imagine the windy dark, but to no avail. The kitten mewed its way under my towel, where it set to lapping at my cheek as if it had discovered a bowl of milk.

I stumbled down the stairs and soaked my head in tepid tap water until at last I felt stable enough to survey the surroundings. Behind the pavilion a clothesline ran to the rusting generator. Chickens strutted inside a coop at the curator's house. Rhenea stirred in the rising mist.

Again I wandered through the ruins, different ruins now, bright with day and the reality of returns: The tourists would return to Delos, and I would return to Mykonos. I ate a solemn breakfast on the terrace with the physicist, then walked past the sacred lake and the marketplace to the Terrace of the Lions. Standing among the five lions of Delos, erected in the seventh century BC to defend the island from invaders, I looked over the crumbling walls and stunted pillars to the temples on the hill. Like priests they presided over the procession of tourists who would surge onto the island, bearing their oblation in cameras and guidebooks. As the trawler approached, a bent figure in a navy blue beret hurried to the dock, and a boy in shorts raced out of the curator's house past the physicist, past me, and into the ruins.

How to get there: The most reliable way to get to Delos is from Mykonos. Caiques depart once each morning (weather permitting) from the pier near the tourist information office, and return once each afternoon to bring visitors back. It is best to inquire on arrival in Mykonos about precise times and also if any other vessels, public or private, are making the trip.

Passage can also sometimes be arranged from other islands in the Cyclades, but such arrangements are subject to the whims of fishermen and sailors.

Where to eat and stay: The Tourist Pavilion offers a small cafeteria and four small and spartan rooms for visitors who want to spend the night. Or, if you prefer to do as I did, you can make arrangements to sleep on the roof. In either case, talk to the pavilion's proprietor.

Guidebooks: A good guidebook is almost essential to understanding the layout and significance of the ruins. My guide of choice was the *Blue Guide: Greece*. Another book that has been highly recommended to me is *Delos: Monuments and Museum*, by P. Zaphiropoulou, which can be purchased on Mykonos.

THE PATH TO SOKKURAM

by Robert Hass

This story by former US Poet Laureate Robert Hass appeared in *Great Escapes*, a quarterly travel magazine published by the *San Francisco Examiner & Chronicle*. In Chapter Four we discussed the article's effective use of *in medias res*, and the interweaving of themes with indelible portraits of people, places, history and culture. Hass's vivid use of language is striking throughout the piece, but what is most impressive is the way he combines a very personal narrative with a much larger explanation and exploration of the country in which that personal tale is unfolding. We finish this account with a rich, multilayered appreciation of Korea as experienced through Hass's eyes and heart. Even more profoundly, we emerge with a renewed appreciation of the power and potential of travel to heal and restore. We come away with a powerfully personified understanding of how every journey can fling unexpected bridges across cultures and offer life-transforming revelations – both interpersonal and intrapersonal. In this masterful tale Hass evokes a full sense of his connection with Korea. And how does he choose to end? Most appropriately, with one final resonant word, written by Hass but spoken by another: a final embodiment of the intercultural connection the story has described and now become.

'The thing you need to understand about Korea,' said the cheerful, dissolute-looking British shipping agent I had run into at six in the morning at the fish market in the harbor at Pusan – we were drinking coffee at an outdoor table in the reek of fish and the unbelievable choral din of the fish merchants, beside tanks of slack-bodied pale squid and writhing pink and purple octopus – 'is that it's Poland. I mean, as a metaphor it's Poland. Caught between China and Japan for all those centuries like the Poles were stuck between the Russians and the Germans. The Japanese occupied the place from 1910 to the end of the war, and in the '30s they simply tried to eradicate Korea as a nation. Outlawed the language. Everybody in the country over 40 went to school when the teaching of the Korean language was forbidden.'

An old woman pushed past with a cart full of fist-sized reddish-green figs. McEwan, the shipping agent, called her over. 'Try one of these,' he said. 'Damned good.' They were, red-fleshed, packed with seeds. McEwan was waving down a waiter with one hand, clutching a torn-open fig with the other. 'They demand soju, don't they?' Soju is a transparent, fiery, slightly sweet Korean brandy, perfect with figs I was sure, but beyond me at that moment. I had been out the night before with a surprisingly hard-drinking lot of professors from Pusan National University, and wandered afterward rather aimlessly through the night market. Just before leaving America I had come to the end of a long marriage, and I had spent my first few days in Korea, when I did not have to concentrate on a task, in a state of dazed grief. In the night market the families had fascinated me, at one in the morning shutting down their produce stalls, loading up

their boxes of fennel and cabbage and bok choy, moving swiftly in and out of the arc of light thrown by a hanging propane lamp, husbands and wives and drowsy children, working easily side by side. I drank beer at a stall and watched the market close down, and then went back to my hotel and couldn't sleep, and so got up again and walked down the hill in the pre-dawn coolness to the wharf.

'A hell of a lot of the Koreans were drafted during the war,' McEwan was saying. The cloud of flies that had risen to reconnoiter the fig cart returned to the gleaming guts of tuna and mackerel that were being eviscerated across the way. 'Either they were pressed into service in factories in Japan or they served in the army. Fellow in my office was conscripted in '44, fought in a Korean unit of the Japanese infantry and ended up in a POW camp in Shanghai, which is where he learned his English.'

I had, so far, only a few definite impressions of Korea: that Koreans were intense, that the country was stunningly, unexpectedly beautiful and that all foreigners who live there and most Koreans had a passion for trying to explain the place. I had liked listening, I noticed, in the way that people made listless by private pain are often stimulated by stories of misfortune. I had particularly liked talking to the students in Seoul who were involved in the demonstrations against the government. They had read the revisionist historians of the Korean War and books on neo-colonialism and 'dependency theory' and were furious at the role the United States had played in the recent history of their country. It isn't always possible to admire what one feels, but like it or not I found the passionate conflicts in Korean politics strangely soothing.

The soju arrived, with a dish of gungju, little charcoal-roasted pond snails that are gathered from the rice field and have a nutty taste. 'The thing is,' McEwan said, 'after the war was over, when they had finally got free of the Japanese, they turned on each other, and they absolutely decimated what was left of their country. Decimated it.' I objected to this interpretation of the Korean War, sipping soju, which I knew was a very bad idea. It was the United States and the Soviet Union that divided the country at the 38th parallel and cut off the possibility of a united and independent state.

McEwan waved me away. 'The Koreans have been lining up foreign help to fight each other since the Chou dynasty. The fact is they lined up the big boys on either side and tore this country the hell apart. In the early '60s, my father-in-law says there wasn't enough food between the used-up winter stores and the summer harvest, and not a cent available to import it. They had "spring hunger," like medieval peasants in wartime. You wouldn't know it now. You know what the average per capita GNP was in 1962? Eighty dollars. Now it's around two thousand.'

I had heard these figures before, quoted by cab drivers, diplomats, bartenders, poets. Koreans seemed to keep track of the per capita GNP as if it were a batting average. When they were not talking about student demonstrations – this was the fall of 1986 – they talked about the 'economic miracle.' And it did seem miraculous. From devastating poverty they had become in twenty years the twelfth most active trading nation in the world, just behind Italy.

McEwan began addressing this subject. 'This wealth was accomplished, of course, with massive infusions of Japanese and American capital, which was attracted by a cheap, hard-working, fairly well educated work force. For which,' he sucked a snail

out of its dark blue shell, 'there's going to be hell to pay. The students are pushing political issues, freedom of speech, free elections. Wait,' he said, 'until the workers start demonstrating. They won't offend the generals' sense of order, they'll offend the actual structure of profits, and that's when the civil war inside the civil war begins.'

'By the way,' he had said, as I was leaving, 'if you're going to Kyongju, there's an old temple outside of town that you'll want to see. Up in the mountain behind it there's an eighth-century Buddha in a cave. Quite famous.' And he gave me what turned out to be very good advice. 'Take the hill path to Sokkuram, if you get a chance. There's a road up that takes you most of the way by car, but if you've got time, take the path. It's not a bad climb.'

He waved his long arm and, fortified by coffee, figs, snails, and two or three shots of soju, made his way down the wharf to work. It was almost seven, and Pusan Bay was steaming in the early heat. I felt alive, though slightly wrecked; back at the hotel, the driver from the American consulate with whom I had arranged a ride to Kyongju was waiting.

It was to be a weekend in the countryside and also a journey into the past. Ancient Korea, the green mountainous peninsula jutting out of the land mass of northeast Asia, was probably settled by successive waves of tribal peoples migrating eastward out of the Altai Mountains. From early on, they had some cultural contact – including war, no doubt – with the Yellow River city-states out of which Chinese culture would evolve. Some of the emigrants made their way to the tip of the peninsula and sailed south across the straits to settle in Japan.

At the most only 30 percent of the Korean peninsula is lowland – river valley and coastal plain. Tribal life must have developed at a slow pace in hill villages and isolated valleys. When Athens was flourishing, at about the time of the birth of Confucius, Korea was, in the historical record, silent. By about 200 BC, when the Roman republic was developing, three centers of power were emerging in Korea, one in the northeast, one in the southeast and one in the southwest.

The southwestern dynasty, Silla, eventually unified the country in the latter half of the seventh century. Its capital, Kyongju, sat in a rather remote and extremely beautiful mountain valley some 55 miles east and north of Pusan. It was there in the eighth century, at about the time of Charlemagne in France and of the great Tang dynasty in China, that old Korea, Confucian in its politics, Buddhist in religion, with a strong undercurrent of shamanism – there were religious ceremonies for the sun and the moon and the spirits of the mountains conducted mostly by a caste of sorceresses or priestesses called mudang – a culture of rice cultivation, rich craftsmanship in gold and bronze, and slavery, reached its highest development. It was now, I was told, a market town of about 130,000 people, surrounded by burial mounds, temples and memorial stones, which, as the economy recovered, the government was attempting to restore and preserve. At the height of Silla, Kyongju had been one of the most civilized cities on earth.

I didn't have much time to brood over this fact, nor did I know exactly what to expect. I was out in the Korean countryside. Nothing before I had come had prepared me for the beauty of it, for the soft, intense green of the rice fields, terraces of them carved into the contours of the valleys like the grain in wood, and the dark green pine forest where the rice fields left off, tangled with wild grape and kudzu; red tile roofs in the villages, or thatch occasionally, or corrugated tin; yellow squash blossoms in the gardens beside the houses; black goats; white egrets in the fields; and the mountains climbing up steeply, mist curling about the peaks. Chiri-san, the highest of them, rose in the distance, a pyramidal granite peak, randomly forested. The mountain villages had blue tile roofs. Everywhere the fields look immaculately tended, and there were vegetable patches in every gully.

This was the life, I knew, that all the young in the cities were fleeing. I saw young women stooped over, weeding or cultivating, and remembered the permanently bowed grandmothers I had seen in the parks of Seoul, come to town for the day, quaint in their traditional, Sunday-best dresses – which looked more or less like kimonos. Their backs were badly bent, and their posture seemed to thrust their chins out. Traveling in packs, muttering to each other, they looked rather like the flocks of large Asian magpies, gatchi, that also populated the parks. The old men – whom one saw in the countryside riding bicycles and wearing broad-brimmed straw hats – ambled along in separate groups; they dressed in traditional loose baggy trousers, tight at the ankle. Both the men and the women seemed to have been freed of their teeth, probably by the famine years of the war. They had had hard lives, and seemed at a loss without the habit of labor. In the city, one saw them peering dutifully at the plaques on public antiquities.

Every ancient building in Korea seemed to be a tale of Japanese militarism. This temple or that pavilion was built in 1395, destroyed by a Japanese invasion in 1592, rebuilt in 1867, taken apart by the Japanese occupying force in 1910, rebuilt as faithfully as possible in 1978. It was a while before I realized that this was ideology. The Japanese had not been the only harriers of Korea. The country had been invaded at one time or another by the Chinese, the Mongols, the Manchurians. But the generation that was rebuilding the temples and palaces and pavilions in Seoul and Kwangju and Pusan had grown up under Japanese domination, so the act of reconstruction was for them at once a celebration of the survival of Korean culture and revenge against the Japanese. It was curious, therefore, to see these old peasants who were being superseded by the new, modernized and vindicated Korea – and who were, to me, far more vivid instances of traditional Korean culture than the buildings they were wandering through bending over to read the solemnly educational public plaques. Which was the historical monument, the old man or the emperor's wife's favorite pagoda?

As the car wound down into the valley of Kyongju – rice fields again, in this milder climate green-going-to-gold, hazy uplands, steep mountains and the town in the distance, which seemed composed mostly of one- and two-story houses with gracefully upward-curving eaves – I thought about the violence of history and the passions of the generations: endless cycles of passion and suffering and response to passion and suffering, division and self-division. The driver pulled up in front of the park that houses the grave barrows of the Silla emperors. A busload of teenagers was filing in; I might be ready to see a statue of Buddha in a cave, I thought, but I wasn't ready for another history lesson.

Still, the park at Kyongju is a haunting place. The tumuli, or royal tombs, what-ever they were, are now great grass-covered mounds, which seem, despite the willow trees and gently curving paths that wind among them, much more ancient than the Silla dynasty. The humped-up earth looks like gigantic wasps' nests or like something very archaic, some impulse to burrow against death, rooted in Korean shamanism perhaps, or simply in the appetite for power; some ghost of the insatiable hunger for life and the vanity of it hovers over the old barrows, and the grassy slopes have not tamed it entirely.

There was much more to see. I took in Punhwangsat'ap, the pagoda built by Queen Sondok (Old Silla: her tweezers and a pair of almost miniature scissors were found inside; I thought of her eyelashes, her nubby royal toes), and the tomb of Kim Yu-shin, the most famous Silla general, with its wonderful zodiacal carvings of wild boars and rams with curled horns dressed in the robes of Confucian scholars. And there was the summer pavilion of P'osokjong, where Silla ended. It was there in 926 that the Silla ruler Kyongae and his family were entertaining when his rival to the east, Kyon Hwon, burst in at the head of an invading army. He had Kyongae butchered on the spot and ordered his men to rape the emperor's wife. But I had had enough of history.

I got a cab to the Kolon Hotel, half an hour outside of Kyongju and within walking distance of Pulguksa, the Buddhist temple that was said to be the crowning achievement of Silla architecture. I took a last look down the valley in the setting sun, had some rice and kimch'i and went to bed. In the morning, I would try to find the path to Sokkuram.

I awoke early, and followed a path that took me to the parking lot where tour buses were unloading schoolchildren to visit Pulguksa. The temple had been built, I knew, in 751 and recently reconstructed. Buddhism came to Korea out of China in the fourth century. It was rich in Mahayana Buddhism with its heavens and hells, its saviors, saints, bodhisattvas and high tolerance for local variation. Pulguksa reflected that tradition. The temple grounds are extensive, built into the hillside and quite peaceful, a rich, complex set of buildings with curving eaves, thickly bracketed, the interlocking, elaborately carved rafters and the wooden pillars painted in bold reds and greens. Inside, tourists were inspecting the weathered pagodas, peering into prayer rooms and the halls where elegant gilt bronze figures sat in the lotus position against brilliantly colored walls. I was not, for some reason, very interested. And neither were the children who began to take turns presenting themselves to me, bowing and saying with great formality, 'Hello, very pleased to meet you.' When I replied, they would run back into their pack of friends, issuing shrill peals of laughter.

I found a guard who spoke some English and he directed me to the hill path, insisting, however, that I should take the bus; it was much too far to walk.

It was, in fact, about five kilometers up the mountain, Toham-san, with wonderful westerly views of the town and the rice fields and the hills on the other side of the valley. The first two or three hundred yards were paved with small squares of worn granite, grass growing up thickly between, with wildflowers in the gullies and shrubs that looked like mulberry on either side of the trail. Soon, however, I was in the forest and felt a flicker of déjà vu. Korea is on the same latitude as Virginia and North Carolina. The landscape felt at first like hollows I had hiked in the southern

part of the Blue Ridge mountains, but the differences were dramatic: soft, deep dust on the trail that had been walked for twelve hundred years; the terraces of rice paddies glimpsed in the distance through spiky pine branches and Japanese maples and gingko-like trees with large palmate leaves; an old gray stone wall on the left side of the trail; and on the steepest parts, granite steps. Lots of wildflowers. A deep forest smell. Tangles of what looked like wild grape in the undergrowth.

I kept seeing birds that looked almost familiar, just as the trees and flowers looked almost familiar. I knew this was the sheer variety and abundance of the gene pool, but it felt as if I were walking in a parallel universe, more ancient than the one I was used to, and more strange: a small woodpecker with a speckled back and a bright yellow head; a chickadee with a black bib and a black stripe down the middle of its white breast; a small finch-like bird, fawn- or copper-colored with delicate black markings over its eye; a lizard with pale blue skin sunning on a rock; everywhere, but rarely visible, a large jay, larger than a magpie, with a buff head, speckled wings and a hoarse cry like the laughing sound a raven makes; and wherever there was water, a wild rose – it looked like a Point Reyes thimbleberry bush but the flowers were a fine, pale lilac.

The shrine itself was an unnerving experience. The trail had taken me over the peak and curved around to the southwest-facing side of the mountain, where it connected with the trail from the parking lot. And then, perhaps fifteen minutes down the road, in a clearing that provided a sudden view of the Sea of Japan glittering in the distance, there was what appeared to be a one-room cottage with sloping eaves wedged into the face of the mountain. It looked like a hermit's shack in an old scroll painting. Sokkuram means Stone Buddha Hermitage, and the little cottage served as an entrance to the grotto. You cannot go all the way in – the main figure having been recently glassed off from the public – but just inside the door, framed by the arch of a short tunnel, this Buddha, Sakyamuni, the young prince, sits, carved out of granite and hugely calm.

The cave is manmade. They must have hollowed out the hillside and then piled up stone slabs until they had fashioned a kind of Norman arch. You walk down the short passageway past guardian figures carved into the wall. They are, I read later in the guidebooks, among the most exquisitely carved bas-reliefs in Asian art, but I hardly noticed them. I was looking at the figure of Buddha, large, about three and a half meters high, eyes closed, right hand resting on his leg, left hand, palm open, in his lap – deeply peaceful, terrifyingly peaceful, so that in the split second of seeing it I had felt my own spirit as a kind of frenetic wind-up toy. I wanted to lay it all down, yearning, grief, anger, operatic sadness, my ragged and insistent passion – the whole idea that something could complete me. I wanted to set it down and leave it there. And I knew that I couldn't do it.

I went outside again. The view across the miles of fields and pine-covered mountains to the sea was hazy, evanescent. There were a few tourists around, all Korean. Most of them stood, like me, silently gazing across the miles toward water. It was intensely quiet. There were slim maples planted against the hermitage and you could hear them rustling against the eaves when the wind came up. My heart hurt. I tried to absorb the information that I was deeply attached to what I was, even if it made me miserable. I had

wanted some brilliant, vindicating spiritual experience; my heart leapt toward it like a dog greeting its master. But this master didn't pet you. It sat still, concentrated, turned inward toward unimaginable freedom, scarcely imaginable peace.

Then I did laugh. There was a sign, in Korean, Chinese, English and Japanese, which said that this figure of Buddha, one of the wonders of the world, faced east toward the rising sun to guard the Silla Kingdom against marauding Japanese pirates. It was the older generation at work again, nailing down the political lesson. They had gotten it wrong, just as I had. This Buddha watched marauding pirates, and the rise and fall of empires, and North Koreas and South Koreas, and economic miracles, from some place in which they all seemed old, sorrowing, repetitive. If he faced outward at all, he simply faced toward the sunrise, toward the endless freshness of the coming into being of things.

When I went back to the hermitage from the opposite side, there was a young girl at a table in the entry. She was doing algebra with a turquoise felt pen. I suppose she was a park ranger; she got up, beckoned me into the cave and slid back the glass door. This time I walked up to the Buddha. He seemed immense, a large lotus carved into the dome above his head, a small one, flame-like, on the floor before him. Many bodhisattvas were carved into the surrounding walls, very simple figures, beautifully plain. I looked up at Sakyamuni. I felt sad and tired, happy to be in that presence.

When I left, and walked back down the mountain in the setting sun, the birds active in the last light, the rice fields almost gold, I tried to think what had happened to me. Nothing I could name. I knew I had been in a very powerful place. And I felt as if

I had been punched very hard in the chest. It was a sobering, not entirely unpleasant sensation. Going down the mountain in the sunset, listening to the jays cackling in the trees, I felt obscurely cheered up.

It was eight o'clock in the evening when I got back to the hotel. I got in a cab and headed for Kyongju. The cab driver, plump, fleshy, mildly hilarious, spoke no English. I didn't know where I was going. He seemed to think 'anywhere' was a particular place, maybe, since I made gestures of eating, a restaurant, and he tried to indicate that he would take me there if I would only pronounce it more clearly. He also stopped at every country bus stop to negotiate fares with the people waiting for the bus. Two women got in, one with a baby. Then an old man and an old woman. There was much animated talk and laughing. The word 'anywhere' kept coming up in various pronunciations. Finally, in the middle of town, the car stopped. They all piled out and gestured for me to get out. One of the women pointed up the street. 'Is Korean custom,' she said. I got out, paid him, waved them all goodbye and found myself in the middle of the night market.

It looked like an English market day crossed with a flea market crossed with an American carnival or county fair. It was jammed with people. The stands, on either side of the street, sold everything from dried squid to woolen socks and pocket calculators. There were games: bingo, ring toss, shooting galleries. I found my way to the open tents where food was being served, pancakes made from corn flour and roasted baby chicks split in half and soaked in ginger and soy sauce. I ordered two pancakes, one chick and a bottle of rice wine, and sat down at an outdoor table. There were several Korean guys in baseball hats, drinking and singing at the next table. I watched them for a while to see if you ate the bones of the baby chicks. You did. I watched the crowd surge through the narrow alley, Saturday night strollers, buying things, all kinds of things, fish, flesh, fowl, try-their-luck. The food arrived. It looked unbelievably good. I was back in the world, I thought, and remembered the birds in the parallel universe on the path to Sokkuram and the silence and power of the figure in the cave, the purity and the quiet.

The waitress returned with a little paper packet of roast silkworms. On the house. She pointed at a shy boy at the next table and bit her lip before proceeding very deliberately. 'My friend is so exciting only to have this opportunity to speak practical English and having sharing Korean culture.' I understood. He was treating me to the silkworms. We were going to argue about politics. I ordered another bottle of wine and gestured him over. He sat down opposite of me. Two of the waitresses joined us. The silkworms tasted vile, and I smiled gratefully trying to get one down. The girls laughed and the wine came. 'Korea,' the young man began, and shook his head. He said the word as if it were a synonym for life. Then he sighed happily and said it again. 'Korea, Korea, Korea.'

Where to stay: An interesting and inexpensive alternative to hotels are the Korean-style inns or *yogwan*. At these, guests sleep in the traditional Korean way – on the floor on a thin mattress called a *yo*, with a quilt-like covering called an *ibul*. Bathrooms are often shared, and meals can be had in the room for an extra charge. Prices run between $6 and $15 per room. The Korea National Tourism Corporation (address below) can supply a list of yogwan throughout Korea.

In Kyongju, a great place to stay is the Han Jin Hotel, run by a very friendly and helpful host who speaks English. Doubles begin at $8 (2-4097 or 2-9679). Near the Pulguksa temple in Kyongju is Sillajang (2-1004/6) and the Kyongju Youth Hostel (2-991/6). In Kyongju town, try Pulguksa Pyoljang yogwan (2-9735).

Home-stays can be arranged through the Korea Tourist Bureau, CPO Box 3533, Seoul, Korea; 011-822-585-4461. At least one member of each family participating in this program speaks English, and breakfast is included in the price of your stay.

Where to eat: Restaurants serving Japanese and Chinese food in addition to traditional Korean fare can be found throughout Korea. Korean meals are buffet-style, with the main courses and eight or nine different side dishes all served at once. One of these dishes is invariably kimch'i, pickled cabbage seasoned with chili peppers.

Koreans like to eat outdoors, and all kinds of food can be sampled in the night markets. Popular drinks are *makkoli*, a rice wine, and *soju*, a strong brandy. Coffee-shops, or *tabangs*, are excellent places to relax and chat.

For more information: Contact the Korea National Tourism Corporation, 510 West Sixth Street, Suite 323, Los Angeles, CA 90014-1395; 213-623-1226/7.

AFTERWORD

These seven examples of successful travel articles are widely varied in tone, setting and subject, but united in their ability to bring a place to vivid life within our minds. We hope these pieces serve as rich illustrations of the principles we have been discussing throughout this book – and of the potential of your own travel writing. We also hope that you took note of how the different service information and fact boxes were tailored to their particular subjects, publications and audiences – these are important parts of the prose package, too.

Now, how do you begin to get your own writing published? We'll explore this territory in Chapter Six.

GETTING PUBLISHED

NEWSPAPERS & MAGAZINES

The three main outlets for travel stories are the travel sections of newspapers, travel magazines and lifestyle magazines with a travel component.

Get a feel for the types of stories they publish. Are the destinations mostly short-haul, long-haul or a mix of the two? Is family travel an important element, or do most stories target the adventurous, independent traveller? Are articles tailored to barebones, mainstream or luxury budgets, or do they cover a spectrum of destinations and options? What is the tone, the approach and the length of the stories? Are most of the articles service pieces, round-ups or destination based? Are there any regular formats that appear each week?

In the UK, for example, the Saturday *Independent* always features a stop-over destination piece called '48 Hours in…' and a two-page spread called 'The Complete Guide to…' If you have some good ideas that could fit such formats as these, you'll be offering copy that you know the travel editor needs each week. Conversely, if you offer a city-break piece that is not in the '48 Hours' format, it is not likely to be considered. Similarly, in Australia the travel pages of papers such as the *Age* and the *Sydney Morning Herald* regularly feature a mix of news and destination pieces, following a clearly identifiable editorial template.

The *New York Times*' travel section includes a half-page personal essay on the penultimate page every week. The length of these essays – 1200–1400 words – is prescribed by the allotted space (and clearly stated in the paper's guidelines), and that space is essentially the only spot in the *Times*' travel section that features essays. So if you send a 2000-word personal essay to the *Times*, you've done yourself a disservice in two ways: you've sent in an essay that's guaranteed to be rejected, and you've signalled to the travel editor that you're not a careful reader of the section, and therefore not a professional travel writer.

Detailed research will pay off. Keep brief notes about the stories your targeted publication has printed. Also make use of the publication's on-line archives – you can search by topic and destination to find any stories similar to the one you're planning to pitch. Such research will enable you to begin a proposal for a piece on Swiss chocolatiers, for example, by saying, 'I'm aware that you published a story on Belgian chocolates a year ago, but…' At the very least, this research will help you tailor your articles to a particular publication. In addition, you will never commit the cardinal sin of offering a travel editor a story which they have just run, and so risk taking a giant step backward in this tricky relationship.

Whether you are targeting a newspaper or a magazine, your first step should be to look on the publication's website for contributor guidelines or a style guide. If this information isn't available on line, ring and request that a copy be posted or emailed to you; in the case of US newspapers, mail a self-addressed stamped envelope (an 'SASE') to the travel editor with a note requesting the guidelines. These guidelines will usually spell out what the editors are looking for in an article and how they prefer to deal with freelance writers. They should also advise on how your submission should be presented, and whether they require accompanying photographs (this is less likely in the UK). Having these contributor guidelines will help you maximise your chances of giving the editors what they want. As examples, we have reproduced the contributor guidelines for the UK's *Wanderlust* magazine and for the Sunday travel section of the US newspaper the *Boston Globe*; see p262 of the Sample Paperwork Appendix.

There are broad differences in the ways writers need to approach and work with newspapers and magazines. There are also significant differences in practice between the UK and the US, while Australian and UK working methods are generally similar. We'll consider these aspects in this chapter, beginning with newspapers.

The UK Newspaper Scene

At the base of the UK's complex newspaper pyramid are the 'freesheets' – local newspapers distributed to every home in a particular area. These rarely carry travel editorial (or, indeed, much editorial copy at all).

At the next level are more than 70 local and regional newspapers – daily or weekly – which are more likely to carry travel stories. Often these papers will be syndicated, but they are always interested in local people doing interesting things, so travel writing opportunities shouldn't be discounted.

The highest circulation newspapers, and therefore those with the highest profile and (usually) rates of pay, are the 'nationals'. These are split into three categories:

▸ The 'red-top' tabloids – the *Daily Mirror*, the *Star* and the *Sun*, and their Sunday counterparts, the *Sunday Mirror*, the *People* and the *News of the World*. Their travel coverage is relatively slim, and is usually handled in-house or by regular freelancers.

▸ Middle-market tabloids – the *Daily Mail*, the *Mail on Sunday*, the *Daily Express* and the *Sunday Express*. These papers have larger travel sections, but again are usually written in-house, by regular freelancers – or by celebrities.

▸ 'Quality' newspapers (previously more commonly called 'broadsheets' because of their larger format, until they began downsizing in 2003) – the *Guardian*, the *Independent*, the *Daily Telegraph* and the *Times*, plus the *Financial Times*. These papers publish their main travel issue on Saturdays, sometimes adding a minor travel section during the week. Their Sunday equivalents – the *Observer*, the *Independent on Sunday*, the *Sunday Telegraph* and the *Sunday Times* – also have substantial travel sections (except for the *Financial Times*, which has a single weekend edition).

A daily paper and its Sunday equivalent are usually compiled by totally different staff; this means that the *Times* and the *Sunday Times*, for example, have separate travel teams and travel editors for you to target. The size of these travel pages or pull-out supplements ranges from four to 40 pages. Wales, Northern Ireland and Scotland also have national newspapers that publish travel stories tailored to their readers' interests.

The US Newspaper Scene

An enormous variety of US newspapers carry some form of travel content; these range from small-town dailies and free weekly city broadsheets to major metropolitan papers. Travel content in the small-town dailies and city broadsheets tends to focus on local getaways; the pay for these pieces is usually minimal, but they do offer writers the chance to get their by-lines in print and to hone their skills.

All major urban newspapers publish travel content on Sunday; some also publish much smaller travel sections mid-week, usually focused on local destinations. The best publishing opportunities are to be found in papers with the largest circulations, which also tend to have the largest travel sections. Such majors include the *New York Times*, the *Los Angeles*

Times, the *Washington Post* and the *Chicago Tribune*. Although these papers publish the largest number of freelance articles every week, and so offer writers the best opportunities to be published, the competition with other freelance submissions is intense. Other newspapers that feature substantial travel sections include the *Boston Globe*, the *San Francisco Chronicle*, the *Dallas Morning News*, the *Miami Herald*, the *Kansas City Star*, the *St Petersburg Times*, the *San Diego Union-Tribune*, the *Philadelphia Inquirer*, the *Seattle Times* and the *Baltimore Sun*. In all, more than 50 papers publish stand-alone Sunday travel sections.

As in the UK, the size of these travel sections runs anywhere from four to 40 pages, depending on the publication, the time of year and the number of advertisements it contains. Opportunities for freelancers vary greatly from paper to paper, and indeed from year to year. It's good practice to regularly analyse how much space is open to freelancers and what kinds of freelance stories are being published.

The Australian Newspaper Scene

Australia has 20 national and metropolitan newspapers, and more than 120 regional and community papers. In general, you'll find the best travel content in the *Australian*, the Adelaide *Advertiser*, the Melbourne *Age*, the *Sydney Morning Herald*, the Brisbane *Courier Mail* and the *West Australian*. Travel is a feature of Sunday editions such as the *Sunday Age*, the *Sunday Herald Sun*, the *Sunday Mail*, the *Sunday Telegraph* and the *Sunday Times*. Travel sections range from four to 24 pages; see the Australian section of the Resources Chapter at the back of this book for details of the various papers' travel section schedules.

Special Sections

Most travel sections feature half a dozen to a dozen 'special' or 'theme' sections a year, presenting an exceptional opportunity for freelancers. Travel editors should include a calendar of special sections in their contributor guidelines; if not, ask the editor to send you a copy.

In the UK, special sections often concentrate on a particular part of the world – more often than not it's somewhere in Europe – and are produced in conjunction with the local tourist board. Typical special sections in the US include Cruising, Mexico, Hawaii, Family Travel, Europe and the Caribbean. In Australia the sections focus on regional and seasonal fare such as snow or other activity-based holidays, mid-winter breaks and European, Asian and domestic destinations.

The themed sections are planned a year in advance, in conjunction with the papers' advertising sales staffs – if the sales team know that a specific section will be devoted to Hawaii, for example, they will have extra leverage to try to persuade a Hawaiian hotel owner to buy an ad in that section. The editorial content in these sections is not directly linked to the specific advertisers (that is, if a particular resort purchases an ad, this does not oblige the editor to publish a story about it), but the editor is obliged to put together a package of stories around that section's theme.

This is where your opportunity comes in. If you know that a particular newspaper will be publishing a special section on a particular date, you'll also know that the travel editor will be sourcing content specific to that destination or theme. In the UK you would contact the travel desk two to three months before publication with a proposal for a couple of articles; in the US you would send in two or three of your best relevant stories three months before the section's publication date.

Themed sections offer particularly good opportunities to publish niche, off-the-beaten-track or reflective essay pieces – an article on studying the hula, for example, or hiking a remote but rewarding trail. It's a good idea to request special section calendars from all the newspapers you're interested in and take full advantage of the expanded editorial possibilities they offer.

Pitching to Newspapers

Travel editors are very busy people. In addition to travelling and writing (they often provide a weekly column and/or a few big stories each month), they also commission, edit and select the content for the weekly travel section; attend weekly editorial meetings; deal with advertising departments; process paperwork; read manuscripts (and return them if they have time); liaise with art and photography departments; and much more. The result of this busy schedule is that although travel editors might like to deal in a humane way with freelance writers, they don't always have the time. The hard truth is that they are not going to call you up and offer advice on how to improve your submission. Basically, if you submit a story to them, they'll read what you've written and if it is a good fit, they'll take it; otherwise, they'll reject it. Do not expect more than that.

Pitching to UK Newspapers

In the UK there are three main ways of pitching a story or a proposal to a newspaper.

UNSOLICITED SUBMISSION

This is when you send a completed article to a travel editor or travel desk out of the blue, on the off chance that they'll publish it. You have little idea whether your story is of interest, whether it fits with future publishing schedules or if a similar article is due to be run this week or is in the pipeline. For all these reasons, this method offers the least likelihood of publication. For you it is also the least financially astute because you've incurred all your costs upfront with absolutely no idea if you'll be able to sell what you have written. In addition, you can send that article to only one newspaper at a time, unless you make it absolutely clear that you are offering it to more than one, and let the other(s) know once it has been accepted; this kind of multiple submission is usually only advisable for a time-sensitive story. Complicating matters further is the fact that travel editors often sit on submissions for months before you learn that it will never be used, or you open up the paper one day and discover that it has been published. On the other hand, there is always the extremely slight chance that your unsolicited article is just what the editor needs to fill an unexpected gap in the travel pages next weekend.

ON SPEC

To avoid many of the unknowns in the first scenario, you could submit your article 'on spec'. To do this, you need to contact the travel editor or travel desk before you travel (or at least before you write) with some story ideas. Most travel editors prefer to receive these proposals by email or post but one or two prefer to be rung; check the contributor guidelines to see if their preference is stated. If the editor likes one of your angles, and can see where it might fit in their paper, they'll ask to see the article when it's finished, but with no obligation. If they like the finished article, they'll publish it. This is a good deal for you and a good deal for them. You know that the editor is interested in publishing your article, assuming your writing is up to scratch. They know that they'll get a story, and if it isn't what they want they won't have to pay you for it. Many freelance travel writers work this way until they've built up a relationship with a travel editor. Of course, after you've written a few articles on this basis, you become more of a known quantity and the travel editor will have enough faith in your abilities to give you a paid commission.

Be warned, however: no travel editor wants to be contacted with vague proposals that haven't been thought through. If you tell them that you're off to Finland, for instance, and ask them if they want a story, you're likely to be told that Finland is a country, not an article. If you are going to Finland, think of a few angles or ways to treat a story that would suit the newspaper you're targeting.

COMMISSION

This is the goal of every travel writer: you come up with an idea that the travel editor likes enough to guarantee that they will publish your story and pay you for it. A paid commission also means that you will have little trouble arranging free facilities such as flights, rental cars and hotels, because the paper's travel desk will usually give you a letter outlining the arrangement (for more information on free facilities etc see the Press Trips & Freebies section opposite). Sometimes, particularly if you have proved your reliability, the desk will contact you and ask you to write a specific piece, though this tends to happen only with the most regular contributors.

Pitching to US Newspapers

For the vast majority of US newspaper travel editors, there is only one way to pitch your story: write it and send it in. The only newspaper travel section in the US that welcomes query letters rather than complete submissions is the *New York Times*. You can read the *Times*' editorial guidelines at www.nytimes.com/ref/travel/SUBMISSION.html.

When you submit your story to a newspaper, enclose a cover letter pithily describing what the story covers and any special experience or expertise you may have that makes you better qualified to write this story than any other writer (ie, 'The enclosed article about where to find and buy the best Japanese pottery synthesises what I learned in the past five years living in Kyoto…'). If you have other writing credits, you should mention those in your cover letter as well. Unless otherwise specified, travel editors in the US still prefer to receive submissions by post rather than email.

Many writers enclose a self-addressed envelope or postcard with their submissions. This is a courtesy for overworked editors, saving them the time of copying the writer's address; the editor can write a quick note on the postcard or stuff a pre-printed note into the envelope. Some writers put three options on the postcard which the editor can simply check, minimising the work even further. For example:

Article: Exploring Korea
1. I plan to use this article on _____.
2. I am holding this article for further consideration.
3. I cannot use this article.

The editor simply ticks the relevant option. Such time-saving gestures may seem trivial, but when you consider that many travel editors receive more than a hundred unsolicited submissions a week, you realise that the amount of time required to scribble all those addresses and notes adds up very quickly. Editors appreciate the gesture and the professionalism it embodies.

In the US, the phrase 'on spec' does not carry the same weight as it does in the UK. If a US travel editor says, 'I'll be happy to consider your story on spec,' it does not necessarily mean that they think your story has a good chance of being published. It means: 'If you send it to me, I'll read it, no strings attached.' Period. Also, note that policies and practices regarding press trips and freebies in the US are extremely different from those in the UK. See the section on Press Trips & Freebies opposite.

How long should you wait to hear about your submission? If you haven't heard back within three months, send a follow-up postcard checking to make sure that the editor received your piece and inquiring about its status. If you don't hear anything for another month or so, consider that the piece has fallen into the vortex of travel editor hell, and move on.

Press Trips & Freebies

Journalists will sometimes be offered an all-expenses-paid trip to a particular destination arranged by travel companies such as tour operators or government tourism organisations, usually in association with an airline. Such press trips can involve travelling with three to 15 journalists and a PR (public relations) consultant: you all fly out together, you all stay in the same hotel, and you are all expected to follow the same pre-arranged itinerary (lunches, dinners, museum and carpet-shop visits etc). A good press trip will build in plenty of free time for journalists to explore the destination independently, so that any ensuing articles won't be based on exactly the same experiences (but not all press trip organisers are so imaginative or enlightened). The sponsors will be hoping that the writers will write favourable stories about the destination or tour for their various publications.

Press Trips in the UK

The press trip has long been an integral part of the UK's travel journalism scene, and most travel editors receive a dozen or so such invitations each week, asking them to nominate a writer.

Many publications prefer not to use pieces based on press trips because they want their writers to take a more independent approach than is often possible on such a subsidised trip. Also, they don't want to run the risk that another publication – whose writer also accepted the press trip – might publish the story ahead of them. Regardless, hundreds of press trips are taken by staffers or freelance journalists each year.

Before a journalist agrees to go on a press trip, it is important for every party – the writer, the publication and the benefactor – to agree on the credit that will be given to the organisations that are providing facilities. This is often less of an issue for tourist boards (who are generally happy simply to see their country/region/city in print), but is of considerable concern to commercial firms. Some publications will mention that 'Joe Bloggs travelled as a guest of Soaraway Vacations, which has holidays to the Costa Brava from £299', but will then go on to suggest other companies. It is very unlikely that an editor will agree to an 'exclusive' mention, although some airlines issue formal contracts to this effect.

FREE FACILITIES

While UK publications rarely pay travel expenses, it's also true to say that very few UK travel writers pay for their own travel. When travel journalists receive a commission from a newspaper or a magazine, it is commonplace for them to negotiate free facilities with tourist boards, airlines, hotels, tour operators and car rental companies, on the understanding that some sort of credit will be given in print.

These freebies exist because travel organisations believe they will gain more of an impact from money spent on a journalist than if they were to spend the cash on advertising – there is even an industry term, 'equivalent advertising spend', which means an estimate of what it would cost in advertisements to procure the same level of media coverage. The effect is to help the journalist make a living.

Press Trips in the US

This is a hot issue in the US these days. Twenty-five years ago press trips were an accepted part of the business of travel writing. They were seen as ways to broaden editorial horizons at minimal expense, and as excellent perks for otherwise under-rewarded staffers.

Since then, however, acceptance of subsidised travel of this kind has changed dramatically because of the all-important issue of impartiality. Most publications do not allow their own staffers to take press trips or to accept freebies, and many do not accept freelance articles that have resulted from accepting such perks.

The development of a special discount rate called a press rate has further complicated matters. This is a reduced rate that sponsors will often offer to writers who want to participate in a trip but who have to show that they have paid for the trip. Essentially, it was developed as a way to get around prohibitions on press trips. Press rates can make an absurdity of the whole situation. For example, if you pay $25 or even $250 for a $2500 trip, is that more valid than getting it for free? It's a tremendously delicate and complicated issue – but the best thing is to be as honest and upfront with your editor as possible, and to be clear about the publication's guidelines and policies. Sometimes the publication's policies on press trips and freebies will be spelled out in their contributor guidelines, but if you are in any doubt whatsoever, be open and honest about the situation before you find yourself in a predicament you could later regret. A few publications still rely on press trips to supplement their own meagre travel budgets, so it is essential to know a publication's position on this issue before you accept any travel offers.

It's not unheard of for sponsors to insist on reviewing any articles that result from the press trip, prior to publication. This is absurd and you should never agree to any such conditions. If a sponsor wants you to go on their trip, they need to give you editorial freedom. Equally, although you need to write your story based on your observations, you also need to ensure that your description isn't coloured by any special treatment you may have received. In most cases, it's futile to write about experiences that would not be available to the general traveller.

Objectivity

Both press trips and freebies introduce the thorny issues of objectivity and impartiality. If a hotel has given you a free room, how objective can you be in assessing it and writing about it? If an airline has flown you across the ocean in business class, won't that prejudice the way you think about the company? Integrity is the editorial bedrock. If you take a press trip, or negotiate free or discounted accommodation or services, you must not feel obliged to write a favourable piece just because someone else is paying your way. Your story will be judged – and your reputation as a travel writer will be based – on your integrity; your primary obligation is to the reader.

Making Contact with Newspapers

A decade ago, snail mail was the standard method of contacting a travel editor with an unsolicited submission or a proposal. These days, however, it is more difficult to know how to proceed because each travel editor has their favourite way of being contacted. Some like to be emailed with submissions or proposals, but might dislike attachments (which clog up their mail box) and prefer the text to be in the body of the email. Others still like to be contacted by post. Very few travel editors want to be contacted by telephone, unless you have built up a relationship with them (and whatever you do, don't call on press day – usually Wednesday, Thursday or Friday – as you'll definitely get short shrift).

Read the contributor guidelines to see if there is a preferred method for submissions. If this information isn't available, play it safe for your first submissions and send them by post. Once you are known to the travel editor or travel desk, you'll most likely be asked to submit your proposals by email.

Rights & Syndicating Your Stories

In order to augment their earnings, many freelance writers syndicate their stories, selling one article or story multiple times. This happy scenario is much more likely to occur in the US than elsewhere, however.

Syndication in the UK

It is normal for a freelance writer to offer an article to a UK newspaper with First British Serial Rights; this is also true for UK magazine submissions. This means that the writer is giving the publication the right to be first to publish their article in the UK. In theory this allows the writer to re-sell the piece later to someone else, either in the UK or abroad, in which case they might be selling Second British Serial Rights or Second EU Serial Rights.

In reality, however, if a newspaper or magazine publishes your piece, it will usually expect to retain syndication rights to your article for a specified period. Some publications will ask writers to sign a contract; others will either verbally, or merely on their website, say that you are bound by their conditions of acceptance. This means that they reserve the right to sell your article on to other publications in Britain or overseas and keep a percentage of the fee (typically 50 per cent). The prospect of earning more cash for no extra work in this way sounds attractive – but the arrangement is unlikely to be as lucrative as it sounds. Very often your article isn't re-sold by the original publication, and you are powerless to sell it yourself.

SELF-SYNDICATION

It is very rare for writers to re-sell their own travel articles in the UK. This is not only because of the rights situation described above but also for the following reasons:

▸ Most UK newspapers and magazines are national, and so their readership overlaps. As such, you would not be able to sell a travel piece to more than one of them.

▸ As most freelance travel writers tailor an article for a specific slot in a specific publication and its readership, the article simply wouldn't be appropriate for another newspaper, magazine or journal.

▸ In reality it is only regional newspapers that might be interested in a syndicated travel piece. However, this will only be worth your while in terms of payment if you have a regular, nonregionally focused column to sell. Re-selling individual pieces just won't be worth the time it takes to do so. Plus there'd be few takers because international travel isn't usually a topic of interest to a regional newspaper, and local travel would be written by a staffer.

Syndication in the US

The US has five 'national' newspapers, to the extent that they buy first national rights to the stories they publish: the *New York Times*, the *Washington Post*, the *Los Angeles Times*, the *Boston Globe* and the *Christian Science Monitor*. All of the nation's other newspapers buy local rights, which means that they want exclusivity within their circulation area but do not care if your piece appears in a paper outside their area. You would be ill-advised, therefore, to submit your story at the same time to the *Chicago Tribune* and the *Chicago Sun-Times*, or the *Sacramento Bee* and the *San Francisco Chronicle*, because their circulation areas overlap. However, you would have no problems sending the same piece at the same time to the *San Diego Union-Tribune* and the *San Francisco Chronicle*. This is called simultaneous submission and most newspaper travel editors in the US recognise that, given the low fees they pay, simultaneous submission is a necessity of freelance life. It is a courtesy but not a necessity to inform an editor in your cover letter if you are simultaneously submitting a story.

The vast majority of freelance writers who sell their stories more than once practise self-syndication. That is, they develop a list of travel editors – anywhere from 10 to 50 – to whom they routinely submit their stories. Well-organised writers have a stack of computerised mailing labels ready to be stuck on envelopes and sent off to their targeted publications. A timely, well-written story may be published by 10 papers, or sometimes even more. Preparing and keeping track of these submissions is both time- and energy-consuming for the writer, and for every story that gets picked up by 10 papers, there are two dozen that may get published by one paper or by none at all. Still, writers who make significant earnings from their newspaper writing all practise some form of self-syndication.

The other syndication option that tempts freelancers is the notion of selling their work through one of the national syndication agencies. The top agencies include King Features Syndicate, Scripps Howard, Knight Ridder, Tribune Media Services, New York Times Syndicate, Hearst News Service, United Media, Universal Press Syndicate, Copley News Service, Newhouse News Service and Gannett. If you peruse newspaper travel sections, you will often see these agencies credited under the by-lines of different writers. The truth, however, is that almost all of these agencies do not accept submissions from freelancers. When you see an agency credited, this means that the writer works for a newspaper that belongs to this syndication group.

The only syndicates that even consider freelance stories are Copley News Service (www.copleynews.com) and Universal Press Syndicate (www.uexpress.com). If a syndicate accepts one of your stories, they will submit it to all of the newspapers that subscribe to their service. If any papers publish your story, you will receive a percentage – often 50 per cent, though terms vary – of the money the syndicate has been paid for your story. This arrangement will be specified in the contract you will have signed with the syndicate.

A relatively new syndication option is via a website called www.itravelsyndicate.com. Travel writers pay $39 a year to belong to this site, and in return they can post articles on the site and set a publication price for each piece. If an editor publishes a piece from the site, the writer receives 60 per cent of the fee. The articles are organised by author and by geography on the site, making them easier for editors to search for content.

The Newspaper Production Process
The UK Production Process
In the UK, the production process followed by most newspapers resembles a sausage factory. As soon as one issue has been sent to bed, production work begins on the next, but many of the ingredients will have been chosen months ahead.

Most newspapers have an editorial schedule that can sometimes extend a year or more in advance. There will be certain topics coming up that the editors know they will want to cover – for example, a trip to Liverpool in 2010 to celebrate the half-century since the Beatles were formed – and these pegs are the building blocks around which each issue's contents are structured. In March, for example, a newspaper may well include a city guide to Dublin for St Patrick's Day, plus a look ahead to Easter breaks in Britain. In addition to these 'time-sensitive' stories, most publications will also carry a range of articles that complement them:

WRITING FOR NEWSPAPERS

A few important tips to remember when writing for newspapers:

▸ Newspaper travel sections are published 52 times a year. That's a lot of pages to fill each week, which is good news for the freelance travel writer.

▸ Weekly deadlines mean that newspapers need stories that have a current, topical or newsy slant. It also means that there's quite a bit of flexibility – if a big story breaks during the week and you can use your expertise to write a fresh, accurate travel piece about it that the editor likes, the story may be run immediately.

▸ Newspaper picture desks tend to be less fussy than magazines about the quality of display photography. This means that if you are a competent photographer as well as a good writer, there is the possibility that you will sell both your story and its accompanying photos. If you have photographs, it is always worth indicating in your proposal or unsolicited submission that you can provide them if required. If you think your photos might help sell your story, by all means submit some representative shots with your text. If you have taken transparencies, make duplicates of half a dozen of your best shots and send them in with your story. Don't send in your original slides, as you'll probably never see them again. If you have taken prints, send in a varied portfolio of six to 10 of your best shots. In the UK it's best to submit sample digital photos on a CD and make it clear that you don't need it back.

– Charlotte Hindle

a long-haul beach holiday, for example, or an overland expedition in Africa. Space can always be made for late-breaking stories, however. If a dengue fever epidemic threatens travellers to Indo-China, or an airline fares war creates incredible bargains for city-breaks, many editors will want to replace a planned story with a fresh article. This is one reason why you may not be told that your piece is definitely being used; weary travel editors try to manage expectations, and a good way to avoid having to call a freelance contributor to say their story has been postponed is by never having made any promises in the first place.

Most of an issue's 'raw' copy will not be read in detail until the previous issue has been finished. Press day, when electronic images of all the pages are transmitted to the print site, is Thursday for travel sections published in national newspapers on a Saturday. For the Sunday travel sections, it can be anything from Thursday to Saturday, depending on how the newspaper prints its different components. Typically, the travel editor will start to look at the stories for the following weekend on Friday morning. They will probably begin with the longer and more prominent articles: the lead story; the comprehensive round-up (for example, a guide to the best Greek islands or beach destinations for young families); the city-break page. Even at this relatively late stage (as it will seem if you submitted your story months ago), you may be contacted for clarifications, embellishments or even a rewrite. If the editorial team cannot contact you, it is possible that your story will be replaced by someone else's – this is why it is essential to provide contact details (ideally your mobile phone number and an email address that you check regularly). If you plan to be away on a long trip, say so – and call the editor a few days before you leave to remind them that they have a limited window if they need any changes, so perhaps they should look at the story ahead of time.

Some editors merely tidy things up a little; others will restructure a story to their liking. But often they will have to cut back a story to fit the available space, and rarely will you get a chance to review their edit – this is a good reason to make sure you don't overwrite.

Most national newspapers have staff (or, increasingly, interns on work experience) who check telephone numbers and websites – and possibly hotel rates, admission prices and hours. Every writer is allowed a little leeway in getting the odd figure wrong, but if a check turns up more than a few errors your reputation could be jeopardised.

Once the editorial staff are confident that the story is in good shape, it is passed to the designers and sub-editors. They are professionals who are concerned with getting the story to look good and to match the house style. They will lay out the page, 'flow in' the story (usually a simple copy-and-paste job), apply the house fonts and add the 'furniture': the headline, 'standfirst' (sub-heading), captions etc.

When their work is done, a proof copy of the page is printed out. The travel editor, features editor and editor will usually look at it, though only the travel editor is likely to study it in detail. Last-minute changes are made, the issue is transmitted, and the whole circus begins again.

The US Production Process

If an editor in the US decides to use your story, you will most likely receive a phone call notifying you one or two weeks before the piece is scheduled to appear. The editor will tell you when your story is going to be published and how much you'll be paid. Depending on the subject, the editor may also ask if you have any photographs to go with the piece (for which you will be paid an extra fee). Do not expect a lengthy style discussion. Newspaper travel editors do not have the luxury of time or staff to go over minute editing changes; in the case of some especially overworked editors, you'll be lucky if you get the opportunity to go over editing changes at all. If editors want to make substantial changes to your story or have serious questions about the content, they'll tell you.

Many newspapers require freelancers to sign a contract, so you should be notified – and you should sign a contract – before a paper publishes your piece. But not all papers require contracts, and at many of those that do, signing a contract once a year is sufficient, meaning that you may not be notified about your second or third published piece. Still, most editors make a great effort to notify writers before their pieces are printed. In the worst case, you will find out when you're paid. (Such 'worst cases' are rare; many newspapers now require writers to send in an invoice before they are paid, so at the very least, the editor or someone from the paper's staff will contact you to request an invoice.)

In general, weekend travel sections are edited on Monday and Tuesday and 'put to bed' by Wednesday or Thursday. Editing will be sharp, quick and usually minimal; fact-checking of only the most potentially troublesome facts – such as phone numbers and prices – will be performed. This is an important detail to note: travel editors in the US rely absolutely on writers to get their facts straight. And if a writer's false 'facts' bring on a deluge of complaining phone calls and emails on Monday morning, you can be sure the editor will not be overly enthusiastic about using that writer's work again.

The Magazine Scene

Magazines with a market for travel stories fall into four basic categories.

Specialist Travel Magazines

These include *Wanderlust*, *Traveller* (the Wexas magazine), *Condé Nast Traveller* and *Sunday Times Travel* in the UK; *Travel & Leisure*, *National Geographic Traveler*, *Condé Nast Traveler*, *Islands*,

Arthur Frommer's Budget Travel and *Town & Country Travel* in the US; and *Vacation and Travel, Luxury Travel, Get Lost!* and *Coast and Country* in Australia.

Trade Magazines

These include the UK and US versions of *Travel Weekly*, Australia's *Travel Week* and the UK's *Travel Trade Gazette*.

Corporate Magazines

The majority of corporate magazines aimed at consumers of travel are in-flight magazines such as British Airways' *High Life*, Virgin Atlantic's *Hot Air*, United Airline's *Hemispheres*, Delta's *Sky*, American Airline's *American Way* and Qantas Airline's *Australian Way*. Leading hotel chains also publish lavishly produced magazines for their customers, as do most train operators, ferry companies and car-rental companies. A number of cruise lines – including Princess, Holland America, Royal Caribbean, Norwegian and Carnival – also publish magazines for their on-board and 'preferred' clientele.

Lifestyle Magazines

The core focus of lifestyle and niche magazines may not be travel, but their content includes a travel element. Examples in the UK include *TNT Magazine, Harpers & Queen* and even *Dogs Monthly*. In the US this spectrum includes high-brow publications such as the *Atlantic Monthly* and *Harper's*; men's/adventure magazines such as *Outside, National Geographic Adventure* and *Men's Journal*; regional and city magazines such as *Caribbean Travel and Life, Coastal Living* and *New York*; bridal and women's magazines such as *Modern Bride* or *Elle*; and subject-focused publications such as *Preservation, Smithsonian* and *Organic Style*. Australian lifestyle magazines with travel content include *TNT Magazine, Inside Out, Vogue Entertaining and Travel* and *Australian Gourmet Traveller*.

The editorial requirements of these publications will differ sharply, and your approach should, as always, be clearly targeted. Specialist travel magazines provide the most promising opportunities, because of their robust appetites for travel stories. Trade magazines are much less useful, unless you have an inside knowledge of the workings of the industry; they would be far more interested in a story on new developments in Cuban resorts, for example, than in pursuing the trail of Che Guevara. Corporate airline magazines provide more encouraging opportunities, particularly for features on the destinations they serve – whether Asian beaches for an international airline, American festivals for a domestic US carrier or British cities located along a main railway line. Numerically, lifestyle and niche magazines take up the most space on the shelves, but they can be tricky to sell to – often their modest travel needs are looked after by a small team of regular freelancers or in-house contributors. However, the range of these publications does offer some alluring possibilities for freelancers, especially in the US; as always, the better you know the publication, the better your chances of pitching the perfect article.

Front-of-the-Book Stories

In the trade, the three parts of a magazine are called the front-of-the-book, the well or middle-of-the-book, and the back-of-the-book.

The 'front-of-the-book' refers to the section of the magazine that appears between the Table of Contents and the feature stories. In this section, along with all the advertisements, you'll find snappy reports of hot hotels, spas, restaurants, bars or boutiques that are just opening in a major city; new galleries or museums; inventive and useful new travel products; and noteworthy news such as a major museum moving to a new location or a change in a venue's status – a new owner, new chef or multi-million-dollar renovation. Slightly longer pieces might include destination news updates or issues-oriented reports.

The 'well', or 'middle-of-the-book', is where you'll find the juicy 2500- to 4000-word feature articles illustrated by lavish photographs. These are the high-profile stories that sell the magazine each month.

The 'back-of-the-book' is reserved for promotions, a few round-up pieces and classified advertisements.

The best way to break into magazines is to start off by writing front-of-the-book stories. Some publications require proposals for these; others are happy to read the entire piece (after all, the proposal may be as long as the piece) – usually this will be spelled out in the contributor guidelines. These days the path to magazine writing success most often proceeds this way. You write a few of these front-of-the-book pieces, get your name published in the magazine, establish a relationship with an editor at the publication and lay the groundwork for further, possibly larger, commissions. You do these well and, after a year or two, you start working on a 'favoured-writer' basis, which eventually results in a big middle-of-the-book feature. You do that well, and you're on your way. Many successful writers have followed this exact path to develop working relationships with different magazines. Never underestimate the power of the front-of-the-book story.

As front-of-the-book stories generally run from only 150 to 300 words, it's important to remember that the subject has to be just right. You have to hit the bull's-eye with your proposal or story, so it's essential to study the front-of-the-book pieces closely to see what the editor is looking for. Unfortunately, it's harder to write 250 words than 2500 words. Every single word has to pull its own weight, yet you need to use zingy language and precise colourful details to convey some feeling for your subject and still get the essential information across. The answer is to edit, edit and edit some more.

The good news is that front-of-the-book stories offer an excellent opportunity to write about your local area. Keep your eyes and ears open, and join a few local travel industry–related mailing lists to ensure that you know what's coming up in your region. And remember, a story that may seem well known to you may be intriguing news to an editor at a publication in another part of the country. Another point to keep in mind is that it's never too early to pitch a story to a national magazine. Editors know about most significant tourism developments before they even break ground. Don't wait until that great new resort or museum opens to propose a story on it; pitch your piece as soon as the plans are announced. Otherwise you're likely to be told, 'Oh yes, we know all about that. We've already commissioned it.'

Pitching to Magazines
Pitching to UK Magazines
In the UK, pitching a story to a magazine is a very similar process to pitching to a newspaper (see p136). However, there are some critical differences between the two types of publications to bear in mind before shaping and submitting a proposal or story.

LEAD TIMES

Magazines work much further in advance than newspapers. Printers' and distributors' deadlines often dictate that the final page proofs are signed off a month before the edition hits the streets. As a result, most magazines have a much longer planning horizon than newspapers – some editors know the main ingredients of their magazines up to 12 months in advance. If you want to write an article with a Christmas angle, for example, you'll need to submit your proposal in February or March.

SUBJECT

Because of these long lead times, it isn't a good idea to base an article around a subject that is highly topical and potentially time-sensitive, as it won't be current when the magazine appears on the shelves. The reason that some magazines appear to be up to date when we buy them is because their writers have become adept at predicting and anticipating travel trends. For example, when the latest group of countries joined the European Union on 1 May 2004, there was a corresponding flood of articles on countries such as Slovenia and Estonia. It had been known years in advance that these countries would be joining on that day, but a clever editorial strategy made these magazines appear timely.

PHOTOGRAPHY

Magazine publishing has a strong photographic component. At its most extreme this could mean that a magazine might turn down your examination of the best choices for changing money because it just isn't interesting visually. They might also reject a good story because the photography will be too expensive (words are cheap in comparison with the photo shoots which are needed for magazines such as *Condé Nast Traveller*).

EDITIONS

Magazines are usually published monthly, which means there are far fewer pages to fill each year in comparison with newspapers. However, there are literally thousands of magazines out there, so that has to be good news.

Pitching to US Magazines

Pitching a story to a US magazine is done by writing a query letter. The query letter is your foot in the door, and as such it's your chance to impress the editor with your perceptiveness and your prose.

Your query letter should be no longer than one page and should propose no more than three article ideas. It should be a pithy, provocative and compelling condensation of your story, illustrating how well you know the magazine you're pitching to, how vividly you can bring your particular idea to life, and why you are particularly suited to writing the best story on this topic. Your letter should always include details of any experience or expertise you might have that distinguishes you from other writers. It can also help to enclose copies of your previously published articles (known as 'clips') – especially articles that are similar in style, subject or tone to the one you're proposing, and that have appeared in reputable publications.

When writing your pitch, it's vital to keep in mind everything you have learned about the publication you are targeting. What kind of tone, angle and subject do they prefer? In addition, think about what might actually help to *sell* the magazine – most editors will tell you that writers rarely give this all-important aspect any consideration, proposing stories that interest *them* rather than stories that will interest a particular publication's readership.

SAMPLE US MAGAZINE QUERY LETTER

Here is a query letter I sent to the articles editor of the US magazine *Signature*, which resulted in a feature assignment.

Dear Ms Shipman

Every month Signature *presents a mix of stories that takes readers beneath the surface and behind the scenes of countries and cultures around the world. One subject that I have not yet seen covered in your magazine – and that I think would intrigue and enrich* Signature's *readers – is a new travel option in Kyoto, Japan: Travellers can now spend the night at a Buddhist temple in the heart of the city. In marked contrast to staying at a hotel, spending the night in a temple can open up entirely new aspects – and bestow an entirely new appreciation – of this ancient capital.*

I know this firsthand because I recently spent an exhilarating night at Myokenji Temple, about 20 minutes from Kyoto's main train station. This night was the highlight of my two-week journey through Japan this spring, and I would like to write about it for Signature.

The article I have in mind would focus on my own experience at the temple: I would describe first impressions of the clean, serene space; a meeting with the koan-quoting, baseball-loving head monk; a glorious evening encounter on the temple's grounds, when the past seemed to spring to life; and an enlightening immersion in incense and chants at a pre-dawn service the following morning.

This little-known alternative is open to all travellers, and I would detail the practicalities as well as the poetry of a temple stay, telling readers exactly how to arrange such a visit, and how to behave at the temple itself.

My own experience in Japan is extensive. I lived in Tokyo from 1977–79 and have visited the country every two years since. I have written about Japan for a variety of publications, including the San Francisco Examiner & Chronicle *and* Winds *magazine, and I speak Japanese fluently. (This is not necessary to enjoy the temple experience, however.)*

Thank you for considering this article proposal. I look forward to hearing from you.

– Don George

SIMULTANEOUS SUBMISSIONS

It is virtually impossible – and definitely not recommended – to send simultaneous queries (that is, copies of exactly the same query letter) to more than one magazine. Your proposal should be closely tailored to fit an individual magazine, and if you are successful, the magazine will be buying exclusive North American Rights. It is absolutely fine to propose quite different stories from the same trip to noncompeting publications (a story on open-air markets for *Saveur*, a hotel review for *Travel & Leisure* and an adventure narrative for *Outside*, for example), but you should not propose the same or similar stories to editorially competing publications.

TIMING

Most magazines close their editorial pages three months before the date on the cover; for example, the contents of the April issue will have been finished in December/January. Editors plan their editorial content at least six months, and in many cases twelve months, in advance. Keep this in mind when proposing time-sensitive stories, and don't be late with your proposal. The best rule of thumb is to send in your proposal as soon as it is finished; if you're writing about a once-a-year festival, the editor will determine when they want to publish it. Many magazines produce an annual editorial calendar that outlines the specific themes they will be focusing on, month by month; for example, March might be the Cruise issue, June the America issue, and November the Island issue. As with newspapers, this schedule helps advertising salespeople target potential advertisers. This doesn't mean that an entire issue will be given over to a designated subject, but it does mean that the editors will be producing a substantial package of articles based on that theme. If a magazine you're interested in has such an editorial calendar (and most of them do), request a copy and propose stories based on the relevant monthly themes as far in advance as possible.

ADDRESSING YOUR PROPOSAL

You'll find a listing of a magazine's editorial staff on the publication's masthead, usually a couple of pages into the magazine. The best practice is to write to an editor three or four rungs from the top of the editorial ladder – this person's title will usually be articles editor, features editor, senior editor or travel editor. If you are unsure which editor to write to, address your submission to the editor in chief or managing editor, who will in turn pass it on to their assistant to assess. Another strategy is to find an editor at the magazine who also writes, and whose articles you admire. Send in your article to them, with a note saying how much you enjoyed the piece they wrote for a recent issue – any writer who has struggled to produce a good story will be happy to hear that at least one reader enjoyed it, and this strategy will help get you noticed and read.

Making Contact with Magazines

As with newspapers, the traditional way of contacting magazines in the past was by snail mail, but today preferences vary from publication to publication and even from editor to editor. Check the magazine's contributor guidelines, and if you're in doubt, use the mail.

Presentation

Professional presentation is all-important when sending in proposals and submissions, whether by mail or email.

▸ The content must be logically set out, legible and neatly presented. It sounds obvious, but it's important to spell the editor's name correctly.

▸ It's also vital to ensure that your grammar, spelling and punctuation are correct throughout, as obvious errors and sloppy presentation can lead to a knee-jerk rejection.

▸ Don't try to use fancy fonts or fussy design elements; just present your story in a simple, clean manner, with ample margins (one inch is fine unless otherwise specified in the contributor guidelines).

▸ Some magazines prefer that you double-space your article submissions; check the contributor guidelines.

▸ If you're submitting a completed story, include the following information on the first page: the story's title (which in most cases will not be the title used if the story is published), your name and your contact information (address, home and mobile phone numbers, and email address), and word count. On subsequent pages, type your last name, one word identifying your story and the page number (e.g., George/Delos – 2) in the upper right-hand corner of each page. For the sake of clarity, write 'The End' at the conclusion of the story.

After the Pitch

If you haven't heard back from a magazine after two months, send a follow-up note to check that the editor received your piece, and ask about its status. In as nice a way as possible, mention that if you don't hear something in the next month you'll assume that the editor is not interested and you'll send your proposal elsewhere. If you don't hear anything in the next month, just move on to the next publication. (Of course, you will probably have to rework your proposal to fit that next publication.)

When you do hear back, the response will bear one of two messages: rejection or acceptance. We'll talk about rejection at the end of this chapter (see p159).

A magazine acceptance will take one of two forms: a provisional acceptance or a commission. In the UK provisional acceptances are rare, as British magazines usually use writers who are known to them and who are respected in the industry to write their big stories – which is why it is recommended that you break into magazine publishing by writing front-of-the-book pieces.

Provisional Acceptance

In the US, if an editor is unfamiliar with your work but intrigued by your idea – or familiar with your work and tempted by but not quite convinced about your idea – they may ask you to write the article without a guarantee that it will be published. The editor will go over the approach, length and deadline of the story with you, but will not offer you a firm contract. This is still an excellent opportunity and you should follow through on it.

Commission

This is what every writer hopes for. If an editor is convinced that they want to buy your story, they'll contact you by phone and discuss the story with you, then send you a contract with a cover, or commissioning, letter. If the editor doesn't send you a follow-up letter, it's a good idea to request one. The letter will reiterate what the editor went over with you on the phone: the angle and approach your story should take, the length, your deadline and your fee. Make sure that your deadline is reasonable, given the amount of research and writing you'll need to do and any other dictates of your personal schedule; it's far better to negotiate the deadline at the beginning of the process than to have to ask for an extension at the end. The contract will re-confirm the subject, length and deadline, the rights the magazine is purchasing, the fee to be paid for the article, the amount of expenses (if any) you will be reimbursed for, and the kill fee you will be paid if the article is not published.

RIGHTS

In the UK, magazine and newspaper rights are handled in a similar fashion; see the section on Newspaper Syndication in the UK on p141. When you sell a story to a US magazine, you're generally selling First North American Rights – meaning your story is appearing for the first time in a North American publication. Your contract will usually give you the right to resell the story after a certain amount of time has passed – often 90 days after publication – but you'll need to read the contract carefully to make sure of this. Some magazines also buy foreign rights and guarantee to pay you a percentage of your original fee if the piece is published by one of its foreign siblings. In theory this means that they will try to sell your story to all of their overseas equivalents, but in practice this rarely results in further publications. If at all possible, you'll want to retain the right to republish your work in another magazine, in any future book of your own or in an anthology. You'll want to sign away as few rights as possible.

Always read the contract you're signing. Don't get so overwhelmed or flattered by acceptance that you neglect to read the fine print or decide not to negotiate on points that make you uncomfortable. You may well regret this later. And if you breach your contract, even unwittingly, you will be legally vulnerable.

FEES

As noted in Chapter Two, the UK rate for magazine articles ranges from £150 to £400 per 1000 words; glossy national US magazines generally pay 50 cents to $1 a word for new contributors; and in Australia magazine fees range from a set fee of $350 to 50 cents or $1 per word. If you continue to write for a publication and establish a regular working relationship, or if you become a celebrated writer yourself, your rate will rise accordingly. Some well-known writers in the US, for example, now command $3 a word.

KILL FEES

'Kill fee' is the rather aggressive expression used by the industry to denote compensation that is given when a commissioned article is submitted (or an article sent on spec is formally accepted) and the editor eventually decides not to publish it – that is, to 'kill' it. There can be many reasons for this. It could be because the subject has been overtaken by events – for example, the destination you wrote about has been devastated by an earthquake or disrupted by internal social upheaval. More often it is because of a change in personnel or policy, which means your story is no longer required. The kill fee is usually between 25 and 50 per cent of the fee agreed upon for your story. If you receive a kill fee, you are free to sell the story to another publication; you may sell the story just as it is or rewrite it to suit a different editor and readership.

Working on Commission

When you score a commission, the real work has just begun. Your obligation and goal is to give the magazine what the editor wants. Every article is a compromise between the writer and the editor, but remember that in this relationship, the editor holds the final power to publish or reject your piece. So take the editor's guidance very seriously.

If you find that your story is deviating from what you had agreed upon, call the editor and talk it over. Don't surprise the editor by turning in a story that is completely different from the one they are expecting. The editing process may go smoothly or bumpily, but either way, your job is to work with the editor to make it as smooth as possible. If an editor asks for a major rewrite, make sure you understand why, and what changes the editor is looking for. Occasionally, an editor may ask for so many changes or so drastic a rewrite that you simply can't agree. In this situation you have the right to say you're not going to do the story after all, but this should be a truly last-case scenario. You'll forfeit the money you were supposed to be paid (including the kill fee and any expenses you may have been promised) and also effectively squander any chance of working with that editor again.

The Magazine Production Process

When a magazine editor accepts a story, they will call you to discuss your article. Sometimes the editor will want a substantial rewrite, and will go over the article in great detail with you, paragraph by paragraph and even sentence by sentence, as necessary. At other times the editing changes will be minimal, but again, the editor will discuss them with you in detail. When your story has been reworked and edited to the editor's satisfaction, you will

NETWORKING

The world of travel is small, and knowing the right people is key to establishing yourself as a travel writer. A contact at a tourist board or PR company can be invaluable in helping you get the information or the interview you require. You also need to meet the travel editors or the publishers who might run your articles or be interested in your book.

A feast of launches, parties, dinners and lunches are held regularly by tourist boards, airlines, bookshops, publishers, travel fairs, hotel chains, travel agents and tour operators to promote anything from countries to new airline routes. It is the aim of these companies to invite as many travel editors and travel journalists along to their event as possible in order to generate coverage. To begin with, you should try to attend as many of these functions as you can, as they all offer opportunities for networking. As you become better known, you'll become more discriminating and probably only attend one a month or less. You can receive invitations to these events by joining a company's press mailing lists or by ringing up the marketing department or PR agency handling the event. Networking is exhausting, and there's a real skill to working a room, but making the right contacts, putting a face to a name and establishing a good relationship with a wide range of travel professionals is central to building a successful travel writing career.

If a prominent travel writer comes to town, the odds are good that members of the local travel writing community will turn out to hear them speak; you can make good connections at such events. Other excellent ways to network include joining a writers' organisation, taking a writing class or attending a writers' conference; for more information on courses etc see the Resources section at the back of this book.

I have taught at a number of writing conferences over the past two decades and have always come away with some helpful new piece of information and a life-enriching new contact or two. Fourteen years ago I co-founded the Book Passage Travel Writers & Photographers Conference in Corte Madera, California. Every August this conference brings together approximately 120 students and two dozen faculty members – prominent newspaper and magazine editors, book publishers, literary agents, travel writers, and travel photographers – for four days of workshops, panels and events devoted exclusively to travel writing and photography. This gathering has proven to be an extraordinary launching pad for travel writers and photographers, dozens of whom have emerged from those intensive four days with magazine assignments and book contracts; a number of these alumni have later returned to the conference as faculty members, with numerous published articles and books to their credit. Such conferences can provide an unparalleled opportunity to interact with top-flight writers, editors and publishers – and to meet like-minded travel-lovers from around the world.

Finally, when you are on the road, you should consider virtually everything you do as an opportunity for networking, fact-finding and story-generating. If you're flying somewhere, talk to the ticket agents about how business is doing, and with the flight attendants about great places to see and things to do in the city you're visiting. Taxi drivers are an endless source of anecdotal entertainment and illumination. Hotel concierges and desk clerks can often give you valuable tips about special places in the neighbourhood. All of these opportunities can enhance your life professionally and personally. And one way or another, they can help you distinguish and develop stories that get published.

– Don George

often be sent a copy of the edited version. This is a final opportunity for you to approve the changes or to raise any final concerns, because you will most likely not be sent a final proof of your story as it will appear on the page.

At some point in the editing process, depending on the publication, you may be contacted by a fact-checker or sub-editor. In the US, the fact-checker will ask you to supply materials that corroborate your information – maps, brochures and pamphlets, pages from guidebooks and other source materials, tapes of quoted conversations and the like. The fact-checker or sub-editor will also contact all of the places mentioned in your story – every hotel, restaurant, shop and museum – and will use independent resources to verify every cultural, historical and geographical fact in your story. So, to avoid humiliation and to cultivate an ongoing relationship with the magazine, be sure to do your own scrupulous fact-checking before you deliver your story. The more errors the editors find in your story, the less likely they will be to use you again.

Magazines have a much more elastic publishing timeline than newspapers. For example, your article could be accepted in May and a photographer sent to shoot photos to accompany your piece in June (photographic conditions permitting); the editor would then contact you about editorial changes in the piece in August, and then work on it with you until the end of September. The magazine would go into production in October, close in November – and hit the newsstands in February or March. Because of the lengthy printing process, magazines work on issues many months in advance – and often on three editions simultaneously.

In another scenario, a piece may sit at a magazine for a year – or much longer – before it appears in print. This might be because the magazine is waiting for the appropriate season to publish your article or because the photographs needed to accompany your piece can't be shot until the following year – or quite simply because space is limited and other stories have higher priority due to the volatility of their subject matter or the celebrity of their author. If this is the case, you won't be contacted to fine-tune your work for many more months. In such cases it is wise to maintain a cordial relationship with your editor, periodically checking on the status of your story and pitching new ideas. Above all, don't be precious about your work – once you've submitted your piece, allow the magazine staff to get on with what they need to do to make it publishable without interference. If the wait is sometimes great with magazine publishing, the rewards are usually great, too.

BOOK PUBLISHING

Proposing a Book

There are two possible scenarios when writing a book-length travel narrative: you can either write the whole manuscript and send it to an agent or publisher, or you can pitch your idea for your book to an agent or publisher and, for those lucky few who are successful, get a publishing house on board from the start.

The first option is full of uncertainties: you don't know if a publisher (approached directly or through an agent) will be interested in what you've written and you'll have to fund all the research and writing yourself. Pitching an idea seems a better choice, but it is extremely rare for a writer to pitch a book idea directly to a publisher and have it accepted. The most common – and desirable – path is to pitch your book idea to an agent, who will then aim to rouse the interest of a publisher. If your proposal is accepted by a publisher, they should pay you an advance – money that will hopefully be recouped from the sales of your finished book and will be deducted from your subsequent royalties. This will go some way to keeping you financially afloat while you're working on your book. As discussed in Chapter Two, this might not amount to much but it is better than nothing: it would be roughly up to

£10,000 in the UK, $15,000 in the US or $20,000 in Australia. For listings of publishers who produce travel literature, see the Resources Chapter at the end of this book.

A proposal for a book-length travel narrative is a much more ambitious package than a simple proposal letter to a newspaper or magazine. You will need to send a short covering letter and include a two- to three-page synopsis summarising your book's themes and structure, a table of contents, a sample chapter or two (usually of around 5000 words) and a little biographical information. Your covering letter will need to establish why you believe your topic and perspective are compelling, why the particular company you've targeted should publish your book and why you think your book will sell. An analysis of any recently published books on a similar theme or covering a similar area is also essential, as is your own best indication of the potential audience for your book. You'll also need to send a stamped, self-addressed envelope if you want to have your work returned. Your whole package should look as professional as possible.

The Role of an Agent

Only a very few publishers will consider book proposals and unsolicited manuscripts sent directly from an author. Most book publishers, particularly the larger ones, will only deal with an agent.

Initially, if an agent likes your book and agrees to represent you, they may work with you to strengthen your book editorially, identifying any narrative weaknesses or suggesting ways to smooth out rough spots in your story and prose. Once your manuscript is finished, your agent will target appropriate publishers. Agents know what interests different publishing houses, and also what different editors within those houses are hoping to find, as they develop relationships with editors over time. Rather than blindly sending your proposal into the vast editorial slush pile, an agent will send your book directly to the person who is most likely to be interested in it.

If a publisher is interested in publishing your book, your agent's next task is to represent you and make sure the publisher's contractual terms are as fair and favourable as possible. If your book attracts interest among multiple publishers, your agent will oversee an auction, with a number of publishers bidding for the right to publish your work. They will also advise you as to which publisher is likely to promote your book the most robustly and generally treat you well. As any published writer knows, getting your book published is only half the battle. If the publisher doesn't allocate any resources to promote it, your beloved tome can quickly sink into literary oblivion.

An important part of negotiating your contractual terms concerns the split of foreign-language publication or screen and other media rights. If you're lucky enough to attract the attention of a film production company, for example, an agent will help navigate you through the tricky waters of rights and fees negotiations.

If you do enter into an agreement with an agent, you will sign a contract. The agent will agree to represent you and your work and you will agree not to seek representation with any other agent and to pay the agent a commission (anything up to 15 per cent) if they find a publisher for your work. Usually, the contract will also spell out circumstances under which one or both parties may terminate the agreement and may include the time period of the mutual commitment.

Finding an Agent

Do you need an agent or do you have the skills and knowledge to do all of this yourself? The answer is up to you, of course, but you will most likely save yourself a great deal of hassle and heartache if you can find a sympathetic and enthusiastic agent. These days, however, finding an agent can be as hard as finding a publisher. Lizzy Kremer, an agent for David Higham Associates Ltd in the UK, comments:

Although agencies often indicate that they don't pay any attention to the manuscripts that are sent to them on an unsolicited basis, my experience is that good writing stands out a mile and will be read. If an agent is not interested in representing travel writing, they might not read past the letter. However, you might have to make some of those submissions in order to find the right agent for you. You can call before sending your work but you probably won't gain anything by it. Make sure your submissions are well presented, professional (no long chatty letters) and always enclose a 2–3 page book outline, first few chapters and an SAE. Work hard at getting yourself published in other ways. If you have had articles printed in papers, magazines or websites, enclose those with your book. When choosing your representation, trust your instincts. Go with the agent who seems passionate about your writing. Make sure the agency has a good reputation within the industry by reading up on them in the various writers' handbooks available. You should take as much care as possible when choosing an agent. If you have written something wonderful, the power is in your hands. I take on new clients when two things fall into place – when I love their writing and when I think I can sell the ideas they have. Apart from that I just have to get a sense we would work well together.

Dealing with Book Publishers

If your book is accepted by a publisher, either as a completed manuscript or as a substantially fleshed-out proposal, your authorial job from that point on is to give the company what they want – just as with newspaper or magazine articles, only on a bigger scale. Your agent will stay in touch with you to monitor your progress, but in effect, once the contract is signed, they will hand you and your book over to the publisher's commissioning editor. This editor is your bridge to the publishing house, the internal champion for your work, as well as the person charged with making sure you deliver a publishable and marketable manuscript on time. Deal with your editor judiciously. Fight for what you believe in, but be as professional and easy to deal with as possible. In the long run, you both share the same goal of bringing out the best – and most successful – book possible.

The Book Publishing Process

Depending upon their location and culture, publishing houses are apt to call their production processes and personnel by different names, but the following is a general overview of the book production process.

Once you have delivered your manuscript, meeting contractual obligations such as length, format and delivery date, your work will be assessed, usually by the commissioning editor or publisher. They will either return the manuscript for further work, discussing any problems in detail and setting a later delivery date, or they'll accept it for publication and authorise the disbursement of any payment-on-acceptance monies. On acceptance, your manuscript will enter the publishing company's editorial and design production process. You will be assigned an editor, who in some situations will be the commissioning editor you've already been dealing with, and it is part of your contractual obligation to work cooperatively with them, responding to suggestions and criticisms in an open and understanding manner. As Bill Bryson has said, 'even the most experienced writers need an editor'. Your book may be your baby, but the editor is the midwife, delivering it to your readers.

The editing process includes a structural edit, which reviews your book's themes and narrative, chapter by chapter. The editor will work directly with you to fix major editorial issues that may arise at this stage. Copy editing is sometimes handled by a different editor, who will ensure that all grammar, punctuation and spelling are correct and consistent.

Once the book has been edited, you will be provided with a copy of the revised manuscript, usually delivered by email or couriered parcel. This version will usually be submitted as draft 'page proofs', meaning that the book has been laid out by a designer: design specifications such as fonts and heading weights will have been imposed, and each page of the printout will contain a double-page spread (emulating the final printed book). Any major alterations, queries or problems should already have been discussed with you, and any remaining minor issues will be clearly indicated for your attention in the edited text. At this point you will have a last chance to make corrections and changes, in consultation with your editor. Once you have returned your author corrections to your editor, and your comments and changes have been taken in, the work will be proofread by a second editor.

You may be able to review the manuscript one more time at final proof stage, shortly before the book heads off to the printer, but any changes made at this stage are expensive and strictly limited. You should also be involved in the cover design process and be shown the back-cover text, summarising your book for the reader – but do not expect that you will have final approval; that usually lies with the publisher.

WRITING FOR OTHER OUTLETS

The Internet

The Internet offers an alluring array of outlets for your writing, and venues where you can share your passion for travel with a like-minded community of travellers and writers. But if you want to support yourself financially, the solutions – at this point, at least – are not on line.

Something of a Wild West atmosphere prevails among sites that publish freelance travel pieces, partly because the Internet is still an evolving publishing territory, and because virtually all Internet outlets pay their contributors little or nothing. Some sites, such as the US-based World Hum (www.worldhum.com) and Travelmag (www.travelmag.co.uk) in the UK, attract excellent writing, but do not compensate contributors. Other sites allow writers to post their own pieces, and some writers prefer to create their own sites where they can freely post their oeuvre of articles and weblogs.

The best practice is to follow the same principles as with newspapers and magazines: study the sites you're interested in and learn as much as you can about how they prefer to deal with writers. All submissions are via email, of course, but you still need to get to know the length and type of articles that different editors or producers are looking for.

Send your story to the editor, and if you don't get a response within a month, email them again to check on the status of your piece.

For pointers on how to write for the Internet as opposed to a print newspaper or magazine, see the interview by Anna Sutton, On-line Travel Editor at Telegraph.co.uk, at the end of this chapter. Also see the Resources Chapter at the end of this book for listings of useful websites.

Anthologies

Another print editorial outlet that deserves mention is travel anthologies, compilations of a mix of previously published and original stories by a variety of writers. San Francisco–based Travelers' Tales specialises in anthologies that are focused either geographically or thematically (women's travel tales, food, humour etc). Seattle-based Seal Press publishes themed travel anthologies that feature women contributors. Lonely Planet also produces anthologies that draw on a wide range of contributors, from best-selling travel writers to never-before-published writers.

Most publishers of anthologies announce their upcoming projects on their websites, and post guidelines on the theme and length of the stories they require. While the monetary prospects are underwhelming – most anthologies pay in the range of £50 to £150 for an original story – they do offer good publishing opportunities, especially for narrative pieces. It's good practice to periodically check the websites of the companies mentioned above for updated information on forthcoming anthologies.

Brochures, Catalogues & Newsletters

Travel-related print materials are not restricted to newspapers, magazines and books. Virtually every travel-related company promotes its products in some kind of printed format. Travel agencies and tour operators, airlines and cruise lines, global hotel chains and family-run guesthouses, urban museums and rural galleries, government tourism organisations and regional visitor information offices – all of these organisations produce brochures, catalogues and newsletters, and all of these products need at least one writer and/or editor. It may not be the *Sunday Times* or *Travel & Leisure*, but it's an excellent way to put baguettes and Brie on the table while you're waiting for the big editors to discover you.

You may want to try to find work as a freelancer with one of these companies to maximise your free time and flexibility, or you may want to try to get a staff job to give yourself some financial stability and security. If you discover a travel company of any kind that intrigues you, contact them and see if they need anyone with your experience and abilities, particularly in the areas of public relations, marketing or advertising. Whichever your goal, keep alive to the possibilities all around you. Think out of the proverbial box.

LEGAL MATTERS

Copyright

Any original text that you write as a freelancer is your intellectual property and is automatically protected by copyright; you don't need to register or apply for it. As the writer, you can grant certain rights or licences to publish your work. Copyright lasts for 70 years after your death. For more information about copyright, contact the British Copyright Council (www.britishcopyright.org), the US Copyright Office (www.copyright.gov) or the Australian Copyright Council (www.copyright.org.au).

Electronic Rights

Electronic rights are an extremely thorny issue. When a newspaper, magazine or journal agrees to publish your article in print, they usually expect to have the right to publish your article on its website, without any further payment. This is especially true in the UK, where electronic rights are usually non-negotiable. These issues should be spelled out in your contract or on the outlet's website. Writers' groups make the compelling argument that if a print outlet posts an article on its website, it effectively takes away the writer's ability to sell that article to a Web-only outlet, and that therefore the writer should be paid separately for the Web posting. Most publishers, however, will try to secure all the rights they can for the lowest possible fee.

If you're absolutely determined to negotiate over these matters, in the US at least, enter into those negotiations with a clear sense of what you think your work is worth, what conditions you will accept and what offers are simply unacceptable – but you should also question whether you are hindering your career more than helping it. Each case will be different, depending on the article, the publication and the pay, but it is always best to have a good idea of your priorities and options in advance, and to know exactly what you want to get out of a negotiation.

Contracts

Most contracts, whether for newspaper or magazine articles or for books, are forbidding. They're written by lawyers and in tiny type. Your mind goes numb when you read them. But they spell out your legal obligations and opportunities, so it is extremely worth your while to plough through them slowly and to make sure you understand every clause. If it is a book publishing contract and you have an agent, they'll explain everything to you and endeavour to negotiate the best possible deal. Otherwise, you may want to consult a friend who has dealt with contracts before or, in extreme cases, a lawyer who can explain the fine print. You can also ask your editor to explain points you don't understand.

In theory at least, most UK newspapers and magazines will email you a contract before you start writing for them. Sometimes this contract will last a year or longer. If you write several articles for the same newspaper or magazine, it is rare that you'll receive a contract for each piece you produce. However, there will be times when you won't receive anything at all because staff on the travel desk are just too busy. In the US, magazines send contracts with each article, while most newspapers send annual contracts.

Most newspaper and magazine contracts are standard, and editors are usually extremely unwilling to deviate from the template. The most crucial considerations are your fee (and whether it will be paid on acceptance or on publication), your deadline, the rights they are buying and the rights you retain, and whether a kill fee will be paid if they do not publish your work. Book publishers send their authors very detailed contracts. One detail you'll want to make sure your contract specifies is the percentage of compensation you will receive if excerpts from your book are published in a newspaper, magazine or anthology.

In the UK and Australia you can ask the Society of Authors (www.societyofauthors.org in the UK; www.asauthors.org in Australia) or the Writers' Guild (www.writersguild.org.uk

in the UK; www.awg.com.au in Australia) to check a contract, provided you are a member. A useful book to consult in the UK is Michael Legat's *Understanding Publishers' Contracts*, where you can compare what you've been offered with a Minimum Terms Agreement and learn more about those clauses which should be questioned. *Australian Book Contracts* by Barbara Jefferis is a helpful resource for Australian writers.

In the US, contact the Authors Guild (www.authorsguild.org) and the National Writers Union (www.nwu.org). The resource book *Writer's Market* also has very helpful chapters on contracts, rights and other aspects of the business of writing.

DEALING WITH REJECTION

Rejection is part of the freelancer's life. To survive, you need to adopt a certain Zen attitude, and accept that your stories or proposals will often be rejected. Above all, don't be derailed by the notion that a rejection is somehow personal, a fundamental rejection of you as a writer or, worse, as a human being. Editors are inundated with stories, the vast majority of which they cannot use; they choose the very few that happen to fit into the particular edition they are currently working on. Becoming a published writer is a job, and you have to approach it with a certain steely professionalism. Prepare your work by following the tips in this book, and persevere by continuing to write and submit your proposals and stories.

If you ever do find yourself sinking into the slough of depression, remember that virtually every writer, even the most legendary, has been rejected at some point in their professional life. For example, when he was starting out as a writer, the National Book Award–winning US writer John McPhee submitted dozens of story ideas to the *New Yorker*; each one was rejected. He persevered until they finally accepted one. A few years later he was a staff writer for that renowned magazine – one of the most coveted writing jobs in the US. Rejection is simply part of the process.

In the UK, many newspapers and magazines don't have the time or staff to send you a rejection note and so you're often left in limbo, not knowing what to do next with your unsolicited submission or proposal. To avoid this situation, it's a good idea to send a covering letter with your article or proposal saying that if you haven't received a response within one month for newspapers, or two to three months for magazines, you intend to submit it elsewhere. If you haven't heard from the publication after this amount of time, write a courtesy letter or email telling them that you will now be submitting your story or proposal to other outlets.

In the US, rejection notes, whether from newspapers or magazines, usually come in the form of either a form rejection or a personal rejection. A form rejection is a pre-printed note, thanking you for your proposal, but letting you know that it can't be used. While this method may seem very cold and impersonal, it's just a practicality for most editors. Much as they might want to add a personal note, they simply don't have the time.

A personal rejection is a printed or hand-written note, clearly addressed personally to you. The editor may write that, while they can't use your submission, you should feel free to send in other articles, or that they liked your article but just published a piece on the same subject. Consider this a major victory, and follow up immediately with another submission or proposal, thanking the editor in your cover letter for the encouraging note they just sent you. If the editor opens the door a crack in this way, keep pushing and open it further. Rejections can and do lead to acceptances. You just have to keep knocking – politely but persistently – on the door.

Form rejection letters are often used by book publishers, but if an editor does include any comments, you should review them carefully. Don't bury your manuscript away after the first rejection. Bear in mind that most of literature's greatest success stories were rejected by at least one publisher – and sometimes dozens – before making it into print.

There are some practical tools that will help you get published, which we'll cover in Chapter Seven.

INTERVIEW WITH SARA WHEELER

Based in the UK, Sara Wheeler is the author of several books, including Travels in a Thin
Country: A Journey through Chile *and* Terra Incognita: Travels in Antarctica.

How did you start off in your career as an author of travel literature?

Like many people, I sent off travel pieces on spec, and amassed a robust collection of
rejection letters, until one day, I opened the *Times*, and there was an article I had sent
them on Prague. They had just whacked it in, without getting in touch with me or
anything. That was my first published travel piece.

How did you get your first book published?

I was approached by a publisher.

How long does it take to write your books?

I would say about three years, all told.

Did you have an agent, and how important do you think they are?

I sold my first book myself, then acquired an agent for the second. I have been with the
same agent ever since (about 12 years). I don't think authors should be afraid of having a direct relationship with a publisher without an intermediary – but on the whole
I think it is best to have an agent. I often hear authors complain that their editor has
left and they feel that they have no supporters in-house – that can be lonely, as an
agent will go in to bat for you. Also, an agent with a good foreign rights department
can generate extra income (publishers do it too, but I think agents on the whole are
better at it). America is a crucial part of the economic equation for me, and I prefer to
have two entirely separate relationships – with a UK house and a US house – with an
agent in the middle.

INTERVIEW WITH SIMON CALDER

Based in the UK, Simon Calder is the Senior Travel Editor of the Independent, *Contributing Editor for* Condé Nast Traveller, *a guidebook and travel book author, and radio and
TV travel broadcaster and presenter.*

How did you start off in your career as a travel writer and journalist?

I have always loved travelling but for many years I had no disposable funds so I used to
hitch-hike a great deal. I had a pretty miserable time going to new destinations, mostly
because I'd spend hours beside a motorway outside Leicester only to find out too late

that one mile away there was a service station where I would have got a ride within minutes. So I began to compile a *Hitch-Hikers Manual to Britain*.

I did things completely the wrong way around and began to look for a publisher only after I'd completed the book. I was put in contact with a radio reporter who interviewed me about the book, or rather manuscript, as it was then. Charles James from Vacation Work heard the interview and invited me to send him the manuscript. He published it, and it was the first of half a dozen guidebooks that I wrote for him. As a spin-off from the research I did, I offered a couple of stories to newspapers.

What is the best way of establishing yourself if you're just starting out in your career as a freelance travel journalist?

Get a reputation for being available and reliable. Don't try to be brilliant – try to be competent and deliver clean copy on time. It is surprising how elusive these apparently simple requirements appear to be to a lot of writers.

How have you managed to get your name known as a freelance travel journalist?

You have to remember that no one reads newspaper by-lines, except possibly the writer's mum, and travel editors scouting for talent. But there is no real substitute for basic competency in delivering clean copy. Once you have demonstrated you can do that, your name will be remembered.

In general, less is more. Targeting a few publications with a single well-thought-out idea that you can see will work perfectly in their pages is a hundred times better and more likely to succeed than coming up with a dozen stories and sending them to dozens of travel editors.

How do you think freelance travel journalists get the numbers to add up in terms of an income?

Very tricky – don't give up the day job, always have another source of income. Often you have to work 15 hours a day and have lots of ideas which come from one trip.

What tips would you give to budding travel writers?

Bear in mind that almost any trip you can think of has already been written about, so instead think about how to cover familiar topics in a fresh way. For example, if you are visiting New York, keep your watch on British time and do everything at the 'wrong' time of day; e.g., finding somewhere to eat breakfast at 2.30 a.m. Or walk the length of Broadway – scary neighbourhoods and all.

Are there any courses or any training that you'd recommend a budding travel writer to undertake?

Competence in written English is the most important quality – if your apostrophes are all over the place, it doesn't bestow a sense of trust in your getting the facts right. But clearly the more training you have in crisp, clear writing, the better.

What are the most common mistakes that travel writers make in their copy?

Simple errors of fact. Of course, we're all human and I make as many mistakes as anybody, but if I read a piece where two or three quotes/facts turn out to be wrong, then I will not be inclined to provide that writer with a great deal of work – especially if I recognise the original source as a guidebook that got its facts wrong.

What are the most common mistakes that travel writers make when pitching to you?

Not reading a number of the *Independent*'s travel sections thoroughly in a row to see the regular categories that we have and offering stories that for a range of reasons do not fit any of the possible segments. I am by no means rigid in the format of the *Independent*'s travel pages, but a 5000-word diary of a trip to Kyrgyzstan is not likely to appear in the near future.

What are the main differences between travel writing for a newspaper as opposed to a magazine?

In both cases you should be writing for the specific publication. That sounds obvious, but a story that works well for *Wanderlust* magazine would not necessarily work for the *Independent*. You can assume that readers of the magazine are intensely interested in travel, and most have probably had more experience than you. But people don't usually buy the *Independent* purely on the strength of its travel section. Therefore you can take nothing for granted about the readership.

What, in your opinion, constitutes 'good' travel writing?

The *Independent* strives constantly for imaginative, informative and inspirational travel pages, demystifying the world – and the travel industry. Usually this means bringing the place and its people to life, and leaving yourself, as the writer, in the background.

What constitutes 'bad' travel writing?

Anything that contains clichés or inaccuracies.

What are the rewards of travel writing as a career?

You have the immense good fortune to travel the world and meet all kinds of fascinating people, while working (or pretending to work).

What has been the downside for you?

Long, stressful hours and time away from my young family.

How did you break into travel radio/TV from travel writing?

After many years of writing about travel you acquire a certain amount of expertise that is sometimes appealing to broadcasters, who may then get in touch.

INTERVIEW WITH SARAH MILLER

Based in the UK, Sarah Miller is the Editor of Condé Nast Traveller *magazine.*

How did you start off in your career as a travel editor?

I started off in features, working on monthly magazines and then 12 years on two British national newspapers – the *Sunday Times* followed by the *Daily Telegraph*. I edited features sections on the weekly paper and was also Assistant Editor of the *Sunday Times Magazine*, followed by working in features across the board for the *Daily Telegraph*, where I was also Arts Editor and Features Editor of the *Saturday Telegraph*. I was approached to launch the UK edition of *Condé Nast Traveller* precisely because I'm an editor and a journalist rather than a 'travel' journalist. Condé Nast wanted someone who understood that travel, rather than being a separate compartment, a section of a newspaper, is part of the mainstream, integral to everyone's lives, from the food we eat to the clothes we pack.

What is the best way of establishing yourself if you're just starting out in your career as a freelance travel journalist?

Starting off your career by being a travel writer is extremely difficult – too many people think that just because they can get about the world, they can write. If you can try getting some work experience, you'll be a remembered name (if you leave your CV and have been willing and enthusiastic) when you make a pitch to an editor you know. Pitching correctly is everything. Editors want good, original journalistic ideas which are timely and relevant to a publication, and its production schedules. Also, don't muddy the pitch by also claiming to be a good photographer. Get your words accepted first.

How can freelance travel journalists get the numbers to add up in terms of an income?

Be flexible but understand that supplying work that appears everywhere may not be as rewarding a financial option as you think. It's better to build relationships with editors of complimentary publications – a monthly travel magazine, a newspaper section, foreign publications – so that each editor doesn't feel you're writing for their direct competitors. Tailor-make your ideas to each. Don't send the same list of ideas to everyone but make each editor feel you are right for their brand. No editor wants to come second or feel that they're being offered second-hand goods. That way you can establish a regular income baseline and build from there. As a general rule, editors prefer working directly with writers rather than through agents, though they are helpful, once you are more established, for expanding your list of outlets. Try to write in areas other than travel – main features, columns, books, scripts. And maximise your earning potential from the four or five 'complimentary' publications through syndication round the world. I prefer to work with writers who will sign rights agreements. And, from a writer's point of view, letting the organisations deal with selling frees up time for pitching and writing.

What tips would you give to budding travel writers?

Ideas are stories, they're not countries. Most people try to cover too much. An entire gap year is a guide book, not an article. The best pieces are relevant, timely and finely focused. And whether you're writing for a newspaper or magazine, think about what would sell it, what is going to make the public buy it. Understanding lead times is essential. It's no good pitching a good idea if by the time it comes out, the peg has gone. It's tough being a freelance writer, particularly in travel. I always say don't specialise only in travel writing unless you're being published really regularly.

Are there any courses or any training that you'd recommend a budding travel writer to undertake?

Good writing is good writing and usually born from experience. This notion that there are 'travel' writers is something I sometimes think was dreamt up by retailers who like to pigeonhole what they display. There are good journalism courses out there – Cardiff School of Journalism or London College of Printing – but I would always see these as an extra to a good degree and interesting life. On the other hand, I don't know a single writer who hasn't benefited from a subbing course. Accurate, clear expression as much as evocation is the essence of being a good writer.

What are the most common mistakes that travel writers make in their copy?

They talk too much about themselves, getting to a place, and imagine a linear narrative of 'and then, and next' etc. Plus, while I don't recommend selling yourself as a photographer at the same time, not enough writers have a sense of what a piece could look like visually – both photographically or how it could be 'packaged' on the page.

What are the most common mistakes that travel writers make when pitching to you?

Spelling mistakes which make you doubt an ability to be accurate. Ideas which are encyclopaedic and undiscriminating. And it's all too obvious when someone hasn't actually read the publication they're pitching to. Travel writers too often rattle off a list of every destination they've ever visited from A to Z and say they could write a piece on any of them. Also, they tend to forget that there are only so many pieces per publication per year. For instance, a monthly magazine only has 12 issues a year, and it's unlikely a writer would appear more than once in an issue, or even in every issue. Good travel writers are also acutely aware of timing and the seasons. It's no good pitching a skiing idea halfway through the season to a monthly because they are already on to their spring/summer issues.

What are the main differences between travel writing for a newspaper as opposed to a magazine?

Newspapers offer more scope to writers in some ways because there are 52 editions a year – so they need more copy. Also, they don't rely on display photography in the same way so a person with three good ideas would stand a better chance of seeing all three get published in the course of a year. But travel magazines can usually run longer pieces.

What, in your opinion, constitutes 'good' travel writing?

Good travel writing shouldn't read like a dissertation. A good destination piece should make you feel you're there. I stop and listen to how a piece 'sounds', 'smells', 'looks' or whether it makes me laugh. I also look for people – too many writers deliver pieces that feel like the *Marie Celeste*. News reports should open my eyes to something I didn't know before. And the very best writing always makes me feel I want to read it again, like a good novel.

What constitutes 'bad' travel writing?

Reliance on where the next free trip is coming from and travel clichés – if I read 'As we banked over Rio...' the piece goes straight in the bin. Also pieces that leave you thinking you could be anywhere in the world. And finally, writing that is trying too hard to be clever.

What are the rewards of travel writing as a career?

Not losing a sense of wonder.

What are the downsides?

It's very hard to succeed and can get quite lonely out there.

INTERVIEW WITH JONATHAN LORIE

Based in the UK, Jonathan Lorie is the Editor of Traveller *magazine.*

How did you start off in your career as a travel editor?

I trained and worked as a professional journalist and then acquired some serious travel experience, especially in unusual places: 41 countries so far! You need both halves of the equation – professional skills and travel experience.

What is the best way of establishing yourself if you're just starting out in your career as a freelance travel journalist?

A good route is to develop a specialism in something – get yourself known to editors for whatever it is, whether it's extreme sports travel or humorous writing or Spanish resorts, or whatever. That way they will come back to you, which is a nice position to be in.

How do freelance travel writers get the numbers to add up in terms of an income?

The smart operators sell three or four stories from each trip, rewritten for different outlets. And of course they get the trips for free by getting themselves known to the PR people who run the press trips.

What tips would you give to budding travel writers?

Come up with the goods and keep your nose clean. Deliver what you promise or what you're asked for, to length and on time. Don't tell people you've got a commission when you haven't, don't leave facts unchecked, don't let editors down. Reliability is as important as talent.

Are there any courses or any training that you'd recommend a budding travel writer to undertake?

Absolutely. There are a very few travel writing courses which are worth attending: I teach the longest-running one, at the Mary Ward Centre (www.marywardcentre.ac.uk) in London, and the difference in people's ability and knowledge and confidence after a term's training is amazing. There are also courses in features writing and photojournalism at some universities, which are good general training opportunities.

What are the most common mistakes that travel writers make in their copy?

Simple things like length and style, and unchecked facts. All these are easy to get right, with a little care and attention.

What are the most common mistakes that travel writers make when pitching to you?

They haven't read my magazine and pitch things that we don't want.

What are the main differences between travel writing for a newspaper as opposed to a magazine?

Increasingly, newspaper articles on travel are consumer guides – how to visit this or that place – whereas some magazines still allow a more personal impression of what a place or journey is like.

What, in your opinion, constitutes 'good' travel writing?

Something that takes you there, leads you through those streets, makes you feel the reality of the journey. I don't think good travel writing has to be complimentary about a place – bad trips often make the best articles.

What constitutes 'bad' travel writing?

Formula writing, where the author either hasn't really been there or else hasn't felt anything about the place. This always shows.

What are the rewards of travel writing as a career?

You'll have some great trips and meet some fascinating people. If you're lucky, you'll also be allowed to write articles that you really like writing.

What is the downside?

You won't earn a fortune and you'll spend a lot of time pitching stories that don't work out. But if you're prepared to persist, you'll make it.

INTERVIEW WITH ANNA SUTTON

Based in the UK, Anna Sutton is the On-line Travel Editor at Telegraph.co.uk.

How did you start off in your career as a travel editor?

I spent a few years post-university writing and researching guidebooks. I was lucky to be in the right place at the right time. I contacted a couple of publishing houses at a time when they needed researchers in the former Soviet Union and Eastern Europe – areas I was planning to travel to in any case.

What is the best way of establishing yourself if you're just starting out in your career as a freelance travel journalist?

To get commissions, you need to get your name in print in the first place, which sounds obvious but can be hard. Editors are generally very reluctant to commission unknown writers. You'll need to submit articles on spec – alternatively try doing some guidebook work first or getting some work experience at a newspaper, travel trade publication or travel magazine.

How do you think freelance travel writers get the numbers to add up in terms of an income?

It's very hard to make a living out of freelance travel writing, as one month or season you may get lots of commissions and then work could dry up for the next few months. I would advise writing for as many different publications as possible – combining guidebook, newspaper and magazine work. If you have any interest in photography, it's definitely worth pursuing that alongside the writing. Unless your photos are professional-standard, they are unlikely to be used on the cover of a book or as the main photo in a newspaper article but they may be used in addition to the main pic, earning you some extra cash on the side.

What tips would you give to budding travel writers?

Persevere. Write articles and submit them on spec to editors of magazines and newspapers. Use any contacts you have in journalism and publishing. Read all the travel press and gain an understanding of current travel trends so that you can pitch articles that pick up on current issues and upcoming destinations.

Are there any courses or any training that you'd recommend a budding travel writer to undertake?

I didn't personally undertake any course but I think I would have benefited from doing some kind of diploma in journalism. Any writing course is likely to be of benefit to a prospective writer.

What are the most common mistakes that travel writers make in their copy?

Common mistakes include: submitting overly long articles, putting too much of your personality or opinions in an article (unless you're a famous person, a very personal account of what you've done is likely to be boring), trying to be funny and not pulling it off, using clichés in descriptions, factual inaccuracies (e.g., wrong phone numbers, mistakes with dates), relating events in exclusively chronological order (with every paragraph beginning with a 'then' or 'the next day' etc).

What are the main differences between travel writing for an on-line publication as opposed to a newspaper?

People tend to have a shorter attention span when they read on line (because they're at work, they're not relaxing, download times are slow etc), so ideally on-line articles should be shorter. Generally people go on line to look for information, for hard facts. They want to find what they need quickly so breaking articles into useful, easy-to-digest sections with self-explanatory headings can make it easier for a reader to navigate to the section they want. In the UK at least, on-line booking patterns show that people use the Web above all to book short breaks, so articles on city destinations, restos, hotels are probably more useful than articles on far-flung but offbeat destinations. As content on the Internet can be updated at any time, there is more of an onus to have up-to-the-minute facts. Newspapers will often publish travel articles several months after submission. On line, the info in the article must be current and should be published quickly. Question and answer formats work well on line, as does any kind of article that draws on reader feedback, as it's easy to ask readers for opinions via email and message boards.

What, in your opinion, constitutes 'good' travel writing?

You need to tell a good story as well as conjure up the destination.

What constitutes 'bad' travel writing?

An article/guidebook that doesn't give you a sense of the place, that bores you or that confuses you.

What are the rewards of travel writing as a career?

If you can make it work financially, it's a fantastic way of travelling to places you might otherwise never be able to get to.

What is the downside?

It is very hard to make a living out of travel writing alone. If you then decide (as some writers do) to do editing instead, you may find yourself frustrated at being deskbound reading about other people's travels rather than being on the road yourself. Striking a balance between having a regular income and enjoying travel writing is very difficult. Another aspect is that in order to make travel writing profitable, you often have to pack a lot into a short time and travel on your own.

INTERVIEW WITH LIZZY KREMER

Based in the UK, Lizzy Kremer is an agent at David Higham Associates Ltd in London.

What is the best way of getting an agent? How do you know that they are right for you and vice versa?

Although agencies often indicate that they don't pay any attention to the manuscripts that are sent to them on an unsolicited basis, my experience is that good writing stands out a mile and will be read. If an agent is not interested in representing travel writing, they might not read past the letter. However, you might have to make some of those submissions in order to find the right agent for you. You can call before sending your work but you probably won't gain anything by it. Make sure your submissions are well presented, professional (no long chatty letters) and always enclose a 2–3 page book outline, first few chapters and an SAE. Work hard at getting yourself published in other ways. If you have had articles printed in papers, magazines or websites, enclose those with your book. When choosing your representation, trust your instincts. Go with the agent who seems passionate about your writing. Make sure the agency has a good reputation within the industry by reading up on them in the various writers' handbooks available. You should take as much care as possible when choosing an agent. If you have written something wonderful, the power is in your hands. I take on new clients when two things fall into place – when I love their writing and when I think I can sell the ideas they have. Apart from that I just have to get a sense we would work well together.

What does an agent exactly do?

A good agent will work with you on your book proposal or manuscript prior to making submissions if she feels it could benefit from some editorial attention. Then she will draw up a list of editors she believes will enjoy your work and will want to publish you. Hopefully she will communicate with you effectively – letting you know who she is sending your work to, why she has chosen those people and what you can expect to happen next. She will encourage swift responses from the publishers and perhaps arrange for you to meet them, so that you have an opportunity to sell yourself in person and in order for you to gain a better understanding of the publishing team you might be working with. She will then negotiate the best possible deal for you. That deal might be the result of an auction between editors competing to become your publisher. Or it might simply be a nice deal with the one editor or publishing house who you and your agent believe will do the best possible job of editing and promoting your work. The agent will then negotiate your contract, using all the precedents available to her from the other contracts she has negotiated with your publisher in the past. An agent might retain certain rights, such as translation rights or newspaper serialisation rights, in order to make those further deals herself. Once your contract has been signed, the agent will continue to act as a middle person on certain aspects of your relationship with your publishers, from encouraging their publicity or marketing efforts to chasing moneys due. Publishers usually prefer to commission agented authors because they realise that agents can provide invaluable advice and support to writers. Publishers only prefer unagented authors if they are trying to save money.

What tips would you give to budding travel literature writers?

Work hard at getting yourself published in other ways – in newspapers, magazines and on line. Enter writing competitions. Don't limit your writing experience to travel writing – the more you write, the more you will develop your own style.

What are the most common mistakes that travel writers make in their first manuscripts?

They probably aren't any different from the mistakes that writers of all genres make. Don't imitate. Don't try too hard. Write from the heart. Don't list everything you did and saw. Remember the book has to have a narrative arc just as a novel does – a story to draw the reader in. Once you think you have finished the book, go back to the start and review the first few chapters again. Inexperienced writers often 'write their way in' to a book, using the first few chapters to find their feet.

What, in your opinion, constitutes 'good' travel writing?

Books which offer a personal or emotional journey as well as a physical one have great appeal. When I pick up a book I want to be moved by it, I want it to change my life. I don't see why I should lower these expectations, even if sometimes it is enough to be entertained.

What constitutes 'bad' travel writing?

Many, many things. It is easier to talk about what is good. Sometimes the best piece of travel writing can be staged between your front door and the local shops. Find your own voice, have confidence in your unique perspective and go with your passions and you give your writing the chance to shine.

INTERVIEW WITH MARGO PFIEFF

Canadian travel writer Margo Pfieff writes for the Los Angeles Times, *the* San Francisco Chronicle, Reader's Digest, Canadian Geographic, *the* Dallas Morning News *and Canada's two national daily newspapers – the* National Post *and the* Globe & Mail. *She has won six Northern Lights Awards from the Canadian Tourist Commission and the Travel Media Award at the 2002 British Columbia Tourism Awards for travel stories on the region.*

How did you start off in your career as a travel journalist?

I started as a photographer trying to sell my photos to magazines in Southeast Asia in the late 1970s. Editors were enthusiastic about the slides, but didn't have the budget to send out a writer for an accompanying text. They asked if I could write something to go with the photos. I've been doing both travel writing and photography ever since and am glad of the joint right brain/left brain exercise.

What is the best way of establishing yourself if you're just starting out in your career as a freelance travel journalist?

Write, write, write, then pitch your best stuff to get enough tear sheets from local newspapers and magazines to allow entry into an established travel writers' organization. If you're good you'll get published eventually; editors are always on the lookout for new talent as travel writers move on to books or scriptwriting.

How have you managed to get your name known as a freelance travel journalist?

As I tend not to be a joiner when it comes to writers' associations it's been mostly by the volume of material I've written and the volume of years I've been in the business. Journalist friends have also been very kind in helping me gain access into the markets for which they have been writing.

As a freelance travel journalist, how do you get the numbers to add up in terms of an income?

I sell stories before deciding on a trip so that I know I will make a reasonable return for my time spent on the road. Then I syndicate my travel stories to a number of newspapers and magazines that do not have overlapping circulations. My photos increase the size of my pay checks and I also write for nontravel publications that pay higher word rates than most newspaper and magazine travel sections.

What tips would you give to budding travel writers?

Study the style and content of the publication you're aiming at until you're very familiar with it. Make sure your idea or destination hasn't recently been covered by that publication. Editors are very busy, so if you can make their jobs easier in any way you'll make a positive impression. Be professional: meet deadlines, pay attention to details. That can mean anything from supplying photos that complement your story to doing a guide box/sidebar that includes all the details the publication requires. Do your homework.

Are there any courses or any training that you'd recommend a budding travel writer to undertake?

The best travel writing courses I've seen offered were at the Book Passage travel writers' conference in the San Francisco area.

What are the most common mistakes that travel writers make in their copy?

Writing first-person journals rather than travel stories. Stories are best told through the writer's eyes and the writer's perspective and personality should come through in the telling, but the writer should not be the focus of the article.

What are the main differences between travel writing for a newspaper as opposed to a magazine?

Magazine stories generally allow the luxury of a longer word count. For me that means the space to develop anecdotes and build a narrative to better put the reader in my shoes. There is less emphasis on the service aspect of travel writing in magazines, more emphasis on literary writing.

What, in your opinion, constitutes 'good' travel writing?

Using anecdotes, characterizations of people you meet, setting scenes to put the reader into the location rather than telling about a place. Dialogue and humor are, for me, good indicators of fine travel writing – and they are too rare in most travel stories.

What constitutes 'bad' travel writing?

Clichés of every sort. Gushing about how wonderful a place is.

What are the rewards of travel writing as a career?

The countries I've had the good fortune to visit and the doors that were opened before and after hours that allowed me such memorable experiences as watching the sun rise as I sat all alone on the Acropolis. The behind-the-scenes glimpses of what makes a Zambian safari camp run. The amazing people I've had the privilege to meet and talk with who probably wouldn't have given me the time of day if I was a tourist. Being paid to do something I love more than anything else in the world.

What has been the downside for you?

Pay rates that have often not changed in two decades. Being treated – primarily by media outside of travel writing – as a hack in a field that is often seen only as a haven for freebie-seekers.

INTERVIEW WITH RANDY CURWEN

Based in the US, Randy Curwen is the Travel Editor of the Chicago Tribune.

How did you start off in your career as a travel editor?

I didn't start off in travel – and neither did any of my travel section staff. Basically, I had 24 years of newspaper experience, including 12 years as a section editor at the *Tribune*, before I got into travel. It didn't hurt, of course, that I'd done a lot of traveling on my own, but it was really the newspaper experience – rather than the travel experience – that got me the job. That's probably true at most newspapers, where travel is considered too much of a plum for beginners.

What is the best way of establishing yourself if you're just starting out in your career as a freelance travel journalist?

'Getting published' is the obvious Answer A. But since it's easier to get published if you already know something about the business (and someone in the business), my Answer B would be: 'Get a [journalism] job!' And be a 'freelancer' on the side. Even if you're just compiling entertainment listings or covering fires, a real job adds a little heft to the résumé – and a little credibility. Plus, it will help pay the bills.

Once you're published, 'the best way of establishing yourself' is to be dependable and – hopefully – talented. (You can also 'get your name known' – negatively – among travel editors by being a real screw-up.)

How do you think freelance travel journalists get the numbers to add up in terms of an income?

It's still a mystery to me how most freelance travel journalists make money.

What tips would you give to budding travel writers?

Don't expect to make a living off this unless you're: 1) very, very good; or 2) very, very driven. Or, better yet, both.

Are there any courses or any training that you'd recommend a budding travel writer to undertake?

You can learn basic writing skills, but you can't learn creativity. While it doesn't hurt to have some writing/journalism courses, you've got to get out and write – and read, read, read. Can you recognize writers who stand out from the crowd – and why? If you can't, you probably should get out of the business.

What are the most common mistakes that travel writers make in their copy?

Sloppiness. Overuse of the 'I' word. Making me figure out what the story is about. Not grabbing my interest in the first paragraph.

What are the most common mistakes that travel writers make when pitching to you?

Confusing their interests with those of my readers (and mine).

What are the main differences between travel writing for a newspaper as opposed to a magazine?

Almost all travel magazine readers subscribe because they're interested in travel, while very few newspaper readers do the same. As a result, newspaper travel stories have to be of more general interest, while magazine stories can be targeted for a better defined, self-selective demographic. Magazines also generally have more time to work on a story, and can tweak it more. But, ultimately, when you look at the very, very best of newspaper travel writing, it can – and should – be just as good as anything written for a magazine.

What, in your opinion, constitutes 'good' travel writing?

I see more than a hundred stories every week, so my first definition of good writing is: would I read this if I didn't have to? That may sound egocentric, but that's the same criterion our readers use every day. There's no formula to a good story, but it should be like the late Supreme Court justice said about porn: I can't define it, but I know it when I see it.

What constitutes 'bad' travel writing?

Let's face it: most travel writing doesn't fall into either category, but rather into the purgatory of 'mediocrity'. Truly bad travel writing has to stand out from the crowd too. Clichés. Inaccuracies. Gross overstatements. Stereotypes. And, oh yes, the criminal misuse of adjectives. Strip a story down to its basic info, and see what you have left. Sometimes a writer just has a way – a *bad* way – with words.

What are the rewards of travel writing as a career?

Traveling!

What has been the downside for you?

None, particularly. But then, I'm not a freelancer.

INTERVIEW WITH CATHARINE HAMM

Based in the US, Catharine Hamm is the Travel Editor of the Los Angeles Times.

How did you start off in your career as a travel editor?

I don't really know how this career happened. I actually think it's because I can recite all 50 states in alphabetical order in less than 30 seconds. I also know that I have so many years in the newspaper business that I'm now starting to repeat jobs. I've been a reporter, a copy-editor, a travel editor, an assistant city editor, an assistant managing editor, a managing editor and the editor of various newspapers. About five years ago, I realized my years in news and features had taught me some lessons, the most important of which was this: do something that makes you happy. I looked back at all the jobs I'd had and realized that travel made me very happy, so I applied for the job as deputy travel editor at the *LA Times* and was lucky enough to be selected and eventually became travel editor.

What is the best way of establishing yourself if you're just starting out in your career as a freelance travel journalist?

Be fresh and bold.

How do you think freelance travel journalists get the numbers to add up in terms of an income?

I'm not sure that they do. The math doesn't add up, unless you can take a story that runs in one newspaper and re-sell it a gazillion times.

What tips would you give to budding travel writers?

1. Good writing begins with good reporting.
2. There is no good writing. There is only good rewriting.

Are there any courses or any training that you'd recommend a budding travel writer to undertake?

For a long time, I thought a liberal arts foreign language degree was about the most ridiculous thing I could have done. Now I think it's the best preparation I could have had for this job.

What are the most common mistakes that travel writers make in their copy?

Not fact-checking, especially dates. Using too many adjectives and adverbs. Telling the reader, not showing him.

What are the most common mistakes that travel writers make when pitching to you?

'I'm going to Rome. Would you like a story?'

What are the main differences between travel writing for a newspaper as opposed a magazine?

About 1500 words. OK, now that that's out of the way, I think we can be a bit more writerly in a magazine piece, particularly if it's a novel approach to a place that's well known. We can paint word pictures with that extra space that we sometimes can't do in the section. But the basics of both are the same: Take me along for the ride.

What, in your opinion, constitutes 'good' travel writing?

The same thing that constitutes any good writing: a good foundation of facts; a commitment to truth and fairness; a desire to educate and entertain and, yes, even amuse.

What constitutes 'bad' travel writing?

When there's no *there* there. Sometimes, as editors, we get seduced by the lovely phrase and the well-crafted paragraph, and when we sit down to edit, we realize it's cotton candy.

What are the rewards of travel writing as a career?

There are many, but the most important is a kinder heart. To know the world makes me a better, more understanding person.

What has been the downside for you?

It's hard to sit still. That might be the travel bug or it might be Adult Attention Deficit Disorder. Either way, the world sings its siren song, and I can hear it so clearly…

INTERVIEW WITH TOM WALLACE

Based in the US, Tom Wallace is Editor in Chief of Condé Nast Traveler *magazine.*

How did you start off in your career as a travel editor?

I knew someone who knew someone who was looking for someone like me. I had been a newspaper editor for 15 years – at the *Stamford Advocate*, a small newspaper in Connecticut; *Newsday* and the *New York Times*. In 1988, a friend who had worked with me at the *Times* but was then writing for *Vanity Fair*, then edited by Tina Brown, who is married to Harry Evans, then the Editor in Chief of *Condé Nast Traveler*, asked me on behalf of Tina, who was inquiring on behalf of Harry, whether I would be interested in coming to the *Traveler*. The rest is history.

What is the best way of establishing yourself if you're just starting out in your career as a freelance travel journalist?

Pitch original ideas. Write great stories. Make friends with commissioning editors, hire well-connected agents.

How do you think freelance travel writers get the numbers to add up in terms of an income?

Very difficult. The writers I know who succeed – who survive – are both widely published and have achieved what's known in the business as vertical integration. Wide publication means their pieces are picked up, translated if necessary, and republished around the world, earning them additional royalties – and attracting yet more commissions. Vertical integration means their pieces lead to book contracts and, even more remunerative, to Hollywood script credits. Writers who cultivate but one outlet, no matter how regularly they are published, are minimizing their exposure and maximizing their risk.

What tips would you give to budding travel writers?

Enjoy life while you can. Keep that business/law/medical school application at the ready.

Are there any courses or any training that you'd recommend a budding travel writer to undertake?

Journalism degrees, particularly graduate degrees, are important, though not as important as a varied life experience and native skill.

What are the most common mistakes that travel writers make in their copy?

Contriving to sound like other travel writers.

What do you look for in a pitch?

We look for good stories – original, compelling, and appropriate – and authors who can tell them well.

What are the main differences between travel writing for a newspaper as opposed to a magazine?

Magazines typically pay more per word and typically buy more words. Beyond that, I would bet that the best newspaper travel writing is, in all aspects, a heck of a lot better than the worst magazine travel writing.

What, in your opinion, constitutes 'good' travel writing?

I don't know if I can get myself to distinguish travel writing from any other kind of magazine writing. All editors want – or should want – good stories well told. Which is to say: a well conceived idea and a genuinely interesting experience presented with above average adjectival invention. Good photo opportunities help.

What constitutes 'bad' travel writing?

Absence of same.

What are the rewards of travel writing as a career?

Seeing the world, learning your place in it.

What is the downside?

Taking too long to learn your place.

INTERVIEW WITH KEITH BELLOWS

Based in the US, Keith Bellows is Editor in Chief of National Geographic Traveler *magazine.*

How did you start off in your career as a travel editor?

By staying away from writing about travel. One of the lucky things was that I was never a travel writer. I had done a lot of actual travel and I had made a living as a writer, but I had never really put the two together. When I was asked to interview for this job, I leapt at the chance, because I'm experienced at putting magazines together and I thought there was an opportunity to apply those skills to making *Traveler* better. Add to that a lifetime of travel and a love of writing and, to me, it added up to the perfect job. Or to the perfect storm, depending on your perspective. But what's important about all this is that

I never set out to be a travel journalist. Some people have done that – and succeeded. But not many. Because it's not a job. It's a passion. And, as we all know, if you pursue your passion – and you're good at what comes from that – then you will succeed.

What is the best way of establishing yourself if you're just starting out in your career as a freelance travel writer?

First of all, I would beg the question a bit. I would say: do you want to be known as a travel writer or do you want to be known as a writer? The really great writers in our genre – Peter Matthiessen, Paul Theroux, Jonathan Raban, Jan Morris – I don't think any of them said, I want to become a freelance travel writer; this is my goal in life. No. They wanted to write, they happened to go to places, places inspired thought and reaction, and that's what they went after. One of the things that gives me the heebie-jeebies is hearing someone say, 'I am a travel writer.' Uh-uh. You're a writer who loves to travel. You're a writer who is very good at getting on the ground, quickly canvassing the territory, surveying the folks and figuring out what the take is, what your angle on the place is and then being able to channel the place to your readers.

What I think is so important is not telling people about the place, it's channeling. And what I mean by that is when you look at a documentary, it channels the place. It's what do the people say about themselves, what do they say about the place they're living in, how do they feel about things, where do they go, and how do you live like the locals. That's the important thing, this sort of packaging, which by the way we do in our magazine. In some respects we tend to do the *Insider's Guide to Boston*, but at the same time we make sure that everybody who says anything about the place is not the writer but the person who lives there.

How do you think freelance travel journalists get the numbers to add up in terms of an income?

First of all, let's define travel journalists. There are two kinds. There are those people who decide they're going to go into this business and work for the *Podunk Times*. They're going to take the press trips. They're going to take the freebies. They're going to do whatever they can, and they're going to write for whoever will take their copy because they really just want to travel. They're not so much interested in becoming celebrated as a writer. That's one class. The other class of people want to write. I am a writer. That's what I do, and I really want to write about places. And they have some passion, and they also have some self-respect in terms of the fact that they want to be proud of what they do.

So back to your question, how do you do this? Lord knows how you do it. I think the number one thing is you have to be a good writer. You have to be a good writer and you really have to have a sense of story. If you come to us or you come to any magazine and you say, I want to do Paris, they're going to say, well, you know, we do too. They all know about Paris.

We have a little thing we say to writers. Why now? Why *Traveler*? Why you? And that's all about how you can make yourself stand out from the pack. And standing out from the pack is how you make a living. I also would say that a lot of the really interesting writers that write for us do a lot of other stuff. They may be covering business in Paris. They may be working for *Wired*. Whatever it is, they're not monosyllabic. They don't just do travel. They're curious about the world. They want to get to other fields. They'll say to me, I'm going to Ethiopia to trace the trail of my daughter. We adopted my daughter. She was found in this place. She was brought to us here. I want to go back and do that. That particular story is a potentially terrific travel story because it's not one note. It's not: I'm going to tell you about the architecture, the food, the hotels, the location, the specialties and the attractions. It's about: I want to put you here through my eyes and set an experience in a place.

What tips would you give to budding travel writers?

I guess I get back to that question of do you want to be a travel writer or do you want to be a traveler and turn your adventures into prose. If you want to get up in the morning and say my goal in life is to be a travel writer, I think first of all you need a second job. I won't say there's nobody – I'm sure there are people – but it gets very difficult to be able to say I'm going to go out and hit home runs where it takes people with 20 and 30 years of experience and with a great deal of tenacity and talent to hit those home runs.

So I think it's wise to start on three fronts. The first thing is to say I'm going to do this as an experiment, but I'm going to have something that roots me, something that's going to put bread on the table. The second thing is that I'm going to really, really, really study what I think is good travel writing. Who are the writers I like? And don't be afraid to mimic them for a while. If you like Tim Cahill or Paul Theroux, look at how they write, and try to imagine yourself writing that way. Then the third thing I think is important is to think about why you love to travel and what personally connects you with a place. You can start to mine those areas. If in fact you have a sub-genre – if you're really, really passionate about the issues that surround sustainable tourism, let's say – become an expert in that. If you really want to mine the travel industry, there are so many sub-genres. There's business travel. There's health travel. There's children and family travel. There's singles travel. There's European travel and Asian travel and so forth. If you can focus on an area where you can become an expert, that expertise will really, really help.

Are there any courses or any training that you'd recommend a budding travel writer to undertake?

Nope. I think the best diploma is to travel.

What are the most common mistakes that travel writers make in their copy?

Trying to mimic guidebooks, or thinking that what editors want is I went there, I saw this, I ate this, I slept here, that kind of stuff. Not paying attention to the basics of writing – writing bad ledes, bad transitions, poor grammar, just bad writing. We see that a lot in queries. We have three curses in a query. Hi, I'm really good, and I notice in your index that you haven't done Tucson lately. I'd like to do it for you. That's number one. Number two is hi, I'd like to write about Tucson, and I live here, and here are the great things about Tucson – wide open boulevards, great buildings, fabulous museums, yada, yada, yada. But no angle. The third is I happen to be going to Tucson; I've never been before but thought you might like an article. There's no I'm from Tucson, I grew up there for 30 years, I've been on the East Coast for 20, I'm going back to find blah blah blah, where there's a real angle so you really get a sense. It's really hard to find a writer underneath all the banalities of what you see in the query.

What are the most common mistakes that travel writers make when pitching to you?

The first is pitching by phone. The second is pitching by email. I get jillions of emails, so please send me a note and include published clips. That's the third thing; they don't include published clips. We have a wonderful phenomenon among our British brethren which is…I'm going out for the next six months and here are the 37 stories that I'm pursuing. Which one would you like? I want one story that you're passionate about. I want it in one page. I want to get a sense of your writing on that page. And I want to know, once again, Why me? Why *Traveler*? Why now?

Also, I really invite people to think cinematically. And what I mean by that is, when you see a movie there are some central characters and lots of dialogue. You know immediately in the first 10 or 15 minutes of the movie either exactly what the movie is about or there's a hook. What am I going to find out? What's the quest? What's the mystery? And you're pulled into it. There's a beginning, middle and end, and you're satisfied, we hope, at the end of the movie. It's all scene setting, dialogue, character and, in terms of magazines or stories, anecdote. You want to see stuff. You don't want to be told about the artesian well that dates back to 1500. You want a story. Most folks don't really realize that. They send manuscripts. We can't take manuscripts because we send people out, and we send photographers with them or pretty much coincident with their trip. So it's not much good to have a manuscript after the fact.

Then of course the cardinal sin is that they don't read the magazine. They don't understand that we're different from our competitors, that we have a very specific mission and a very specific way of expressing our take on travel, and they don't really give us a sense that they know the magazine. That's death.

What are the main differences between travel writing for a newspaper as opposed to a magazine?

Money is probably the biggest difference. And to put that in very crass terms, when we do a story on Africa, we're sending a writer and a photographer into the field collectively for about a month. The writer's going to come back with a manuscript, and the photographer is going to come back with anywhere from 300–500 rolls of film. That trip could cost us $40K. We're not going to say, Hey Betty, we loved your lede, and we're going to send you off on a $40K goose chase. We've got to be darn sure of what we're doing. We define everything from the get go. We're very clear about what we're looking for. I don't mean that from the point of view that we say here's what we want the story to be. But we certainly want to point an angle that the writer can work around. We plan from the inside out, which is to say that before you leave we're trying to nail down all the details. The photographer is going to be there for eight days between these dates for this amount of money. The writer is going to be…same kind of thing. The contract says, in general terms, this is what the story is about.

A newspaper, which has far less resources, will say you're going to Berlin. Let us know what's going on when you get back. Or they'll say it's the 50th anniversary of the bratwurst, and we want you to do a bratwurst piece. And of course we hope you know that we can't afford to pay you to go there, so you're going to have to figure out how to get there on your own. The really good newspapers are very imaginative. They try to tap a very far-flung resource pool of writers and so forth. They don't have the budgets. The smaller newspapers really don't have the budgets.

What, in your opinion, constitutes 'good' travel writing?

First of all, a sense that you're in sure hands, that the person on the ground who's writing the piece is a writer – not an observer, but a writer who can filter things out.

The second thing is that I want to meet the people. I want to smell the place. I want to hear the place. I want to taste the place. I want a sense of place, of atmospherics. I'm much less interested in the litany of wonderful things to see and do in a place, unless it's a service piece. But in a narrative story, I want a slice of the place. I want you to make me understand the place, not by telling me everything you know about it, but by showing me some aspect of it that makes me excited about wanting to know more. And that's about meeting the people, hearing their voices, listening to the cadence of their voices, getting a sense of what they eat, getting a sense of how they conduct their day. This is the wonderful thing about the slice of life approach, which is where I want to move the magazine. I don't want a piece that says: Well, I got off the plane, and I got in the taxi, and I went into London, and I checked into my hotel, and the hotel room was blah, blah, blah, and then I went downstairs and had a meal, and I went to…You just don't do it that way. You say: The most amazing thing that happened to me was this gypsy woman who came up to me in Piccadilly. And she said, death be on your soul, and you went, what? And you sat down with her, and she told you this story, and you bonded with her, and she took you to this place, and you had an experience. That's the essence of travel. It's the surprise, the unpredictable.

What constitutes 'bad' travel writing?

Paint by numbers. What you really want is a story. I went to Dubai because 20 years ago I had lost a watch there in a market, and I wanted to go back and find out what that market was like. Whatever you're doing, it's a quest. Travel is all about a quest, and when the quest is to find that next 400-thread-sheet bed linen set, it just doesn't work. So what it's about, I think, is what's the movie? What's the story? The bad stuff is the predictable stuff: these are the markets we visited, this is what we did during the day, this is the shopping district, this is the hotel, these are the restaurants. It's just like paint by numbers.

What are the rewards of travel writing as a career?

I don't think you can make a career of travel writing. I think you can make a career of traveling and then doing things around that passion. The people that I have the most respect for are people who just figure out how to build their lives around the process of traveling. The good ones express themselves through writing. It's not so much I want to be a travel writer because I want to make a bunch of money, because that's a very difficult proposition. What it is is I'm traveling. How do I take that passion that I have and mutate it into bank funds? One of the things that has astounded me from Rangoon to Hong Kong to Sydney to Vancouver is the amazing people in the travel business. They got into the business because they're passionate about traveling, and they figured out how to take that passion and make a living out of it.

Writers can do it too. Maybe not just writing…I just spent some time doing research on line, and I was looking at all the websites that are directed to expats. There are a lot of them. I found at least 30 in just an hour. What that told me is that a lot of people have a lust for life, love wanderlust, want to get out there, and they're figuring out how to live in places other than the US and sort of leverage that lust for the other, for the foreign. And writing is just a part of it. So I think that if you just think about how you're going to make a living off of writing about travel, that might be a little one-dimensional.

How can I make a living off travel and then, the sidebar is, can I write about it? If I'm living in Paris and I'm a banker, but I'm having extraordinary experiences and feeling some sort of simpatico with the local community, then I start to look overseas (ie the States), and say how can I sell my experience to markets there? So, in other words, if I'm from Pittsburgh and living in Paris, is there a way to connect those two places because of who I am and the fact that I'm living in Paris? I'm not a travel writer; I'm a banker. But maybe I can make people in Pittsburgh understand the foreignness of France.

What is the downside of travel writing as a career?

I think the problem with travel writing as a career is, first of all, you get a lot of competition. Second, sometimes travel writing gets tough in the way of traveling. You're so caught up in taking notes and interviewing people and taking pictures and looking at things because you've got to learn how to turn them into saleable prose or saleable pictures that you miss the place. I've had this happen to myself where I've been so fanatically looking at some particular thing, because I wanted to get the take, that I missed something that I should've gotten.

I think the best way to become a travel writer is to travel and let the experiences accumulate and aggregate in your notebook. In a way you almost have to be just experiencing and not constantly documenting.

The other thing that's really interesting to me is that we're getting more and more queries from people who have what I would call international connectivity. I mentioned the guy from Ethiopia who's going back there to trace the trail from where his daughter was born to where he picked her up. And there's another one that we got which is really terrifically crafted about a guy who met his wife in Hue in Vietnam about 20 years ago. Magical descriptions of the place then. Two kids now, going back. That idea of the foreignness seen through the eyes of the domestic. I think that what's going to happen now, that more and more people are really interested in this multicultural mix. And I think that's an important thing for writers to mine. When I get a query that says I lived in Country X for 20 years, and this is something that happened to me, and this is what I want to investigate – there's a connectivity there which I think is very, very important and which I gravitate toward. I think that what we all gravitate toward is people. Travel is about people. It's not just about place. I think we all tend to fixate on explaining the place and not experiencing the people.

INTERVIEW WITH AMY RENNERT

Based in the US, Amy Rennert is the former Editor in Chief of San Francisco *magazine and the founder and president of the Amy Rennert Agency, Inc.*

What is the best way of getting an agent? How do you know that they are right for you and vice versa?

The best way to get an agent is to do your research first. *Publishers Marketplace* is a great resource, as is Jeff Herman's *Guide to Book Publishers, Editors and Literary Agents*. It's also a good idea to check the acknowledgements pages in appropriate books. It's important to take the time and care to follow specific submission guidelines. Some agents want a query first, others will accept sample pages; some will accept email submissions, others won't. It shows that you've done your research and respect the agent's practices if you follow their guidelines.

What does an agent exactly do?

An agent has many roles, but the most accurate definition of a literary agent is the person who guides you and acts as your advocate – from start to finish – through the publishing process. I'm a former national magazine editor and I consider myself an author's first editor before we sell the book. Agents send proposals and manuscripts to appropriate publishers and then make deals on the authors' behalf. They also provide critical feedback during the editorial process and then help promote, market and advertise your work after publication. Many agents, myself included, have a wide range of media contacts, so we often help sell sub-rights, including first serial and film. As an agent I don't just represent the book. I represent authors and I'm very involved in career management as well.

What tips would you give to budding travel literature writers?

Travel! And write while you travel, so you don't forget about specific thoughts and experiences once you return home. Also, it's always smart to try to establish a name for yourself – try to get articles or essays published in smaller, regional magazines, and gradually you'll make a name for yourself. And *read!* Read other travel writing to see what works and what doesn't. Know the marketplace so you aren't trying to sell something that's been done numerous times. Also, it's important to determine what kind of travel writing you want to do.

What are the most common mistakes that travel writers make in their first manuscripts?

They give too many details about the trip, the preparation for it, getting visas, packing their bags, telling people about the upcoming trip, why they are taking it, getting to the airport – rather than concentrating on the real heart of the story. Often these are facts and incidents that happen to pretty much everyone who travels – they don't have a unique perspective or point of view. I think new writers feel they need to give all of the background up front. That may be a good and useful writing exercise for the writer but it's not appreciated by the reader. They should go back and cut judiciously – start where the story really starts.

What, in your opinion, constitutes 'good' travel writing?

A strong voice – Pico Iyer, Simon Winchester and Jan Morris are some of my personal favorites. We see a lot of travel writing that doesn't have any real voice. I look for compelling narrative nonfiction that reads like great fiction.

THE TOOLS OF THE TRADE

Most serious travel journalists carry three items with them wherever they go: their journal or notebook, an audio recorder, and a camera. Depending on the circumstances of the trip, they also sometimes carry a laptop computer.

JOURNAL

Don't go anywhere without your journal. It's where you record your first-hand experiences, impressions and reflections. Sometimes you will just need to jot down a word or phrase that will help you remember an experience; at other times it will be whole paragraphs of description. This is also where you'll feverishly copy down all the practical information you'll need for your travel pieces, such as restaurant or museum opening and closing times, costs and transport timetables. It's best to write down everything you want to remember while you're right there. You may think that you won't forget, but you will, and your notes will be especially important if you want to draw out a memory at a much later date.

MY JOURNAL

I've been using the same particular style of journal since I discovered it in Tokyo in the late 1970s. It measures about 10 inches by seven inches and has a durable but soft cover so that I can roll it up and stuff it in a pocket when I need to. At the same time, it's stitched so that the pages don't fall out and there's no awkward metal spine. Many travel writers use a standard reporter's notebook, roughly five inches by three inches, but its rigid cardboard covers aren't as adaptable as my soft-cover version, although it is a handy, stuff-in-your-shirt-pocket size.

Notebook entries are very powerful portals that transport you back to a place and to your experience there. Try to make time at least every other day to sit in a café or other suitable place and write about the world around you for an hour. The peripatetic Pico Iyer has told me that when he is travelling, he sets aside time every night before going to bed to record the most important experiences and impressions of the day. There is absolutely no substitute for words written on the day, in the place, as close to the experience as possible, so the details and your reactions and thoughts are fresh.

Use your journal as a friend and confidant, sounding board and *aide-mémoire*, all in one. Number your notebooks and, whatever you do, make sure you don't lose them. I always write a big note on the first page of each notebook: 'If found, please return to:...', and then my name and address. When I finish a notebook, I note the dates of the first and last entries, and put it in storage with all my other notebooks.

– Don George

AUDIO RECORDER

For many years travel journalists have relied on microcassette recorders as an indispensable tool of their trade; these recorders are now being replaced by minidisc recorders or MP3s (which are becoming cheaper by the minute). It's critical that the recorder you use is hardy, portable and practical; easy to slip in a pocket; and easy to use in virtually

◀ **Short-lived water calligraphy on a Jingshan Park pathway, Beijing – Phil M. Weymouth** any kind of situation. Size, weight, sound quality and simplicity of use are all important considerations. You might want to try a few different kinds to see which one works best for you. And whichever you choose, don't forget to carry spare batteries.

The downside of using an audio recorder, of course, is that you have to play back everything you've recorded and transcribe all the notes you'll need for your article. This is a major pain, requiring you to stop and start the recorder over and over and over again. If you can afford it, you could pay a transcription service to do this for you – or perhaps you could ask a sympathetic touch-typist friend to help you out in exchange for a far-flung souvenir or home-cooked meal.

Interviews
An audio recorder is vital when carrying out interviews, whether informal or with officials such as museum curators or hoteliers. You might also want to record what locals or fellow travellers think of a certain situation, be it their reaction to a new restaurant or a new travel advisory. In the trade, these short interviews are called Vox Pops. It's good practice to get the names of the people you interview on tape, together with any tricky spellings; you may not end up using the person's name even if you do quote them – depending on the context, it may be fine to write simply, 'A tourist from London told me that…' – but it's good to have the name in case you do need it. Recorded interviews are very helpful when you're writing up your story, and indispensable when publications ask to fact-check quotes; see the section on interviewing techniques on p47.

Too Much Too Soon
It's also useful to start recording if you find yourself in a situation where someone is dispensing valuable information too quickly for you to take notes. This can be especially handy in a museum, for example, where a guide is talking about the history and technique of a particular painting or sculpture. Another situation where an audio recorder comes in handy is on the guided city walks which many tourist offices or private individuals run these days. Using a recorder will help you capture important details that you might need later on when you're writing up – there is nothing worse than coming to a crucial spot in your writing and realising that you've missed a particular piece of information.

Replacing Written Notes
Audio recorders are a useful way to record what's happening in a situation where taking notes is impractical – such as bumping through the African bush on a safari, for example, when your written notes are likely to start looking like the profile of Mt Kilimanjaro. You

Twenty years ago, I accompanied a tour group on a three-week journey along Pakistan's Karakoram Highway. When we stopped in Hunza, we were visited by an impromptu band of musicians. I don't know how it happened that they materialised at the moment we entered the village, but there they were, and they began to play. I quickly got out my tape recorder and stuck it into the air to capture their spontaneous performance. Even now, 20 years later, when I begin to play that tape, I am transported back to that scene: the marvellous musicians, the snow on the peaks around us, the crisp sunshine, the muddy fields, the neat stone walls and the rows of poplars all around.

– *Don George*

can orally jot down words or phrases just as you normally would in your notebook – 'vast golden savanna', 'elephants running, ears flapping', 'gurgling roar of lion' – and they'll help re-create the scene when you're back in front of your computer.

Sound is also a powerful key that can open up all kinds of stored-away memories, and bring a place back to life. It's a good idea to record evocative background noise, if appropriate.

CAMERA

On the most basic level, a camera can be used to make a visual record of a place you want to write about later. Use it to take photographs of particular features you may want to re-member in detail, and which might figure in an article or story. When writing your piece, you can surround yourself with images of your destination or journey to help transport you back to a situation or place.

Photos can also be used to record information you may want to use in your story, such as details provided in a historic plaque, temple marker or store sign, or in the printed explanatory text hung beside a work of art in a museum or gallery.

These 'memory snaps' can be taken on any camera, although disposable ones aren't generally recommended as they are an expensive and ecologically unfriendly way of working. Consider carrying a cheap, light, everyday 35mm film or compact digital camera for taking shots when you don't want to risk damaging or losing your good camera. Ideally, however, you want to be taking photos of publishable quality, so that if the opportunity arises you can sell both your words and your pictures to a publication. This is a very different ball game and demands rather more sophistication in terms of equipment and photography skills.

Adding Photography to Your Skills

Photography and writing are two very different arts, requiring completely different skills. However, it does make sense to think about developing your photography skills if you are a travel writer. You are there, *in situ*; you know what you're going to write about and you're in a unique position to illustrate your words.

If you are writing for a newspaper, photos could help you get published. Your story might be good but not so great that the editor simply *has* to run it, and having compelling photos can sometimes push the editor into deciding to publish your package. Photographs taken by guidebook authors are sometimes published in the guidebook they're writing, particularly if they're researching a remote location or have pictures of unusual or infrequent events (festivals or rituals, for instance). As mentioned in Chapter Six, glossy travel magazines are very photo-led, and employ a stable of professional photographers who are sent into the field to illustrate middle-of-the-book feature stories. The glossy magazines might occasionally be interested in competent photos for front-of-the-book or back-of-the-book stories, but you have a better chance with more down-to-earth travel magazines. In fact, many tighter-budget magazines actually rely on their writers to provide photos. The better your photos, the better your chances of getting published. Every magazine, large or small, needs a cover shot – if you work on your skills and study the kinds of shots that feature on magazine covers, this coveted slot might someday be within your reach.

Photographic Rates

While good photos may sometimes help your story get published, the strongest incentive to add photography to your CV or repertoire is, to put it bluntly, money. Selling both a story and photos to a publication is obviously more lucrative than selling the story alone.

In the UK, most newspapers and magazines have arrangements with picture agencies and tend to favour these sources (not least because they have attractive commercial arrangements with them). If your picture is used it will probably be paid at 'space rates', which might be in the region of £40 to £65 for a small 'drop in' photo and £150 to £180 for a half-page shot. Rates also depend on the circulation (and budget) of the newspaper or magazine, and where your photo is being placed; cover shots for a travel supplement or magazine cover would obviously attract a greater fee. A UK magazine with a circulation of around 10,000 would pay around £80 for half a page and in the region of £200 for a front cover; a magazine with a circulation of 150,000 might pay anything from £100 for a half-page and £325 for a cover shot.

US newspapers generally pay from $25 to $50 for a black-and-white shot, and $50 to $100 for a colour photo. As in the UK, glossy magazines tend to assign favoured photographers to shoot stories, but they occasionally publish noncommissioned photos, and pay from $200 to $1000 for a single shot.

In Australia, words and photos are often commissioned as a package. For photographs alone, based on a print run of 50,000, newspapers pay $265 for up to half a page and $310 for a full page; magazines pay $240 for up to a quarter page, $290 for a half-page and $338 for a full page.

Photographic Equipment

If you're going to get serious about trying to shoot for publication, you'll need to invest in some good photographic equipment. To offer pictures that are up to the highest professional standards, you'll need a film or digital 35mm SLR (single lens reflex) camera with at least a 28–80mm lens. As you get more ambitious, you will probably want to purchase a second 80–200mm lens as well. Second-hand cameras are certainly worth considering, but lenses are best bought new. A light tripod is optional. If you're shooting on film you'll need to use 100 ISO slide film; while some publications will publish from prints as well as slides, virtually all publications prefer transparencies to prints or print negatives.

Digital photography is becoming more and more popular, and all newspapers and most magazines are accepting digital files captured on digital SLRs with six megapixel or more sensors. In fact, it's becoming increasingly common for publishers to only accept digital files, no matter how you captured the image. It's extremely important to check the photography submission guidelines before approaching a publisher, as they will usually have a preference, whether it be for transparency film, negative, print or digital files.

The advantage of digital photos is that you can avoid the high costs of developing your film, and you can either email individual pictures or burn a CD with an entire trip's worth of images on it. For considerably more information on digital photography – and on traditional photography as well – see the second edition of Lonely Planet's *Travel Photography* guide by Richard I'Anson, published in September 2004.

Taking Shots

As a travel photographer, what kinds of photos should you be taking? Try to think like an editor, and take photos that will help readers to *see* your story, complementing and enhancing your words. Your photos should illustrate the highlights and main points of your story – the landscapes or cafés, people or animals, ferries or *tuk-tuks*, fossils or flowers. To maximise your chances, submit a wide variety of photos, from close-up details to expansive vistas, and shoot a robust mixture of horizontal and vertical images, because you never know what size space will be available in a publication. If you're photographing a building, event or landscape that is absolutely crucial to your story, be sure to take both vertical and horizontal shots.

When composing your photos, look for interesting angles and perspectives to give a twist on the standard view of a particular scene or subject. Also, make sure that your shot has a clear visual focus – a central element that the eye is drawn to and that helps centre the image. Be aware of the full frame of your picture, and of the elements you are using to frame the scene. Frame your shot so that the entire photo is the tableau you want the editor to publish, but if this is not possible, include too much in your photo rather than too little, as the image can always be cropped.

Light is the most important element of any photo, and in order to capture the best effects some professional photographers shoot only in the early morning, just after sunrise, and in the late afternoon, just before sunset (the so-called 'Golden Hours'). The harsh light of midday tends to wash out or drain the colour and definition in photos. If you are serious about your photographs, plan to shoot in the early morning and late afternoon, and use the middle of the day for your article research or for interior shots.

Photos that include local people are important to an article portfolio, but these can be tricky because if the person can be identified, you may need them to sign a model release form; see the Sample Paperwork Appendix for an example form. How do you decide if you need to ask someone to sign a release form? This is an ambiguous area, but if you want your shot to appear on a magazine cover or to be used for advertising purposes, or you want your work to be represented by a photo agency, you've got to have a model release form. You won't need permission to publish photographs for editorial purposes.

Beyond this, the issue is a combination of legal, practical and contextual concerns. On the legal front, you can be sued for defamation or invasion of privacy if you publish a photo of a person who can convincingly claim that they have been damaged by that publication. Let's say you take a shot of a Parisian café scene; the photo appears in a major national magazine, and the couple romantically clasping hands and looking deeply into each other's eyes in the left-hand corner of the frame catches a woman's eye – because the man in the photo is clearly her husband and the woman is clearly not herself. Bring on the lawyers!

To complicate matters even further, it isn't just people who pose potential legal liabilities – publishing unauthorised photos of certain buildings and logos can cause problems, too.

For detailed information about the intricacies of this issue, consult the second edition of Lonely Planet's *Travel Photography*.

Ultimately, you can take photography as far as your resources and energies permit you. You add to your income if your photos are published, but you have to weigh the costs of film, developing, equipment, preparation of digital files and the time involved – particularly the time it takes to sort and label your slides when you get home – against the income you make from your photos. The important thing is to decide what you want your photography to do for you, and then to work toward that goal.

LAPTOP COMPUTER

Travel writers generally have a bit of a love-hate relationship with their laptops. On balance, most of them take their laptops with them on the majority of their trips – but there are pros and cons. Whatever you decide, for whichever trip, bear in mind the sometimes life-saving ubiquity of Internet cafés. If you decide to keep your laptop safe at home, you can still do some writing on the road and email it to yourself or to your editor. And in some cases, even when you do have your laptop with you, it may prove far less frustrating to email your work home from the Internet café on the corner than having to untangle the idiosyncratic intricacies of connecting to the Internet from your hotel room.

The Advantages of Travelling with a Laptop

The biggest advantage of all is the most obvious: you can write your article while you're travelling. This may sound pretty basic, but there's nothing like writing your article while you're *in situ*, or working on chapters of your guidebook while you're actually staying in the particular city you're updating. If you've already sent in your article by email, you can answer any questions that may arise or gaps that may appear in your research right on the spot – plus it's a wonderful feeling to walk in your front door at the end of a trip knowing that your story is already done.

A laptop computer is also essential for emailing from a hotel room (though this can be technologically challenging and, if you don't watch the connection costs, financially ruinous). Plus you can type more quickly into a laptop than you can write longhand or even shorthand in a notebook. If you're taking digital photos as 'memory snaps', you'll need a laptop so you can download your images on an ongoing basis and free up your camera's memory card.

The Disadvantages of Travelling with a Laptop

A laptop can be a significant impediment to the kind of travelling you plan to do. Hard travel, difficult environments and long periods away from electricity supplies don't bode well for a computer. In this sense, a general rule of thumb is that laptops make good companions when you're on urban excursions but are probably best left at home if you're going on an adventure trip. Even though laptops are meant to be portable, the reality is that only a few are robust enough to survive life on the road. A well-travelled laptop will probably need to be replaced every year or two, depending, of course, on how you treat it.

OTHER ESSENTIAL ITEMS

Other useful tools in the travel writer's on-the-road repertoire include a mobile phone (make sure your service will work in the area you're visiting before you pack your phone, extra battery and recharger); a currency converter or calculator; your address book, either the old-fashioned paper variety or a modern handheld PDA; and of course a good guidebook or two. To save valuable space, consider photocopying the relevant pages of your guidebooks – you can also use the pages for your notes, writing in the margins and on the reverse side of the photocopied pages. Finally, always be sure to pack extra batteries and the appropriate plugs and adapters.

As technology evolves, more and more products will emerge that may have uses for the travel writer's lifestyle. As you assess these products, keep in mind the equation of convenience and cost. What do you absolutely need to do your job? Is that particular new product suitable for the kinds of travelling you will be doing? High-tech products are great when they do more work for us – but not great when we end up doing more work for them.

If you carry your laptop around the streets with you, as many travel writers do, it can make you a target for muggers. Then again, if you leave it in your hotel room or car, there is also a chance that it will be stolen, taking all your notes (and your story!) with it.

Travel journalists are always searching for places to recharge their laptops, whether this be in hotel rooms, at restaurants or in airport lounges. You need to carry suitable plugs or adapters with you at all times, and keep track of how much time your battery has left so you don't lose any priceless prose if your laptop suddenly shuts down.

Finally, even under favourable conditions, laptops can be a literal pain in the neck to lug around. Even the most lightweight laptop doesn't feel so light after you've been carrying it around on your shoulder all day.

COURSES

Writing Courses

Writing courses, workshops and conferences are often overlooked as tools of the trade, but they can be an invaluable means of recharging your professional batteries and refining and expanding your expertise and skills. The attendees usually comprise a good mix of professional and amateur writers.

The majority of courses in the UK and Australia are for Creative Writing, but they shouldn't be discounted, as travel writers old and new can learn a lot from courses such as these. Some courses offer travel writing as a component of a more general course, while others, such as those run in the UK by the Arvon Foundation, TNT or London's Mary Ward Centre, specialise exclusively in the genre of travel writing. Learndirect (☎ 0800-100 900; www.learndirect.co.uk) is an invaluable resource for finding out what courses are available in the UK. For part-time and full-time study opportunities in the Greater London area, consult www.floodlight.co.uk. Grants are sometimes available to help less-privileged students cover costs, so it is always worth asking the course organisers about funding opportunities. In Australia, Good Guides (www.thegoodguides.com.au) publishes a print and on-line guide to every university and college course available in the country.

In the US a good resource for classes (especially for freelancers) is www.mediabistro .com, a professional journalists' organisation that offers writing classes around the country. The Book Passage Travel Writers & Photographers Conference is a four-day conference that focuses exclusively on travel writing and photography, and is held every August in the San Francisco area. I co-founded the conference in 1991, and act as chair every year. Numerous other summer writers' conferences offer nonfiction writing classes and workshops that can include travel writing.

Travel writing classes are offered across the globe through community colleges, universities, writers' centres and independent learning organisations; they can also be held in conjunction with bookstores. See the Resources Chapter at the back of this book for more details on courses offered in the UK, the US and Australia. For information on writing courses available worldwide, take a look at http://writing.shawguides.com, which lists almost 1500 writers' conferences and workshops, and is searchable by country, state, date and genre. The Internet offers virtually inexhaustible information about writing classes – including some virtual courses that take place entirely through on-line classes, submissions and critiques. Don't just consider courses on writing; learning how to edit, how to find and work with an agent, and how to work with editors can also be very beneficial in helping you understand the pressures and requirements of the publishing world.

When you're considering a particular workshop, course or conference, find out as much as you can about the presentations and course structure. What topics are covered? Who are the guest speakers? What are their credentials? How much interaction is there between lecturers and students? What kinds of opportunities are there for close critiquing of your work, and for one-on-one or small-group contact? Do the topics correspond to your interests? Ask for feedback from past students, and find out what former students have gone on to achieve.

Typing & Shorthand Courses

Being able to touch-type is an invaluable skill for any writer. When the words are coming thick and fast, your fingers need to keep up with them on the keyboard. If you can't type, or if your typing skills are poor, a typing course may be one of the best investments you make. It takes only around 40 hours to learn how to touch-type, and courses are inexpensive.

Before the advent of audio recorders, shorthand was an essential journalistic skill. There can still be situations when an audio recorder isn't appropriate and old-fashioned shorthand comes into its own again. It can be particularly useful when you are interviewing someone by phone or when the presence of an audio recorder is making an interviewee feel ill at ease. UK and Australian journalists use a form of shorthand called Teeline, which is based around the consonants of the alphabet and is therefore easy and fast to learn. As with typing courses, Teeline shorthand courses can usually be found wherever there's an adult-education centre or secretarial college. Depending on how many words per minute you want to achieve, Teeline shorthand can be learnt in anything from 70 to 100 hours. Most US journalists simply devise their own abbreviated note-taking method – but all agree that having some way to quickly and easily jot down notes is essential.

SETTING UP YOUR HOME OFFICE

Working from Home

One of the essentials for a writer is a comfortable and compatible place to work, and ideally one that is a dedicated work space. In the UK it is best to have your work space as part of a room that's used for another purpose – for example, a bedroom or living room; if you set up your home work space in a separate room, you could become liable for business tax rates (that is, nondomestic rates). In the US and Australia it is actually a tax advantage if you can set aside a separate room as your workplace.

Wherever your work space is, you want it to be truly your office. When you go there, even if you are simply stepping from one part of a room into another, you have to have the mindset that you are now entering your workplace. You are there to work and not to watch TV, listen to music or chat to friends on the phone. If at all possible, it should be free of all such distractions – except the telephone, of course, which you'll be using to check travel information for fact boxes and the like. Of course, you have to set up a schedule that works best for you, and if that means periodic TV, music or phone calls to friends, that's up to you. But to get the most out of your workplace, wherever it may be, you need to adopt it in your mind as the place where you focus on your work.

In terms of equipment, you will need:

▸ a reasonably powerful and up-to-date computer and computing software

▸ a phone and voicemail (or an answering machine)

▸ a letter-quality printer

▸ at least one filing cabinet

▸ broadband Internet connection (you'll be doing a lot of research on line, so you need a fast connection that allows you to be on line and make phone calls at the same time)

▸ a scanner (particularly in the US, for emailing images from print photos to newspaper editors)

▸ a fax machine (this technological dinosaur is still important for chasing unpaid invoices)

▸ a world atlas

▸ English and foreign-language dictionaries

▸ a thesaurus

▸ a small library of guidebooks, travel literature books and other editorial and reference works: for example, an up-to-date copy of the *Writers' & Artists' Yearbook* in the UK; a copy of *Writer's Market* or *Literary Market Place* in the US; or *The Australian Writer's Marketplace*. For listings of other useful reference tools, see the Resources Chapter at the back of this book.

Basic Administration

Once you start earning money as a freelance travel writer there are certain administrative and legal steps which you will need to take, such as filing taxes, keeping careful records and taking out insurance.

Taxes

TAXES IN THE UK

Whether you start writing full time, part time or on weekends and evenings after your 'proper' job, you will need to register with the Inland Revenue as being self-employed.

You need to register within three months of receiving your first cheque (regardless of how small it might be), as otherwise you'll incur a fine of £100. Once you become self-employed, you will have to pay your own National Insurance contributions, but only when your net travel writing income is more than £4215 a year. While you're earning less than this, you can apply for a Certificate of Small Earnings Exception. To register with the Inland Revenue and talk through all your options, ring the Newly Self-Employed Helpline on ☎ 08459-15 45 15. You should also be sent a useful leaflet called 'Thinking of Working for Yourself?' (P/SE/1). The Inland Revenue publishes another helpful booklet called 'Starting up in Business'; ask for this to be sent, too, or download it at www.inlandrevenue.gov.uk/startingup.

As a self-employed writer, you will also have to pay your own tax (see www.inlandrevenue.gov.uk for more information). Each April, at the end of the tax year, the Inland Revenue will send you a Self-Assessment Tax Return; if you return it to them before 30 September, the Inland Revenue will work out your tax bill. You will be required to pay your tax and National Insurance contributions in two instalments, on 31 January and 31 July. If you haven't given up your day job, you will be required to pay tax on any travel writing income from the outset because your tax-free allowance of £4745 will already have been used up. The tax rate of either 22 or 40 per cent will be worked out on your total earnings. If your travel writing income reaches £57,000, you'll have to register for VAT. (Note that all figures quoted above are for the tax year 2004–05, and usually change annually.)

TAXES IN THE US

The situation is a bit less formalised in the US. If freelance writing is a source of income, in addition to the 1040 standard tax form, you'll need to fill out the Schedule C tax form for self-employed individuals, 'Profit or Loss from Business'. For your freelance income, you'll use the 1099 forms you have received from all the publications that have paid you to fill out the Schedule C form's earnings information.

If you are filing as a freelancer, you should also fill out a Schedule SE Self-Employment Tax form. The SE tax is a Social Security and Medicare tax primarily for people who work for themselves; it is similar to the Social Security and Medicare taxes withheld from salaried employees. Regulations and rates vary from year to year, so the best advice is to research the current rules and requirements by reading the IRS's concise and helpful Publication 334, 'Tax Guide for Small Business (For Individuals Who Use Schedule C or C-EZ)'. You can download this publication and peruse a wealth of other tax-related information on the IRS website (www.irs.gov).

TAXES IN AUSTRALIA

In Australia freelance writers need to apply for an Australian Business Number (ABN), which must be included on all business-related invoices and stationery. If you do not have an ABN, any payments you receive may be subject to a Pay As You Go (PAYG) withholding tax of 48.5 per cent. If your annual income reaches or exceeds $50,000 you'll also need to be registered for GST, and will be required to lodge quarterly Business Activity Statements (BAS) specifying the GST payable or refund receivable, and any quarterly income tax payable or receivable.

If you keep a distinct separate office in your residence, you can claim a proportion of heating and lighting, rates, insurance and interest payable on your home loan. You are also able to claim for stationery consumables, plus depreciation on your computer, printer, modem, desk and library etc. You need to be rigorous about keeping documentation such as invoices, fees, contractual agreements, purchase contracts and receipts. It's also a good idea to keep a running diary of your expenses and income, detailing your working hours and any time spent using your computer for private use, and to keep track of business phone calls, emails and faxes. For more information, go to the Australian Tax Office website (www.ato.gov.au).

HIRING AN ACCOUNTANT

It's highly recommended that you engage an accountant to prepare your taxes. An accountant can handle (and educate you about) the intricacies of your tax return, give you up-to-date advice and ensure you are not over- or underpaying income tax. A possible alternative to hiring an accountant is to use one of the popular tax software programs, such as Quicken or TurboTax, to prepare and file your returns. The best of these feature a step-by-step 'interview' process that will record and analyse your answers and then generate the required tax forms.

However you choose to prepare your taxes, it is very important to bear in mind that you may be able to deduct many of your business-related expenses. These include your office expenses (stationery supplies, postage, phone calls, Internet connection etc) and a portion of your heating, lighting and other home expenses. You may also be able to deduct expenses for books, newspapers and magazines, as long as they are genuinely for research purposes, and of course research-related travel expenses such as transportation, accommodation, meals and some work-related entertainment expenses. As each individual's circumstances and options are different, hiring an experienced tax accountant is a good idea to ensure that you take full advantage of your qualifying deductions.

RECORD-KEEPING

Clearly, all of this means that you have to be a meticulous record-keeper. As a travel writer you'll incur a wide range of expenses – air tickets, hotel bills, car mileage, meals, equipment, entrance fees – and virtually all of these may be tax deductible. From the outset you need to make sure you understand what is an allowable expense and what isn't. In the UK, for example, you can claim travel expenses only on a work trip and not for a holiday which may also result in your writing a travel piece. In order to prove your legitimate business expenses, you need to keep all your receipts, and to have a thorough, well-organised calendar of your travels and other work-related activities during the year. You must keep all your records for six years in the UK, for seven years in the US and for five years in Australia.

With regard to expenses and deductions, you should be aware that the government will expect your business to become profitable at some stage. If you are incurring a business loss year after year, you should consult with a tax accountant because you will be permitted to lose money for only a certain number of years in a row. In the US and Australia, for example, you must make money in any three out of five years or your travel writing will be classified as a hobby rather than a livelihood, and your travel-related expenses will be disallowed (but any travel-related earnings, of course, will still be taxable).

Record-keeping is important not only when it comes to taxes, of course. If you are travelling on assignment for a US publication, and that publication is paying your expenses, you will have to turn in a record of your expenses with related receipts in order to be reimbursed. Keep all your receipts in a safe place, and carry a blank receipt book so you can supply your own receipts in situations where the local establishment doesn't have a form. To avoid the nightmare of sorting through dozens of scraps of paper days or even weeks after a trip, try to record all your expenses at the end of each day – you'll then have the date, the place, the reason for the expense and the amount, all ready to be categorised and submitted when you get home. It's also a good idea to keep a running tab of your expenses, because if you go over your expense limit, you'll be responsible for the difference.

Record-keeping is also fundamental when it comes to income. Having a story published doesn't automatically guarantee that a cheque will appear in the mail. These days most publications expect or require you to submit an invoice after your piece has been published; the invoice should include the subject of the article, the date of publication, the agreed-upon payment for the piece, your address, and your social security number (if in the US) or ABN (if in Australia). It is also a good idea to include your phone number and/or email address so you can be contacted if necessary. And even after you've submitted your invoice, it isn't the editor's responsibility to keep track of whether you've been paid for your piece; they have far too many other balls to juggle. You are the only person who will be watching out for *you* – and you can be sure that at some point your payment will slip through the cracks. Keep track of your publications and payments rigorously, and follow up on any outstanding invoices. The best practice is to create a table or spreadsheet that tracks all of your proposals and story submissions – where and when you submitted them and what responses you received, plus any commissions and deadlines, expenses submitted (if in the US), dates of publication and payments received.

As a freelancer you have to be a businessperson, too. Your writing is your livelihood and you need to keep your business records up to date, as if your life depended on them – and it usually does. If you are absolutely hopeless at record-keeping but sufficiently successful, consider taking on an intern or hiring a well-organised friend to keep your records for you.

Travel Insurance

It's also extremely important to make sure you are covered by insurance when you travel. In the UK and Australia, you will need business travel insurance if you are travelling to research and write. Most travel writers take out annual policies so they don't have to worry about this aspect of their trip each time they travel. In the US, writers should check to see what kind of coverage they already have through their personal insurance and what kind of supplemental travel coverage they may need. Consult with your insurance agent to make sure you have protection for all the potential hazards of your professional world-wanderings, from trip disruption or cancellation to loss of business equipment and medical emergencies.

Now that we've covered the essential tools of the trade, let's turn our attention to a specialised area of the travel writer's world: writing for travel guidebooks.

WRITING FOR TRAVEL GUIDEBOOKS

Much of the foregoing advice about writing travel articles for magazines and newspapers can also be applied to writing for travel guidebooks – and, indeed, many freelance writers combine guidebook writing with magazine or newspaper work – but there are some major differences, too. To focus on the particular skills required for writing or contributing to travel guidebooks, we turned to one of Lonely Planet's most seasoned guidebook writers, David Else, who has more than 20 years' experience researching and writing for a variety of travel guides. Here are David's tips and tales from the trenches.

WHAT IT TAKES TO BE A GUIDEBOOK WRITER

What abilities do you need to be a guidebook writer? First, you must employ the same artistic skills as a travel literature author or travel journalist. Your words must capture the nature, spirit and ambience of a place, whether it's a whole country, a small town or a single café. Your words must be engaging or entertaining where appropriate, and authoritative or serious where required.

Second, you need the temperament of a detective. You need to be inquisitive and fastidious as you seek out details and carefully record them, from obscure facts about local customs to bland hotel rates or restaurant phone numbers. The information you provide to your publisher, and eventually to your reader, has to be 100 per cent accurate and reliable.

Third, you need the mind of a poet. Space is always short in guidebooks, and you must transmit the detail and description in a concise, engaging and economic manner. When you've got just a few pages to cover a city with 20 hotels, 10 restaurants, three museums and four galleries, plus some introductory paragraphs to reflect the atmosphere of the place, you simply don't have the space for long reviews or elaborate articles enjoyed by magazine writers. As with poetry, every word must count. But we're not talking *Paradise Lost* here; think more along the lines of a haiku.

And finally, you must have the attitude of a publishing professional. You must adhere to your editors' requirements and produce the work according to their guidelines, rather than making up your own. You might think your 'artistic freedom' is hobbled – and sometimes it is – but freedom is a luxury enjoyed by the novelist. As a guidebook writer, you are a provider of information, and you must present it in an accessible style and in a prescribed format as laid down by the publisher who hires you for the assignment.

If you can combine all these skills and attributes, and – most important – if you simply love travel, then guidebook writing could be the job for you.

Why Write Guidebooks?
Although it's not a major concern for every writer, a good reason to write guidebooks is that compared to many other genres, guidebook work can sometimes offer a fair chance of actually

earning enough money to make freelance writing a full-time career. That's a major advantage. But you should never do it just for the money – not least because in many cases the money isn't that good, and not always constant enough to keep the wolf from the door.

So before you buy that air ticket, before you phone that editor, and even before you put pen to paper (or fingers to keyboard), you must be very clear on your own reasons for wanting to write guidebooks. Do you think that guidebook writing might suit your personality? Do you have an urge to seek out new places, and a desire to spread the word? Do you want to write guidebooks for pleasure? For the satisfaction of seeing your work in print? Is it just a desire for subsidised holidays, or simply to make a small amount of money while seeing interesting parts of the world, escaping the nine-to-five rat-race, and generally having a good time?

Of course, you often have to ask yourself the same questions about writing literary works or magazine pieces, and all or any of the above are perfectly good reasons for wanting to write guidebooks. The key point is that you have to be clear about *your* reason for wanting to write travel guides. This chapter will help you make that decision.

APPROACHING A PUBLISHER

Rule Number One: get a publisher. Only on very rare occasions should you write a guide-book without having contacted a publisher beforehand. You should secure an assignment or commission (and, in most cases, a contract) from the publisher before you start researching and writing, at least in detail. Writing a book that nobody wants would be a huge waste of your time. Also, you need clear instructions from the publisher (such as which areas they want you to cover, or which angle they want you to take) before you go out on your travels. Even if you decide on the destination and the nature of the book, and a publisher agrees with your proposal, it's still not possible to write a book after returning from a 'normal' holiday; you must travel specifically to do your research.

Study the Market

As with magazine and newspaper writing, before approaching guidebook publishers you need to study the size, style, range and coverage of the market. Get to know the specialities of each company, and tailor your applications accordingly. It's important to note that not all guidebook publishers are the same, and they vary considerably in their methods of dealing with new writers. You can't send out identical email applications or form letters to a batch of publishers and expect any of them to take you seriously. In fact, if a publisher feels you're sending out form letters, that's the surest way for your mail to end up in the rubbish bin.

Some publishers concentrate on a certain sector of the travelling public and produce only one type of book; they could be aimed at adventure tourists, overland drivers, cul-ture buffs or wildlife fans, for instance. Other publishers produce a wide range of series aimed at different markets; Lonely Planet, for example, publishes Shoestring guides for backpackers, City guides for urban aficionados and Best Of guides for business and short-break travellers.

Invest your time and effort wisely, and do some serious research in libraries and travel bookshops. Make sure you look at publishers' most recent products, as the style and content of guidebooks can change over the years. Publishers who once covered the backpacker scene might now be publishing guides for mid-market travellers, too; they may have introduced a new series, such as mini city guides for business travellers or recreation guides for families, or perhaps trimmed their range right back. Wherever possible, take a look at the different publishers' catalogues (either in print or on line) to see what new series they are publishing right now – and what they will be bringing out next year, too.

Pitching Yourself As a Writer

Having done your homework, and decided which company you want to approach, the next step is to write your pitch. Tell the publisher what you can offer them. Asking for a job because you've 'always wanted to travel' is unlikely to be successful.

While you're researching the market, you'll also discover the sort of initial information the publisher will need, the name or title of the person you should write to (usually a managing editor, commissioning editor, publishing recruitment administrator or similar) and whether the company prefers written or emailed applications.

Whatever their specific preferences, you'll generally need to briefly outline your background, skills and qualifications. Emphasise your experience as a writer or your knowledge of certain destinations. Keep your main message short and sweet. Include some examples of your writing and a more detailed CV or résumé.

Pitching an Idea

If you have an idea for a brand-new book, something no other publisher currently has on their list, you'll need to pitch both your idea and yourself as a writer. Once again, it's essential to study the market, and make sure you take your proposal to the right place. Ask yourself why your book is required. Does it cover a new subject; an emerging destination, such as Ethiopia, North Korea or the Arctic; an unusual niche, such as Iraq; or an unusual angle, such as travelling the railways of Africa or a guide to South American ski resorts? You need to be very clear about the reasons why a publisher should take up your idea and why it should sell. (Incidentally, all these examples of possible new titles already exist.)

Also consider the different types of destination, and your readership. Is your book targeted at low-budget travellers visiting a wider area (a backpacking guide to Southeast Asia, for example); high-rolling tourists stopping off at a compact destination (a Tokyo city guide, perhaps); or a guide for all budget levels but with a particular specialist bias (such as a guide to trekking in Nepal)?

Do some research into the number of tourists travelling to the destination you propose covering. Are there enough potential travellers out there to buy the book and make it commercially viable? A 'remote island paradise' may appear the perfect subject for a guidebook, but if it can only be reached by a three-day canoe trip, it's unlikely to be flooded with visitors.

Maybe there are books which are similar to the one you're proposing, but you feel that yours will be much better. You may persuade a publisher with a well-researched, detailed and confident pitch, but only the big companies can take up a full-frontal assault on the opposition in this way.

Finally, be relevant. Don't contact a publisher of backpacker titles offering a book on five-star restaurants, or send a publisher of smart hotel guides a pitch about travelling around Europe on a dollar a day.

Replies & Rejection

As with many other types of travel writing, contacting guidebook publishers can be a soul-destroying affair. Every month the major guidebook publishers receive literally hundreds of applications from eager wannabees, and even the smaller outfits have a steady steam of enquiries coming in, so a reply along the lines of 'Sure, we'd love to hire you, can you go to Cuba tomorrow?' is very unlikely (but not unknown). It's much more likely that you'll be sent a standard response asking for more details of your skills, experience and qualifications (formal or otherwise) for writing a book. However, some publishers may not even reply at all.

Self-Publishing

If you don't receive a commission, but you still believe in your guidebook idea and remain convinced that there's an eager travelling public out there just dying to buy it, then you could consider taking the path of self-publishing. Many of the well-known travel guidebook publishers of today started out by self-publishing just one title. However, while it's still possible, the nature of travel publishing has changed considerably since then. The writing and printing aspects of self-publishing are relatively straightforward, but in order to actually *sell* books you'll probably end up having to self-market and self-distribute, too.

PUBLISHERS & NEW WRITERS

Whether you're totally new to guidebook writing or just new to dealing with a particular company, you'll find that publishers fall into two main camps when dealing with new writers. In the first camp are the publishers looking for writers with the skills and travel experience to work on new editions of existing titles. In the second camp are the publishers looking for new writers who also have ideas for brand-new titles. For most aspiring guidebook writers, publishers in the first camp provide the best opportunities.

For example, Lonely Planet is one of the largest independent travel publishers in the world, with several hundred staff and a pool of around 250 freelance guidebook writers who are regularly contracted (plus a few hundred more who are hired less frequently), spread across the globe. While Lonely Planet encourages writers to submit ideas for brand-new books, most ideas for new titles are put forward by in-house publishing staff, and freelance writers are hired to do the research and produce the text. The same applies to new editions of titles which already exist: publishing staff decide what's needed, and freelance writers are hired. Writers of the previous edition may be hired to write the next edition, or the book may be handed over to a new writer, particularly if the previous edition needs a totally new author perspective. For titles involving teams of writers, a new edition will most likely be written by a mix of first-timers and experienced writers who worked on the previous book.

All writers who join the Lonely Planet 'author pool' must pass a rigorous selection procedure: they must produce a sample of writing which shows a talent for writing engaging text and an ability to follow Lonely Planet's house style closely, and they must pass a mapping test. Many of the people (but by no means all) who pass Lonely Planet's selection process are already trained or experienced writers. Most successful applicants also have knowledge about or expertise in certain destinations, and are usually commissioned to work on books covering those areas. Sometimes, applicants who show considerable research and writing skills may be hired to join an author team in a country they've never visited before. Viewing a country through the eyes of a first-timer (like most readers) is seen as an advantage in this instance.

Having passed Lonely Planet's tests, a new writer could experience the following scenario: their first contract might be to update a relatively small part of a book with a large team of writers covering a major area (for example, *Western Europe* or *South America on a Shoestring*); the second contract could be for a larger part of a similar book; a third contract might be for work on a book covering a smaller area (for example, *Slovenia* or *Kenya*) as part of a smaller team of writers; and a fourth contract might be a major role in a key country title or a city title (*India* or *Bangkok*, for instance). The path would be similar at other publishers who have this approach to new writers.

In contrast to Lonely Planet's approach, other publishers such as Bradt and Trailblazer in the UK and Wilderness and Sasquatch in the US are as likely to give assignments to keen amateurs as to full-time professionals; this is often true of smaller companies, but not always. In addition, in the US some larger publishers such as Moon and Globe Pequot, though they generally prefer experienced writers, will sometimes commission authors with special knowledge and passion, even if they have little or no publishing background. The key aspects these companies are looking for are proven knowledge of and genuine enthusiasm for a destination. Good writing is also valued very highly – prospective authors are usually asked to submit a sample of writing for approval.

For aspiring travel writers, approaching a smaller publisher can seem like a great way of getting a foot in the door of the freelance travel writing business, but most companies of this nature are less likely to have titles in need of new contributors, especially if their current writers hold the copyright to their books (and are guaranteed work on each new edition), and so in reality there are usually fewer options here than at a larger publishing company. There may be occasional opportunities to update existing guides, usually arising when the original author doesn't have the time to work on the new edition, but most companies would be very unlikely to commission someone to update a guide who had neither travel writing experience nor previous knowledge or understanding of the destination.

Taking all the above into account, if you approach a smaller publisher looking for work, they may well expect you to come equipped with ideas for brand-new titles to add to their range. If there is initial interest in your suggestion for a new title, a detailed proposal covering the destination concerned would then be required. Working for a smaller publisher often means more freedom, but unfortunately they usually (although not always) sell fewer books – and that means lower fees. If money is a prime factor, you should probably look for work with one of the larger publishers. If the sheer enjoyment of writing is your goal, then you might be happier with a smaller organisation.

COMMISSIONING & BRIEFING

You have received a commission: the publisher likes what you do, and wants you to write all or part of a book. What happens next? In most cases, your point of contact at a publishing house is a commissioning editor. In general, this is the person who decides which books to publish, and which writers to hire (although different publishing companies have different structures and various titles for the people in this position). If you've had only outline discussions so far, you and your editor will now start to discuss in full the work you're expected to do.

The destination area you're expected to cover, the style you're required to use and all other aspects relating to the book will be laid out in a document called a 'title outline' or 'brief'. As the name implies, a title outline is an overview of what the editor requires from you the writer, whereas a brief (despite the name) is usually a longer, more detailed document. Larger companies with a huge range of books place great importance on a homogenous style recognisable by readers and bookstore buyers across the globe, and so tend to produce very precise briefs, carefully describing the areas to cover, the tone and style required, the intended readership and other instructions based on the strengths and weaknesses identified in previous editions. Smaller companies are likely to be more flexible when it comes to briefing, and to allow the writer to use a style which works best for the subject in hand. Either way, the brief may go through several drafts as you and the editor work together to form a final version.

Most guidebook publishers expect their writers to gather material for the maps which will appear in the book. Again, requirements vary: a brief from a larger publisher may contain many instructions regarding mapping, whereas smaller publishers are likely to be far less demanding.

You'll also be given a deadline – the date when you must finish the book and deliver it to the publisher as a 'manuscript'. (This quaint term is still used, even if you send in your work as an email attachment.) The work must be ready for publication as far as you're concerned, or as far as the brief requires, although copy-editors and proofreaders will still have a role to play – querying, fine-tuning or rewriting your text where necessary.

At some stage in the proceedings – ideally, early on – you'll also receive a contract or letter of agreement, which clearly sets out your obligations to the publisher, and their obligations to you. The contract will also specify the amount you will be paid – and when you'll get it.

FEES, ROYALTIES & COPYRIGHT

There are some key points to be aware of when considering guidebook fees, royalties and copyright.

Fees & Royalties

Guidebook publishers have two main options when paying writers. The first option is to pay a royalty, where the writer receives a share of every book sold. This might be 10 per cent of the cover price, five per cent of the total net sum received by the publisher, or a similar arrangement. For example, if the book's cover price is £10, and you're on 10 per cent, then you earn £1 for every book sold. If the book sells 100 copies, you earn £100; if it sells a million, you make a million. It's important to discuss the expected sales figures with your publisher before you sign a contract, but be aware that the publisher's estimates are no guarantee of actual sales.

The second option is to be paid a flat fee. This is a single payment which is guaranteed to the writer, whatever the book's sales performance, although the amount of the fee is still likely to be determined by how well the publisher thinks the book will sell. Fees vary widely from publisher to publisher, and project to project. For example, the fee for a single author working on a major guidebook to a city or country might be anything between £2500 and

£15,000, depending on the work required; for a team of authors working together on a book, individual fees can range from £1500 to £10,000.

Both payment methods have advantages and disadvantages. With royalties you stand a chance of making more money, but also a chance of making less. A flat fee takes out the guesswork and helps with your financial planning, especially if you're trying to make guidebook writing a full-time job. The larger companies generally offer deals based on fees while smaller publishers tend to work on royalties. Writers usually have no choice in the matter, and are obliged to accept each publisher's method.

Viewed on a per-word basis, guidebook writing fees do not always compare favourably with the rates you can be paid for travel articles in magazines or newspapers. However, guidebook commissions tend to be larger assignments and therefore pay more overall. To make a living from freelance magazine work, you'd need to be given two to four decent commissions each month, and that can be rare. In contrast, for a good, reliable writer, receiving two to four guidebook commissions a year is quite feasible, and that can be enough to make a living.

THE UPS & DOWNS OF FEES & ROYALTIES

In the 1990s I was commissioned to write a guidebook called *Walking in Britain*. The editor did not foresee massive sales, and I was unsure of just how many people would buy the book, so I was happy to accept a flat fee of around £20,000 for the job. Over the next four years the book exceeded all expectations and sold about 125,000 copies. Had I been on a royalty deal I would have earned over £100,000. It was frustrating, but I had to remind myself that at the time I signed the contract I was happy with the fee, and over the following years I just had to dream of my 'lost wealth'.

At about the same period, a friend of mine was writing a guide to the USSR. Again, this was based on a flat fee, not a royalty. After months of hard research and write-up the book was published. Then, about three days later, the cold war finally ended, the USSR ceased to exist and the book was immediately out of date. The publisher had to start again, producing new books to the 'new' countries of Russia, Ukraine, Azerbaijan and so on, while thousands of copies of the USSR book went unsold and were eventually pulped. If my friend had been on a royalty deal he'd have earned virtually nothing. As it was, he still got his fee, as per the contract, and the publisher took the full financial hit.

– David Else

Advances

If you're paid on a royalty basis, some publishers pay an advance. This means that you'll receive some money in the early stages of your work, and won't have to wait until the book is in the shops being bought by the public before your payment arrives. You might be given an advance on signing the contract, on delivering your work or on publication (or staggered amounts across all three stages), but it's important to remember that it's an up-front payment, which will be deducted later from your royalties. It's not an extra payment.

If you're paid on a fee basis, you might receive the whole payment in a lump sum (on publication, for example). Alternatively, the fee might be divided into four instalments, with 25 per cent being paid on signing the contract, on delivering your work, on the date the book goes to the printer and on the day it's published.

Copyright

Some guidebook publishers allow writers to keep the copyright of the text (and sometimes the maps) they produce; others will take ownership of copyright. If you sign over copyright to the publisher, you lose all rights to your own words, and the publisher can do what they like with them, including re-selling them to another user such as a website or foreign publisher. You cannot reuse the words you created without permission from the publisher who now holds the copyright.

There are advantages and disadvantages to both systems (for example, the extra re-sale opportunities gained by your publisher in taking copyright ownership can be reflected in higher fees for you, although rarely directly), and often you don't have a choice anyway, but it's important to be clear on the legal situation regarding your carefully crafted text, before signing the contract.

Generally – though not always – books commissioned on a royalty basis tend to remain the copyright of the author, while the copyright in fee-based books passes to the publisher.

Expenses & Freebies

Whether you're paid on a royalty or fee basis, it's important to remember that what you earn will most likely have to cover all the costs you incur while you're specifically researching the guidebook; for example, flights, surface travel and accommodation, as well as general business items such as your computer, stationery and phone calls. Only rarely will a publisher pay a fee and then make additional payments to cover your research costs, or allow you to submit a claim for expenses.

Some guidebook publishers may allow their writers to negotiate complimentary or discounted services (free hotel nights, special rate car hire and so on), while other publishers take a dim view of this. It goes without saying that accepting 'freebies' should not cloud your independent judgment as a guidebook writer. If you're accepting deals in exchange for positive write-ups you're on very dodgy ground, as it is a practice most guidebook publishers positively forbid.

MAKING IT PAY

Assuming you're working as a travel guidebook writer at least partly for the money, you have to make sure that all the earnings you make from writing a guidebook cover your research costs and your general business items, and still leave you with enough money to live on. And that means your rent or mortgage, food, clothes and all the other stuff you'd buy with your salary from any other type of job.

But how does a guidebook writer know if the fee being offered is fair or reasonable? This is a question commonly asked by new writers. There is no easy answer, as there are no hard and fast rules in the world of freelance travel writing. The fee for a job might seem fair to one author, too low to another, and generous to yet another. To help a little, here are a few pointers:

Work Out Your Costs

To work out your costs, take into account the following:

Research Days

Decide if a town with 12 hotels and 10 restaurants plus beaches, museums and clubs is going to take you one day or three to research. Decide how long bigger cities, villages or places like national parks will take. Work out your travel time (in some countries it can take a whole day just to get from Town A to Town B), then add it all up – that's how long you'll be on the road.

Long-Haul Travel Costs
This is usually a plane fare. Scan the Internet or newspapers for sample fares, then add 20 to 50 per cent because those travel agent bargains are always hard to find in reality.

Ground Travel Costs
Costs for travel by bus, train, boat, rental car, camel or dug-out canoe will depend on the destination, but are easy to calculate based on the number of days you'll be in the destination, the number of days you'll actually be travelling, and the average costs (per day, per 100 kilometres, or whatever) of travel in your destination. If you have no idea of average costs in the country you're about to write about, ask yourself if you're the right person for the job.

Accommodation Costs
This cost is easy to calculate, based on the number of days you'll be on the road, the type of book you're writing and the type of accommodation you intend to sample.

Food Costs
Once again, this cost is easy to calculate, based on the number of days you'll be on the road. Don't forget that you've got to eat wherever you are, so deduct your normal 'at home' food bills from this amount.

Other Costs
This includes miscellaneous expenses such as phone calls, Internet time, postage, photocopying, laundry and local guides, and will depend on the destination you're covering and the amount of time you're away.

Work Out Your Profit
Add together all the costs listed above to work out your total cost. Look at the fee offered by your publisher, deduct the total cost, and that's your profit or earnings.

Work Out How Long the Project Will Take
You've already worked out how long you'll be on the road; now calculate the number of days you'll spend writing up. Consider the number of pages you're responsible for, the amount of brand-new text that's required, and how much rewriting of old text you'll have to do.

Add together the research and writing-up time, then add another week or two to set up flights, arrange meetings and familiarise yourself with your editor's requirements, plus about a week at the end of the project to handle editorial queries.

Is it Right for You?
Consider the profit as a whole (guidebook writers get paid by the job, not by the hour) or view the sum as a daily or weekly rate according to the time it will take you to earn it. It could work out at £5 per day; it could be £150 per day, or more. Then ask yourself: does that seem reasonable, and will the earnings cover your cost of living? What surplus does it leave for essentials such as new equipment or a pension for the day you hang up your backpack and laptop for good?

If you're single, footloose and fancy-free, you might not care too much about profit. You might want to be a travel guidebook writer for the thrill of visiting exotic destinations. For you, as long as your costs are covered, that's enough.

Maybe you can combine the book research with other freelance opportunities, such as photography or writing for magazines. Or perhaps you realise that because you are new to travel writing, you've got to get a gig or two under your belt before you can start expecting (or demanding) higher fees.

Approaches to fees vary considerably among writers, and everyone has their own parameters. A lot depends on your attitude to writing and your attitude to life, but the key question is always this: is the fee reasonable for *you*?

GROUND RESEARCH

You've finally managed to find a publisher, scored a commission, negotiated a payment that you're happy with and worked your way through various briefs and contractual documentation. At last, after jumping all these hurdles, you can begin the next stage of the guidebook process: the on-the-ground research.

Ground research for guidebooks can take anything from two to 20 weeks, depending on the size and nature of the book. About six to eight weeks on the road is average, but your first gig could be five days in Berlin checking out clubs for an entertainment listing, or three months covering several countries in Africa. The size and nature of the destination to be covered can have a major impact on your research time: a country with a good transport network, or just good roads (such as Switzerland), will be much easier and quicker to get around than a country with neither of these features (such as Mongolia).

Your level of experience also has an effect on the amount of time you'll be away: writers new to guidebook writing have to learn the ropes, and will inevitably work more slowly. As your experience grows, you'll figure out ways to work faster and more efficiently. And when you start working on repeat editions, you can incorporate information and knowledge from previous trips, which will also save you considerable time, money and effort.

Destination Coverage

Successful travel guidebooks are accurate, up to date, well written and relevant to the reader, and as a writer you'll have a great many things to cover on the ground.

Collecting Key Information

There are four key elements in every guidebook: information on transport, accommodation, food and places to visit.

Everything you research for the section on transport will depend on the nature of the guidebook, which in turn is determined by the intended readership, but you will certainly get to know a lot about planes, trains, boats, buses, bikes, taxis, cars and – sometimes – camels or mules. You'll have to research timetables, frequencies, quality, reliability, rental opportunities, rules of the road and so on.

For the accommodation section you'll visit everything from cheap dives to five-star hotels. Often you'll have to visit 20 hotels, just to see which are best (or best to mention), even though you'll only be writing about five or six of them in the book. It can be particularly difficult to work up the energy to trek out to distant city suburbs, or travel for hours through the jungle, just to visit a single place to stay. But when you reach that luxury hotel or backpackers' lodge and realise it's just the type of gem your readers will love to visit, it makes the slog worthwhile.

If you've only got three days in a town you won't be able to stay in all of those 20 hotels, just as you won't be able to eat in every single restaurant. That's where the guidebook writer's skill really comes into its own, and where techniques vary. Usually, your first stop will be the person working on the hotel's reception desk. You'll ask for the room rates, and if there are any seasonal differences, and maybe pretend that you are coming back next week or checking options for a friend who's due to visit. To complete your review you can ask the receptionist to show you a few rooms, talk to other guests sitting in the lobby, look at the bar, note any interesting features and take in the general ambience of the whole place. Usually you won't reveal that you're writing a guidebook, although sometimes coming clean can be beneficial (for example, the manager might tell you that a new bar is about to open or that that the delightful old wing with the ornate balconies is about to be demolished). Often you'll most likely end up using a combination of all these approaches, but the key is to collect accurate information as efficiently as possible.

It's the same deal for the section on food, where you'll cover anything from street food to silver-service restaurants, depending on the nature of the book. As with hotels, remember to keep your research relevant, and be careful to follow the instructions you've been given by your editor in the book's brief. A common mistake is to 'over re-search' – to spend lots of time finding and assessing places that don't require coverage. If you're writing a guide for budget travellers, make sure you cover places only in that price bracket. If your readership is mid-market, include a couple of bargain and splurge options in the mix.

While readers need to know the prices and phone numbers of all the places to sleep and eat, they also want your opinion. Simple listings are available everywhere – on the Web or in a brochure from the tourist office – but it's the guidebook writer's opinion that adds value, and makes the guidebook stand out from other, sometimes free, information. Include your first-hand knowledge, noting if a hotel is 'friendly and welcoming', 'opulent with excellent service' or 'spartan but good value'; if a restaurant has 'a great lunch-time buzz', 'impatient waiters' or 'a calm atmosphere'; and if a café is 'noted for its oysters', 'a local favourite' or 'intimate, verging on the cramped'.

You might think that the section on entertainment is a guidebook writer's perk. Checking out those drinking dens down by the docks and the finest cocktail lounges in town sounds like fun, but the reality is that you've got to stay sober and check three nightclubs, the theatre and the traditional dance show in one night, plus see what time they show English-language movies at the cinema. And then get up at dawn the next day to catch the early train to the next destination in the chapter.

Other Destination Details

In addition to researching transport, accommodation, food and entertainment there's all the other practical information that readers need when visiting a place for the first time. You'll have to research banks, change bureaus, post offices, telephone centres, Internet cafés, embassies, pharmacies – and note their opening hours, phone numbers, postal rates, visa regulations and so on.

For the section on places to see, you'll need to visit a destination's markets, museums, palaces, temples, churches and tombs, plus all the venues for football matches, bull fighting, local ceremonies and so on. Once again, you'll have to note the opening hours carefully, but also pass comment where appropriate. Is this museum worth a detour, or is it actually rather dusty and boring? Is the market lively and fun, or will you have your bag snatched (or possibly both)?

Most guidebooks have an activities section, so you'll need to find out where readers can go fishing, surfing or mountain biking (and where to hire wetsuits or bikes). Once again, you need to give the reader some idea of quality: if a visitor has only one day in a city, which activity is the most fun? What is a must-do, what is best-value and what could be skipped?

You'll also need to describe excursions around the city or trips and safaris further afield, collecting prices, departure times and destinations. It's a good idea to speak to other travellers to get some ideas on quality.

Feeling tired? Sorry, you're not done yet. You've got to cover the shopping section by visiting craft shops, designer stores and markets, and dig out any quirky places selling local spices or gifts.

Regional Information

Most of the key elements and other destination details apply to cities and towns (although they won't all apply to the smaller places). If you're researching a country or regional guide, there are other things to cover beyond the urban environs. You'll need to visit and collect details on places such as vineyards, chateaux, beaches, wildlife reserves and national parks.

Wildlife areas can be a massive topic, especially in Africa or Central America. As well as a selection of safari lodges or camping grounds to visit, you'll need to research the park's access and entrance regulations. You must be up to scratch on your wildlife knowledge, too, informing the reader about the various species that can be seen, and including details such as the seasonality of sightings. Simply writing 'the Kruger Park has a wide range of birds and animals' just will not do.

Introductory Information

If you're writing a whole book, or some introductory chapters, you might also be asked to provide sections on getting to the country you're writing about – from the UK, the USA, Australia or whatever the publisher requires. This means covering the wide choice of international flights and other aspects of transport such as self-driving or overland trucks. You must also cover getting to the country or region you're writing about from neighbouring countries. This means finding out about local transport, border crossings, regulations, and so on.

Other introductory chapters provide the reader with essential background information on the country, region or city being covered. This means researching and writing about history, politics, economics, geography, climate, ecology, people, government, language and culture. In some places that last aspect can be a world in itself: you need to find out about everything from ancient carvings to the latest craze in local pop music.

Timeliness

If you're updating a previous edition, you won't have to write everything from scratch; you'll be able to reuse some of the existing material (although you'll have to check it all, as the previous author may have been less rigorous than yourself). If you're writing a brand-new book, however, you'll have to cover all the material described above. When you're weighing up the fee or the terms the publisher is offering, make sure you're clear on what you have to cover in your research and writing, and be sure to have a good estimate on how long it will take.

To gather all the necessary information, the guidebook writer must be an independent traveller and cover the same ground in the same way as the reader. The difference is that while the reader can pick and choose, or just take a day or two to laze on the beach, the guidebook writer must cover every town, every hotel and every bus station, every national park and every major attraction (and some of the minor ones, too) – and cover them fast as well. You can't stay in bed because you're feeling a bit tired, or not leave your room because the weather looks bad. And it's no good just dabbling here and there, missing out important or interesting places – that way the book will take longer to write and the information will become out of date. Much more importantly, the book will not be submitted on time: you'll miss your deadline, breach your contract, lose part or all of your fee, and be much less likely to be offered work by the publisher again. Writing guidebooks slowly is financially unviable, as guidebook writers are paid by the job, not by the hour. The more projects you can pack into a year (without skimping, of course), the more likely you'll be able to make a living as a guidebook writer.

Research Tools

Unfortunately, you won't have a huge range of tools to assist you as you collect and record the huge amount of information you'll be dealing with while researching. Essentially, you've got the option of pen and paper, an audio recorder, a PDA or other hand-held electronic device, or a laptop computer.

You'll usually find yourself using a combination of all the above – although a lot depends on the nature of the job. Carrying a laptop isn't a problem if you're working in a more developed part of the word, such as Europe or North America, where you might be travelling in your own vehicle. But pen and paper is the best way to go if you're working on a book covering a large area where conditions are hard, such as India or West Africa, where you'll probably be travelling on public transport.

The exact form of your paper can vary: big or small notebooks, hard or soft cover, stitched, ring binder or clipboards. For writing you can choose from ball-point pens, roller-tips or pencils (they work in the wet, and even upside down). The best thing is to try a few options, then stick with what works best for you.

PDAs and audio recorders can have their uses, but using them on city streets might get you unwanted attention. Back at your hotel, though, they can be useful for recording a summary of your day's work as a backup to your notes.

Many authors use a pocket camera to quickly record such things as departure boards in bus stations or restaurant menus, or to snap the outside of a hotel or a city's main market to help bring back the memories when it comes to crafting those reviews and introductory paragraphs. If you use a digital camera you can play back the images or download them straight onto your computer, and have them right there when you're writing.

For checking maps, you'll need a pocket compass and maybe a small ruler for working out scales (or just make some marks on the edge of a slip of cardboard). Some authors use a GPS for updating and correcting maps of cities and countries, and this can be particularly useful if original source maps are unreliable.

Research Techniques
Paperwork

Whatever tools you use, it's essential when researching to be very well organised. It's vital to keep all your notes and maps in order, and to set yourself an itinerary for each day or week (depending on the nature of the book). Even if you break away from the itinerary, at least you've got a structure to your work, and it's much better than working at random.

If you're using pen and paper, the best basic research tool in cities is a map, ideally a photocopy, possibly from the previous edition of the guidebook. Make several copies, blown up to about 150 per cent of the original size, and use a new copy every day. Section off blocks of the city and visit all the items shown (restaurants, hotels, places of interest) in a logical route. If the place has closed down, or is no longer worth recommending, cross it out. For existing or new places, put your notes on prices, hours, quality and ambience on the back of the photocopy.

At the same time, carry photocopies of the relevant pages from the book (never the book itself) with enough white margin all round to add additional corrections to the text, where necessary. Thus, with just a few sheets of paper, you can refer to both map and text easily, often while walking. You can add notes quickly without having to flip between different pages or constantly switch between guidebook and notebook.

Every hour or so, take a break from pounding the streets and sit down in a bar or coffee shop, or anywhere with a table, to quickly review the information you've gathered so far, and to check for any gaps. If you have missed anything, it's much easier to go back while you're still in the area. It's a real pain to have to cross town again the following day, and even more of a disaster to find you've missed the phone number of that great new hotel you discovered, and there's no way of checking now that you're writing up back at home.

It's essential to note down every pertinent fact or observation on the spot. Don't rely on your memory. There's just too much to remember, and without proper notes you can't produce accurate text. To save note-taking time, pick up every map, leaflet and brochure you can from tourism offices and travel agencies. They won't all be useful, and tourist office hand-out maps are notoriously inaccurate, but don't worry. Sort them out every day or so, and throw away the ones you don't want. To save weight, consider sending home the ones you do want by mail or courier.

TIP OF THE TRADE

Along with my pens and paper, my other most valuable research tool is a big shirt pocket. Sounds boring, but all my travel shirts have large chest pockets – preferably two – for carrying my trusty pens, a few sheets of paper, a map, a compass and highlighter, and a few other odds and ends. I never carry a bag in cities, which means one less thing to worry about. I can move quickly, keep my notes instantly accessible and refer to them on the hoof. It also avoids drawing attention to myself, as some of the cities I've had the pleasure to research have some fairly nasty crime rates, and the 'travel light, travel safe' advice I give my readers makes a lot of sense for the writer, too.

– *David Else*

Local Assistance

When you're researching a large city in developed, well-organised parts of the world, maps are easy to find, road signs exist and the streets have names. But in parts of Africa, Southeast Asia and South America there may be no such luxuries as these, and simply getting around can be a very time-consuming aspect of the guidebook writer's day. This is when you have to think a bit more imaginatively.

If the city sprawls or the road layout is confusing, consider hiring the services of a local guide to help speed up your research process. This might be a professional, arranged through the tourist office; it might be a local person such as an off-duty hotel receptionist or a schoolboy who wants to practise his English; or it could be one of the hustlers who always seem to hang around tourist hotels.

Local guides can stop you getting lost among the alleys, markets and narrow streets; they can help you to decipher the local bus network and may take you to tiny local bars and restaurants that would be impossible to find otherwise; and they can explain the complicated queuing system at the train station. Many of them also become good friends.

Although most guidebook writers work incognito, it's worth explaining to the guide what you're doing, and that you're not a normal tourist; otherwise they'll soon begin to wonder why you're spending all day looking at hotels where you never want to stay, and then spending only five minutes looking at the museum, sultan's palace or other major attraction.

For the larger cities with sprawling suburbs, it's also worth picking up some form of private transportation. For flexibility you can't beat a bicycle – especially in places with traffic jams or tricky parking. A moped or motorbike might be a better option if you need to cover a bit more ground, either hired officially or borrowed from a contact. It will

---

LIFE ON THE ROAD

When researching in Africa, I sometimes hire a local guide to sit in my rental car or on the back of a borrowed motorbike. Occasionally, this passenger has to provide a more elaborate service.

On one trip I was in a town in Mali, and had arranged to hire a moped from the brother of one of the cleaners at my hotel. When the moped turned up, it was in a sorry state, with no stand, no lock and a very dodgy starting mechanism. I was worried that it could be stolen while it was parked outside a shop or restaurant I was checking. And I didn't like the thought of being stranded in the suburbs if I couldn't get the bloody thing started. I didn't fancy having to push it anywhere either, as most of the streets were made of sand and the temperature was uncomfortably hot.

'No problem,' said the cleaner, 'I have another brother.' The youngest member of the family was sent for, and your intrepid guidebook writer set off to research the town with an eight-year-old boy sitting on the back of my moped. When I pulled over to conduct some research, my young companion put his legs down to stop the moped falling over. He also acted as guard. Then, after completing my visit to each hotel, shop and restaurant, the hapless fellow pedalled the moped around in the heat and dust, until the engine fired and I could step nonchalantly into the driving seat. We made a great partnership, and he seemed to enjoy his day as my 'guide and assistant'. Of course, I tipped him generously and got my day's work done more quickly – so we were both happy.

– David Else

also come in useful if there are several places of interest in the surrounding countryside. Alternatively, you can charter a city taxi for the day (a tip: hire the car for the day, and pay for petrol separately), or hire a self-drive rental car and arrange a local guide to ride shotgun.

Taxi drivers can be a very useful source of information, once they've grasped what you're doing. They'll also take you to nice hotels, good local markets or interesting sights which you might otherwise have missed. As always, the end result of hiring transport is speed. If it means you can research the area more quickly – and more comprehensively – than on foot, and get on to your next destination more quickly, it's normally worth the outlay.

Protecting Your Material

Whichever way you collect and store your information when researching on the road, there's always the dreaded matter of protecting it: your bag could be stolen, your hotel could burn down or your canoe could be attacked by ravenous crocodiles and your notebook polished off by piranhas.

If you're using a laptop you can copy material onto a disc once every week or so, and send it home by mail or courier. If the technology of the country allows, you can also send the material to yourself (or a friend) as an email attachment.

If you're not using a laptop, it's essential that you regularly photocopy the notes and maps you've been busily scribbling on all day, and send these copies home every week or so. Alternatively, you could leave the copies with someone reliable, to be called upon in case of an emergency. If photocopying isn't possible, consider using your audio recorder to make a backup, simply by reading the key points from your notes straight onto the tape.

One final safety technique that some guidebook writers employ when staying in less-reputable hotels is to scatter their notes and maps around the room, rather than leaving them carefully filed in a smart-looking bag or briefcase. That way, if someone breaks in they'll steal your bag and other gear but hopefully leave the papers – priceless to you, but valueless to the thief – untouched. This also proves that although you don't have to be paranoid to be a guidebook writer, it certainly helps.

WRITING UP

The final major aspect of being a guidebook writer concerns the practicalities of the writing itself.

Writing Tools

While a few novelists may prefer to work in longhand, with quill and parchment no doubt, for the professional guidebook writer a computer with good word-processing software is essential. It makes your writing better, and helps you work faster. It also allows you to make electronic backups. Most important, publishers generally insist that your work is submitted electronically, either on a disc or via email or FTP (file transfer protocol). A few publishers still insist on receiving a printed manuscript too, even if you also have to deliver the work electronically.

Word Counts

One other reason for using a good word-processing program is that you can measure your word count as you write. Nearly all guidebook publishers will specify the number of words (or sometimes pages) they require, and this will be stipulated in your brief or contract. It is paramount that you keep to this figure. If you genuinely feel you can't fit everything in, you should inform your editor as early as possible – sometimes they may budge and give you a few extra pages or a few extra thousand words.

It can have major financial implications for your publisher if you deliver over length. Extra editors may need to be employed, the production time may be delayed, print deadlines and bookstore deliveries may be missed, and orders may be lost. It also has financial implications for you: deliver over length, or late, and you'll be much less likely to be hired again.

Where to Write Up

On the Road

Some guidebook writers do their writing as they go: every night, at their hotel or in their tent, they write up the day's research onto a laptop. This sounds fine but the theory often breaks down as most evenings you'll need to be out researching restaurants, bars and nightclubs. It's hell, but someone has to do it. Even if you don't go out on the town, after a full day on the streets of London, Lima or Lusaka, you'll probably be too exhausted to face a few more hours staring at a computer screen. And you can't write effectively if you're tired.

A lot depends on the nature of the book. If you're working on a city guide, you might be based in the same hotel room for a month, and find you can do a lot of writing when you're not pounding the streets. If you're covering a large country, moving on every day or so, you'll probably find very little time for writing.

A solution might be to take two days off from your research every week to turn raw data into text. Other writers take a middle course, getting their notes down at least in rough draft form, to be honed and polished back at the ranch.

At Home

Most guidebook writers get their ground research finished as quickly as possible and then head home to do the writing up. Most agree that it's much easier to write at their own desk, with all the maps, notes and other research material near at hand, and coffee bubbling nicely in the kitchen.

Assuming you're writing at home (it's very unusual for freelance writers to be given a desk at their publisher's office), it's important to create a proper work environment where you can avoid distractions. Ideally, you should set aside a dedicated desk in a bedroom or another room. Convert the garden shed if you have to, and lock yourself away. You can't write a good guidebook on the kitchen table with the TV blaring in the background.

As when you're researching, discipline is essential. It's no good having spent three months on the road, collecting loads of good information, if you can't turn it into engaging and accurate text in time to meet your publisher's deadline.

In Country

A few writers take the interesting course of staying 'in-country' after finishing the ground research, renting a room or apartment in the capital for a month or two and doing their writing there. It certainly helps when it comes to recalling local atmospheres, or using the phone to check an overlooked hotel tariff. And depending on where you're researching and where you live normally, it can save you money on rent, too.

TAKING THE PLUNGE

On the assumption that you're not immediately going to make a million from your first endeavour, how do you combine guidebook writing with everyday life, and how do you survive for a year or so with no income from the guidebook you're still hammering out on your computer?

The answer may be hard to swallow, but until you reach a stage where you *can* live off guidebook writing alone, you'll almost certainly have to combine it with another job. This leads to its own problems as, unfortunately, it's not normally possible to research and write a book in the two to four weeks of annual leave that most people can take from their work.

An option might involve taking a short commission such as updating a small part of a book. This can require just a couple of weeks of ground research, and you can write it up back at home in the evenings when you've finished your day job. This can be a very useful way of getting a feel for the world of guidebook writing, without having to commit fully right from the start.

Ideally, of course, you need the sort of job which gives you long holidays, but there aren't many of those about. You're more likely to take a series of temporary jobs, and use the time in between for writing. Many guidebook writers – in fact, many writers, whatever their speciality – combine writing with jobs such as supply teaching, locum medicine, night security, agency nursing, taxi driving, motorbike dispatch, short-term secretarial or accountancy, and so on. These jobs keep some money coming in, and allow you to take guidebook jobs at pretty short notice. This course can seem a bit risky or unsettling if you're used to the comforts of a secure full-time occupation – and income.

Perhaps the most practical option is to combine guidebook writing with a job which is somehow compatible. As mentioned earlier, many guidebook writers also write for magazines or newspapers; others sell their photographs, drive overland trucks, or work as leaders and guides for tour companies. Perhaps the most perfect option is to find a job that pays so well that you can afford to work only half the year and then concentrate on writing guidebooks in the other half.

However you work it out, the bottom line is still the same: travel guidebook writing is not a job to be taken lightly. You need to have the right attitude; you need to be able to combine the skills of author, poet, detective and publishing professional; you need to be flexible and adventurous; and you need to be able to work hard and fast. Meet these requirements, and after a year or two you'll have the pleasure of seeing your guidebook on the bookstore shelves and in the hands of eager travellers. You'll be able to visit the places you love, and you might even make some decent money along the way.

That's it! Hopefully, we've given you all the information and inspiration you need to embark on your own travel writing adventures – and for a wealth of further practical information, consult the Resources appendix at the end of this book. Before you set off on those adventures, here's one final wish: wherever you go and whatever you endeavour to do, may you always map your dreams, journey fully every day and impassion your path in your own special way. Good luck, and whatever you do – don't forget to write.

AFTERWORD

Jan Morris is one of the world's most respected writers about places, with some 40 books ranging in subject from her native Wales to Venice, Trieste, Manhattan, Hong Kong and Sydney. When we sent her the interview questions for this book, she replied as follows.

Lines to a Publisher in Response to Interview Questions Concerning Theories and Practices of Writing

Dear Publisher, I've thrown away
The form you sent to me today.
Theorizing's not my line –
It sends a shiver down my spine.
And as to agents, proper fees,
Writing methods – please, Sir, please,
Excuse me from this dismal chore!
O, let's take a car down to the shore
(Convertible would be the best),
Follow the sun into the west,
And sit, and drink, and spread our wings,
And talk about less dreary things.
Writing should be a happy art,
Springing, like love, but from the heart…

– *Jan Morris*

APPENDIX: RESOURCES

US RESOURCES

GENERAL GUIDES TO PUBLISHERS, EDITORS & LITERARY AGENTS

BookWire
www.bookwire.com/bookwire/publishers/Travel-Publishers.html

This website provides a list of and links to various travel publishers.

Jeff Herman's Guide to Book Publishers, Editors, and Literary Agents
by Jeff Herman (Writer, Inc)

A who's who for the publishing industry. Provides contact information for hundreds of top editors and agents. Published annually.

LMP: The Directory of the American Book Publishing Industry (Literary Market Place)
compiled by Information Today Inc staff (Information Today)
www.literarymarketplace.com

Over 2000 pages of book publisher listings. Published annually. An international directory is also available.

Publishers Marketplace
www.publishersmarketplace.com

This resource is especially helpful for writers looking for an agent. Users pay $15/month to access the on-line databases.

Travel Publishers Association
www.travelpubs.com

This website provides links to various independent travel publishers who are members of the Travel Publishers Association. Many of these publishers specialize in books targeted to niche markets (eg RV travelers, gay/lesbian market).

The Writer's Handbook
edited by Efreida Abbe (Writer, Inc)

An annual guide to literary agents, book publishers, consumer magazines, contests and awards, and more. Edited by the editor-in-chief of *The Writer* magazine.

Writer's Market
edited by Kathryn S. Brogan (Writer's Digest Books)
www.writersmarket.com/index_ns.asp

Another annual guide to literary agents, book publishers, consumer magazines, contests and awards, and more, from the publishers of *Writer's Digest* magazine. The subscription-based website ($29.99 annual fee) also offers information regarding travel publishers and links to their websites.

Yahoo! Directory
http://dir.yahoo.com/Business_and_Economy/Shopping_and_Services/Publishers/Travel

Provides links to the websites of over 75 travel guidebook and travel literature publishers.

MAJOR TRAVEL PUBLISHERS
Travel Guidebooks
As the aforementioned reference books illustrate, there are dozens of guidebook publishers. Following are nine of the most prominent:

Avalon Travel Publishing
1400 65th St, Suite 250, Emeryville, CA 94608
☎ 510-595 3664, Fax 510-595 4228
info@travelmatters.com
www.travelmatters.com, www.avalonpub.com

Publishers of the Moon Handbook series and of Rick Steves' guidebooks.

Fodor's Travel Publications
Researcher Writer Positions, 1745 Broadway, New York, NY 10019
☎ 212-782 9000
www.fodors.com

Publishers of the Fodor's guidebook series. Proposals should be mailed to their New York office at the address listed above.

The Globe Pequot Press
246 Goose Lane, PO Box 480, Guilford, CT 06437
☎ 203-458 4500
info@globepequot.com
www.globepequot.com

Publishers of a variety of theme and destination guides.

Let's Go Publications
67 Mt Auburn St, Cambridge, MA 02138
☎ 617-495 9659, Fax 617-496 7070
www.letsgo.com

As a wholly-owned subsidiary of Harvard Student Agencies, employs only Harvard students.

Lonely Planet Publications
150 Linden St, Oakland CA 94607
☎ 510-893 8555, Fax 510-893 8572
info@lonelyplanet.com
www.lonelyplanet.com

Independent travel media company, publishing over 600 titles in 17 different languages.

Rough Guides
80 Strand, London WC2R 0RL, UK
UK ☎ 020-7010 3700
US ☎ 212-414 3635
write@roughguides.com
www.roughguides.com

The company has offices in both the US and UK, but mailed proposals and inquiries should be directed to the UK address.

Sasquatch Books
119 S Main, Suite 400, Seattle, WA 98104
☎ 206-467 4300, 800-775 0817, Fax 206-467 4301
www.sasquatchbooks.com

Publishers of guides to the Pacific Northwest, Alaska and California.

Wilderness Press
1200 5th St, Berkeley, CA 94710
☎ 510-558 1666, 800-443 7227
www.wildernesspress.com
mail@wildernesspress.com

Publishers of outdoor activity–oriented guides to California, Alaska, Hawaii, the US Southwest and Pacific Northwest, New England, Canada, and Baja.

Wiley Publishing
111 River St, 5th fl, Hoboken, NJ 07030
☎ 201-748 6000
www.wiley.com
www.frommers.com

Publishers of Frommer's guidebooks and other travel products as well as the Frommers .com website.

Travel Literature
Numerous publishing companies produce travel literature. Here are 11 of the most prominent.

Broadway Books
1745 Broadway, New York, NY 10019
☎ 212-782 9000
bwaypub@randomhouse.com
www.randomhouse.com/broadway

Broadway's Broadway Abroad division specializes in a particular area of narrative travel books: travelogues and memoirs of authors' experiences living in (as opposed to visiting or journeying through) the world's most seductive and unusual places. Authors include Frances Mayes, Bill Bryson and Tony Cohan.

Crown Journeys
1745 Broadway, New York, NY 10019
☎ 212-782 9000
crownbiz@randomhouse.com
www.randomhouse.com/crown

Crown publishes a selection of popular fiction and nonfiction by both established and rising authors. Travel titles are part of the Crown Journeys series.

Harcourt Trade Publishers
15 East 26th St, 15th fl, New York, NY 10010
☎ 212-592 1000
www.harcourtbooks.com/default.asp

Under the Harcourt name, Harcourt Trade Publishers publishes hardcover editions of fine fiction and literature, nonfiction, poetry, and belles-lettres from authors worldwide.

HarperCollins
10 East 53rd St, New York, NY 10022
☎ 212-207 7000
www.harpercollins.com

HarperCollins has published over 150 travel-related titles, including literary nonfiction and the Access guidebook series. Manuscripts must be submitted through an agent.

Houghton Mifflin Company
222 Berkeley St, Boston, MA 02116
☎ 617-351 5000
www.houghtonmifflinbooks.com

Publishes Paul Theroux.

Lonely Planet Publications
150 Linden St, Oakland CA 94607
☎ 510-893 8555, Fax 510-893 8563
info@lonelyplanet.com
www.lonelyplanet.com

Lonely Planet publishes literary travel anthologies, single-author narratives and pictorial books, in addition to its guidebooks. Proposals for travel literature titles may be sent to the US office or the UK office.

Penguin Group
375 Hudson St, New York, NY 10014
☎ 212-366 2000
http://us.penguingroup.com

Penguin Group publishes an extensive list of travel literature titles, as well as the Rough Guide and Time Out guidebook series.

Random House Group
1745 Broadway, New York, NY 10019
☎ 212-782 9000
editor@randomhouse.com
www.randomhouse.com

Several imprints that publish travel narratives.

Seal Press
300 Queen Anne Ave N #375, Seattle, WA 98109
☎ 206-524 4257, Fax 206-285 9410
www.sealpress.com

Seal Press, an imprint of the Avalon Publishing Group, publishes fiction and non-fiction books by women across the globe.

Travelers' Tales
330 Townsend St #208, San Francisco, CA 94107
☎ 415-227 8600, Fax 415-227 8605
ttales@travelerstales.com
http://travelerstales.com

Travelers' Tales publishes a variety of anthologies and travel advice books. The company currently has more than 60 titles in print, and publishes approximately eight to 12 titles per year. Travelers' Tales also publishes stories on its website.

Vintage
1745 Broadway, New York, NY 10019
☎ 212-782 9000
www.randomhouse.com/vintage

This imprint of Random House has published the works of some of the most popular American travel writers, including Tim Cahill, Pico Iyer and Bill Bryson. A list of travel writing titles can be found at www.random house.ca/vintage/travelwriting.htm.

Travel Magazines

WRITERS RESOURCES

In addition to *Writer's Market* and *The Writer's Handbook*, the following resources provide valuable information on magazines and newspapers that publish travel writing in the US:

Bacon's Newspaper/Magazine Directory (2 volumes)
www.bacons.com/research/nwspprmagdir.htm

Lists editors and contact information for nearly 15,000 magazines and newsletters and all US, Canadian, Mexican and Caribbean daily newspapers. Published annually. Includes travel editor pitching profiles for most papers. This directory costs $375; it is available at many public libraries.

Editor & Publisher International Year Book, Part 1
www.editorandpublisher.com/eandp/resources/yearbook.jsp

The encyclopedia of the newspaper industry, with listings for all dailies worldwide and all community and special interest US and Canadian weeklies. Published annually. This directory costs $140; it is also available at many public libraries.

ehotelier.com
www.ehotelier.com/browse/magazines.php

This website offers a variety of resources for people in the hospitality industry and provides an extensive list of travel trade publications, linked to their websites.

Travel Marketing Sources
3 Monroe Parkway, Suite P, Lake Oswego, OR 97035.
☎ 503-534 9960
travelmarkets@comcast.net

Publishes *Travel Publications Update*, a compilation of travel material, both editorial and photographic, for nearly 650 magazines and 160 US and Canadian newspaper travel editors. Most listings include editors' names, contact information, descriptions, submission requirements, pay rates, photo requirements and other useful information. Cost is $32. The *Survey of Newspaper Travel Editors* is a printed version of the newspaper-only section of *Travel Publications Update* for $14.

Travel Publications Update
Marco Polo Publications, 1299 Bayshore Blvd, Suite B, Dunedin, FL 34698
☎ 800-523 7274, 727-735 9455, Fax 727-735 9534
http://main.travelwriters.com/tpu/about/index.asp

The Travel Publications Update offers concise information about more than 500 travel magazines and 200 newspaper travel sections. Each listing includes editorial contact information, a description of the publication, article and photography guidelines, pay rates and other essential data. Listings are updated continuously (but you need to buy a new copy to get updated information). Cost is $39. Even if you don't buy a copy it's worth browsing this site for market news and press releases.

Travelwriter Marketletter
PO Box 1782, Springfield, VA 22151
Voicemail/Fax 208-988 7672

A monthly newsletter of current market information, news and tips for travel writers and photographers. A sample issue is available on line. A one-year on-line subscription costs $65.

World Hum
www.worldhum.com

This site features links to many of the major travel magazine websites, newspaper travel section websites (in the US and abroad) and a host of other great travel links.

Writer's Market
www.writersmarket.com/index_ns.asp

This subscription-based website ($29.99 annual fee) offers information for consumer and trade magazines and links to their websites. This resource is also available in a print version that is updated each year.

Yahoo! Directory – Travel Magazines
http://dir.yahoo.com/Recreation/Travel
/News_and_Media/Magazines

Provides links to over 100 major print and on-line travel magazine websites, including major travel magazines, as well as in-flight magazines, regional publications and publications targeted to specific travel niches.

MAGAZINES
Hundreds of magazines publish travel writing. Following are seven of the most prominent that specialize in publishing articles on travel. If publications welcome email queries, we include the appropriate email address.

Arthur Frommer's Budget Travel
530 Seventh Ave, New York, NY 10018
☎ 646-695-6700
monique.lewis@newsweekbt.com

Published 10 times a year. Submission information at www.msnbc.com/modules/bt/info/contact.asp; writer's guidelines at www.msnbc.com/modules/bt/info/writer guidelines.asp.

Condé Nast Traveler
The Condé Nast Publications, 4 Times Sq, New York, NY 10036
☎ 212-286 2101
www.concierge.com/cntraveler

Condé Nast Traveler is a monthly magazine seeking stories that appeal to upscale, sophisticated travelers.

Islands
Islands Media Corp, 6267 Carpinteria Ave, Suite 200, Santa Barbara CA 93140
☎ 805-745 7100, Fax 805-745 7102
editorial@islands.com
www.islands.com

Islands focuses on islands around the world, and seeks informative, insightful, personal pieces that reveal the essence of the place; it is published eight times a year.

National Geographic Adventure
104 West 40th St, New York, NY 10018
☎ 212-790 9020
adventure@ngs.org
www.nationalgeographic.com/adventure

The magazine covers the world of adventure, from exciting travel destinations and outdoor pursuits to accounts of cutting-edge expeditions and profiles of modern-day explorers.

National Geographic Traveler
Query Editor, 1145 17th St NW, Washington, DC 20036-4688
☎ 202-857 7000 (ask for National Geographic Traveler's editorial office)
www.nationalgeographic.com/traveler

Traveler's publishing goals are to find the new, to showcase fresh travel opportunities, and to be an advocate for travelers.

Outside
Editorial Department, 400 Market St, Santa Fe, NM 87501
☎ 505-989 7100
http://outside.away.com

Outside is a monthly national magazine dedicated to covering the people, sports and activities, politics, art, literature and hardware of the outdoors.

Travel + Leisure
1120 Ave of the Americas, 10th fl, New York, NY 10036
☎ 212-382 5600
tlquery@aexp.com
www.travelandleisure.com

Monthly publication targeting sophisticated, active travelers who plan both pleasure and business trips. About 95 per cent of the magazine is written by freelance writers on assignment.

Newspapers
WRITERS RESOURCES
Online Newspapers
www.onlinenewspapers.com

This free site has links to the websites of thousands of US and international newspapers.

Travel Publications Update
http://main.travelwriters.com/tpu/about/index.asp

See p224-5 for more information.

World Hum
www.worldhum.com

See p225 for more information.

Some of the newspapers that regularly feature substantial travel coverage:

NATIONAL
The *Christian Science Monitor*
1 Norway St, Boston, MA 02115
☎ 617-450 2000
lowej@csmonitor.com
www.csmonitor.com

The Monitor publishes a monthly travel section. Contributor guidelines can be found at http://www.csmonitor.com/about us/guidelines.html.

The *Los Angeles Times*
202 W First St, Los Angeles, CA 90012
☎ 213-237 5000
travel@latimes.com
www.latimes.com

Sunday travel section of 16 to 24 pages; publishes articles on a wide variety of international and domestic destinations. 'Our stories are first-person experiential – travel stories as opposed to travel features. As we used to say in Missouri, show me, don't tell me.'

The *New York Times*
229 West 43rd St, New York, NY 10036
☎ 212-556 1234
travelmail@nytimes.com
www.nytimes.com

One of the largest travel sections in the US Publishes articles on a variety of international and domestic destinations.

The *Washington Post*
Travel Section, 1150 15th St NW, Washington, DC 20071
☎ 202-334 7750
travel@washpost.com
http://washingtonpost.com

Sunday section of 10 to 12 pages; publishes articles on a wide variety of international and domestic destinations.

LOCAL
Atlanta Journal-Constitution
72 Marietta St, Atlanta, GA 30303-2804
☎ 404-526 5151, 800-846 6672
travel@ajc.com
www.ajc.com

Sunday section publishes articles on regional, national and international destinations.

The *Baltimore Sun*
501 N Calvert St, Baltimore, MD 21278
☎ 410-332 6633
travel@baltsun.com
www.baltimoresun.com

Sunday section of 6 to 12 pages. The best way to break in is by pitching regional articles.

The *Boston Globe*
Travel Editor, 135 Morrissey Blvd, Boston MA 02107
☎ 617-929 2000
travel@globe.com
www.boston.com

Sunday section of 16 to 20 pages. The Globe buys first North American rights to articles; they will not publish articles that have previously appeared in North America.

The *Chicago Tribune*
435 North Michigan Ave, Chicago, IL 60611
☎ 312-222 3999
rcurwen@tribune.com
www.chicagotribune.com

Only deals with completed manuscripts; does not accept queries by phone. Sunday section of 10 to 22 pages. Interested in the Midwest and shorter stories.

The *Dallas Morning News*
Travel Editor, PO Box 655237, Dallas, TX 75265
☎ 214-977 8222
travelsection@dallasnews.com
www.dallasnews.com

Sunday section of 8 to 16 pages. Requests that stories be submitted via regular mail and that stories have a tight angle or focus.

The *Denver Post*
1560 Broadway, Denver, CO 80202
☎ 303-820 1010, 800-336 7678
travel@denverpost.com
www.denverpost.com

Sunday section of 8 to 14 pages. Submissions that are timely, newsy and compelling will have a better chance of making it.

The *Miami Herald*
One Herald Plaza, Miami, FL 33132
☎ 305-350 2111, 800-437 2535
travel@herald.com
www.miami.com/mld/miamiherald

Sunday section of 10 to 18 pages.

The *Philadelphia Inquirer*
PO Box 8263, Philadelphia, PA 19101
☎ 215-854 2000
inquirer.travel@phillynews.com
www.philly.com/mld/inquirer

Sunday section publishes articles on regional, national and international destinations.

The *San Diego Union-Tribune*
350 Camino de la Reina, San Diego, CA 92112-4106
☎ 619-718 5200
travel@uniontrib.com
www.signonsandiego.com

Sunday section of 8 to 10 pages.

The *San Francisco Chronicle*
901 Mission St, San Francisco, CA 94103
☎ 415-777 1111
travel@sfchronicle.com
www.sfchron.com

Sunday section of 10 to 20 pages. The best way for freelancers to break in is to send Californian stories.

The *Seattle Times*
Travel Dept, PO Box 70, Seattle, WA 98111
☎ 206-464 2111
travel@seattletimes.com
http://seattletimes.nwsource.com

Sunday section of 8 to 14 pages.

The *South Florida Sun-Sentinel*
200 E Las Olas Blvd, Fort Lauderdale, FL 33301-2293
☎ 954-356 4731
tswick@sun-sentinel.com
www.sun-sentinel.com

Sunday section of 10 to 18 pages. Interested in stories with characters, dialogue and humor, that focus more on the people who live in a place than on the tourists who visit.

On Line

Online Markets for Writers
by Anthony Tedesco and Paul Tedesco
www.marketsforwriters.com

Online Markets for Writers is a database of submission guidelines and pay-rate and policy information for over 200 paying on-line magazines, electronic newsletters and custom corporate on-line publications, plus advice from confidential writer surveys about specific markets. Available only as an e-book through MarketsForWriters.com Press. Includes free updates. A free newsletter on on-line markets and a free e-book are also available through the website.

Writer's Online Marketplace: How and Where to Get Published Online
by Debbi Ridpath Ohi (Writer's Digest Books)

Lists 161 paying on-line publications, 10 potentially lucrative alternative markets and 26 commercial e-publishers. Includes interviews with 12 industry insiders.

The following websites have comprehensive links to other on-line travel sites:

BootsnAll
www.bootsnall.com

Billed as the 'ultimate resource for the independent traveler,' this site offers travel booking information, discussion groups, travel guides and traveler's resources. The site also accepts story submissions and publishes travel articles.

Joe Sent Me
www.joesentme.com

A website for business travelers that contains a wealth of information useful to travel writers. Look for the link to Travel Newsstand (www.travelnewsstand.com), where you'll find links to newspaper travel sections and travel magazines worldwide. Also click on

Fellow Travelers (www.fellowtravelers.com), another Joe Sent Me site that provides links to all the travel commentators currently published on the Web.

Travelers' Tales
www.travelerstales.com

The Travelers' Tales website features weekly stories from freelance writers, along with information about Travelers' Tales anthologies, upcoming titles and submission guidelines.

World Hum
www.worldhum.com

This website publishes articles, essays and first-person stories that 'reveal the heart of a beating travel experience.' It also provides links to dozens of travel-related journals, magazines, communities, blogs, newspaper sections, book publishers, bookstores, TV and radio stations, and other helpful sites.

WRITERS GROUPS & ASSOCIATIONS

In your local area, you may find travel writing and/or general writing groups and organizations that are open to writers of all levels. If writing becomes your career, the following national organizations may add clout to your resume, and provide various benefits such as networking opportunities, insider market information and discounted health insurance.

American Society of Journalists and Authors
1501 Broadway, Suite 302, New York, NY 10036
☎ 212-997 0947
www.asja.org

Founded in 1948, this is the US's leading organization of independent nonfiction writers. Their monthly member newsletter provides valuable information on writing markets. To become a member of ASJA, you must have published a minimum of six by-lined articles written on a freelance basis in major magazines. Non-members can still receive the *Contracts Watch* newsletter, a free source of information about the latest terms and negotiations in the world of periodicals, print, and electronic publishing.

International Food, Wine and Travel Writers Association
PO Box 8249, Calabasas, CA 91372
☎ 818-999 9959, Fax 818-347 7535
ifwtwa@aol.com
www.ifwtwa.org/index.html

This association has more than 300 members, including travel and food journalists and broadcasters, representatives of tourism boards and convention and visitor bureaus, and other public relations professionals. Their membership standards include a minimum of 10 published travel articles per year.

National Writers' Association
3140 Peoria St, #295MB, Aurora, CO 80012
☎ 303-841 0246, Fax 303-841 2607
execdirsandywhelchel@nationalwriters.com
www.nationalwriters.com

Members of the National Writers' Association receive discounts on health and dental insurance, car rentals, office supplies, and other products and services. NWA also provides services such as contract reading, editing, and manuscript criticism from other members. Email or call for information on how to join.

National Writers' Union
113 University Pl, 6th fl , New York, NY 10003
☎ 212-254 0279, Fax 212-254 0673
nwu@nwu.org
www.nwu.org

The National Writers' Union (NWU) is a trade union for freelance writers of all genres who work for American publishers or employers. You are eligible for membership if you have published a book, a play, three articles, five poems, a short story, or an equal amount of newsletter, publicity, technical, commercial, government or institutional copy. You are also eligible for membership if you have written an equal amount of unpublished material and are actively writing and attempting to publish your work.

North American Travel Journalists Association
International Headquarters, 531 Main St, #902, El Segundo, CA 90245
☎ 310-836 8712, Fax 310-836 8769
headquarters@natja.org
www.natja.org

A professional organization of writers, photographers and editors dedicated to the travel and hospitality industries. You must submit 10 clips of your writing published in the last year to join. Member dues are $125 per year.

Society of American Travel Writers
1500 Sunday Dr, Suite 102, Raleigh, NC 27607
☎ 919-861 5586, Fax 919-787 4916
satw@satw.org
www.satw.org

The leading organization for travel writers and other travel professionals, SATW works to raise the standards of the profession, guard the right of freedom to travel, and encourage conservation and preservation of historic sites and natural wonders. You must fulfill membership publishing requirements and be sponsored by two SATW members to join.

Travel Journalists Guild

PO Box 10643, Chicago, IL 60610
☎ 312-664 9279, Fax 312-664 9701
www.tjgonline.com

Guild members include freelance writers, photographers, artists and film-makers who focus on travel. To become a member, you must be a self-employed freelance travel journalist in the field of writing, photography, lecturing, art, radio or television who has worked in the field for at least three years in the past five. You must also be sponsored by two current members and provide at least 12 clips of articles published (or broadcast, distributed etc.) for each of the past three years.

Information on additional writers associations and groups can be found at:

The Writer Gazette

www.writergazette.com/linksclubs.shtml

This website also provides links to writer-related articles, paying calls for submission and freelance job postings, contests, tips and other resources to help induce, improve and promote your writing career.

WRITING COURSES

Writing classes are offered through community colleges, adult education schools, universities, writers' centers, independent learning organizations and bookstores. Check these local organizations in your area for the most up-to-date schedules and offerings. Courses on related topics such as learning how to edit, how to find and work with an agent, and how to work with editors can also be very beneficial in helping you understand the pressures and requirements of the publishing world. The websites listed below may also be useful in identifying relevant courses, conferences and on-line workshops.

Travel Writing Classes & Conferences

Your home town is a good place to start looking for classes and conferences on travel

writing. The relationships you build with other writers and writing instructors provide rewards long after the class is over. At your local community colleges, adult education schools, libraries and bookstores, look for classes on travel writing, creative writing, journalism, researching, touch-typing, editing and other writing-related skills. The Internet offers nearly inexhaustible information about writing classes – including some virtual courses that take place entirely through on-line classes, submissions and critiques. Magazines like *Writer's Digest* (www.writersdigest.com), *The Writer* (www.writermag.com), and *Poets & Writers* (www.pw.org/mag) are also good sources of information on classes. Here are some additional resources to help you start your search for the right class:

The Association of Writers and Writing Programs

www.awpwriter.org/aboutawp/index.htm

The association is dedicated to the promotion of writers and creative writing programs at universities in the US, Canada and the UK. Its website features information on writing programs, conferences and contests. Membership benefits include a subscription to the association's *Writer's Chronicle* magazine, job lists and discounted registration fees for contests and conferences.

Media Bistro

www.mediabistro.com

Media Bistro is dedicated to anyone who creates or works with content, including editors, writers, television producers, graphic designers, book publishers and people in production and circulation departments in industries including magazines, television, radio, newspapers, book publishing, on-line media, advertising, PR and graphic design. It provides opportunities (both on line and off line) to network, share resources, become informed of job opportunities and interesting projects, improve career skills and showcase work, and also runs a variety of writing and related courses in major US cities.

Poets & Writers

www.pw.org

The mission of Poets & Writers is to support and promote the literary community in the US, and to foster communication among and professional development for poets and writers of fiction and non-fiction. The organization publishes *Poets & Writers* magazine and its website offers links to writer's resources including national and regional organizations, writing programs and conferences.

ShawGuides' Guide to Writers' Conferences and Workshops
http://writing.shawguides.com

This website lists almost 1500 writers' conferences and workshops and is searchable by country, state, date and genre.

Writer's Digest
www.writersdigest.com

This 'on-line guide to the writer's life' publishes the monthly *Writer's Digest* magazine and offers a 24-month Writer's Digest school and various on-line workshops.

Writing-World.com: Writing Classes, Conferences and Colonies
www.writing-world.com/links/classes.shtml

This website provides links to websites, schools, colleges and universities that offer writing classes.

WRITERS WEBSITES & TOOLS

The following websites contain extensive lists of links to resources for writers:

The 101 Best Websites for Writers by WritersDigest.com
www.writersdigest.com/101sites/2004_index.asp

This is a selective list of helpful websites for writers.

Google Directory of Writers' Resources
directory.google.com/Top/Arts/Writers_Resources

Google's collection of links to writing-related websites.

Internet-Resources.com
www.internet-resources.com/writers

A huge collection of links to resources for writers.

Writers Write Links and Resources for Writers
www.writerswrite.com/writinglinks

Assorted links for writers organized by genre and type.

Writing-World.com
www.writing-world.com/links/index.shtml

Provides well-organized lists of hundreds of links for writers.

The Zuzu's Petals Literary Resource
www.zuzu.com

Contains '10,000+ organized links' of resources for writers, artists, performers and researchers.

Here are a few specific sites for writers:

Absolute Write
www.absolutewrite.com

A place for professional writers to meet, this website offers market listings, a newsletter, discussion forums, editorial services, articles and classes, plus a warnings page to keep you from making bad decisions.

Alibris
www.alibris.com

This website connects people to thousands of independent book, music and movie sellers around the world. It offers over 35 million used, new and hard-to-find titles to consumers, libraries and retailers.

Bartleby.com
www.bartleby.com

Bartleby.com publishes classics of literature, nonfiction and reference free of charge for visitors to its site.

Bibliofind
www.bibliofind.com

Bibliofind, through a partnership with Amazon.com, provides millions of rare, used, and out-of-print books through their community of booksellers.

Carnegie Library of Pittsburgh
www.carnegielibrary.org/subject/travel/guides.html

This website provides information and links to numerous print and on-line travel guide publishers as well as booking agents. Links to specialty guides covering subjects from dining out to cruises are included along with general travel guides.

Common Errors in English
www.wsu.edu/~brians/errors/index.html

This site provides information to help avoid common word usage errors.

Creativity for Life
www.creativityforlife.com

This site offers hints, tips and tricks to keep your creativity alive.

Freelance Writers
http://freelancewrite.about.com

Part of the about.com network, this site includes articles, relevant links, how-to information, forums, and answers to questions.

iTravelSyndicate
www.itravelsyndicate.com

iTravelSyndicate is an on-line marketplace that allows editors worldwide to search for and purchase the articles they need. Writers pay a fee to post articles, and editors buy nonexclusive reprint rights, which include digital reprint/archive rights.

OneLook Dictionary Search
www.onelook.com

OneLook easily helps define, translate or determine the accurate spelling for over five million words by linking visitors to more than 900 on-line dictionaries.

Writer's Weekly
www.writersweekly.com

Writer's Weekly is an e-zine dedicated to freelance writers. The site features articles, a forum, and sections on markets and writers' 'warnings'. There is also a section dedicated to new writer resources and one dedicated to self-publishing.

Research-Related Websites
CLIMATE & THE ENVIRONMENT
Intellicast.com
www.intellicast.com

Intellicast.com provides extensive specialized weather information to help plan outdoor and weather-sensitive activities, such as golfing, sailing, hiking, skiing or relaxing at the beach. The site offers free, accurate and up-to-date weather information and forecasts for most US and featured international destinations.

The Weather Channel
www.weather.com

The Weather Channel's website features current conditions and forecasts for over 77,000 locations worldwide, along with local and regional radars. The site also offers a variety of maps, along with weather-related news, educational material, a weather glossary, a storm encyclopedia, seasonal features, and other resources for travel planning.

ECOTOURISM & RESPONSIBLE TRAVEL
Ethical Traveler
www.ethicaltraveler.com

A grass-roots alliance whose goal is to unite the travel community in the fight to strengthen human rights and to protect the environment. Offers links to other organizations and companies concerned with the same issues.

The International Ecotourism Society
www.ecotourism.org

The largest and oldest ecotourism organization in the world, TIES is dedicated to generating and disseminating information about ecotourism. The website has links to other ecotourism organizations around the world, and information about how you can travel responsibly to natural areas while conserving the environment and sustaining the wellbeing of the local people.

EMBASSIES, CONSULATES & PASSPORTS
Embassy World
www.embassyworld.com

Embassy World is designed to provide a comprehensive directory of and search engine for contact resources for all of the world's embassies and consulates.

US Department of State
http://travel.state.gov/passport/index.html
http://travel.state.gov

These two sections of the US Department of State website provide information to US citizens about passports and visas required to visit other countries.

FACTS, FIGURES & STATISTICS
The Audit Bureau of Circulations
www.accessabc.com

Among other things, provides magazine and newspaper circulation figures.

CIA World Factbook
www.odci.gov/cia/publications/factbook

This section of the US Central Intelligence Agency website offers access to maps and general information including geography, people, military, government and economy about virtually every country in the world.

Country Calling Codes
www.countrycallingcodes.com

International telephoning made easy.

Encyclopaedia Britannica
www.britannica.com

You can search through the 32-volume Encyclopaedia Britannica on line.

European Travel Commission
www.etc-corporate.org

Extensive country information for Europe.

Firstgov.gov: Reference Shelf
www.firstgov.gov/Topics/Reference_Shelf.shtml#statistics

Links to data and statistics from the US government's official web portal.

IATA
www.iata.org

The International Air Transport Association site features interesting reports, facts and figures.

Nation Master
www.nationmaster.com/index.php

This website contains information from the CIA Factbook as well as other sources and allows users to generate graphs based on numerical data that compare countries across various statistics. Information can be analysed based on health, politics and ecology.

Office of Travel and Tourism Industries
tinet.ita.doc.gov/research

This office functions as the US federal tourism office. A core responsibility is to collect, analyse and disseminate international travel and tourism statistics for the US Travel and Tourism Statistical System.

time and date.com
www.timeanddate.com

Includes the times of sunrise, sunset, international country codes, and city coordinates.

Travel Industry Association of America
www.tia.org/Travel/default.asp

This website provides an authoritative and recognized source of research, analysis and forecasting for the entire industry. Information on statistics and trends is offered, with enhanced services for TIA members.

Universal Currency Converter
www.xe.com/ucc

Converts the values of nearly every currency using current market rates.

The World Heritage List
http://whc.unesco.org/pg.cfm?cid=31

The 754 properties which the World Heritage Committee has inscribed on the World Heritage List.

World Information
www.worldinformation.com

Business, economic and political information on every country in the world.

World Tourism Organization
www.world-tourism.org

There's a wealth of statistics on tourism available on this site; some are for free and others will cost you.

GENERAL TRAVEL INFORMATION & ADVICE
Cybercafes
www.cybercafes.com

Contains a database of more than 4200 Internet cafés in 140 countries.

ehotelier.com
www.ehotelier.com/browse/conventions.php#visitorbureaus

This website, which offers a variety of resources for people in the hospitality industry, provides an extensive list of convention and visitors bureaus in the US and abroad

Frequent Flyer
www.frequentflyer.oag.com

The website of *Frequent Flyer* magazine offers a free e-newsletter with the latest business travel news, updates on travel loyalty programs and book reviews. The site also provides addresses/phone numbers of major airlines, airline clubs, rental cars and hotels around the world and other information relevant to business travelers.

Joe Sent Me
http://biztravelife.com/m/jsm.htm

Joe Brancatelli's site targets business travelers with free access/links to everything from pharmacy and cybercafé locations to travel warnings and airport/flight information. Additional benefits including travel tips and a newsletter are offered to contributors. Four levels of annual membership ranging from $25 to $150 are available.

The Thorn Tree
http://thorntree.lonelyplanet.com
www.lonelyplanet.com/subwwway

The Thorn Tree section of Lonely Planet's website is a bulletin board used by travelers from all over the world to exchange information about a wide variety of travel topics and destinations. You'll also find cultural, literature, food, and political discussions. The site also provides links to other important travel resources in its Subway section.

The Practical Nomad Resource Guide
http://hasbrouck.org/links/index.html

Edward Hasbrouck, author of *The Practical Nomad: How to Travel Around the World* and *The Practical Nomad Guide to the Online Travel Marketplace*, features this page on his website with links to travel planning and research, logistics and practicalities, tickets and reservations, and tips and resources for using the Internet on the road.

Tourism Offices Worldwide
www.towd.com

The Tourism Offices Worldwide Directory provides links to official US and international tourist information sources: government tourism offices, convention and visitors bureaus, chambers of commerce, and similar organizations that provide free, accurate and unbiased travel information to the public.

Travel Ticker
www.lonelyplanet.com/travel_ticker

Lonely Planet's travel advisory service.

Travel Weekly – The National Newspaper of the Travel Industry
www.twcrossroads.com

This website offers travel industry news features, as well as a forum and stories on destinations.

US Department of Homeland Security, Transportation Security Administration: Travelers and Consumers
www.tsa.dot.gov
www.tsatraveltips.us

The mission of the Transportation Security Administration is to protect the nation's transportation systems to ensure freedom of movement for people and commerce. The 'Travelers & Consumers' section of its website offers information, links, tips and requirements for air, rail, passenger vessel, highway and mass transit travel. Consumers can sign up to receive Homeland Security Alerts which notify travelers of changes in the Homeland Security Alert status, TSA Policy updates and other critical information to assist with travel plans.

US Department of State
www.state.gov

US Department of State travel warnings provide updates about risks abroad such as civil unrest, natural disasters or outbreaks of serious diseases. The site also provides information about visa requirements and consular details for visiting other countries.

World Travel Guide
www.columbusguides.com/country.asp

Provides histories and travel information on virtually every country in the world.

World Travel Watch
www.worldtravelwatch.com

Larry Habegger and James O'Reilly have been reporting on issues that affect travelers for major newspapers since 1985. Their World Travel Watch site reports on developments around the globe, from crime waves, disease outbreaks and transit strikes to political upheaval and cultural quirks. It also provides links to major news resources.

HEALTH

Travel Health Online
www.tripprep.com

A resource of travel medicine and practitioners around the globe.

US Centers for Disease Control (CDC)
www.cdc.gov/travel

CDC is the federal agency for developing and applying disease prevention and control, environmental health, and health education activities designed to improve the health of the people of the United States. The website provides health information on specific destinations as well as on outbreaks that may affect international travelers.

World Health Organization
www.who.int/en

The website provides information on health risks around the world as well as recommended precautions, immunizations and vaccines when traveling.

MAPS

Atlapedia
www.atlapedia.com

This site provides facts, figures and statistical data on geography, climate, people, religion, language, history, economy and also full color physical maps and political maps for regions of the world.

MapQuest
www.mapquest.com

MapQuest provides basic maps of US and select international cities. Visitors can also utilize this site to get directions between two points in the US or Europe.

Mapsonus.com
www.mapsonus.com

This site provides advanced mapping and driving directions throughout the US.

Multimap.com
www.multimap.com

One of Europe's most popular mapping websites, this website has maps and information valuable to travelers from any country. Key features include street-level maps of the US, the UK and Europe; road maps of the world; door-to-door travel directions; aerial photographs; and local information.

WORLD EVENTS
Artrepublic
www.artrepublic.com/WOW

Search over 1250 museum listings to find out what exhibitions are on now.

City Search
www.citysearch.com

This local search service allows users to find up-to-date information on businesses, from restaurants and retail to travel and professional services, for major US cities and some international locations.

Whatsonwhen
www.whatsonwhen.com

A world-wide directory of upcoming events.

YOU ON THE WEB
Backflip.com
www.backflip.com

'My Daily Routine' organizes all the websites you regularly visit and speeds up the process of browsing through them.

Blogger
www.blogger.com

Site allows you to build and maintain your own on-line diary.

Buildfree.org
http://buildfree.org

Build your own website for free.

My Trip Journal
http://lonelyplanet.mytripjournal.com

Build an on-line journal of your trip with maps, photos and email notification of updates for your friends.

Yahoo! GeoCities
http://geocities.yahoo.com

This web hosting site enables you to create your own personal web page. Instructions guide you in using the site's design tools, viewing your web page on the Web, and promoting your web page to your family and friends.

REFERENCE PURCHASES
Every writer must have a good dictionary such as *Merriam-Webster's Collegiate Dictionary* or *The American Heritage Dictionary of the English Language*. A thesaurus such as *Roget's Thesaurus* is also essential. In addition, consider purchasing the following books:

The American Directory of Writer's Guidelines, 3rd Edition: A Compilation of Information for Freelancers from More than 1,400 Magazine Editors and Book Publishers by Brigitte M. Philips, Sussan D. Klasson and Dorris Hall

AP Stylebook and Briefing on Media Law (Associated Press)

The ASJA Guide to Freelance Writing: A Professional Guide to the Business, for Nonfiction Writers of All Experience Levels edited by Timothy Harper

Bartlett's Familiar Quotations by John Bartlett

Bird by Bird: Some Instructions on Writing and Life by Annie Lamott

The Chicago Manual of Style, 15th Edition (University of Chicago Press)

The Elements of Style by William Strunk Jr and E. B. White

Literary Law Guide for Authors by Tanya Marie Evans, Susan Borden Evans and Dan Poynter

On Writing Well by William Zinsser

Rand McNally Goode's World Atlas by J. Paul Goode et al

The World Almanac and Book of Facts (World Almanac; annual)

A Writer's Legal Guide: An Author's Guild Desk Reference by Tad Crawford and Kay Murray

Library References

These useful references are available in many libraries:

Bacon's Newspaper/Magazine Directory (2 volumes) by Bacon's Media Directories; annual

The Complete Guide to Literary Contests by Literary Fountain

Editor & Publisher International Year Book by Editor & Publisher; annual

Encyclopaedia Britannica by Encyclopaedia Britannica Inc

LMP: The Directory of the American Book Publishing Industry (Literary Market Place) by Inc Staff Information Today; annual

Poets & Writers magazine

The Writer magazine

Writer's Digest magazine

TRAVEL LITERATURE CLASSICS

Don George's list of top 20 works of travel literature by US authors:

Arctic Dreams by Barry Lopez

Blue Highways by William Least-Heat Moon

The Colossus of Maroussi by Henry Miller

Coming Into the Country by John McPhee

Desert Solitaire by Edward Abbey

The Great Railway Bazaar by Paul Theroux

The Inland Sea by Donald Richie

Innocents Abroad by Mark Twain

Jaguars Ripped My Flesh by Tim Cahill

Notes from a Small Island by Bill Bryson

On the Road by Jack Kerouac

Pilgrim at Tinker Creek by Annie Dillard

The Snow Leopard by Peter Matthiessen

The Solace of Open Spaces by Gretel Ehrlich

Travels with Charley by John Steinbeck

Two Towns in Provence by M. F. K. Fisher

Video Night in Kathmandu by Pico Iyer

Walden by Henry David Thoreau

Westward Ha! by S. J. Perelman

Zen and the Art of Motorcycle Maintenance by Robert M. Pirsig

UK RESOURCES

GENERAL GUIDES TO PUBLISHERS, EDITORS & LITERARY AGENTS

The Directory of Book Publishers and Wholesalers
by The Bookseller's Association

This is an annually updated guide to publishers in the UK and Ireland, containing details of over 3000 publishers in an A-Z listing. Details include named contacts, business type and email and web addresses. You can order from www.booksellers.org.uk or email mail@booksellers.org.uk.

Writers' & Artists' Yearbook
by A&C Black

Revised and updated annually, this is the bestselling reference guide that all UK writers and artists have on their bookshelves – whether you are looking at writing a book or a magazine or newspaper article. It gives comprehsive listings of magazines, newspapers, book publishers, literary and artists' agents, theatre, television and radio producers, picture agencies, societies, prizes, creative writing courses, festivals and much more.

MAJOR TRAVEL PUBLISHERS
Travel Guidebooks

AA Travel Publishing
Fanum House, 16th fl, Basing View, Basingstoke, Hampshire RG21 4EA
☎ 01256-493138, Fax 01256-492440
connie.austen-smith@theaa.com
www.theAA.com

Over 300 travel guides, plus atlases, maps, walking books, phrasebooks and restaurant and hotel guides.

Berlitz
58 Borough High St, London SE1 1XF
☎ 020-7403 0284, Fax 020-7403 0290
insight@apaguide.co.uk
www.berlitzpublishing.com

Over 120 pocket guidebooks to the world put together by the team that also produces the Insight Guides.

Bradt Travel Guides
19 High St, Chalfont St Peter, Buckinghamshire SL9 9QE
☎ 01753-893444, Fax 01753-892333

info@bradt-travelguides.com
www.bradt-travelguides.com

Bradt Travel Guides focuses on emerging travel destinations. The company has over 70 titles in print.

Cadogan Guides
Network House, 1 Ariel Way, London W12 7SL
☎ 020-8740 2050, Fax 020-8740 2059
info@cadoganguides.co.uk
www.cadoganguides.com

Around 100 titles covering the following series: country & regional guides, city guides, Buying Property Abroad guides, Working & Living Abroad, Take the Kids, and Flying Visits. In 2003 Cadogan introduced a travel literature series.

Dorling Kindersley
Penguin Group (UK), 80 Strand, London WC2R 0RL
☎ 020-7010 3000, Fax 020-7010 6060
travelguides@dk.com
www.dk.com

Highly visual Eyewitness country, city and regional guidebooks and a Top Ten series for world cities.

Footprint Handbooks
6 Riverside Ct, Lower Bristol Rd, Bath BA2 3DZ
☎ 01225-469141, Fax 01225-469461
discover@footprintbooks.com
www.footprintbooks.com

Travel guides for independent and adventurous travellers with a list of over 90 titles.

Insight Guides
58 Borough High St, London SE1 1XF
☎ 020-7403 0284, Fax 020-7403 0290
insight@apaguide.co.uk
www.insightguides.com

Over 200 highly pictorial guides to the world plus pocket guides and compact guides. Also a range of thematic guides.

Itchy Media
Unit 2, Whitehorse Yard, 78 Liverpool Rd, London N1 0QD
☎ 020-7288 4300, Fax 020-7359 9611
all@itchymedia.co.uk
www.itchymedia.co.uk

Pocket-sized UK city guides for those aged between 18 and 35. May look at doing city guides to overseas destinations in the future.

Lonely Planet Publications
72–82 Rosebery Ave, London EC1R 4RW
☎ 020-7841 9000, Fax 020-7841 9001
go@lonelyplanet.co.uk
www.lonelyplanet.com

Independent travel media company, publishing over 600 titles across 17 different languages.

Rough Guides
Penguin Group (UK), 80 Strand, London WC2R 0RL
☎ 020-7010 3701, Fax 020-7010 6767
write@roughguides.co.uk
www.roughguides.com

Over 200 travel guidebooks, plus music and other reference guides. Go on line to find details on how to write for them.

Thomas Cook Publishing
PO Box 227, Units 15/16 The Thomas Cook Business Park, Peterborough PE3 8SB
☎ 01733-416477, Fax 01733-416688
books@thomascook.com
www.thomascookpublishing.com

Over 160 titles to cities, countries and regions aimed at a variety of travellers from soft backpackers to more mainstream holiday-makers.

Time Out Guides
Universal House, 251 Tottenham Court Rd, London W1T 7AB
☎ 020-7813 3000, Fax 020-7813 6153
guides@timeout.com
www.timeout.com

Around 40 overseas city guides, separate guides to London shopping, eating, children, sport, pubs and bars, plus national eating and drinking guides and a bi-annual guide to Europe by air.

Trailblazer Publications
The Old Manse, Power Rd, Hindhead, Surrey GU26 6SU
Enquiries by fax or email only
Fax 01428-607571
info@trailblazer-guides.com
www.trailblazer-guides.com

A range of route guides for the adventurous traveller including walking guides and rail guides.

Vacation Work
9 Park End St, Oxford OX1 1HJ
☎ 01865-241978, Fax 01865-790885

info@vacationwork.co.uk
www.vacationwork.co.uk

Series include: country guides, Living & Working Abroad, Jobs Abroad, and guides to Buying a House overseas.

Travel Literature

Bloomsbury Publishing
38 Soho Sq, London W1D 3HB
☎ 020-7494 2111, Fax 020-7434 0151
aspectguides@bloomsbury.com for the travel guidebooks
www.bloomsbury.com

Bloomsbury does not have a large travel literature list but is always interested in manuscripts with 'legs'. The company also publishes a small range of guides to hotels and restaurants in France.

Eye Books
51a Boscombe Rd, London W12 9HT
☎/Fax 020-8743 3276
book@eye-books.com
www.eye-books.com

Small publishing house specialising in travel books about personal journeys and growth – ordinary people doing extraordinary things.

Faber and Faber
3 Queen Sq, London WC1N 3AU
☎ 020-7465 0189, Fax 020-7465 0034
editorial@faber.co.uk
www.faber.co.uk

Publisher of Jan Morris, Tobias Jones and Benedict Allen. Travel literature appears within its non-fiction list.

HarperCollins Publishers
77–85 Fulham Palace Rd, London W6 8JB
☎ 020-8741 7070, Fax 020-8307 4440
webcontact@harpercollins.co.uk
www.harpercollins.co.uk

Most travel literature is published under the Flamingo imprint.

Hodder Headline
338 Euston Rd, London NW1 3BH
☎ 020-7873 6000, Fax 020-7873 6024
clientservices@bookpoint.co.uk
www.madaboutbooks.co.uk

Group consisting of Headline, Hodder & Stoughton, and John Murray: travel writing is included in all of their lists.

John Murray (Publishers)
338 Euston Rd, London NW1 3BH
☎ 020-7873 6000, Fax 020-7873 6442
clientservices@bookpoint.co.uk
www.madaboutbooks.co.uk

Publishers of distinguished travel literature authors like Dervla Murphy and Patrick Leigh Fermor. The list continues to be built with new travel literature authors.

Lonely Planet Publications
The Market Building, 72–82 Rosebery Ave, Clerkenwell, London EC1R 4RW
☎ 020-7841 9000, Fax 020-7841 9001
go@lonelyplanet.co.uk
www.lonelyplanet.com

Lonely Planet's travel literature series was launched in 1996, and features a mix of single-author narratives and anthologies. The company generally publishes four to six titles per year. Proposals for travel literature titles may be sent to the UK office or the US office.

The Orion Publishing Group
Orion House, 5 Upper St Martin's Lane, London WC2H 9EA
☎ 020-7240 3444, Fax 020-7379 6158
info@orionbooks.co.uk
www.orionbooks.co.uk

Weidenfeld & Nicolson is the imprint where travel literature is published.

Pan Macmillan
20 New Wharf Rd, London N1 9RR
☎ 020-7014 6000, Fax 020-7843 4640
www.panmacmillan.co.uk

Travel Literature is published in all imprints. Only manuscripts submitted by an agent are considered.

Penguin
80 Strand, London WC2R 0RL
☎ 020-7010 3000, Fax 020-7010 6060
customer.service@penguin.co.uk
www.penguin.co.uk

Publishers of Paul Theroux and Redmond O'Hanlon, Penguin does not accept any unsolicited manuscripts.

Random House Group
20 Vauxhall Bridge Rd, London SW1V 2SA
☎ 020-7840 8400, Fax 020-7233 8791
www.randomhouse.co.uk

Publishes travel literature in a range of imprints including Jonathan Cape, Chatto &

Windus, Vintage, Ebury and Arrow. All need to be contacted separately – ring the main telephone number for details.

Time Warner Books UK
Brettenham House, Lancaster Pl, London WC2E 7EN
☎ 020-7911 8000, Fax 020-7911 8100
sandra.wood@timewarnerbooks.co.uk
www.timewarnerbooks.co.uk

Travel literature is usually published by the imprint Little Brown or Time Warner. It is best to send manuscripts by post.

Transworld
61–63 Uxbridge Rd, London W5 5SA
☎ 020-8231 6771, Fax 020-8579 5479
info@transworld-publishers.co.uk
www.booksattransworld.co.uk

Publishers of Bill Bryson; most travel literature comes out in the Black Swan, Bantam and Doubleday imprints.

Virgin Books
Thames Wharf Studios, Rainville Rd, London W6 9HA
☎ 020-7386 3300, Fax 020-7386 3360
info@virgin-books.co.uk
www.virginbooks.com

As from 2004 a travel literature list is being built by Virgin. Please send enquiries by post or ring. They are interested in accessible destinations by authors based in the UK.

Travel Magazines

ABTA Magazine
197–199 City Rd, London EC1V 1JN
☎ 020-7253 9906, Fax 020-7250 0955
editorial@abtamagazine.co.uk
www.absolutepublishing.com

Monthly travel trade publication with in-depth analysis of issues affecting the travel trade from an industry perspective.

ABTA Travelspirit
197–199 City Rd, London EC1V 1JN
☎ 020-7253 9906, Fax 020-7250 0955
editorial@abtamagazine.co.uk
www.absolutepublishing.com

Bi-monthly publication aimed at the travelling public but not at the higher end of the market.

Adventure Travel
PO Box 6254, Alcester B49 6PF
☎ 01789-450000

No enquiries by fax
alun@atmagazine.co.uk

Bi-monthly travel magazine aimed at the 25–45 age group, particularly to trekkers and aspiring mountaineers.

Business Traveller
Euromoney Pl, Nestor House, Playhouse Yard, London EC4V 5EX
☎ 020-7778 0000, Fax 020-7778 0022
editorial@businesstraveller.com
www.businesstraveller.com

Monthly consumer magazine with destination features which are business or lifestyle related.

Condé Nast Traveller
Vogue House, Hanover Sq, London W1S 1JU
☎ 020-7499 9080
No enquiries by fax
cntraveller@condenast.co.uk
www.cntraveller.co.uk

Glossy, monthly travel/lifestyle magazine aimed at the high end of the market.

Food & Travel
Fox Publishing, Lion House, 1 Red Lion St, Richmond TW9 1RE
☎ 020-8332 9090, Fax 020-8332 9991
info@fox-publishing.com
www.foodandtravel.com

The best in food and travel from around the world; comes out monthly.

France Magazine
Archant Life Ltd, Cumberland House, Oriel Rd, Cheltenham, Glos GL50 1BB
☎ 01242-216050, Fax 01242-216074
editorial@francemag.com
www.francemag.com

Monthly magazine for people passionate about France. No unsolicited copy; send ideas by email.

French; Spanish; Portugal; and Greece magazines
Merricks Media, Cambridge House South, Henry St, Bath, Somerset BA1 1JT
☎ 01225-786800, Fax 01225-786801
info@merricksmedia.co.uk
www.merricksmedia.co.uk

Either monthly or bi-monthly, these magazines all have culture, lifestyle and buying a propery features in them.

Geographical (magazine of the Royal Geographical Society)
Campion Interactive Publishing Ltd, Unit 11, Pall Mall Deposit, 124–8 Barlby Rd, London W10 6BL
☎ 020-8960 6400, Fax 020-8960 6004
proposals@geographical.co.uk
www.geographical.co.uk

Monthly magazine for members of the RGS and for the wider public.

Global
Castle House, 97 High St, Colchester CO1 1TH
☎ 01206-505921, Fax 01206-505929
dom_global@aceville.com
www.globalmagazine.co.uk

A magazine with eight issues a year, aimed at young and adventurous travellers. Writers' guidelines are available on request.

Globe
Globetrotters Club, BCM/Roving, London WC1N 3XX
☎ 020-8674 6229 (information line only)
danjames@ntlworld.com
www.globetrotters.co.uk

This is the bi-monthly magazine of the Globetrotters Club (see General Travel Information & Advice, p246 for details). Articles can be posted or emailed; there's no financial remuneration.

High Life and Business Life
Cedar Communications, 37–43 Sackville St, London W1S 3EH
☎ 020-7534 2400, Fax 020-7534 2553
high.life@cedarcom.co.uk
www.cedarcom.co.uk

High Life is the monthly in-flight magazine for British Airways passengers. Business Life is carried only on short-haul British Airways flights and carries lifestyle stories with a business twist.

Holiday Which?
Consumers' Association, 2 Marylebone Rd, London NW1 4DF
☎ 020-7770 7000, Fax 020-7770 7663
holiday@which.net
www.which.net

Published four times a year (in January, March, May and September), Holiday Which? provides independent travel features, investigative articles, and hard news on all aspects of holidaying and travelling in the UK and abroad. Many of the articles are written by Holiday Which? staff; occasionally freelancers are employed. Unsolicited manuscripts are not accepted.

Living France
Archant Life Ltd, Cumberland House, Oriel Rd, Cheltenham, Glos GL50 1BB
☎ 01242-216050, Fax 01242-216094
editor@livingfrance.com
www.livingfrance.com

Monthly magazine on France and French property.

The Sunday Times Travel Magazine
River Publishing, Victory House, 14 Leicester Pl, London WC2H 7BZ
☎ 020-7306 0304, Fax 020-7306 0314
travel@riverltd.co.uk
www.sundaytimestravel.co.uk

Bi-monthly travel magazine from the Sunday Times covering a broad range of holiday and short-break destinations. Submissions by email.

TNT Magazine
TNT Group, 14–15 Childs Pl, Earls Court, London SW5 9RX
☎ 0870-752 2701, Fax 0870-752 2720
tnttravel@tntmag.co.uk
www.tntmagazine.com/uk

A bi-weekly free magazine for UK-based travellers, TNT Magazine is distributed in London and Edinburgh. Email submissions. The magazine is interested in photographs too.

Travel Trade Gazette
CMP Information, 7th fl, Ludgate House, 245 Blackfriars Rd, London Se1 9UY
☎ 020-7921 8005, Fax 020-7921 8032
www.ttglive.com

A weekly newspaper for the travel trade.

Travel Weekly
Quadrant House, The Quadrant, Sutton, Surrey SM2 5AS
☎ 020-8652 3799, Fax 020-8652 3956
martin.lane@rbi.co.uk
www.travelweekly.co.uk

A weekly newspaper for the travel industry.

Traveller
Wexas Ltd, 45–49 Brompton Rd, London SW3 1DE
☎ 020-7589 0500, Fax 020-7581 1357
traveller@wexas.com
www.traveller.org.uk

Quarterly travel magazine for the Wexas travellers' club aimed at a 35+ age group. Guidelines for submissions are on the website.

Wanderlust
PO Box 1832, Windsor SL4 1YT
☎ 01753-620426, Fax 01753-620474
info@wanderlust.co.uk
www.wanderlust.co.uk

Leading magazine for independent-minded and adventurous travellers, published eight times a year. Writer guidelines are on their website.

Newspapers

The Daily Mail
Associated Newspapers, Northcliffe House, 2 Derry St, London W8 5TT
☎ 020-7938 7153
travel@dailymail.co.uk
www.thisistravel.co.uk

Main travel section of between eight and 12 pages is published on a Saturday. There's also a small travel section on Wednesdays. Do not fax enquiries.

The Daily Telegraph
1 Canada Sq, Canary Wharf, London E14 5DT
☎ 020-7538 6195/6484, Fax 020-7538 6802
dttravel@telegraph.co.uk
www.travel.telegraph.co.uk

The Saturday travel section ranges from between 12 and 42 pages but usually comes out at 18.

The Guardian
119 Farringdon Rd, London EC1R 3ER
☎ 020-7239 9591, Fax 020-7239 9935
travel@guardian.co.uk
www.guardian.co.uk/travel

Twenty-four page travel supplement on a Saturday.

The Independent
Independent House, 191 Marsh Wall, London E14 9RS
☎ 020-7005 2834, Fax 020-7005 2428
travel@independent.co.uk
www.independent.co.uk

Thirty-two page travel tabloid on a Saturday.

Independent on Sunday
Independent House, 191 Marsh Wall, London E14 9RS
☎ 020-7005 2271, Fax 020-7005 2428
sundaytravel@independent.co.uk
www.independent.co.uk

Twelve page travel section on a Sunday.

Mail on Sunday
Associated Newspapers, Northcliffe House, 2 Derry St, London W8 5TS
☎ 020-7938 6000, Fax 020-7938 2894
www.thisistravel.co.uk

About 12 pages of travel on Sunday. Please mail any article proposals.

The Observer
119 Farringdon Rd, London EC1R 3ER
☎ 020-7278 2332, Fax 020-7713 4794
escape@observer.co.uk
www.observer.co.uk/travel

From 16 to 30 pages of travel on a Sunday. Occasionally, the paper produces an *Observer Travel Magazine*. Please fax all travel story proposals, rather than ring.

The Sunday Telegraph
1 Canada Sq, Canary Wharf
London E14 5DT
☎ 020-7538 6195, Fax 020-7538 6802
traveldesk@telegraph.co.uk
www.travel.telegraph.co.uk

Sunday travel section of up to 28 pages.

The Sunday Times
News International, 1 Pennington St, London E98 1ST
☎ 020-7782 5000, Fax 020-7782 5540 (travel)
travel@sunday-times.co.uk
www.sunday-times.co.uk/travel

Sunday travel section of up to 30 pages.

The Times
News International, 1 Pennington St, London E98 1TT
☎ 020-7782 5173, Fax 020-7782 5927
travel@thetimes.co.uk
www.timesonline.co.uk/travel

Saturday travel section of up to 26 pages.

On Line
Please bear in mind that some of these publications pay for stories and some don't.

Globetrotters e-newsletter
beetle@globetrotters.co.uk
www.globetrotters.co.uk

As it says on the site: if you enjoy writing, enjoy travelling, why not write for the free monthly Globetrotters e-newsletter. 'The

Beetle' would love to hear from you: your travel stories, anecdotes, jokes, questions, hints and tips up to 750 words, together with a couple of sentences about yourself and a contact email address. Over 8,000 people currently subscribe to the Globetrotter e-news.

Handbag.com
151 Oxford St, London W1D 2JG
☎ 020-7292 0020, Fax 020-7292 0021
travel@handbag.com
www.handbag.com

A site that provides information and advice for busy women on line. Travel writers are sometimes employed to contribute to the travel pages.

Highbury Columbus Travel Publishing
www.travel-guide.com
☎ 01322-660070 (ask for Head of Editorial)

Comprehensive on-line information on every country, 101 major cities and 200 airports worldwide. An in-house editorial team and a network of freelance travel writers update this on a daily basis.

Teletext Holidays
traveldesk@teletext.co.uk
www.teletextholidays.co.uk

Extensive bank of travel guides and information – mostly uses in-house staff to update travel information but occasionally uses freelance travel writers.

This Is Travel
www.thisistravel.co.uk

The on-line travel site of Associated Papers. Original pieces are sometimes commissioned. Contact them with ideas through the website.

Travel Intelligence
www.travelintelligence.net

A travel site founded by travel writers for travel writers acting as an outlet for material as well as an on-line agent. Strict writing guidelines and contact details are given on the site. They are also interested in hotel reviewers.

TravelMag
ed@travelmag.co.uk
www.travelmag.co.uk

An on-line travel magazine supported by Wexas, the travel club. Interested in both articles and pictures. Contributor guidelines are found on-line. There's no payment but it's a good way of getting your name in print.

TravelMole
editor@travelmole.com
www.travelmole.com

On-line network of over 90,000 members of the travel and tourism industry. There's a lot on this site including daily trade news reports, chat forums and reference directories. The site uses travel trade writers from time to time.

TravelNotes
www.travelnotes.org

A US on-line guide to travel. The site needs Roving Reporters, Country Correspondents, Credible City Guides and Cyberspace Travellers. Contributor guidelines and contact details are on line and you can gain exposure for your work (and maybe earn a little extra money) by being published by them.

ViaMichelin UK
www.viamichelin.com

This website mostly offers travel assistance but freelance travel writers are used to update and compile the monthly on-line magazine section.

Whatsonwhen
91 Brick Lane, London E1 6QL
☎ 020-7770 6050, Fax 020-7770 6051
jobs@whatsonwhen.com
www.whatsonwhen.com

Global events and activities website. Freelance writers are hired to write feature articles, and field stringers are also employed.

World Rover
editor@worldrover.net
www.worldrover.net

A US site which takes contributions from UK writers, although unpaid.

WRITERS GROUPS & ASSOCIATIONS

Arts Council England (National Office)
14 Great Peter St, London SW1P 3NQ
☎ 020-7333 0100, Fax 020-7973 6590
enquiries@artscouncil.org.uk
www.artscouncil.org.uk

The Arts Council England is the national development agency for the arts. Between

2003 and 2006 it will invest £2 billion of public funds in the arts to both individuals and organisations. It supports writers through Grants for the Arts, through the annual Arts Council England Writers' Awards scheme, through International Fellowships and a range of literary prizes.

British Guild of Travel Writers
BGTW Secretariat, 51b Askew Cres, London W12 9DN
☎/Fax 020-8749 1128
charlotte.c@virtualnecessities.com
www.bgtw.org

Over 200 members of journalists, authors, editors, photographers and broadcasters involved in the world of travel. Strict membership criteria are detailed on the guild's website.

The English Centre of International PEN
Lancaster House, 33 Islington High St, London N1 9LH
☎ 020-7713 0023, Fax 020-7713 0005
enquiries@englishpen.org
www.englishpen.org

A membership organisation for writers and literary professionals founded in 1921, providing an active and supportive focus in the home community for writers and other professionals working in the literary sector.

National Association of Writers' Groups
Mike and Diane Wilson, 40 Burstall Hill, Bridlington, East Yorkshire YO16 7GA
☎/Fax 01262-609228
michael.wilson@tesco.net
www.nawg.co.uk

Launched in 1995, there are over 150 affiliated groups and over 100 associate (individual) members spread across the UK. The Association aims to bring cohesion and fellowship to isolated writers' groups and individuals, promoting the study and art of writing in all its aspects. On its site there's a list of writers' groups, details of the competitions, festival of writing and bi-monthly magazine.

National Union of Journalists
Headland House, 308–312 Gray's Inn Rd, London WC1X 8DP
☎ 020-7278 7916, Fax 020-7837 8143
info@nuj.org.uk
www.nuj.org.uk

The biggest journalists' union in the world, with 34,000 members. There are offices in Dublin, Glasgow and Manchester. You can find help with training, legal services, advice on what freelance writers should be paid, and much more. Ten times a year the union publishes a magazine called the *Journalist*.

Outdoor Writers' Guild
37 Sandycoombe Rd, Twickenham, Middlesex TW1 2LR
☎/Fax 020-8538 9468
info@owg.org.uk
www.owg.org.uk

Membership is open to writers, journalists, photographers, illustrators, broadcasters, film-makers, artists, publishers and editors, actively and professionally involved in sustainable activities in any outdoor setting.

Public Lending Right
Richard House, Sorbonne Close, Stockton-on-Tees TS17 6DA
☎ 01642-604699, Fax 01642-615641
authorservices@plr.uk.com
www.plr.uk.com

Under the United Kingdom's PLR Scheme authors receive payments from government funds for the free borrowing of their books from public libraries in the United Kingdom. To qualify for payment, you must apply to register your books with them.

Society of Authors
84 Drayton Gardens, London SW10 9SB
☎ 020-7373 6642, Fax 020-7373 5768
info@societyofauthors.org
www.societyofauthors.org

You have to be a published author/writer to join. Benefits include: clause-by-clause contract vetting, advice on professional issues or problems, opportunities to meet other authors, publishers and agents, invitations to talks and seminars, plus you get the quarterly journal called *The Author*.

Travelwriters UK
www.travelwriters.co.uk

A site where travel writers, broadcasters and photographers can advertise (for a fee) their experience and expertise. It might be worth a go but don't hold your breath.

Writers and Photographers Unlimited
PO Box 520, Bamber Bridge, Preston, Lancashire PR5 8LF
☎ 01772-321243, Fax 0870-137 8888
mail@wpu.org.uk
www.wpu.org.uk

WPu is an electronic membership service to English-language professional writers and photographers specialising in all aspects of travel, tourism, the outdoors, adventure sports, food and drink. Membership is by invitation only but you can apply on line to be considered. There is an annual fee.

writers-circles.com
Diana Hayden, 39 Lincoln Way, Harlington, Bedfordshire LU5 6NG
☎ 01525-873197, No Fax
diana@writers-circles.com
www.writers-circles.com

There are over 1000 writing circles in the UK and Ireland, you can contact Diana by email or phone and she'll tell you of the nearest writing circle to you. She also publishes a directory of writing circles which you can buy.

Writers' Guild of Great Britain
15 Britannia St, London WC1X 9JN
☎ 020-7833 0777, Fax 020-7833 4777
admin@writersguild.org.uk
www.writersguild.org.uk

This is a trade union for writers working in television, radio, film, theatre, books and multimedia. They've got Minimum Terms Agreements and advice services plus professional, cultural and social activities.

Yr Academi Gymreig – The Welsh Academy
3rd fl, Mount Stuart House, Mount Stuart Sq Cardiff CF10 5FQ
☎ 029-2047 2266, Fax 029-2049 2930
post@academi.org
www.academi.org

The Academi represents the interests of Welsh writers and Welsh writing both inside Wales and beyond. It works in partnership with Ty Newydd, the Cricieth-based residential writers' centre. It runs events, courses, competitions, tours by authors, lectures, international exchanges, readings, literary performances and festivals. It offers bursaries and administers the annual Book of the Year award.

WRITING COURSES

The Arvon Foundation (National Administration Office)
2nd fl, 42a Buckingham Palace Rd, London SW1W ORE
☎ 020-7931 7611, Fax 020-7963 0961
london@arvonfoundation.org
www.arvonfoundation.org

This registered charity has some of the best writing courses in the country, including ones specifically on travel writing. Courses usually run for 4½ days between April and December.

Cardiff School of Journalism, Media and Cultural Studies
Bute Bldg, Cardiff University, King Edward VII Ave, Cardiff CF10 3NB
☎ 029-2087 4041, Fax 029-2023 8832
jomec@cardiff.ac.uk
www.cf.ac.uk

Runs courses in journalism and other contemporary media including international media, media technologies, media development, film, radio, television, magazine journalism and public and media relations.

London College of Printing
Elephant & Castle, London SE1 6SB
☎ 020-7514 6569, Fax 020-7514 6535
info@lcp.linst.ac.uk
www.lcp.linst.ac.uk

Over 240 courses on design, media, printing, publishing, travel and tourism. Long, short or summer courses are available.

Mary Ward Centre
42 Queen Sq, London WC1N 3AQ
☎ 020-7269 6000, Fax 020-7269 6001
info@marywardcentre.ac.uk
www.marywardcentre.ac.uk

One of the writing courses run by this college is called Travel Writing Beginners and lasts for 12 weeks.

National Council for the Training of Journalists (NCTJ)
Latton Bush Centre, Southern Way, Harlow, Essex CM18 7BL
☎ 01279-430009, Fax 01279-438008
info@nctj.com
www.nctj.com

One- to four-day courses on aspects of journalism from Sharpening Your English to Successful Freelancing. Also full-time or weekend courses lasting from 40 weeks to three years.

The Open University
Walton Hall, Milton Keynes MK7 6AA
☎ 01908-653231, Fax 01908-654806
enquiries@open.ac.uk
www.open.ac.uk

With a network of centres throughout the UK, the Open University runs several writing courses a year.

Skyros

92 Prince of Wales Rd, London NW5 3NE
☎ 020-7267 4424, 020-7284 3065, Fax 020-7284 3063
enquiries@skyros.com
www.skyros.com

Skyros is a specialist holistic holiday company offering courses that engage the mind, body and spirit. A variety of writing courses run all year round on the island of Skyros, Greece, or on the island of Ko Samet, Thailand.

The TNT Group

14–15 Childs Pl, Earls Court, London SW5 9RX
☎ 020-7341 6729, Fax 020-7341 6756
events@tntmag.co.uk
www.tntmagazine.com/uk

TNT runs at least three travel writing courses per year – usually before the summer. One always coincides with their London travel show for independent travellers held each spring. Courses combining travel writing with photography may run from 2004 onwards.

trAce Online Writing School

The Nottingham Trent University, Clifton Lane, Nottingham NG11 8NS
☎ 0115-848 3533, Fax 0115-848 6364
traceschool@ntu.ac.uk
www.tracewritingschool.com

If you want to study writing as you travel then why not sign up to learn on line. There are courses on around 12 subjects per year including Article Writing. A general writing workshop runs continually or if you want personal on-line tuition then this can also be accommodated.

University of East Anglia

Norwich, Norfolk NR4 7TJ
☎ 01603-592283, Fax 01603-593799
eas.admiss@uea.ac.uk
www.uea.ac.uk/eas

Many universities offer writing courses (see www.ucas.ac.uk or www.postgrad.hobsons.com) but UEA's MA in Creative Writing is famous, set up by Angus Wilson and Malcolm Bradbury.

Ways with Words

Droridge Farm, Dartington, Totnes, Devon TQ9 6JQ
☎ 01803-867373, Fax 01803-863688
admin@wayswithwords.co.uk
www.wayswithwords.co.uk

A family business running a number of writing courses as well as organising three large literature festivals a year. One- and two-week creative writing courses are run in Italy in September. There are also day courses in a Devon farmhouse.

WRITERS WEBSITES & TOOLS

ABCtales.com
www.abctales.com

Set up by the guy behind the *Big Issue*, and Gordon Roddick (of Body Shop fame), this is a site where you can get published for free.

Askaboutwriting
www.askaboutwriting.net

Useful site aimed at British and Irish writers.

Association of Authors' Agents
www.agentsassoc.co.uk

There's an on-line directory of members.

author.co.uk
www.author.co.uk

A site offering all sorts of services to writers, and information on writers' circles, agents, literary festivals and much more.

Author Network
www.author-network.com

Provides an extensive range of resources for writers.

Bartleby.com
www.bartleby.com/62

Loads of reference books on line, like *Roget's Thesaurus*, the *World Factbook* and *Brewer's Dictionary of Phrase & Fable*.

Bloomsbury Publishing
www.bloomsbury.com/WritersArea

Bloomsbury's writers' area includes a guide for unpublished writers, a research centre for writers, a web directory, a writers' noticeboard and a calendar of literary events.

The Booksellers Association
www.booksellers.org.uk

Contains info on events and on-line directories of publishers and members.

Booktrust
www.booktrust.org.uk

A site devoted to books, publishing and the booktrade with listings of events, publishers, prizes, writers, finance and factsheets.

The Independent Publishers' Guild
www.ipg.uk.com

The membership organisation for independent publishers with an on-line directory.

The Literary Consultancy
2nd fl, C/o Diorama Arts, 34 Osnaburgh St, London NW1 3ND
☎/Fax 020 7 813 4330
swifttlc@dircon.co.uk
www.literaryconsultancy.co.uk

Independent assessment of your manuscript for a charge.

The Publishers Association
www.publishers.org.uk

There's a useful 'Getting Published' section on here.

WriteLink
www.writelink.co.uk

Writers' website with an outstanding list of possible markets, a chat room, opportunities to write for them (in return for small gratuity) and a great deal more.

Writer's Services.com
www.writersservices.co.uk

A site for writers with reproduced sections from the *The Writer's Handbook* by Barry Turner.

Research-Related Websites
CLIMATE & THE ENVIRONMENT
Climate Care
www.co2.org

A site which calculates the amount of carbon dioxide you generate by travelling, then offsets it by funding projects that reduce this major greenhouse gas. Besides allowing you to compensate for your own emissions as a travel writer, it's also a useful resource for writing about ethical travel.

The Met Office
www.metoffice.com

UK and world weather forecasts.

ECOTOURISM & RESPONSIBLE TRAVEL
responsibletravel.com
www.responsibletravel.com

Holidays that give the world a break, backed by Anita Roddick.

Tourism Concern
www.tourismconcern.org.uk

Campaigning for ethical and fairly traded tourism.

EMBASSIES, CONSULATES & PASSPORTS
Thames Consular Services
www.thamesconsular.com

A leading independent passport and visa agency.

UK Foreign & Commonwealth Office
www.fco.gov.uk

Provides details of all embassies and consulates in the UK.

UK Passport Agency, The Home Office
www.ukpa.gov.uk

On-line passport applications and advice.

FACTS, FIGURES & STATISTICS
The Audit Bureau of Circulations
www.abc.org.uk

Amongst other things, magazine and newspaper circulations figures.

The British Library
www.bl.uk

The national library of the United Kingdom and one of the world's greatest libraries.

CIA World Factbook
www.cia.gov/cia/publications/factbook

Everything you ever wanted to know about countries but never dared to ask. It's obviously a US site but every travel writer has this site marked down as a Favourite.

Country Calling Codes
www.countrycallingcodes.com

International telephoning made easy.

Encyclopaedia Britannica
www.britannica.com

You can search through the 32-volumed Encyclopaedia Britannica on line.

European Travel Commission
www.etc-corporate.org

A wealth of country information.

IATA
www.iata.org

The International Air Transport Association site features useful reports, facts and figures.

National Statistics Online
www.statistics.gov.uk

Some of these reports have to be bought.

VisitBritain
www.visitbritain.com

Click on to the UK Tourism Industry section of this site for all manner of facts and figures.

The World Heritage List
http://whc.unesco.org/pg.cfm?cid=31

The 754 properties which the World Heritage Committee has inscribed on the World Heritage List.

World Information
www.worldinformation.com

Business, economic and political information on every country in the world.

World Tourism Organisation
www.world-tourism.org

There's a wealth of statistics available on this site, some are for free and others will cost you.

GENERAL TRAVEL INFORMATION & ADVICE

ABTA
www.abta.com

The Association of British Travel Agents.

AITO
www.aito.co.uk

The Association of Independent Tour Operators.

ANTOR
www.antor.com

Association of National Tourist Offices in the United Kingdom.

ATTA
www.atta.co.uk

African Travel & Tourism Association.

British Tourist Authority
www.visitbritain.com

VisitBritain is the site of the British Tourist Authority.

Cybercafes
www.cybercafes.com

Contains a database of 4208 Internet cafés in 140 countries.

Globetrotters Club
BCM/Roving, London WCIN 3XX
☎ 020-8674 6229 (information line only)
Email through website
www.globetrotters.co.uk

International travel club founded in 1945. It meets on the first Saturday of every month in London where guest travellers speak about their adventures. There's a bi-monthly printed magazine called *Globe* and a monthly e-newsletter.

National Rail Enquiries
www.nationalrail.co.uk

Information about Britain's appalling train services.

RAC
www.rac.co.uk/travelservices

Use this site to plan routes for the UK and Europe by car.

Steve Kropla
www.kropla.com

One of the Web's most comprehensive listings of worldwide electrical and telephone information.

The Thorn Tree
http://thorntree.lonelyplanet.com
www.lonelyplanet.com/subwwway

The Thorn Tree section of Lonely Planet's website is a bulletin board used by travellers from all over the world to exchange information about a wide variety of travel topics and destinations. You'll also find cultural, literature, food and political discussions. The site also provides links to other important travel resources in its Subway section.

TIA
www.tia.org

This is the site of the Travel Industry Association of America.

Tourist Office Worldwide Directory
www.towd.com

The Tourism Offices Worldwide Directory provides links to official US and international tourist information sources: government tourism offices, convention and visitors bureaus, chambers of commerce, and similar organisations that provide free, accurate and unbiased travel information to the public.

Travel Lists
www.travel-lists.co.uk

Independent travel directories for British travellers.

TravelMole
www.travelmole.com

On-line network of over 90,000 members of the travel and tourism industry. There's a lot on this site including daily trade news reports, chat forums and reference directories.

travel-quest
www.travel-quest.co.uk

Travel directory – adventure holidays and activity holidays worldwide.

Travel Ticker
www.lonelyplanet.com/travel_ticker

Lonely Planet's travel advisory service.

time and date.com
www.timeanddate.com

And also the times of sunrise, sunset, the international country code and city coordinates.

UK Foreign & Commonwealth Office
www.fco.gov.uk/travel

Country by country travel advice.

Universal Currency Converter
www.xe.com/ucc

Calculate your dwindling finances on line in any number of different currencies.

Wanderlust Magazine
See p240 for contact details.
www.wanderlust.co.uk/travclub/clubs01.html

If you follow this link on Wanderlust's website you'll find a good list of UK travel clubs.

Warrior
www.warrior.com

Specialist in laptop and mobile equipment.

HEALTH
Department of Health
www.doh.gov.uk/traveladvice

Health advice for travellers.

London Hospital for Tropical Diseases
www.uclh.org/services/htd/index.shtml

Health advice for tropical destinations.

MASTA Travel Health
www.masta.org

For the latest health news, travel clinics, chat room and advice.

World Health Organization
www.who.int/en

The website provides information on health risks around the world as well as recommended precautions, immunisations and vaccines when travelling.

MAPS
Multimap.com
www.multimap.com

One of Europe's most popular mapping websites, offering a range of free, useful services to assist with everyday life. Key features include street-level maps of the UK, Europe and the US; road maps of the world; door-to-door travel directions; aerial photographs; and local information.

WORLD EVENTS
Artrepublic
www.artrepublic.com/WOW

Search over 1250 museum listings to find out what exhibitions are on now.

Whatsonwhen
www.whatsonwhen.com

Don't miss out on what event is being held where.

YOU ON THE WEB
Blogger
www.blogger.com

Have your own on-line travel diary to share with your friends.

My Trip Journal
http://lonelyplanet.mytripjournal.com

Build an on-line journal of your trip with maps, photos and email notification of updates for your friends.

Yahoo!GeoCities UK & Ireland
http://uk.geocities.yahoo.com

Build your own website for free.

REFERENCE PURCHASES
An Author's Guide to Publishing by Michael Legat

Brewer's Dictionary of Modern Phrase revised by Adrian Room

Brewer's Dictionary of Phrase & Fable revised by Adrian Room

The Cassell Dictionary of Slang edited by Jonathan Green

The Concise Oxford Dictionary of Quotations edited by Elizabeth Knowles

A Dictionary of World History compiled by Market House Books

The Freelance Writer's Handbook – How to Make Money and Enjoy Life by Andrew Crofts

The Internet: A Writer's Guide by Jane Dorner

Mind the Gaff by R. L. Task

Modern English Usage by Henry Fowler

The Modern Law of Copyright & Designs by Justice Laddie Prescott, Peter Vitoria, Mary Lane and Lindsay Lane

From Pitch to Publication by Carole Blake

Quick Guides by The Society of Authors – see the website (www.societyofauthors.net /publications/index.html) for details

Roget's Thesaurus edited by Betty Kilpatrick

Starting in Business (IR28) from the Inland Revenue (download from www.inlandrevenue .gov.uk).

The Teleworking Handbook by Alan Denbigh

The Times Comprehensive Atlas of the World, 11th edition – rather expensive at £150 but well worth it

The Times Concise Atlas of the World, 8th edition – slightly cheaper at £60

Understanding Publishers' Contracts by Michael Legat

User's Guide to Copyright by Michael F. Flint

Library References

The Bookseller Magazine (weekly magazine for the bookselling and publishing world – twice a year there's a special travel issue)

The Directory of Writers' Circles by Diana Hayden; annual

Encyclopaedia Britannica by Encyclopaedia (UK) Ltd

Publishing News (weekly newspaper for the bookselling and publishing world – twice a year there's a special travel issue)

Whitaker's Almanack by A&C Black; annual

Who's Who by A&C Black; annual

TRAVEL LITERATURE CLASSICS

Following is a list of 20 travel literature classics by UK authors compiled with help from Lonely Planet co-founder Tony Wheeler and the staff members of Stanford Bookshop, London:

Arabia Through the Looking Glass by Jonathan Raban

Arabian Sands by Wilfred Thesiger

Frontiers of Heaven by Stanley Stewart

Full Tilt by Dervla Murphy

Holy Mountain by William Dalrymple

I Came, I Saw by Norman Lewis

In Patagonia by Bruce Chatwin

Into the Heart of Borneo by Redmond O'Hanlon

Journey Into Cyprus by Colin Thubron

A Pattern of Islands by Arthur Grimble

The Road to Oxiana by Robert Byron

A Season in Heaven by David Tomory

A Short Walk in the Hindu Kush by Eric Newby

South From Granada by Gerald Brenan

Southern Gates of Arabia by Freya Stark

Terra Incognito by Sara Wheeler

A Time of Gifts by Patrick Leigh-Fermor

An Unexpected Light: Travels in Afghanistan by Jason Elliot

Venice by Jan Morris

The Worst Journey in the World by Apsley Cherry-Garrard

AUSTRALIAN RESOURCES

GENERAL GUIDES TO PUBLISHERS, EDITORS & LITERARY AGENTS

The Australian Writer's Marketplace
(Queensland Writers Centre, www.qwc-asn.au)

The prime resource for Australian writers, this annually updated, practical guide to markets and resources includes advice from leading local authors and separate indexes to publishers, literary agents, awards and courses.

Australian Books in Print
(Thorpe-Bowker, www.thorpe.com.au)

This hefty reference provides contact details and summaries of all Australian publishers and distributors, local distributors of overseas publishers and information on literary associations.

OzLit
http://home.vicnet.net.au/~ozlit/lists.html

OzLit's useful website includes a database of books and writers, and links to literary agents, prizes, publishers, references, magazines and organisations.

MAJOR TRAVEL PUBLISHERS
Many publishers' websites provide detailed information and advice for writers on topics such as writing tips, unsolicited manuscripts, style and presentation; agents, contracts and manuscript services.

Travel Guidebooks
Explore Australia Publishing
C/o Hardie Grant, 12 Claremont St, South Yarra Vic 3141
☎ 03-9827 8377
explore@hardiegrant.com.au

This publisher of road maps, activity guides and the state-based 'Explore' guides has been in business for 25 years.

Little Hills Press
3/18 Bearing Rd, Seven Hills NSW 2147
☎ 02-9838 4373, Fax 02-9838 7929
lhills@bigpond.net.au
www.littlehills.com

This small, locally owned publisher produces regional and activity-based travel guides. A publisher of travel guides since 1987, Little Hills also produces general trade titles in fields such as languages, cooking and gardening.

Lonely Planet Publications
Locked Bag 1, Footscray Vic 3011
☎ 03-8379 8000, Fax 03-8379 8111
talk2us@lonelyplanet.com.au
www.lonelyplanet.com

Head office of the independent travel media company, covering every country in the world in over 600 titles across 17 different languages.

New Holland Publishers (Australia)
Locked Bag 516, Frenchs Forest NSW 1640
☎ 02-9975 6799, Fax 02-9452 6255
www.newholland.com.au

This branch of the international New Holland company focuses on nonfiction Australiana including pictorials, natural history and regional travel destinations. Also publishes reference, cookery, gardening, health, lifestyle and current affairs.

Universal Publishers
PO Box 1530, Macquarie Park, North Ryde NSW 2113
☎ 02-9857 3700, Fax 02-9888 9074
www.universalpublishers.com.au

Australia's largest publisher of local mapping and travel-related products, Universal's titles include the Gregory's leisure guides and UBD maps and references.

Travel Literature
Allen & Unwin
PO Box 8500, St Leonards NSW 1590
☎ 02-8425 0100, Fax 02-9906 2218
recept@allenandunwin.com.au
www.allenandunwin.com

Distributed worldwide by its UK parent company, Allen & Unwin publishes a wide-ranging list of nonfiction Australian titles including memoir and travel writing.

Duffy and Snellgrove
PO Box 177, Potts Point NSW 1335
☎ 02-9386 0280, Fax 02-9386 1530
info@duffyandsnellgrove.com.au
www.duffyandsnellgrove.com.au

This small, independent publishing house produces around 30 fiction and nonfiction titles each year. It specialises in Australian literary nonfiction.

Five Mile Press
PO Box 177, Ferntree Gully Vic 3156
☎ 03-8756 5500, Fax 03-8756 5588

A small, independent publisher of nonfiction Australiana such as literary anthologies.

Hardie Grant Books
Private Bag 1600, South Yarra Vic 3141
☎ 03-9827 8377, Fax 03-9827 8766
www.hardiegrant.com.au

Publisher of the best-selling guide to fictional Molvanîa, Hardie Grant also publishes books on contemporary issues and popular culture.

HarperCollins Publishers
PO Box 321, Pymble NSW 2073
☎ 02-9952 5409, Fax 02-9952 5555
www.harpercollins.com.au

HarperCollins Australia's list of contemporary nonfiction titles includes travel and memoir, lifestyle and Australian issues.

Hodder Headline Australia
Level 17, 207 Kent St
Sydney NSW 2000
☎ 02-8248 0800, Fax 02-8248 0810
auspub@hha.com.au
www.hha.com.au

Part of the Hodder Headline group, HHA publishes travel nonfiction by Australian authors.

Lonely Planet Publications
All travel literature and travel pictorials are commissioned out of Lonely Planet's UK office; see p237 for contact details.

Lothian Books
Level 5, 132–136 Albert Rd, South
Melbourne Vic 3205
☎ 03-9694 4900, Fax 03-9645 0705
books@lothian.com.au
www.lothian.com.au

Established in 1888 and still independently owned today, Lothian publishes adult nonfiction Australiana, including travel literature and pictorials.

Pan Macmillan Australia
Level 18, St Martins Tower, 31 Market St,
Sydney NSW 2000
☎ 02-9285 9100, Fax 02-9285 9190
panpublishing@macmillan.com.au
www.panmacmillan.com.au

Publishes and distributes a range of imprints, including Australian adventure travel and travel literature titles.

Penguin Australia
PO Box 701, Hawthorn Vic 3122
www.penguin.com.au

Penguin Australia's Books for Adults list includes travel and memoir, short stories and fiction.

Random House Australia
20 Alfred St, Milsons Point NSW 2061
☎ 02-9954 9966, Fax 02-9954 4562
random@randomhouse.com.au
www.randomhouse.com.au

Australian travel titles published by Random House Australia and its many imprints include Sarah Turnbull's *Almost French* and Sarah Macdonald's *Holy Cow*.

Spinifex Press
PO Box 212, North Melbourne Vic 3051
☎ 03-9329 6088, Fax 03-9329 9238
women@spinifexpress.com.au
www.spinifexpress.com.au

Nonfiction published by this small feminist press includes travel literature and memoirs.

Text Publishing Company
171 La Trobe St, Melbourne Vic 3000
☎ 03-9272 4700, Fax 03-9272 4854
books@textpublishing.com.au
www.textpublishing.com.au

The publisher of prestigious Australian authors such as Murray Bail, Tim Flannery and Anna Funder, Text recently joined forces with the UK's Canongate Books.

Wakefield Press
1 The Parade West, Kent Town SA 5067
www.wakefieldpress.com.au

This small, independently owned publishing company from South Australia produces travel anthologies, Australian travel stories, autobiographies and books on food, history, culture and art.

Travel Magazines
WRITERS RESOURCES
The Australian Writer
PO Box 3036, Ripponlea Vic 3183
☎ 03-9528 7088, Fax 03-9528 7088

Bimonthly interviews and articles for writers, published by the Victorian branch of the Fellowship of Australian Writers (FAW).

Margaret Gee's Australian Media Guide
Crown Content, Level 2, 141 Capel St, North
Melbourne Vic 3051
☎ 03-9329 9800, Fax 03-9329 9698
www.mediaguide.com.au

Available in both print and on-line format, the guide includes listings and details of Australia's newspapers and magazines.

MAGAZINES
4x4 Trader
Locked Bag 12, Oakleigh Vic 3166
Email using form on website
www.carpoint.com.au

This monthly publication includes freelance articles by 4WD enthusiasts.

AFTA Traveller Magazine
Level 3, 309 Pitt St, Sydney NSW 2000
☎ 02-9264 3299, Fax 02-9264 1085
afta@afta.com.au
www.afta.com.au

The Australian Federation of Travel Agents' free quarterly trade magazine highlights destinations and provides updates on campaigns and programs conducted by tourist offices, airlines and hotels, reflecting current tourism trends worldwide.

Air New Zealand
Private Bag 47920, Ponsonby, Auckland, New Zealand 2001
☎ 9-379 8822, Fax 9-379 8821
editorial@pol.net.nz

A monthly in-flight magazine covering regional destinations serviced by Air New Zealand.

Arena Magazine
PO Box 18, North Carlton Vic 3054
☎ 03-9416 5166, Fax 03-9416 0684
magazine@arena.org.au
www.arena.org.au

An independent leftist bi-monthly forum for the discussion of political, cultural and social issues.

Art Almanac
PO Box 915, Glebe NSW 2037
☎ 02-9660 6755, Fax 02-9660 6799
info@art-almanac.com.au
www.art-almanac.com.au

Monthly reviews of current local exhibitions and news from the international art world.

Aussie Backpacker Magazine
PO Box 1264, Townsville Qld 4810
☎ 07-4772 3244, Fax 07-4772 3250
info@aussiebackpacker.com.au
www.aussiebackpacker.com.au

Bi-monthly collection of information, articles and stories for budget travellers. Also publishes the *Aussie Backpacker Attractions and Accommodation Guide*.

Australian 4WD Monthly
Locked Bag 111, Silverwater NSW 2128
☎ 02-9741 3800, Fax 02-9748 3856
4wd@expresspublications.com.au
www.4wdmonthly.com.au

Monthly articles and reviews for outback travellers.

Australian Alpine News
PO Box 1523, Surrey Hills Vic 3127
☎ 03-9888 4834, Fax 03-9888 4840
alpinenews@nenews.com.au

Produces three issues per year for skiing enthusiasts.

Australian Geographic
PO Box 321, Terrey Hills NSW 2084
☎ 02-9473 6711, Fax 02-9473 6701
editorial@ausgeo.com.au
www.australiangeographic.com.au

Quarterly articles for lovers of adventure and discovery.

Australian Gourmet Traveller
PO Box 4088, Sydney NSW 1028
☎ 02-9282 8758, Fax 02-9264 3621
nley@acp.com.au
www.ninemsn.com.au/gourmettraveller

Monthly magazine devoted to wine, food and travel.

Australian House & Garden/Getaway Magazine
PO Box 4088, Sydney NSW 1028
☎ 02-9282 8456, Fax 02-9267 4912
h&g@acp.com.au
www.houseandgarden.acp.com.au

Lifestyle and travel magazines. *Getaway Magazine* is a free supplement with *Australian House & Garden* twice a year.

Australian Table
PO Box 4088, Sydney NSW 1028
☎ 02-9282 8000, Fax 02-9267 5462
atable@acp.com.au

Monthly magazine focusing on food, lifestyle and travel.

Backpacker Essentials
GPO Box 5276, Sydney NSW 2001
☎ 02-9261 1111, Fax 02-9264 4516
backpacker.essentials@yhansw.org.au
www.backpackeressentials.com.au

A YHA-focused print and on-line magazine for Australia's budget and independent travellers. Topics include destination guides, transport and book reviews.

Backpackers Magazine
Level 4, 46–48 York St, Sydney NSW 2000
☎ 02-9299 4811, Fax 02-9299 4861
www.tntmagazine.com/au

A free monthly publication for independent travellers.

The *Bulletin*

GPO Box 3957, Sydney NSW 1028
☎ 02-9282 8227, Fax 02-9267 4359
bulletin@itechne.com
www.ninemsn.com.au/bulletin

Australia's oldest news and current affairs weekly.

Coast & Country

PO Box 1045, Ivanhoe Vic 3070
☎ 03-9490 1417, Fax 03-9499 9122
office@coastandcountry.com.au
www.coastandcountry.com.au

Bimonthly magazine focusing on country living in Victoria and Tasmania.

Cuisine

PO Box 1101, Potts Point NSW 2011
☎ 02-9360 9380, Fax 02-9360 3568
jacom@bigpond.net.au
www.cuisine.co.nz

Trans-Tasman food and lifestyle quarterly from New Zealand; also available in Australia.

Get Lost!

www.getlostmag.com

A new quarterly focusing on travel lifestyles and culture, targeting the backpacker and youth markets.

Inside Out

Level 5, 2 Holt St, Surry Hills NSW 2010
☎ 02-9288 3272, Fax 02-9288 2788
insideout@newsltd.com.au
www.insideout.com.au

Monthly home and lifestyle magazine.

Luxury Travel

1st fl, 645 Harris St, Ultimo NSW 2007
☎ 02-9281 7523, Fax 02-9281 7529
www.luxurytravel.net.au

Quarterly magazine focusing on four- and five-star travel.

Melbourne Magazine

Level 1, 6 Palmer Pde, Richmond Vic 3121
☎ 03-9429 8866, Fax 03-9429 8155
info@melbournemag.com
www.melbournemag.com

This glossy design and lifestyle magazine published 11 times a year welcomes contributions for publication.

On the Road

PO Box 310, Williamstown Vic 3016
☎ 03-9397 2611, Fax 03-9397 2711
editor@ontheroad.net.au
www.ontheroad.net.au

Monthly magazine for camping, 4WD and eco-tourism enthusiasts.

Outdoor Australia

PO Box 1014, Haymarket NSW 1240
☎ 02-9581 9400, Fax 02-9581 9570
outdoor@emap.com.au
www.emap.com.au

Bi-monthly magazine for lovers of bushwalking, camping and other outdoor pursuits.

Overland

PO Box 14428, Melbourne Vic 8001
☎ 03-9688 4163, Fax 03-9687 7614
overland@vu.edu.au
www.overlandexpress.org

A leftist literary and political quarterly focusing on culture, current affairs, history, reviews and new writing.

Qantas: The Australian Way

PO Box 4088, Sydney NSW 1028
☎ 02-9282 8549, Fax 02-967 4361
www.qmedia.acp.com.au

Qantas Airline's in-flight magazine is published monthly.

Quarterly Essay

5/289 Flinders Lane, Melbourne Vic 3000
☎ 03-9654 2000, Fax 03-9654 2290
quarterlyessay@blackincbooks.com
www.quarterlyessay.com

Award-winning current affairs quarterly providing serious and significant reflections on contemporary issues.

TNT Magazine Australia

Level 4, 46–48 York St, Sydney NSW 2000
☎ 02-9299 4811, Fax 02-9299 4861
editor@tntmag.com.au
www.tntmagazine.com/au

A free monthly publication for independent travellers and backpackers.

Tracks

PO Box 1014, Haymarket NSW 1240
☎ 02-9581 9400, Fax 02-9581 9570
tracksmag@emap.com.au
www.tracksmag.com

This monthly surfing magazine includes travel tips and travel stories.

Travel Australia
Level 7, 275 Alfred St, North Sydney NSW 2060
☎ 02-9964 0103, Fax 02-9964 0102

Monthly trade publication.

Traveltrade
Locked Bag 2999, Chatswood NSW 2067
☎ 02-9422 2999, Fax 02-9422 2921
www.travelbiz.com.au

Traveltrade publishes *Travel Week*, a weekly wrap-up of industry news and stories; *Traveltrade*, a fortnightly travel news magazine for travel professionals, including news and feature articles on local and international destinations; and the *Traveltrade Year Book*, published twice a year and presenting up-to-date contact details of agents, wholesalers, cruise lines, airlines, accommodation and national tourist offices.

Vacation and Travel
F16/1–15 Barr St, Balmain NSW 2041
☎ 02-9555 7477, Fax 02-9555 1436
ag.cpg.@bigpond.net.au

Quarterly targeting adventurous travellers.

Vogue Australia
180 Bourke Rd, Alexandria NSW 2015
☎ 02-9353 6666, Fax 02-9353 6699
vogue@vogue.com.au
www.vogue.com.au

Monthly fashion and beauty magazine; includes travel articles.

Vogue Entertaining + Travel
180 Bourke Rd, Alexandria NSW 2015
☎ 02-9964 43888, Fax 02-9906 5016
vogueent@vogue.com.au
www.vogue.com.au

Lifestyle, food and travel magazine published bi-monthly.

Newspapers

The *Advertiser*
GPO Box 339, Adelaide SA 5001
☎ 08-8206 2000, Fax 08-8206 3669
mailedit@adv.newsltd.com.au
www.theadvertiser.news.com.au

This South Australian newspaper has a colour travel section on Saturdays.

The *Age*
PO Box 257C, Melbourne MC Vic 8001
☎ 03-9601 2250, Fax 03-9601 2332
newsdesk@theage.com.au
www.theage.com.au

Victoria's major newspaper includes an eight-page travel section on Saturday and a 20-page full-colour section in the *Sunday Age*. Topics include feature stories, specialist city guides, travel tips and advice.

The *Australian*
GPO Box 4245, Sydney NSW 2001
☎ 02-9288 3000, Fax 02-9288 2250
travel@theaustralian.com.au
www.theaustralian.news.com.au

Saturday's *Weekend Australian* includes a travel and indulgence lift-out, edited by Susan Kurosawa.

The *Canberra Times*
PO Box 7155, Canberra MC ACT 2610
☎ 02-6280 2122
www.canberratimes.com.au

The capital's newspaper includes a Sunday travel section.

The *Courier Mail*
PO Box 130, Brisbane Qld 4001
☎ 07-3666 8000, Fax 07-3666 6696
cmletters@qnp.newsltd.com.au
www.thecouriermail.com.au

Australia's second-bestselling broadsheet features special interest sections on travel and a regular section on Saturday. The *Sunday Mail* features the 'Escape' 24-page full-colour travel lift-out.

The *Daily Telegraph*
GPO Box 4245, Surry Hills NSW 2001
☎ 02-9288 3000, Fax 02-9288 2300
dtnews@matp.newsltd.com.au
www.news.com.au

This Sydney newspaper includes a travel section every Tuesday.

The *Herald Sun*
HWT Tower, PO Box 14999
Melbourne City MC Vic 8001
☎ 03-9292 1226, Fax 03-9292 2112
hseditor@hwt.newsltd.com.au
www.heraldsun.com.au

Melbourne's tabloid includes a travel feature section on Fridays.

The *Sun-Herald*
201 Sussex St, Sydney NSW 2000
☎ 02-9282 1679, Fax 02-9282 2151
shnews@mail.fairfax.com.au
http://sunherald.com.au

The Saturday edition includes a 20-page full-colour travel magazine.

The *Sunday Herald Sun*
PO Box 14634, Melbourne City MC Vic 8001
☎ 03-9292 2000, Fax 03-9292 2080
sundayhs@hwt.newsltd.com.au
www.news.com.au

Includes the full-colour, 24-page 'Escape' travel feature lift-out.

The *Sunday Mail*
GPO Box 339, Adelaide SA 5001
☎ 08-8206 2000, Fax 08-8206 3646
mailedit@adv.newsltd.com.au

South Australia's Sunday paper features the expanded 'Escape' full-colour travel section.

The *Sunday Telegraph*
GPO Box 4245, Surry Hills NSW 2001
☎ 02-9288 3000, Fax 02-9288 2307
letters@sundaytelegraph.com.au
www.sundaytelegraph.news.com.au

Includes the full-colour 'Escape' and 'Body & Soul' lift-outs.

The *Sydney Morning Herald*
GPO Box 506, Sydney NSW 2001
☎ 1300 85 8058, Fax 02-9282 3253
travel@smh.com.au
www.smh.com.au

Sydney's major newspaper contains similar travel coverage to the *Age*. Both papers welcome freelance submissions about unsubsidised travel.

The *West Australian*
GPO Box D162, Perth WA 6001
☎ 08-9482 3111, Fax 08-9482 9070
westinfo@wanews.com.au
www.thewest.com.au

The *West Australian* was first published in 1833, and features travel in Saturday's weekend edition.

On Line

Crikey
www.crikey.com.au

Australia's leading independent on-line news service promises to 'fill the gaps the Australian media seem unable or unwilling to fulfil' and accepts contributions from journalists who might 'think the Australian media is too cautious, under-resourced, unadventurous and too concentrated'.

National Library of Australia
www.nla.gov.au/npapers

The NLA's huge resources include links to Australia's newspaper media, searchable both by state, town and title.

News Medianet
http://newsmedianet.com.au

Provides an on-line guide to News Media's titles, including circulation figures and market research.

Online Newspapers
www.onlinenewspapers.com/australi.htm

This international guide to on-line newspapers includes a comprehensive listing of Australia's urban and regional newspaper websites.

Reportage
www.reportage.uts.edu.au

The Australian Centre for Independent Journalism's Web magazine focuses on national and international issues, including travel.

Travel News
http://travel.news.com.au

News Limited's on-line travel magazine includes features culled from its national newspapers and some news agency content.

Tourism Victoria
www.tourismvictoria.com.au

Tourism Victoria publishes *Pieces of Victoria*, a monthly electronic news bulletin for travel writers highlighting special events, tours, accommodation and other travel products.

WRITERS GROUPS & ASSOCIATIONS

Asia & Pacific Writers Network
bmj@net2000.com.au
www.pen.org.au

Members have access to a database and on-line forums to develop a better understanding of the writing, cultures and issues of the Asia-Pacific region.

Australian Society of Authors (ASA)
PO Box 1566, Strawberry Hills NSW 2012
☎ 02-9318 0877, Fax 02-9318 0530
asa@asauthors.org
www.asauthors.org

Promotes and protects the professional interests of Australian writers. Members receive the association's journal, *Australian Author*, and regular newsletters.

Australian Society of Travel Writers
www.astw.org.au

This website is largely for members only, and is dedicated to reporting news for the travel industry and serving the interests of the travelling public. The website includes useful hints for becoming a travel writer, accessible by nonmembers.

Australian Writers' Guild
www.awg.com.au

The professional association for performance writers provides members with access to industry information and a wide range of services. It has a number of branches:

New South Wales
8/50 Reservoir St, Surry Hills NSW 2010
☎ 02-9281 1554, Fax 02-9281 4321
admin@awg.com.au

Queensland
QPIX 33A Logan St, Woolloongabba Qld 4102
☎ 07-3391 2809, Fax 07-3391 2809
awgqld@powerup.com.au

South Australia
PO Box 43 Rundle Mall, Adelaide SA 5000
☎ 08-8232 6852, Fax 08-8232 6852
sa@awg.com.au

Victoria
42 Courtney St, North Melbourne Vic 3051
☎ 03-9328 5671
vic@awg.com.au

Western Australia
PO Box 492, Leederville WA 6903
☎ 08-9201 1172, Fax 08-9201 1173
wa@awg.com.au

Copyright Agency
Level 19, 157 Liverpool St, Sydney NSW 2000
☎ 02-9394 7600, Fax 02-9394 7601
pr@copyright.com.au
www.copyright.com.au

This not-for-profit copyright-collecting society seeks to secure fair payment for authors and publishers; membership is free.

Fellowship of Australian Writers (FAW)
A nonprofit membership-based group dedicated to supporting, promoting and advocating the needs and interests of Australian writers.

Australian Capital Territory
9 Bage Pl, Mawson ACT 2607

☎ 02-6286 1773, Fax 02-6262 9191
www.actwriters.org.au

New South Wales
PO Box 448, Rozelle NSW 2039
☎ 02-9810 1307, Fax 02-9810 1307
faw@bigpond.com

Northern Territory
PO Box 37512, Winnellie NT 0821
☎ 08-8948 1216

Queensland
PO Box 6338, Upper Mt Gravatt Qld 4122
☎ 07-3343 7654

South Australia
1a Billabong Rd, Goolwa SA 5214
☎ 08-8555 2092

Tasmania
PO Box 234, North Hobart Tas 7002
☎ 03-6234 4418, Fax 03-6239 6991

International PEN
www.pen.org.au

A member of the international association of writers, founded in 1921 to promote friendship and intellectual cooperation among writers worldwide.

Australian Captial Territory
PO Box 261, Dickson ACT 2603
☎ 02-6251 7438

New South Wales
PO Box 123, Broadway NSW 2007
☎ 02-9514 2738, Fax 02-9514 2778
sydney@pen.org.au

Queensland
PO Box 328, Annerley Qld 4103
☎ 07-3359 8647

Victoria, South Australia & Tasmania
PO Box 2273, Caulfield Junction Vic 3161
☎ 03-9509 7257

Western Australia
PO Box 1131, Subiaco WA 6715
☎ 08-9225 6715

Varuna – The Writers' House
141 Cascade St, Katoomba NSW 2780
☎ 02-4782 5674, Fax 02-4782 6220
varuna@varuna.com.au
www.varuna.com.au

Twenty-six fellowships are offered annually to writers in all genres and of all levels of experience.

Writers Centres
The various writers centres provide support for Australian writers, including local advice

and the use of resource libraries and facilities.

Australian Capital Territory
Gorman House, Ainslie Ave, Braddon ACT 2612
☎ 02-6262 9191, Fax 02-6262 9191
admin@actwriters.org.au
www.actwriters.org.au

New South Wales
PO Box 1056, Rozelle NSW 2039
☎ 02-9555 9757, Fax 02-9818 1327
nswwc@nswwriterscentre.org.au
www.nswwriterscentre.org.au

Northern Territory
GPO Box 2255, Darwin NT 0801
☎ 08-8941 2651, Fax 08-8941 2115
ntwriter@octa4.net.au
www.ntwriters.com.au

Queensland
Level 2, 109 Edward St, Brisbane Qld 4000
☎ 07-3839 1243, Fax 07-3839 1245
qldwriters@qwc.asn.au
www.qwc.asn.au

South Australia
PO Box 43, Rundle Mall PO, Adelaide SA 5000
☎ 08-8223 7662, Fax 08-8232 3994
sawriters@sawriters.on.net
www.sawriters.on.net

Tasmania
77 Salamanca Pl, Hobart Tas 7000
☎ 03-6224 0029, Fax 03-6224 0029
admin@tasmanianwriters.org
www.tasmanianwriters.org

Victoria
1st fl, Nicholas Bldg, 37 Swanston St, Melbourne Vic 3000
☎ 03-9654 9068, Fax 03-9654 4751
info@writers-centre.org
www.writers-centre.org

Western Australia
PO Box 891, Fremantle WA 6160
☎ 08-9432 9559, Fax 08-9430 6613
slo@fremantle.wa.gov.au
www.writerswritingwa.org

WRITING COURSES

Good Guides (www.thegoodguides.com.au) publishes a print and on-line guide to every university and college course available in Australia. Also check Griffith University's frequently updated list of creative writing programs (www.gu.edu.au/school/art/text/cwcourses.htm).

Australian College of Journalism
PO Box 80, Bondi Junction NSW 2022
☎ 02-9389 6499, Fax 02-9389 4277
principal@acg.edu.au
www.acj.edu.au

Travel writing is included as a component of this correspondence course. Tutors include industry professionals.

Centre for Adult Education
Arts Centre, 21 Degraves St, Melbourne Vic 3000
☎ 03-9652 0611, Fax 03-9652 0748
writing@cae.edu.au
www.cae.edu.au

Offers short entry-level courses and professional-development courses in travel writing and professional writing and editing.

Macleay College
PO Box 433, Paddington NSW 2021
☎ 02-9360 2033, Fax 02-9360 9589
study@macleay.edu.au
www.macleay.edu.au

Provides full- or part-time courses in journalism and editing at diploma level.

Massey University
School of English and Media Studies, Private Bag, Palmerston North, New Zealand
☎ 6-356 9099 x 2601
http://writery.massey.ac.nz

Offers courses in travel writing; its interactive website is open to all writers.

Offbeatrips Travel & Tourism Journalism
9 Compass Close, Edge Hill, Cairns Qld 4870
☎ 07-4032 1708
info@offbeatrips.com
www.offbeatrips.com

On-line, part-time distance education course specialising in freelance travel journalism.

Open Learning Australia
PO Box 18059, Collins St East, Melbourne Vic 8003
☎ 03-9903 9855, Fax 03-9903 8976
advisers@ola.edu.au
www.ola.edu.au

Australia's distance learning university offers a Bachelor of Communications with media studies components including journalism and new media.

Open Learning Institute of TAFE
Adult Community Education, GPO Box 1326, South Brisbane Qld 4101

☎ 07-3259 4111, Fax 07-3259 4377
oli.info@tafe.net
www.oli.tafe.net

The short, vocationally oriented correspondence courses include freelance journalism levels I and II.

OTEN Distance Education
51 Wentworth Rd, Strathfield NSW 2135
☎ 02-9715 8333, Fax 02-9715 8445
oten.courseinfo@tafensw.edu.au
www.tafensw.edu.au/oten

Correspondence courses include a one-year
Writing for Publication commercial certificate and Writing in Plain English communications course.

Southern Cross University
School of Arts, PO Box 157, Lismore NSW
2480
☎ 02-6620 3000, Fax 02-6622 1683
stuadmin@scu.edu.au
www.scu.edu.au

The School of Arts offers distance, full- or
part-time training in journalism as part of a
BA or associate degree via its Lismore, Coffs
Harbour and Tweed Heads campuses.

University of Newcastle
School of Design, Communication and
Information Technology, University Dr,
Callaghan NSW 2308
☎ 02-4921 5000, Fax 02-4921 6944
www.newcastle.edu.au

A journalism major is included in the university's communications program.

University of Technology, Sydney
PO Box 123, Broadway NSW 2007
☎ 02-9514 1222
info.office@uts.edu.au
www.uts.edu.au

One of Australia's leading undergraduate
and postgraduate schools of journalism, UTS
hosts the Australian Centre for Independent
Journalism.

University of Sydney
Centre for Continuing Education, Locked
Bag 20, Glebe NSW 2037
☎ 02-9351 2907, Fax 02-9351 5022
info@cce.usyd.edu.au
www.cce.usyd.edu.au

The centre's short courses for adults include
How to Get Published and Writing for Cash.
It also operates a writing retreat in Italy.

WEA Sydney
72 Bathurst St, Sydney NSW 2000
☎ 02-9264 2781, Fax 02-9267 6988
info@weasydney.nsw.edu.au
www.weasydney.nsw.edu.au

Short courses run by this nonprofit educational organisation include travel writing
and writing articles.

Writers Centres
The various writers centres also offer short
courses and workshops in all aspects of writing and publishing. See p255-56 for contact
details.

WRITERS WEBSITES & TOOLS

Aboriginal Languages of Australia
www.dnathan.com/VL/austLang.htm

A guide to on-line language resources for Aboriginal and Torres Strait Islander languages.

Aboriginal Studies Virtual Library
www.ciolek.com/WWWVL-Aboriginal.html

An on-line guide to Aboriginal studies, including history, native title, art and culture.

Australian Copyright Council
www.copyright.org.au

All the information you'll ever need to know
about copyright, plus a guide to the organisation's training programs, publications and
information sheets.

Australian Law Online
www.law.gov.au

This government-run site provides Australians with access to information about the
Australian legal system.

Australian Publishers Association
www.publishers.asn.au

Includes useful information for getting published and general trade information.

Australian Writers Online
http://groups.yahoo.com/group/Australian
_Writers_Online

Includes useful links and a chat room for
Australian writers.

Australia's Copyright Act 1968
www.austlii.edu.au/au/legis/cth/consol
_act/ca1968133

View the Act on line.

Department of Communications, Information Technology & the Arts
www.dcita.gov.au/arts

The Australian government's guide to arts and culture.

Go Australia
http://goaustralia.about.com/cs/language/a/strinea.htm

An on-line guide to Aussie colloquialisms and slang. See also http://library.trinity.wa.edu.au/subjects/english/aust/austlang.htm for comprehensive links to Australian linguistics sites.

Macquarie.Net
www.macquariedictionary.com.au

Provides access to a range of information and images on history, science, geography, literature and the arts, with a strong Australian emphasis. You can also subscribe to the on-line Macquarie Dictionary.

National Library of Australia
www.nla.gov.au/oz/litsites.html

A guide to Australian literature on the Internet. The site also lists Australian booksellers and publishers with an on-line presence at www.nla.gov.au/libraries/resource/bookpub.html, and information on recent Australian publications at www.nla.gov.au/kinetica/rap.html.

Ozguide
www.journoz.com

A comprehensive list of Internet information sources for Australian journalists.

PATA Award for Travel Writing
www.pata.org

The Pacific Asia Travel Association's annual awards in the fields of journalism, photography, guidebook writing, websites and electronic newsletters.

Text – The Journal of the Australian Association of Writing Programs
www.gu.edu.au/school/art/text

An electronic journal for writers published twice a year.

Writers on the Web
www.toadshow.com.au/rob/webwriting/skills.htm

Articles, advice and links on writing for the Web, plus an extremely useful cliché thesaurus.

Writing Centre
www.allen-unwin.com.au/writing/writingcentre.asp

Allen & Unwin's on-line compendium of inspirational tips and practical advice for writers includes author interviews, useful links and competition news.

Research-Related Websites
CLIMATE & THE ENVIRONMENT
Bureau of Meteorology
www.bom.gov.au

Weather forecasts, warnings and observations nationwide.

CSIRO
www.dar.csiro.au

The atmospheric research division of the Commonwealth Scientific & Industrial Research Organisation studies Australia's weather, climate and atmospheric pollution.

ECOTOURISM & RESPONSIBLE TRAVEL
Big Volcano Ecotourism Resource Centre
www.bigvolcano.com.au/ercentre/eaacode.htm

Includes guidelines for operators, the Code of Practice for Ecotourism Operators and tips for how to choose an ecotourism holiday or program.

Earthlink
www.earthlink.org.au

A green directory including information on ecotourism, environmental groups and resources.

Ecotourism Australia
www.ecotourism.org.au

Heaps of information on Australia's ecotourism industry.

Natural Heritage Trust
www.nht.gov.au

The government's initiative to restore and conserve Australia's environment and natural resources.

Wilderness Society
www.wilderness.org.au

Community-based environmental advocacy organisation committed to defending and protecting Australia's wild country.

EMBASSIES, CONSULATES & PASSPORTS

Australian Embassies
www.dfat.gov.au/missions/index.html

Includes details of overseas high commissions, consulates and representative offices. The Department of Foreign Affairs & Trade site also includes travel advisories and passport advice.

Visas
www.info.dfat.gov.au/protocol

If you're travelling, contact the relevant foreign embassies before you leave Australia to check the latest visa regulations. Also check out www.travel.com.au/tools/visa.html.

FACTS, FIGURES & STATISTICS

Australian Automobile Association
www.aaa.asn.au/default.htm

Includes a statistics database of motoring-related topics.

Australian Bureau of Statistics
www.abs.gov.au

Australia's official statistical organisation publishes a range of information including national economic and social indicators, the consumer price index and papers from the 2001 census.

Australian Heritage Council
www.ahc.gov.au/index.html

Up-to-date news on heritage issues in Australia.

Australian Honours List
www.itsanhonour.gov.au/honours_list.html

A who's who of esteemed Australians.

Australian National Museum
www.austmus.gov.au

Includes an on-line guide to the museum's research and collections.

Australian Places
www.arts.monash.edu.au/ncas/multimedia/gazetteer/index.html

A gazetteer of Australian cities, towns and suburbs.

Commonwealth Parliamentary Library
www.aph.gov.au/library/pubs/mesi

Publishes monthly economic and social indicator reports.

Country Calling Codes
www.countrycallingcodes.com

International telephoning made easy.

Datacard
www.btr.gov.au/service/datacard/index.cfm

All the numbers on Australia's tourism industry, including visitor statistics and travel patterns.

Geoscience Australia
www.ga.gov.au/education/facts

All kinds of fabulous facts about Australia.

National Library of Australia
www.nla.gov.au/oz/stats.html

Links to all kinds of Australian statistical information on the Web.

National Trust of Australia
www.nationaltrust.org.au

Includes links to state branches and information on properties and collections.

Register of the National Estate
www.ahc.gov.au/register

A listing of more than 13,000 places of natural, historic and indigenous significance.

Tourism Australia
www.tourism.australia.com

The Research & Stats section includes a breakdown of visitor arrivals data and other market intelligence.

Universal Currency Converter
www.xe.com/ucc

Calculate your dwindling finances on-line in any number of different currencies.

GENERAL TRAVEL INFORMATION & ADVICE

Atlas Travel Club
http://atlas-club.com.au

A nonprofit travel and leisure club.

Australian Automobile Association
www.aaa.asn.au/default.htm

Includes links to state-based motoring organisations.

Australian Federation of Travel Agents
www.afta.com.au

The representative body of Australia's travel agents, highlighting industry events and hot deals.

Australian Internet Cafes
www.gnomon.com.au/publications/net access

Where to go on line across Australia.

Australian Regional Tourist Associations
http://members.ozemail.com.au/~fnq/rta

Tourist information websites and organisations across the land.

Australian Wireless Hotspots
www.wi-fihotspotlist.com/browse/au

State-by-state listings of cafes, restaurants and businesses with WiFi access.

Civil Aviation Safety Authority
www.casa.gov.au

Includes aviation industry information and air travel safety tips.

Cybercafes
www.cybercafes.com

Contains a database of 4208 Internet cafés in 140 countries.

PATA (Pacific Asia Travel Association)
www.travelwithpata.com

A travel guide to the Asia-Pacific region, with destination features, travel deals and advice.

The Thorn Tree Australasia and Pacific
http://thorntree.lonelyplanet.com
www.lonelyplanet.com/subwwway

You can post a question on Lonely Planet's destination-specific Thorn Tree travel forum, which includes a page devoted to Australia and the Pacific. You'll also find cultural, literature, food, and political discussions. The site also provides links to other important travel resources in its Subway section.

Tourism Offices Worldwide
www.towd.com

The Tourism Offices Worldwide Directory provides links to official US and international tourist information sources: government tourism offices, convention and visitors bureaus, chambers of commerce, and similar organisations that provide free, accurate and unbiased travel information to the public.

Travel Biz
www.travelbiz.com.au

Highlights breaking news in Australia's travel industry, with links to airlines, travel agents and hotels.

Travel Ticker
www.lonelyplanet.com/travel_ticker

Lonely Planet's travel advisory service.

HEALTH
My Doctor
www.mydr.com.au

A comprehensive health information resource provided by the MIMS Consumer Health Group.

Smart Traveller
www.smartraveller.gov.au/tips/travelwell.html

Health tips and recommendations from the Department of Foreign Affairs & Trade.

Travel Doctor
www.tmvc.com.au

The Traveller's Medical & Vaccination Centre site features health advice, clinic details and current health alerts for overseas travel.

World Health Organization
www.who.int/en

The website provides information on health risks around the world as well as recommended precautions, immunisations and vaccines when travelling.

MAPS
Australian Coastal Atlas
www.deh.gov.au/coasts/atlas

Interactive maps of Australia's coastline from the Department of the Environment & Heritage.

Australian Place Name Search
www.ga.gov.au/map/names

Discover just where in Australia you'll find Burrumbuttock.

Geoscience Australia
www.ga.gov.au/map

Free downloadable topographic and geophysical maps of Australia.

Street Directory.com
www.street-directory.com.au

A virtual street directory.

Whereis
www.whereis.com.au/whereis/home.jsp

A virtual street directory.

WORLD EVENTS

City Search

www.citysearch.com.au

A guide to what's on where and when throughout Australia.

Culture and Recreation

www.acn.net.au/events

Reviews, previews and listings of Australian events.

YOU ON THE WEB

My Trip Journal

http://lonelyplanet.mytripjournal.com

Build an on-line journal of your trip with maps, photos and email notification of updates for your friends.

REFERENCE PURCHASES

Aboriginal Words edited by Nick Thieberger and William McGregor (Macquarie Library)

Aussie Slang by Sarah Dawson (Penguin Books Australia)

The Australian Oxford Dictionary edited by Bruce Moore (Oxford University Press)

Australian Book Contracts by Barbara Jefferis (Keesing Press)

The Australian People: An Encyclopedia of the Nation, Its People and Their Origins by James Jupp (Cambridge University Press)

A Dictionary of Australian Colloquialisms by G. A. Wilkes (Oxford University Press)

The Dictionary of Australian Quotations edited by Stephen Murray-Smith (Mandarin)

A Guide to Australian Law for Journalists, Authors, Printers and Publishers by Geoffrey Sawyer (Melbourne University Press)

The Little Aussie Fact Book by Margaret Nicholson (Penguin Books Australia)

Macquarie Dictionary (Macquarie Library)

Macquarie Slang Dictionary (Macquarie Library)

Macquarie Thesaurus (Macquarie Library)

Macquarie Writer's Friends (Macquarie Library)

Modern Australian Usage (Oxford University Press)

The Oxford Companion to Australian History, edited by Graeme Davison, John Hirst and Stuart Macintyre Oxford (University Press)

The Penguin Working Words: An Australian Guide to Modern English Usage edited by Barrie Hughes (Penguin Australia)

The SBS World Guide, 11th edition (Hardie Grant)

Style Manual for Authors, Editors and Printers, 6th edition (John Wiley)

Writing as a Business by Ken Methold (ABC Books)

Writing Feature Stories by Matthew Ricketson (Allen & Unwin Australia)

Library References

Australian Books in Print (DW Thorpe)

Australian Bookseller & Publisher (DW Thorpe)

Australian Dictionary of Biography (Melbourne University Press)

Australian Literary Awards & Fellowships (DW Thorpe)

Directory of Australian Booksellers (DW Thorpe)

Guide to New Australian Books (DW Thorpe)

Weekly Book Newsletter (DW Thorpe)

Who's Who in Australia (Information Australia)

International Literary Market Place (Information Today)

AUSTRALIAN TRAVEL LITERATURE CLASSICS

The following 10 travel literature titles reveal quite different responses to Australia and its culture, penned by both locals and visitors.

Down Under by Bill Bryson

In the Land of Oz by Howard Jacobson

One for the Road by Tony Horowitz

Sean & David's Long Drive by Sean Condon

A Secret Country by John Pilger

The Songlines by Bruce Chatwin

Thirty Days in Sydney by Peter Carey

Tracks by Robyn Davidson

Sydney by Jan Morris

The Winners' Enclosure by Annie Caulfield

APPENDIX: SAMPLE PAPERWORK

THE *BOSTON GLOBE* TRAVEL SECTION (US)

Guidelines for Contributors

The *Sunday Globe* Travel Section accepts freelance articles submitted on speculation. Manuscripts will be considered and, if accompanied by a stamped self-addressed envelope, will be returned to the sender, usually within two months, if they do not meet our needs.

Our preferred length is 1000 to 1500 words. Photographs are desirable and should accompany manuscripts or be available via email. (Please do not send slides or negatives unless they are copies. Things sometimes get lost here, so you should keep the originals. The same is true of manuscripts.)

We want articles to be well written and generally positive in tone, but also candid, honest, and helpful. Writers are expected to be personally familiar with the destinations and subjects they are writing about, and to double-check all facts in the story. We sometimes – though infrequently – accept first-person pieces, but only when the writer's own experience helps illuminate a larger point about the destination; we want our readers to hear not just the voices of our writers, but of the people that give a destination its character. We are always in the market for offbeat stories, particularly ones with fresh approaches to familiar destinations such as New England, Atlantic Canada, Great Britain, etc. Begin each story with an appropriate dateline.

It is the policy of the Travel Section not to print articles paid for or subsidized by agencies or organizations with a direct or indirect interest in the subject written about. We also do not print articles about places or subjects in which the writer has any professional stake or other personal or professional interest that could compromise – or appear to compromise – his or her objectivity. In other words, no press trips, no freebies from resorts or travel agencies, no writing about the resort owned by your cousin. We also require that all freelance writers and photographers sign a contract, which is available for reading and signing online at www.bostonglobe.com/freelance.

Contributors are asked to include a one- or two-sentence biographical description, including occupation and place of residence.

In destination pieces, we include service information such as recommended restaurants and hotels with price ranges and rates, airline service, special attractions, and bargains, etc. (See below.) We regard this information as a service to readers and expect it to be objective and reasonably comprehensive. If three airlines serve a destination, for instance, the rates and packages of all three should be given, not just of those used by the writer. Similarly, the room rates of a representative selection of hotels should be given, as should the range of entrée prices of a representative selection of recommended restaurants.

Please list this information separately so it can be used as a box or sidebar. We can email a template for our If You Go information if requested.

We prefer to deal with finished manuscripts rather than queries, outlines, or rough drafts, and we prefer electronic submissions to paper. If mailed, however, manuscripts should be neatly typed, preferably double or triple spaced, with one inch margins. If emailed, they should be embedded directly into the message or sent as a Microsoft Word attachment. Please include your full name, address, telephone number, and Social Security number. And always retain a copy of the manuscript.

Photographs

Each photograph submitted should have an identifying caption, either written separately or on the back of the print, or both. There must be a return address on each print and an indication of who should get the credit for the photo. We can work with prints, slides, and high-resolution jpeg files sent one per email. Again, please do not send your only negatives or slides; send copies. We cannot be responsible for unsolicited photos or for those with no return address.

Contributors will be notified if their manuscripts and/or photos are accepted, but payment is not made until publication. Rates vary, depending on how the story and photos are used, and checks are usually mailed out within 30 days of publication. Tearsheets, too, can be sent out after publication.

Exact publication dates of articles cannot be given in advance. Repeated inquiries neither improve chances of acceptance nor accelerate publication.

Manuscripts should be mailed to Wendy Fox, Travel Editor, *Boston Sunday Globe*, Box 55819, Boston, MA 02205-5819, or emailed to travel@globe.com.

If You Go Boxes

Writers of travel stories must supply this additional information in condensed and graphic form. Depending on the scope of the story, we try to give readers as much practical information about how to enjoy a destination as possible. For major destination pieces, that includes the following categories:

HOW TO GET THERE

▸ The length of the flight, train ride, car ride, boat ride, etc
▸ Range of recent plane fares and airlines
▸ If train or boat, its name and starting location
▸ If driving, some basic directions from a major landmark
▸ If a far-flung destination, time difference from Boston time

WHERE TO STAY

▸ Names, phones, and websites for a reservation service that deals in the area, if there is one
▸ Names, addresses, phones, websites, and room rates for hotels that you like, at a good range in prices

WHERE TO DINE/EAT

▸ Names, addresses, phones, websites, and the range of dinner entrée prices for restaurants that you like, of varying price ranges

WHAT TO SEE

▸ Name, phone, and website for any kind of visitors' bureau that lists events or resources

▸ Name, address, phone, and website for any attraction that you mention in the story

▸ Any other music, drama, art, dance, religious festivals; other scheduled events; predictable events (northern lights, eclipses, moose-hunting season)

WHERE PLACES ARE

▸ If you have a map, please mark it up and mail/fax it or copy the area relevant to your story and mark that up and mail or fax it. This is especially important for major destination pieces.

Stories with a narrower angle may not need all the above information. For instance, a story on bargain shopping in Paris may require only a listing of the stores mentioned; a story on a honeymoon expedition to a specific lodge in Belize may require all the above information except where to eat and where to stay if the package is all-inclusive.

WANDERLUST MAGAZINE (UK)

Guidelines for Contributors

With only six issues a year, the opportunities for getting work published in *Wanderlust* are very limited – yet we receive more than 100 articles and proposals each week. Realistically, you have a one in 800 chance of a manuscript or photograph being accepted for publication. Please read our guidelines carefully and note that we do not accept enquiries or proposals by telephone or email. *Due to the overwhelming number of submissions received, we do not respond to postal contributions unless a self-addressed envelope (SAE) is enclosed, which must be stamped or accompanied by sufficient International Reply Coupons (IRCs).*

Subject & Format

Our mission is simple – we want to provide our readers with the best writing, the best photographs and the most authoritative facts.

Wanderlust aims to cover all aspects of independent, semi-independent and special-interest travel. We do cover 'soft' adventure but leave the crampons and adrenalin stuff to other magazines. Off-the-beaten-track destinations, secret corners of the world and unusual angles on well-known places are always of particular interest. We are particularly interested in local culture and try to provide more of an insight than travel articles in other publications – hence, we prefer pieces to be written by someone with an in-depth knowledge of a topic or destination.

You should make yourself familiar with the style, tone and content of *Wanderlust*, and be aware of recent articles to ensure your chosen subject has not been covered in the past year or so.

If tackling a topical subject then do bear in mind that we plan the contents of each issue up to a year ahead.

Always ask yourself what makes your article different from all the others that may have been sent to us on the same topic.

Wanderlust includes the following formats of articles on a regular basis:

1. FEATURES

Covering a specific destination – a country or a region – or an activity, eg, horseriding in Chile, walking in Italy. Should be both anecdotal and informative, written in the first person and in the past tense, and between 1800–2200 words. A factpage should be provided when requested, but not with unsolicited manuscripts (a style sheet will be provided if the article is accepted).

2. TRAVEL BLUEPRINTS

Trip planner articles designed to give a practical and inspirational overview of a country – a mini-guide to help readers decide the basic outline of their trip before buying a detailed guidebook. Usually written by guidebook authors or someone with in-depth knowledge of the destination. Send a proposal first.

3. SPECIAL INTEREST FEATURES

Do you have specialist knowledge on a travel-relevant subject? Topics covered to date include safaris, cycling holidays, New Zealand walks, family adventure trips. Must be authoritative – authors should have in-depth regional or global knowledge.

Between 1500 and 2200 words (scene-setting intro, followed by factual article). Send a proposal first.

4. CITY GUIDES

A descriptive intro (750 words approx), followed by a two-page up-to-date factual guide (around 1200 words), totalling about 2000 words. Send a proposal first. A style sheet will be provided if we are interested.

5. ROOM SERVICE

Special places to stay, either a focus on one option or a round-up of several. Can be a hotel, a lodge, a tree-house or even a campsite. Round-ups to date have included Cuban hotels, Zambian safari lodges, cave hotels of Andalucía and special UK seaside stays.

Around 1000 words for an individual place, 1200–1500 words for a round-up. We also publish regular short pieces on unusual or special UK places (around 400 words).

6. AD-HOC FEATURES

Short anecdotal snapshots or observations, arts, culture, food and wine, issues, viewpoints, etc.

Up to 1400 words.

7. DISPATCHES

Brief, topical pieces (700–800 words) describing a recent development in a destination of interest to our readers. Recent Dispatches have included the demise of the Mallorca ecotax, resumption of whaling in Iceland, knitting circles in New York and the introduction of mobile phones in Bhutan.

8. WATERING HOLES

Short (250 words) structured articles describing unusual and eccentric bars around the world. Photos are required to accompany Watering Hole pieces.

Style

Study a copy of the magazine *before* considering a submission. It is no coincidence that the majority of our contributors are regular readers. Single issues are currently £3.60 in UK shops, or £4.50 (incl. UK postage and packing) ordered direct from us. Annual subscription (six issues) costs £19 in the UK.

With the exception of Travel Blueprint trip planners, factpages, the factual sections of City Guides or purely practical articles, do not disrupt your text with facts and figures. *Wanderlust* aims to be an entertaining read, even for those who have no intention of travelling to the destinations described, so keep your narrative flowing by cutting down on statistics and including personal observations, anecdotes and conversations. We also aim to be as unbiased as possible so we never 'plug'. Make sure the opening paragraph draws readers in.

The Wanderlust *Reader*

Our readers encompass all ages and budgets, and at least 50% are female. They are well educated and reasonably affluent, and are mostly active travellers, perhaps more experienced
than you. Although most are British we have readers in more than 80 countries worldwide.

Handy Hints

▸ Your article should have a beginning, a middle and an end – do not just tail off. Make the opening
paragraph one of your strongest, in order to pull the reader in. You do not have to tell a story in
chronological order – you can open with a tense situation and then flashback to how it began.

▸ Ensure that your piece has a strong central theme that moves the reader forward and provides a
point to it all.

▸ Do not try to cover too much in one article – there may be several different articles hiding inside
one large piece. You should be able to sum up the contents of your article in a single sentence.

▸ Show the good and bad side. Disasters and tricky situations often make for a more entertaining read
than harmonious, straightforward trips.

▸ Present an honest account – *Wanderlust* is not a travel brochure. If you hated a place, then say so
(and why).

▸ Feature articles should have personality – though often not yours; dialogue and comment from local
people add colour to a story.

▸ Think about how you can avoid blandness in your descriptions of a destination – recounting a seem-
ingly unimportant incident can bring a place to life more than a detailed adjectival description of its
physical appearance. And don't forget smells, sounds, flavours and even temperature or air quality
as well as sights and emotions.

▸ Be aware of the political, environmental and social background to the places you describe –
they may not be pertinent to your story, but be sure of this, especially if you are going to allude to
them.

▸ Be aware of the consequences of what you write – for example, ecological issues such as the damaging effect that snorkellers may have on a coral reef. Be wary of endangering the subjects of your
article if describing an illegal activity or political views.

▸ Avoid Americanisms (unless you are recounting speech or quotations from an American!), jargon,
foreign terms that are not generally understood, and the numerous travel clichés that many writers fall back on – snow-capped mountains, lands of contrast, kaleidoscopes of colour and seething
masses of humanity will all get the chop.

▸ If we have recently run an article on a particular destination or topic then it will probably be some
time before we cover that area again.

▸ Check your facts and be wary of making generalisations that you cannot be sure of.

▸ It goes without saying that *Wanderlust* will not tolerate any racist, sexist or otherwise discriminatory
writing, but be careful too of patronising the peoples you describe and making generalisations about
characteristics that could be deemed insulting.

▸ We have readers in 80+ countries worldwide – try to avoid references that would confuse other
nationalities.

Proposals & Unsolicited Submissions

Proposals and unsolicited submissions are always considered, but please do not waste our
time or yours! Make sure you understand the style of the magazine and who its readers
are. Please don't ring or email the editor to discuss your idea – we are a small team and she
simply doesn't have the time. Any correspondence should be by mail and addressed to the

Editor, Lyn Hughes. *Sorry, material will not be acknowledged or returned unless a self-addressed envelope (stamped or with sufficient International Reply Coupons) is included.*

PROPOSALS

Send a synopsis, cuttings of any previously published work, and return postage. Faxed proposals will not be acknowledged unless they are of definite interest. Do not phone or email with proposals unless we ask you to.

MANUSCRIPTS

Manuscripts should be clearly typed on A4 paper, on one side only. A cover sheet should be attached detailing your name and address, the title of the article, the number of words, and whether relevant slides are available.

Faxed articles are not considered.

We receive up to 100 manuscripts *each week* so there may be several months' delay responding to you. Please don't ring to check the status of your article – if you haven't heard anything, it hasn't yet been read.

PHOTOGRAPHS & ILLUSTRATIONS

Guidelines for Photographers are available. Transparencies (slides) are used, and must be pin-sharp and ideally on professional film (eg, Fuji Velvia). Prints, whether from negatives or digital cameras, are not suitable. Otherwise, in the first instance send a summary of available work addressed to the Picture Editor, Hayley Lawrence. Any samples should be kept to a minimum and can be in the form of duplicates, laser copies or prints.

We recommend that valued or original material is sent by registered or recorded mail.

Commissioned & Accepted Work

While the editor may ask for material to be submitted, this does *not* guarantee acceptance for publication.

If accepted, manuscripts should be made available in electronic format via email or on a Mac-readable CD-Rom. You will also be asked to confirm in writing that the article has not been previously published in the UK.

Payment

Current rates (as of 1/2/04) for most features are £200 per 1000 published words. Unless otherwise agreed, the fee is based on printed, not submitted, words. Factpages are paid at £90 per page (approx 750 words) pro-rated. Fees for other sections (including Dispatches, Watering Holes and interviews) are set per-article rates, agreed on commissioning.

These rates are based upon copy being available on disk or email, and First British Serial Rights being offered.

An invoice request and complimentary copy of the magazine will be sent upon publication. Payment will be made within 30 days.

Wanderlust Publications Ltd, PO Box 1832, Windsor, Berks SL4 1YT. Editor: Lyn Hughes

SAMPLE RELEASE FORMS

Model Release

By signing this document:

I irrevocably consent to the Photographer (and its licensees and assigns) incorporating my image or likeness in photographs or illustrations in any form or media (images) and reproducing, publishing and communicating the Images in any form and media for any purpose, whether commercial or otherwise (including advertising), and to the use of my name and any other text or works in connection with the Images. I waive any right to inspect or approve the Images or any publication incorporating the Images and any right to compensation for the use of the Images by the Photographer, its licensees and assigns. I release the Photographer, its licensees and assigns from any or all claims, actions, proceedings, demands and expenses and other liability that may arise in connection with the use of the Images by any person. I confirm that I am either over 18 years of age or that my parent or guardian has also agreed to these terms by signing in the space provided below.

I understand and agree to the above.

Signed: _____ Signed by parent/guardian: _____

Print name: _____ Print name: _____

Address/email/phone number: _____

Date: _____

Description of image: _____

Property Release

By signing this document:

I irrevocably consent to the Photographer (and its licensees and assigns) incorporating an image or likeness of the property described below in photographs or illustrations in any form or media (images) and reproducing, publishing and communicating the Images in any form and media for any purpose, whether commercial or otherwise (including advertising). I waive any right to inspect or approve the Images or any publication incorporating the Images and any right to compensation for the use of the Images by the Photographer, its licensees and assigns. I release the Photographer, its licensees and assigns from any or all claims, actions, proceedings, demands and expenses and other liability that may arise in connection with the use of the Images by any person.

I warrant that I am the owner of the property and/or am fully authorised to enter this property release.

Signed: _____ Print name: _____

Address/email/phone number: _____

Date: _____

Property description: _____

Property address: _____

Description of image: _____

ACKNOWLEDGMENTS

This Book

This first edition of *Travel Writing* was written by Don George with Charlotte Hindle. David Else wrote the Guidebook Writing chapter, and Janet Austin wrote the Australian resources section. The book was commissioned and developed in Lonely Planet's Melbourne office by Janet Austin and Laetitia Clapton, and the project was managed by Bridget Blair. It was edited by Janet Austin with assistance from Emma Koch, Andrea Dobbin and Meladel Mistica. The book was designed by Annika Roojun, and it was laid out by Michael Ruff and Margie Jung. Brendan Dempsey also assisted with design. The cover was designed by Annika Roojun and Wendy Wright.

Thanks from the Authors

Don George

This book represents the accumulation of five decades of experience, and it is impossible to name all the people to whom I am indebted for the inspiration and education embodied herein. But a few people deserve special mention. First of all, I want to thank my parents for setting me on the right path with our family adventures when I was still a young and impressionable traveller, and for encouraging me to follow that path all the way to the present day.

I want to thank Tony and Maureen Wheeler for making dreams – theirs and mine – come true at Lonely Planet. I'd also like to thank Roz Hopkins, Peter d'Onghia, Janet Austin and Laetitia Clapton of Lonely Planet for believing in this book from the beginning, and for guiding and supporting it throughout its own journey. My extended Lonely Planet family in the Oakland office also deserve thanks for their understanding and cheer-giving in this and all my adventures.

I want to thank Charlotte Hindle for reading the entire text – multiple times – and for congenially contributing excellent, extensive counsel and information that has helped invaluably to shape and complete the book. Thanks also to David Else for writing the eloquent and authoritative guidebook chapter. I'd like to thank Judy Tierney and Jennica Peterson, who tirelessly researched the US resources section and offered thoughtful, valuable suggestions and insights on the entire text. And I want to thank all the distinguished travel editors, writers and agents who took the time to contribute their perspectives, experiences and wisdom to these pages.

Thank you to the hundreds of students who have endured my classes over the years and whose boundless curiosity and passion have taught and re-taught me in ways large and small. I also want to thank the wonderful writers and editors with whom I have had the privilege of working over the past 25 years, who have honed my own appreciation of good writing – and good beer! And to the innumerable travellers – at home and on the road – I have encountered in my wanderings, who have enriched and enlightened my life beyond measure.

Finally, I want to thank my own intimate circle of fellow travellers – Kuniko, Jenny and Jeremy: you fill my journey with magic, and meaning, and love.

Charlotte Hindle

I would like to thank Simon Calder from the *Independent*, freelance writer Harriet O'Brien and Steven Wood from *Condé Nast Traveller* for their professional advice and help. Paul Bloomfield and Lyn Hughes from *Wanderlust* magazine assisted with Chapter Five and allowed us to reproduce their Contributor Guidelines. I'd like to thank Cath Urquhart from the *Times* for digging out such a fine example of a UK proposal. Thanks also to all the UK travel literature authors, travel journalists, travel editors and agents who gave such informative and detailed interview copy. Finally, thanks to LP commissioning editors Janet Austin and Laetitia Clapton.

Janet Austin

Many thanks to Bridget Blair in Lonely Planet's Melbourne office for technical and timely support. Thanks to Andrew Bain for the great interview and friendly words of advice, and thanks also to Michelle Bennett, John Weldon and Leonie Mugavin for their helpful suggestions.